GREAT BATTLES AND LEADING FIGURES OF THE CIVIL WAR

GREAT BATTLES AND LEADING FIGURES OF THE CIVIL WAR

John S. Bowman
General Editor

Published by World Publications Group, Inc.
140 Laurel Street
East Bridgewater, MA 02333
www.wrldpub.net

ISBN 1-57215-009-2
978-1-57215-009-6

Printed and bound in China by SNP Leefung Printers Limited.

1 2 3 4 5   06 05 03 02

Page 1: *Confederate pickets at Fredericksburg.*

Page 2: *Robert E. Lee and his generals (top) and Ulysses S. Grant and his generals (below).*

Pages 4-5: *Union cavalrymen of Pleasonton's Corps in 1863.*

CONTENTS

INTRODUCTION

It is common knowledge by now that there exists a paradox involving books about the Civil War: On the one hand, there are more than one can imagine the public ever "digesting," while on the other hand, there seems to be no let up in the public's appetite for such books. To be sure, there is a hard core of Civil War aficionados, devotees, fans—"buffs" seems to have become the favored term. There is even a bestseller of recent years about some of these very individuals—specifically, those who make or obtain authentic replicas of uniforms and weapons and re-enact battles. Very likely these re-enacters read a different set of the books on the war than, say, academic historians, but they are no less serious about wanting to get things right. In any case, the public for Civil War books is far larger than those two extremes might suggest and the books go on being published and bought.

Clearly there are many and quite diverse reasons why such a wide spectrum of individuals are so fascinated by the Civil War, and it would be beyond the scope and ability of this introduction to analyze and explain them. But there must be some underlying and shared reasons, some really bedrock interests and motives, behind this persistent phenomenon. Something about it taps a deep chord in the American experience, sounding many motifs: slavery, states' rights, Abraham Lincoln, Jefferson Davis, horrendous casualties, heroic actions, Gettysburg (both battle and address), Robert E. Lee, Ulysses S. Grant, "John Brown's Body," and the Lost Cause. It is a long litany of names and words and phrases that one can merely drop into any speech, each of which evokes vivid and meaningful repercussions in many minds.

All that said, it then follows that no single book could hope to capture all those motifs, and this work is no exception. But what it does encapsulate are two of the most resonant aspects of the Civil War: the major battles and the major individuals. And in both instances, the separate sections go far beyond what might at first be associated with such subject matter.

Thus the section on great battles is more than just another retelling of a series of battles—set pieces of military operations, tactical operations, units, casualties, and the like. Jackson's Valley Campaign, Shiloh, Fredericksburg, Vicksburg, Chancellorsville, Gettysburg, Chickamauga—these and other major battles and campaigns are put into the context of the surrounding events, the decisions and strategies that led up to them, the personalities involved, and the impacts that ensued. It can not and does not claim to be a complete history of the military operations of the Civil War, but in providing the series of dramatic narratives of these great battles, this volume conveys a sense of just how terrible and tragic this war was. The division of these battles into those generally conceded to be victories for the Confederate forces and those generally conceded to be victories for the Union forces is not done to revive or exacerbate the regional differences that lay behind this war; it is intended solely to allow readers to focus on particular "subplots" in this great drama—to concentrate on the strategies and leaders that led each of these great armies to moments of triumph and moments of defeat.

Meanwhile, the second section, the one devoted to an alphabetized directory of individuals—this goes far beyond the standard list of well-known military and governmental figures. The sheer numbers and range of these entries end up providing a true overview of the Civil War in all its dimensions. Many readers may be surprised, for instance, to see so many women included in this section; since, for the most part, they did not participate in the battles and on the field of combat, these women often get overlooked. Our volume has made sure that they receive their just recognition for the varied roles they played, and the same holds for countless others who get entries here. By ranging beyond the traditional and conventional selection, this part of the book provides a glimpse into the length and breadth and depth of American society in this era and event of the nation's history. Along with soldiers and sailors of every rank, there are the statesmen and spies, nurses and newspapermen, authors and artists, plantation owners and abolitionists—they are all here.

With more than 500 illustrations—many in full color—and 15 valuable maps, this volume also provides a pictorial dimension to the subject matter that many will find most revealing—photographs of events and individuals who have heretofore been only names on the printed pages of books. Among other things, it is a reminder of the role that the relatively recently acquired technology of photography was to play in this war. Photographs also serve to bring to life some of the other new technologies that came into play in this war—railroads, balloons, steel-clad ships, and weaponry of all sorts.

Written in an engaging and accessible style that makes both the battles and the individuals come alive, this is a volume for those who bring all levels of knowledge to the grand yet tragic story that is America's Civil War.

GREAT
BATTLES OF THE
CIVIL WAR

Southern Victories

THE OPENING GUNS

On 20 December 1860, a convention of delegates meeting in Charleston, South Carolina, unanimously voted to pass this ordinance.

We, the people of the State of South Carolina, in Convention assembled, do declare and ordain, and it is hereby declared and ordained, that the ordinance adopted by us in Convention, on the 23rd day of May, in the year of our Lord 1788, whereby the Constitution of the United States of America was ratified, and also all Acts and parts of Acts of the General Assembly of this State ratifying the amendments of the said Constitution, are hereby repealed, and that the union now subsiding between South Carolina and other States under the name of the United States of America is hereby dissolved.

It happened at last, the thing long predicted and long feared: the United States, which had fought so fiercely for nationhood and felt themselves to be the hope of the world, were beginning to fall apart. A state had seceded from the Union. Others were ready to follow its lead.

The issues swirling around slavery had, beginning from the inception of the country, tended increasingly to split the nation along sectional lines. Among other corollary issues were the contending doctrines of federalism and of states' rights. Federalism, strongest in the North, proclaimed the primacy of the federal government and its laws; while states' rights doctrine, strongest in the South, upheld the primacy of each state's government and the states' right to nullify Federal laws they did not like – and, in extremity, to sever their bonds with the Union entirely.

Thus over the years two sections of the country pulled apart in economy (the North was more industrialized), in temperament and in culture. On both sides, fear and suspicion gradually supplanted goodwill and reason. Eventually the situation had grown out of control of even the wisest of men. The divisiveness came to a head with the election of Abraham Lincoln, whom the South perceived as a rabid abolitionist. In reality, Lincoln was comparatively a moderate on the issue. He regarded slavery as a great evil, writing at one point, "If slavery is not wrong, then nothing is wrong." But

Below: *An early cotton gin. It made cotton the staple crop of the South, increasing the demand for slaves.*

Opposite: *Jefferson Davis, US senator and former cabinet officer, became president of the CSA.*

Lincoln was willing to go to any lengths to resolve tensions peacefully; if that meant tolerating slavery for the time being, he would tolerate it.

By the time of Lincoln's inauguration, on 4 March 1861, he was faced with a rival government of seven Southern states calling themselves the Confederate States of America: South Carolina, Mississippi, Florida, Alabama, Georgia, Louisiana, and Texas. Following the lead of South Carolina, these states had responded to Lincoln's election by seceding from the Union, had drawn up a constitution, appointed a president, and claimed all Federal property within their borders.

Lincoln's opposite, Confederate President Jefferson Davis, was already occupying his office and planning how best to take over Union garrisons in the South. There were three of these in Florida, far from the centers of government; it was on the fourth garrison that the attention of the whole country came to rest – Fort Sumter, in Charleston Harbor.

The importance and the vulnerability of Fort Sumter had become clear even before Lincoln or Davis had taken office. After South Carolina seceded, state authorities sent a commission to President James Buchanan to arrange for transfer of Federal property to the Confederacy. Buchanan, who was not entirely unsympathetic to the South, met the commissioners unofficially and told them he would not change the status quo in Charleston Harbor. But soon after this the status quo did change ominously. Acting on his own, Major Robert Anderson, Federal commander in the harbor, loaded his men on boats and took them from the old Revolutionary Fort Moultrie, near the mainland, to the more defensible Fort Sumter, an unfinished pentagonal brick edifice three miles out in the harbor. The significance of Anderson's move was

Above: Major Anderson left Fort Moultrie on Christmas night 1860. The troops moved to Fort Sumter.

Opposite: A Currier & Ives print of the attack on Fort Sumter in Charleston Harbor, 12 April 1861.

not lost on Confederate authorities. In January President Buchanan sent a boat of provisions to the fort, which was low on both food and munitions; the boat was fired on from the South Carolina mainland and turned back. The state government decreed that no supplies of any kind were to be allowed in. By the time Lincoln took office Fort Sumter was isolated and running out of food.

The president decided neither to abandon the fort nor to initiate hostilities, but rather to send a boatload of provisions to the garrison. In notifying the governor of South Carolina of that action Lincoln was in effect challenging the Confederates to respond: if hostilities were to begin, it must be the South's doing. The next day, 7 April, the response came: General Pierre G T Beauregard, Confederate commander in Charleston, cut off communications between Charleston and the fort and began to organize Confederate forces in the harbor. On 11 April Beauregard sent a demand for evacuation to Major Anderson. Sumter's commander, realizing the terrible momentum that was gathering about his command, replied that he would evacuate on 15 April unless he was attacked or received further orders from Washington. Suspecting, correctly, that this would not satisfy the Confederate authorities, Anderson assured the aides who delivered the ultimatum, "Gentlemen, if you do not batter the fort to pieces about us, we shall be starved out in a few days."

The momentum of events rolled on, pulled by the seem-

ingly irresistible magnet of war. At 3:20 in the morning on 12 April the next note came to Major Anderson: We have the honor to notify you that [Beauregard] will open the fire . . . in one hour from this time." Greatly upset, Major Anderson accompanied the Confederate messengers back to their boat. Pressing their hands in farewell, he choked, "If we never meet in this world again, God grant that we may meet in the next." (Among Anderson's acquaintances on the other side was Beauregard, his artillery instructor at West Point.)

Surrounding Fort Sumter in a wide circle on the mainland and islands around the harbor, the guns of the Confederacy were aimed and ready. Learning of Anderson's final words, General Beauregard sent firing orders at about four in the morning to Captain George S James and the James Island battery. Captain James positioned his men. When they were ready he turned to his friend Roger A Pryor and said to him, "You are the only man to whom I would give up the honor of firing the first gun of the war." Shaken, Pryor declined. At 4:30 in the morning of 12 April 1861, Captain James pulled the firing lanyard of a ten-inch mortar, and the first shot of the war arched into the sky.

It was not until after daylight that Federal guns began responding from within the fort. The slow rate of return fire showed the Confederates that the Federals were low on ammunition and were mounting only token resistance. After three hours of steady firing there were no casualties to either side.

Three Federal warships appeared outside the harbor in midmorning. The defenders in the fort cheered and flag salutes were exchanged, but after a few hours the ships turned and sailed away. Federal firing ceased at dusk. All through the night the Confederate batteries kept up their pounding while the defenders anxiously tried to sleep. About dawn on 13 April the batteries of Fort Moultrie began pouring hot shot into the fort, and the effects were soon seen: the

Above: *Interior of Fort Sumter during the bombardment. The shelling produced no casualties but the defenders' position was plainly impossible.*

Below: *The Confederate commander of Charleston, P G T Beauregard, accepted the surrender of Fort Sumter on 13 April. The Union evacuated the next day.*

Union barracks, supposedly fireproof, were in flames. The weak Federal return fire slowed still further, to one shot every five minutes, as soldiers in the fort were detailed to fight the flames and try to keep them from spreading to the magazine. Shortly after noon, the flagstaff of the fort was shot away and quickly repaired. But soon the Stars and Stripes were hauled down and replaced by a white flag.

A detachment was sent by boat to offer aid to the fort. They arrived to find that they had been preceded by ex-Senator Wigfall of Texas, who had apparently rowed out on his own to demand surrender. Wigfall had appeared in front of one of the fort's gun embrasures, to the considerable surprise of the Federal gunners. They had finally pulled Wigfall in before he was killed by his own side's fire. The ensuing negotiations were confused, what with two separate Confederate delegations and Major Anderson's uncertainties and anxieties – he and his men were begrimed with smoke and cinders and near exhaustion. But the outcome was inescapable. The garrison had taken some 4000 shells in 34 hours of nearly continuous bombardment and the Federals had few shells left to fire in reply. Finally Anderson capitulated, saying he would evacuate Fort Sumter on 14 April. Beauregard generously agreed that the Federals could salute their flag with cannons before leaving. By that point there still had been no casualties on either side.

As an ironic fate would have it, men were nonetheless destined to fall as a result of this battle. As the Federals fired their salute to the flag on 14 April, some sparks from the smouldering fire in the fort set off a paper-wrapped cannon cartridge as it was being loaded. The explosion killed Private Daniel Hough and wounded five other soldiers, one of whom soon died. These were the first casualties of the Civil War.

The fighting seemed rather dashing and decorous at Fort Sumter; to the Southerners it seemed the realization of all their fantasies of how easy it would be to send the Yankees running. All over the South there was revelry, dancing in the streets, young men joining up in thousands, showing off their grand new uniforms and guns to their families. They dreamed of glory and immortality and the romantic excitement of battle.

But elsewhere in the South one woman of Virginia, living in sight of Washington, wrote eloquently of her fears and heartbreak:

I heard distinctly the drums beating in Washington. As I looked at the Capitol in the distance, I could scarcely believe my senses. That Capitol of which I had always been so proud! Can it be possible that it is no longer *our* capitol? Must this Union, which I was taught to revere, be rent asunder?

Right: *The Confederate flag flew over Fort Sumter throughout the war, despite several major Federal assaults. Confederate troops finally abandoned the ruined fort on 17 February 1865 before the approach of Union General Sherman's army.*

FIRST AND SECOND MANASSAS

After the fall of Fort Sumter war fever swept across the country – or rather, the two countries. President Lincoln called for 75,000 three-month volunteers to suppress the Southern rebellion. Four more states seceded – Virginia, Arkansas, Tennessee, and North Carolina. The border states – Delaware, Maryland, Kentucky, and Missouri – stayed shakily loyal to the Union, even though the latter three were slave states. Both sides expected a short war, to be won in one or two decisive battles. Certainly no one foresaw the four years of agony that were to come.

There were essential differences in the strategy and aims of the two sections. The more formidable task was the Union's – in order to conquer the South the North had physically to invade, occupy, and hold its entire territory. This involved unprecedented commitments of men and supplies. On the other hand, the Confederacy's strategy seemed to call

Left: *Robert E Lee during his tenure as Superintendent of the US Military Academy (1852-55). Offered command of all the Federal forces on 18 April 1861, Lee declined, having decided that he could not raise his hand against his home state of Virginia.*

Opposite: *The young army officer Thomas J Jackson would earn his nickname "Stonewall" at First Manassas, where his brigade stoutly defended its position on Henry House Hill.*

for the defensive. As Northern armies advanced into the South their supply lines would steadily become longer and more tenuous as their numbers shrank due to attrition and the necessity of guarding lines of communication. The South thus had the advantage of fighting on and for its own territory, and also had, theoretically at least, the advantage of *interior lines* (because an invading army must stretch around and contain its enemy, that enemy, being more compact, can shift its forces much faster to any point on the perimeter along interior lines of communications).

At the beginning of the war the South probably had at least as good a chance of winning its war as the American colonies had of winning theirs. Moreover, Jefferson Davis confidently expected Great Britain and France to come to the rescue of the Confederacy; the threat of losing Southern cotton, Davis said, would bring them to the Confederate cause. In this, as in many other things, Davis miscalculated seriously. Great Britain at the beginning of the war had enough surplus cotton to last two years, and after that time found other sources.

(However, a good deal of Southern trading with Great

Britain – cotton out, arms and supplies in – did go on during the war. The North imposed a blockade of Southern ports from the outset, but it did not become effective until later in the war. In the South, blockade-running developed into a fine maritime art.)

Nearly all the commanding generals on both sides were West Pointers; as the war went on, a number of untrained leaders of genius arose, among them Nathan Bedford Forrest. But since military tradition was stronger in the South, the Confederacy got more than its share of the best military minds of the time; at the beginning of the war the North had no one to compare to Robert E Lee, Jackson, the two Johnstons, and Beauregard. This superiority of Confederate generalship in the early part of the war was clear to all concerned in the two great battles fought on a little stream called the Bull Run, near Manassas, Virginia.

Having resigned his commission in the US Army – and in the process declining an offer to command all Union forces – Robert Edward Lee was made a general in the Confederate army and given overall command of operations in his beloved home state of Virginia. In June and July of 1861 Americans began killing one another: Union forces were defeated near Fort Monroe, Virginia, and Federal general George B McClellan secured the western countries of Virginia for the Union (this area was soon to achieve statehood). Lee sent 11,000 men under General Joseph E Johnston to Harpers Ferry, near the entrance to Virginia's Shenandoah Valley, and 22,000 under General Pierre G T Beauregard to Manassas Junction, some 25 miles southwest of Washington. Lincoln,

despite objection that Union forces were too green, ordered General Irvin McDowell to drive Beauregard away from the important Manassas rail junction. Most of McDowell's 30,600 men were three-month volunteers and militia; only 800 were regular army. In support of McDowell, General Robert Patterson was ordered to keep Johnston in the Shenandoah in order to prevent his reinforcing Beauregard.

On 16 July, McDowell began advancing from Washington toward what everyone seemed to know would be the first great convulsion of the war. Many felt it would be the last. Confidently, the Union soldiers shouted, "On to Richmond!" Accompanying the Federal army were swarms of reporters, Congressmen, ladies with parasols and picnic baskets, and assorted sightseers – all off to see the war as if it were a fireworks show.

Marching on the Warrenton Turnpike, McDowell's Federal army reached Centreville, near Manassas, Virginia, on 18 July. At that point Beauregard's forces were vulnerable, though McDowell had no idea of that fact. Since the Union forces had become highly disorganized during the march, McDowell did not try a fullscale offensive (if he had, it might well have been successful). Meanwhile, Beauregard had received thorough intelligence concerning Union dispositions from a network of spies in Washington. He asked General Johnston to bring his forces over from the Shenandoah, where Patterson proved unable to contest their departure. On the 18th McDowell did try a reconnaissance in force against Beauregard's right. After a brisk skirmish at Blackburn's Ford on the Bull Run, the Federals were sent running

Right: *Confederate and Union movements toward Manassas Junction on 18 and 19 July.*
Right bottom: *Troop positions on 21 July 1861.*

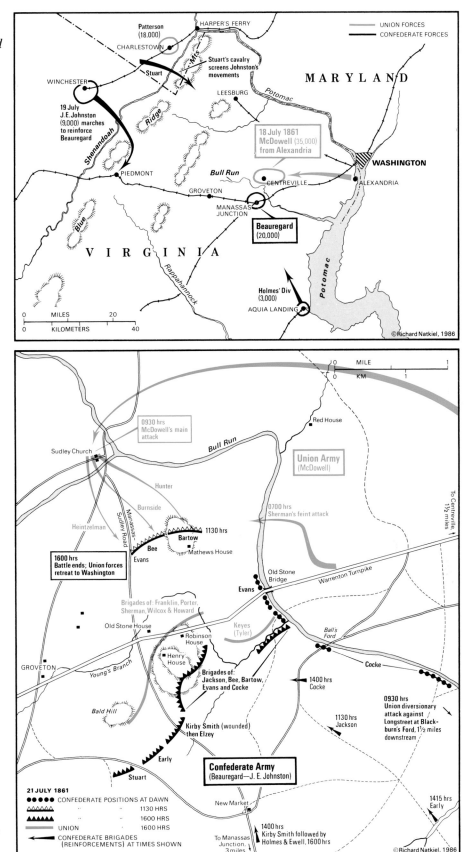

Opposite: *Confederate blockade-runners entering the harbor at St George, Bermuda. At first the Union blockade of the South was not very effective, but it became ever more so as the war progressed.*

back by the Confederates. The Southern commander in that skirmish was General James Longstreet, soon to be one of the great corps leaders of Robert E Lee's army. (In the South the affair at Blackburn's Ford is called the First Battle of Bull Run' to add to the confusion, the Northern names for the two large battles around the stream are the First and Second Bull Run).

McDowell's hesitation on the 28th allowed time for Johnston to move his 12,000 men east from the Shenandoah Valley. Most of that journey was made by railroad – the first

major strategic troop movement by railroad in history. Among Johnston's generals was a strange, laconic brigade commander named Thomas J Jackson.

McDowell and Beauregard had been classmates at West Point and had studied the same tactics. Perhaps for that reason, they made identical plans for an offensive on 19 July: feint with the left, attack with the right. If both had been successful, the results could have been strange indeed – after brushing past each other like a swinging door, the Con-

federates might have continued right into Washington and the Federals march into Richmond. But on the morning of the 19th, McDowell got his offensive underway first, and thereafter Beauregard and Johnston were on the defensive. McDowell made his feint on the Southern right, mounted a secondary attack on the enemy center, and took his right wing on a wide envelopment, marching the troops 15 miles through the broken and difficult landscape to attack the Rebel left flank.

Union general McDowell's plan was a perfectly good one, but it ran afoul of several problems. First, his troops were too inexperienced to execute with dispatch the intended wide envelopment of the Southern left flank. Second, Confederate observers on Signal Hill saw the movement and sent word to Beauregard: "Look out for your left; you are turned." Third, Beauregard had seen a cloud of dust on his left and realized the attack along the Warrenton Turnpike was a bluff to cover the move on his left. He began shifting divisions over to his left to oppose the oncoming Federals in the vicinity of Henry House Hill. As the Federals marched they could hear the whistles of the trains bringing Johnston's men to the battlefront. These arrivals were formed up on the railroad platform and marched directly into line.

Confident that every one of them could whip seven Yankees, the Confederate troops advanced from Henry House Hill towards the enemy. But then the Federals smashed into the Rebels, driving them back on to the hill. It seemed that the Federals were going to sweep the Rebels back down Henry House Hill. But defending that position was Thomas J Jackson and the brigade he had trained. He formed his men into a defensive nucleus on the hilltop. Seeing that stand, Confederate general Bernard E Bee entered history in his last moments of life. "Look at Jackson's Brigade," Bee shouted to his men, "It stands like a stone wall! Rally behind the Virginians!" And rally they did, stopping the advancing Federal troops in their tracks. And forever after, the general who led that stand would be called Stonewall Jackson, his men the Stonewall Brigade.

As Beauregard continued to strip his right and send men to the left, the Confederate line firmed up around Jackson on Henry House Hill. Finally Jackson led a counterattack on the Union right flank; sweeping around the hill in support rode the Rebel cavalrymen of young J E B ("Jeb") Stuart, another leader of that day destined for greatness. Jeb's men tore into a battalion of red-pantalooned New York Zouaves inflicting heavy casualties. At the most critical moment, just after two o'clock in the afternoon, on the Southern left, a Union artillery officer held his fire, mistaking blue-clad Rebel troops in his front for Federals; as a result, two powerful batteries fell into Southern hands and the Federals began to retreat. Now was Beauregard's great chance to pursue the enemy and annihilate them. However, at just that moment, Beauregard echoed the mistake of the Federal artillery commander: receiving a report that a large Federal force was moving on his supplies near Manassas, Beauregard pulled troops from his attack force to meet this threat. But the threat was a false alarm – it was Confederates marching towards the supplies, not Yankees. As Beauregard's advance slowed, dusk came on. The Confederacy had won the field that day of the first Manassas, but it was too late to pursue the enemy.

The Federals commenced an orderly retreat from the battlefield, moving up the Warrenton Turnpike. The Federal column, including numbers of civilian spectators who had not found the battle to be as much fun as they had expected, had to constrict to pass over a stone bridge over the Bull Run. Suddenly a Rebel battery dropped a few shells into the dense column near the bridge. There was an instant panic that quickly snowballed into a chaotic rout. By 22 July, Washington was inundated by the broken remains of its great army, which had become a mob of jaded, dirty, and demoralized men.

On the Confederate side there was a great and understandable jubilation over the triumph at Manassas. But the victory led to a dangerous overconfidence. Rebel soldiers had been confirmed in their illusion of invincibility.

Perhaps the South should have studied the casualty figures; they would have found the Union army had not been seriously damaged. Indeed, by the later standards of the war the First Manassas was not a particularly bloody contest – the South had 387 killed, 1582 wounded, 12 missing, for a total of 1981 casualties of the 32, 232 engaged; the Union suffered 418 killed, 1011 wounded, 1216 missing, for a total of 2645 casualties of 28,452 engaged. The contrast in the numbers of missing is notable; but the fact remained that the Union army was only marginally more hurt than the Confederate – and the North had virtually endless supplies of manpower, whereas the South was severely limited in that regard. The day after the First Manassas, a young Federal general named George B McClellan took command in Washington and from the shattered Union forces of the First Manassas began rebuilding the army.

As will be described in the next chapter, Stonewall Jackson went on to his Shenandoah Valley Campaign of summer 1862. During that operation, Jackson kept three Federal armies tied up in the Valley and thereby helped to stymie Union General McClellan's Peninsular Campaign on Richmond with his new Army of the Potomac. During the Seven Days Battles that surged around Richmond during McClellan's campaign, Confederate General J E Johnston, one of the heroes of the First Manassas, was severely wounded. Johnston was replaced by General Robert E Lee; it was Lee who finished the job of driving the Army of the Potomac away from Richmond and, before long, out of Virginia entirely.

After tying up the enemy armies in the Shenandoah and keeping them from reinforcing McClellan, Stonewall Jackson hurried east to join Lee in the Seven Days Battles. As soon as Jackson's forces left the Shenandoah, new orders went out from Washington: the three Federal armies that had futilely chased Jackson were to be consolidated into one army under General John Pope, who was then to march South from

Above: *Stonewall Jackson directs his brigade at First Manassas, where he earned his nickname.*

Below: *Union marines, stationed to defend Washington, march outside their barracks.*

Washington and draw the Confederate army away from Richmond. But the plan was soon changed in light of Union failures in the Seven Days, and a new plan developed: McClellan was to move his forces around by water to unite with Pope; with the resulting army of 130,000 men, the Federals would descend into Virginia to annihilate Lee's army of 50,000. Federal intelligence estimates had more than doubled Lee's actual numbers; in contrast, Lee had a per-

Opposite top: *Confederate artillery repels a Union attack at First Manassas.*

Opposite bottom: *Rebel Black Horse Cavalry under assault by Union Zouaves.*

Above: *Artist Alfred R Waud sketched Union General McClellan crossing Bull Run on 29 March 1862.*

Right: *General George B McClellan would regain command of the Union army after Second Manassas.*

fectly clear idea of the daunting prospect he was up against. It was the first great challenge of his career.

The new commander of the Confederate Army of Northern Virginia was an unusual man for a soldier. So soft-spoken, courtly, and religious was Lee that many of his soldiers dubbed him "Granny." It was not long before they saw him more accurately: this mild-mannered Virginian aristocrat was one of the most aggressive and brilliant fighting generals who ever lived. But it is a strange position he occupies. Later called by Winston Churchill "the greatest of Americans," Lee was a primary leader of a rebellion that aimed to destroy the United States. Yet he believed neither in slavery nor in secession, and was certainly patriotic enough before the war. Like many Americans of that era, Lee placed loyalty to this home state above loyalty to the United States. In his resignation from the US Army, Lee said he could not raise his hand against Virginians; if they seceded, so must he.

It was not long before Lee was virtually deified by his Army of Northern Virginia. Moreover, the Army of Northern Virginia had an outstanding staff of subordinates. The great Stonewall Jackson was known as Lee's right arm. In addition there were the over-cautious but hard-fighting James Longstreet, impetuous A P Hill, choleric Daniel H Hill, and 25-year-old Jeb Stuart, one of the greatest cavalry-men of all time, who ful-

Opposite above: *At Cedar Mountain, in the first battle of the Second Manassas campaign, A P Hill halted a Union advance under Nathaniel Banks on 9 August.*

filled his function of being the eyes of Lee's army with extra-ordinary effectiveness and dash.

Such generals combined with a fighting body of the highest spirit made for one of the great armies of history, one already legendary during its own brief existence. But it is also true that there were deep and abiding weaknesses in both the command structure and army. Chief among these weak-nesses was that both Lee and the Confederate government paid too little attention to logistics, especially the need to feed and clothe the army properly. For much of the war Southern soldiers marched and fought hungry, ragged, and often shoeless, even when the Confederacy had abundant supplies. The availability of arms and powder was remark-ably dependable throughout the war, but soldiers need more than weapons to fight. Beyond that, Lee often gave vague orders, leaving much leeway for his generals; with a sub-ordinate of genius like Stonewall Jackson, the results could be spectacular, but with lesser generals there were often mis-understandings. And Lee arguably gave too much of his

attention to his beloved home state of Virginia, leaving large-scale strategy to the unreliable attentions of Jefferson Davis (though this was more the fault of Davis than of Lee).

But all these things were unknown in July of 1862. By then Lee had driven McClellan from the gates of Richmond, but he faced the prospect of a grand combination of McClellan and Pope's forces that would, if successfully accomplished, spell almost certain doom for the Confederacy. On 14 July Pope began moving his forces south in Virginia, intending to take over the railroad junction at Gordonsville and then attack Lee, who for the moment was still protecting the Confederate capital from further efforts by McClellan. An observer watched Lee as he grappled with this daunting situation:

When contemplating any great undertaking or a vast stra-tegic combination, General Lee had an abstracted manner that was altogether unlike his usual one. He would seek some level sward and pace mechanically up and down with the regularity of a sentinel on his beat; his head would

be bent as if in deep meditation, while his left hand unconsciously stroked his thick iron-grey beard.

Soon Stonewall Jackson was summoned; Lee now knew what he was going to do. Jackson and A P Hill were ordered north with 24,000 men to confront Pope and draw him away from the safety of Washington. Above all Pope had to be dealt with before McClellan could reinforce him, and time was running short it that was to be done. As always, Lee had examined his opponent carefully and knew his man. In this case, he knew he was dealing not with a worthy opponent but with a blustering fool. This may be seen in Pope's first address to his new command, in which he crowed, "Let us understand each other. I come to you from the West, where we have always seen the backs of our enemies." Lee took an uncharacteristically angry attitude towards this particular opponent; the "miscreant" Pope, Lee said, must be "suppressed."

Jackson set off with his and Hill's divisions to execute Lee's orders. He first planned to smash Pope's vanguard at Culpeper, Virginia, then to defeat the rest in detail, one corps at a time. But due to unwonted slowness, Jackson fumbled this initial strategy. On 9 August the advancing Confederates found themselves opposed by General Nathaniel Banks at Cedar Mountain. The Federals came on strongly and pushed Jackson's men back, but a crashing counterattack by A P Hill ended the enemy advance.

Pope's advance had been slowed, but no more. And now McClellan began pulling his Army of the Potomac away from Richmond by water and moving to combine with Pope. The immediate threat to the capitol over, Lee moved with Longstreet's division to join Jackson and march to the east of Pope's army, trying to maneuver to a position between him and both Washington and McClellan. This plan miscarried; because of poor staff work and a surprise attack on Jeb

Below: *General John Pope commanded Union forces at Second Manassas. General Lee considered him an unworthy opponent.*

Overleaf: *Federal troops, protected by a determined rear guard, begin their retreat at First Manassas.*

Right: *A column of Federal cavalry along the Rappahannock River in Virginia in August 1862.*

Below: *A Union brigade fails in its attempt to force strongly entrenched Confederate troops from the woods at the battle of Cedar Mountain.*

Stuart's camp (18 August) that captured Lee's plans, the Confederates were unable to march east of Pope. Finally both armies came to rest facing one another across the Rappahannock River, both making probing attacks with their cavalry. The report came to Lee that McClellan was now five days away from the juncture with Pope. In effect, the Confederates were racing with McClellan to get to Pope first. At that critical juncture in the history of the Confederacy, the combination of Lee and Jackson first revealed the genius for which history remembers them.

For the first, but not the last, time, Lee contradicted an ancient and virtually ironbound rule of military strategy: do not divide forces in the face of the enemy. In this case, it was an enemy that outnumbered Lee 75,000 to 55,000. The extraordinary bold plan was this: holding Pope in place on the Rappahannock with Longstreet's thinly spaced forces, Lee sent Jackson and Jeb Stuart on a wide envelopment, first northwest, then east, around Pope's army. Jackson's command left on 25 August; his foot soldiers duplicated the feats of marching they had demonstrated in the Valley Campaign, when they earned the title "foot cavalry." On the first day they marched 26 miles, the second day 36 miles.

At least McClellan had the sense to expect the unexpected from Stonewall Jackson. In the ensuing days that led up to the convulsion of the battle of Second Manassas, General Pope resolutely refused to believe that Jackson was behaving in anything but a timid and predictable fashion.

Pope's first surprise came on the evening of 27 August, when Jackson's men swamped the Union supply dump at Manassas. There the hungry Confederates had themselves the feast of a lifetime. After torching the remaining supplies, Jackson and Stuart pulled their forces away and, as far as Federal intelligence was concerned, vanished into thin air. General Pope, finding Jackson unexpectedly on his rear and the Federal supply line at Manassas destroyed, pulled his army away to the north on 26 August. This was what Lee had been waiting for; he took Longstreet's corps away from the Rappahannock, marching to meet Jackson. Meanwhile, Pope's blustering confusions continued; insisting that Jackson was retreating toward the Shenandoah Valley, Pope vowed to find and destroy him. Finally the Union army of 75,000 men was concentrated squarely between Jackson's force of 24,000 and Longstreet's still-distant 30,000. Here was a golden opportunity for the North: crush Jackson and then

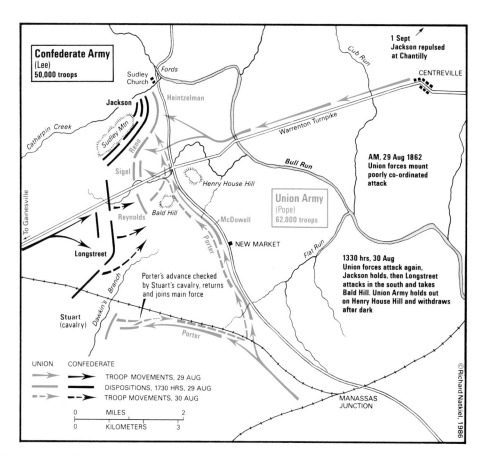

Confederate Army
(Lee)
50,000 troops

1 Sept
Jackson repulsed
at Chantilly

CENTREVILLE

Sudley Church   Fords

Jackson   Heintzelman

Warrenton Turnpike

Catharpin Creek   Sudley Mtn   Reno

Bull Run

AM, 29 Aug 1862
Union forces mount
poorly co-ordinated
attack

Sigel

Henry House Hill

Union Army
(Pope)
62,000 troops

To Gainesville   Reynolds   Bald Hill   McDowell

Porter

NEW MARKET

Longstreet   Flat Run

1330 hrs, 30 Aug
Union forces attack again,
Jackson holds, then Longstreet
attacks in the south and takes
Bald Hill. Union Army holds out
on Henry House Hill and withdraws
after dark

Dawkin's Branch

Porter's advance checked
by Stuart's cavalry, returns
and joins main force

Stuart
(cavalry)

Porter

UNION   CONFEDERATE

TROOP MOVEMENTS, 29 AUG
DISPOSITIONS, 1730 HRS, 29 AUG
TROOP MOVEMENTS, 30 AUG

0   MILES   2
0   KILOMETERS   3

MANASSAS
JUNCTION

© Richard Natkiel, 1986

Left: *Map of Confederate
and Union positions and
movements at the Second
Manassas.*

Opposite: *An A R Waud
sketch of the defeat of the
Federal Army of the
Potomac under General
Pope at the Second
Manassas on 30 August
1862.*

turn on Longstreet. The trouble was, Pope could not find
Jackson, despite frantic efforts to do so. Too, from start to
very near finish, Pope ignored Longstreet entirely.

Nonetheless, with a large enemy between their divided
forces the Confederates were in a desperate situation, one
that might well have proven fatal if their opponent had possessed a modicum of sense. Jackson's problem was: how to
hold Pope at bay until Longstreet arrived, how to attack, if
possible, and still leave room to retreat. About 27 August
Jackson found the place to do both those things – an unfinished railroad cut at the foot of Stony Ridge. It was an ideal
defensive position, attackers having to make their way across
a deep excavation. Behind the cut were mountain passes serviceable for retreat. On 27-28 August Jackson moved his
forces to that position circuitously, in three detachments,
and then literally hid his army in the woods behind the railroad cut.

On 28 August the Federals were in Groveton, unaware of
Jackson's presence nearby. At that point Jackson made a historic gamble, a bigger one than Lee had made in dividing his
army. With less than a third of the forces of the enemy, Jackson moved out and attacked the Federals, thereby revealing
his position. It was a decision so bold as to seem foolhardy.
The reason for it was that Jackson wanted to make sure Pope
stayed away from strong defenses at nearby Centreville; if
they pulled back to that position, the Federals could wait for
the oncoming McClellan with impunity.

So Jackson moved out and struck the Federals near Groveton. A fierce skirmish developed as Pope turned his army to
smash the supposedly retreating Jackson, meanwhile sending telegrams to Washington proclaiming victory over Jackson and saying Lee was in precipitate retreat to Richmond.
Some of his officers tried to warn him of Longstreet's
approach; Pope refused to listen. Now the Confederates were
ready to engage the enemy before McClellan could arrive.
The stage was set for the Battle of Second Manassas.

On the morning of 29 August 1862, General Pope threw
62,000 men against 20,000 Confederates, most of whom were

again entrenched behind the railroad cut. All morning long
the Union attacks continued; all were driven back with heavy
losses. But the Confederates were increasingly desperate as
the morning wore on.

As ammunition ran out, the Confederate defenders began
hurling rocks at the attackers. General Maxcy Gregg walked
up and down behind his troops, a sword of Revolutionary vin-
tage in his hand, shouting "Let us die here, my men, let us die
here!" Then, at about 11 in the morning, Longstreet's corp
arrived on the Confederate right. In fact, Longstreet was
squarely athwart a large gap in the Federal line; he could have
fallen on the Union flank with devastating effect. But as was to
be the case so often in the future, Longstreet was over-
cautious, worried about the Union corps on this right. Rather
than mounting a fullscale attack, then, Longstreet moved
some men over to make a demonstration on the Federal
center. This sufficed to relieve the pressure on Jackson and
to ensure the failure of Pope's offensive.

At the end of the day on 29 August Jackson pulled back
from some of his advanced positions. Obtuse as ever, Pope
declared that Jackson was retreating (the Federal commander was still oblivious to the presence of Longstreet).
Pope ordered his men to pursue the enemy the next day. Lee
encouraged Pope's illusions by letting some carefully-misin-
formed Federal prisoners escape back to their own lines;
these returned prisoners assured Pope that the enemy was
indeed retreating.

Next day, 30 August, the Federals, renewed their assault on
the Southern lines, which now contained the entire Army of
Northern Virginia. Lee let Pope hit Jackson's left, then sent
Longstreet against the opposite Union flank. Longstreet remembered that morning:

A heavy fire of shot and shell was being poured into the
thick column of the enemy, and in ten minutes their stubborn masses began to waver and give back. For a moment
there was chaos; then order returned and they re-formed,
apparently to renew the attack. Meanwhile my other eight

pieces reported to me, and from the crest of the little hill the fire of twelve guns cut them down. As the cannon thundered the ranks broke, only to be formed again with dogged determination. A third time the batteries tore the Federals to pieces, and as they fell back under this terrible fire, I sprung everything to the charge. My troops leaped forward with exultant yells, and all along the line we pushed forward.

Now the Federal army was pincered between Longstreet and Jackson. Lee proceeded to swing his forces shut around the enemy like a gate.

Pope and his army were routed, but a stout Federal defense at Henry House Hill saved the army and made an orderly retreat possible. Lee and Jackson had created the first great victory of their immortal partnership.

There was much more to their success than a battle won, however. The Seven Days Battles, Jackson's Shenandoah Valley Campaign and the Second Manassas had really been one gigantic and ultimately victorious campaign of three months' duration. In that time Lee had sent two enormous Federal armies running back to Washington and virtually cleared Virginia of enemy forces. When Lee took command the North had been at the gates of Richmond. Now Lee was only 25 miles from Washington.

Yet in the end, the Second Manassas proved to be an incomplete victory. After driving the North from the field Lee tried to maintain the offensive, sending the corps of Jackson and Longstreet around the Federal west flank at Centreville. In this effort the exhausted Rebels discovered their enemy was still ready to fight. Jackson struck the Federals, but they resisted strongly even after two corps commanders were killed. In the end the Federals got away to Washington. On the next day Pope's forces were merged into McClellan's command, and that general once again took over operations in the East. Pope was never to command in the field again.

The Second Manassas was the first really devastating engagement of the Civil War. Now the soldiers and civilians of the contending nations were to learn the real costs of war. Confederate casualties were 1481 killed, 7627 wounded, 89 missing, a total of 9197 out of 48,527 engaged – 19 percent casualties. Federal losses were 1724 killed, 8372 wounded, 5958 missing, a total of 16,054 of the 75,696 engaged – 21 percent casualties.

Now Lee had to do something. He could not stay put; his army was in an exposed position near the enemy capital, where there were enormous masses of soldiers who would sooner or later be coming at him again. Lee knew he did not have sufficient strength to mount a siege of Washington. But it was not in his nature to pull back to safety near Richmond. Lee was above all an aggressive general; thus he decided to keep going, to invade Maryland. In this decision he underestimated his enemy and overestimated his own men. It was Pope, not the Federal soldiers, who had lost the Second Manassas; in battle the Northern men had fought with the same valor as their enemy.

JACKSON'S VALLEY CAMPAIGN

Stonewall Jackson showed his mettle in the Battle of Second Manassas. It was one of his greatest moments, but it was an earlier campaign in the Shenandoah Valley of Virginia that has forever stamped Jackson's genius in the annals of military history.

Thomas Jonathan Jackson had not seemed so promising at the outset of his military career. He arrived at West Point an awkward, taciturn mountain boy clad in rough homespun. With great effort he managed to rise from the bottom to nearly the top of his class during his four years. When the

Right: *Union General John Charles Frémont, commander of the Frederal Mountain Division in western Virginia, was defeated by Jackson in the Shenandoah Valley Campaign.*

Opposite: *General Thomas Jonathan ("Stonewall") Jackson, one of the greatest generals of the Civil War. His death on 10 May 1863 was a devastating blow to the Confederate cause.*

Civil War began he was a professor of mathematics and natural philosophy at the Virginia Military Institute and was already viewed as a strange character. He was a fanatical, brooding, and humorless Presbyterian, who never smoked or drank or played cards. He was obsessed with his health and with eccentric remedies: during the war he sucked lemons constantly, shunned pepper, claiming it made his left leg weak, and kept his right arm raised a good deal of the time, saying it improved the circulation.

So peculiar was Jackson that some of his own subordinates questioned his sanity. His obsessive secrecy drove his men close to madness themselves; not only did the enemy never know where Jackson was going, neither did any of his command, much of the time. But it was not long before everyone on both sides understood the military genius of Stonewall Jackson, and thereafter his men were happy to accept any

odd notion he devised. He was to become the indispensible right arm of Robert E. Lee, who described Jackson thus:

> A man he is of contrasts so complete that he appears one day a Presbyterian deacon who delights in theological discussion and, the next, a reincarnated Joshua. He lives by the New Testament and fights by the Old.

The Shenandoah Valley of Virginia was one of the vitally important stretches of land in the Confederacy. It is the most fertile farmland imaginable, and was thus the breadbasket of the South. Beyond that, it was the ideal route for Confederate armies marching North for Maryland or Pennsylvania. To the Union, the Shenandoah was strategically useless; marching south in it took them nowhere in particular. The Valley was important to the north only because it was so important to

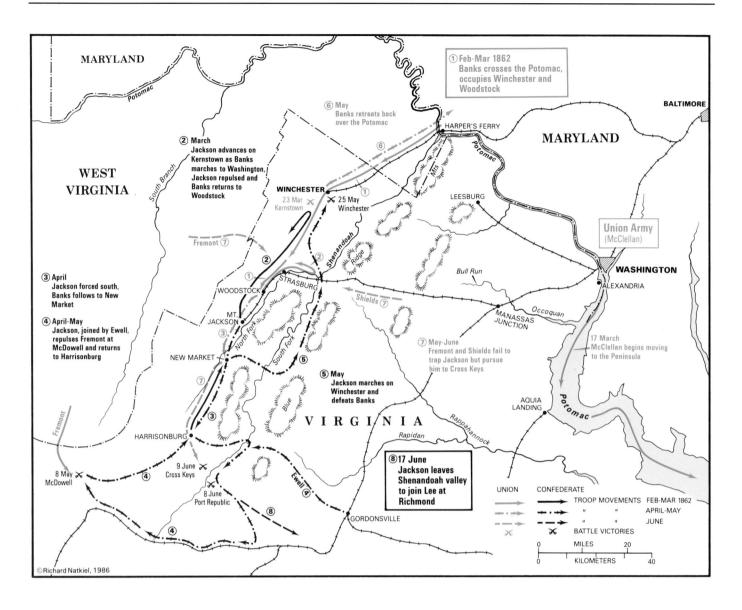

① Feb-Mar 1862
Banks crosses the Potomac,
occupies Winchester and
Woodstock

⑥ May
Banks retreats back
over the Potomac

② March
Jackson advances on
Kernstown as Banks
marches to Washington,
Jackson repulsed and
Banks returns to
Woodstock

③ April
Jackson forced south,
Banks follows to New
Market

④ April-May
Jackson, joined by Ewell,
repulses Fremont at
McDowell and returns
to Harrisonburg

⑤ May
Jackson marches on
Winchester and
defeats Banks

⑦ May-June
Fremont and Shields fail to
trap Jackson but pursue
him to Cross Keys

17 March
McClellan begins moving
to the Peninsula

⑧ 17 June
Jackson leaves
Shenandoah valley
to join Lee at
Richmond

UNION   CONFEDERATE
TROOP MOVEMENTS FEB-MAR 1862
"   "   APRIL-MAY
"   "   JUNE
BATTLE VICTORIES

MILES   20
KILOMETERS 40

© Richard Natkiel, 1986

the Confederacy. Thus in October 1861 a Federal army occupied Romney, in the northern part of the Valley, and threatened Winchester; the Union was preparing to clear the Shenandoah of Confederates. In response, Stonewall Jackson and his brigade were sent to take charge of operations in the Shenandoah. With his Stonewall Brigade, some militia, and other troops, Jackson (now a major-general) commanded around 10,000 men. The main Union forces in the area were some 10,000 men under General Nathaniel P Banks.

After a winter of mostly fruitless maneuvering by both sides, Bank occupied Winchester in March of 1862, chasing Jackson's forces away and sending a Federal division south to occupy Strasburg. From that position Banks prepared to leave the Valley and join General McClellan's Federal Army of the Potomac, which was marching towards Richmond.

On 21 March Jackson learned of the planned Federal move from his cavalry commander, Turner Ashby. It was clear to Jackson as it was to his superiors that this must not happen: if Banks or any other major Union forces joined McClellan (a Federal army under McDowell was just east of the Valley and also slated to reinforce McClellan) they would gain overwhelming strength, and the Confederacy would be doomed. Lee, who at that time was overseeing operations in Virginia rather than commanding in the field, ordered Jackson to make a strategic diversion to keep Union forces, especially Banks's and McDowell's, in the Shenandoah and away from McClellan. In the process, he was to try to lead the Union high command into scattering their armies and also defend Richmond from the west. In all those requirements Jackson was to prove successful beyond anyone's expectations.

Hurrying to keep the Federals in place, Jackson ordered Ashby's cavalry to attack Shields's division of Banks's army at Kernstown on 22 March 1862.

Next day Jackson arrived and followed up with his infantry (after searching his soul about fighting on Sunday). The Confederate attack went well for a while, until Shields moved some concealed forces into line. Then, outnumbered and low on ammunition, Jackson's men retreated, with Ashby covering the rear. Casualties in the fighting were disproportionate: the South had lost 700 of 4200 engaged; the Union 590 of 9000 engaged. It seemed a most unpromising beginning for Jackson's campaign.

In fact, Kernstown proved to be as good as a major victory for the South. Federal authorities assumed that Jackson's command was far larger than it actually was, and simply threw over the entire plan to reinforce McClellan, to that general's great disgust (for all his mistakes, McClellan understood better than his superiors in Washington that Jackson's campaign was a diversion). Orders went out from Washington: Banks and McDowell were to stay in the Shenandoah to deal with Jackson; indeed, some additional troops were stripped from McClellan for the purpose. At length there were three uncoordinated Federal commands trying to clear the Shenandoah Valley – Banks, McDowell, and, to the west, the army of John C Frémont.

As the Federal armies prepared to pursue him, Jackson

Opposite: *Troop movements in the Valley Campaign, February–June 1862.*

Right: *General Richard S Ewell led a division of Confederates in Jackson's Valley Campaign.*

Below: *Union General Frémont taking command of the Department of the West. He was removed for political and military errors but, owing to his popularity, was reassigned to western Virginia.*

withdrew gradually up the Valley (that is, to the south) with his 6000 men; Banks cautiously followed with 15,000. Then Jackson suddenly made a forced march to Swift Run Gap, in the eastern mountains. There his command was on the flank of Banks's army at Harrisonburg. Banks thus could not continue on up the Valley, for Jackson would be behind him, on the Union supply line. At Swift Run Gap in late April, Jackson was reinforced by 8000 men including the command of General Richard S Ewell; added to earlier reinforcements, this brought Rebel strength to 17,000 (which was as high as it would be in the campaign).

Of course the Federals were not standing still; Frémont began moving his forces east to join Banks in operating against Jackson. Learning of this Jackson made plans to stop that conjunction, which would likely to be fatal to his efforts. As he would so often in the future, Lee wisely gave Jackson fre rein. With a series of brilliant and lightning-quick maneuvers Jackson began his momentous campaign.

Leaving Ewell at Swift Run Gap to keep Banks in place, and sending Ashby's cavalry to make some feinting attacks, Jackson moved to strike Frémont's advance. In the most rigorous secrecy the Confederates began their march. Only Jackson knew that his destination was the town of McDowell, where R H Milroy's division was just pulling in. Driving his troops in continuous forced marches, Jackson moved to the attack. So fast did his men march that they began to be called "foot cavalry"; they made 92 miles in four days of wet and muddy weather. On 7 May they drove Federal outposts back into McDowell. There the Federal command numbered some 6000, under Milroy and Schenck, to Jackson's 10,000. With classic skill, Jackson had maneuvered his small army to gain local superiority over his enemy.

On 8 May 1962, the Federals took the initiative at McDowell, attacking in the afternoon. Despite heavy losses, the Confederates repulsed the attack and sent the Yankees running west. Though the wet weather and enemy resistance made pursuit most difficult, the Rebels managed to chase their enemy to Franklin, West Virginia. Then Jackson withdrew, using Ashby's cavalry as a screen. The South had lost 498 men to the Union's 256, but they had won the day. Jackson, however, was by no means ready to rest. On 14 May he marched his command for Harrisonburg.

As the Confederates marched, Banks dug his army in at Strasburg and sent troops to reinforce General McDowell to the east. Thus Banks left himself with only 8000 men, a most dangerous position to be in with Stonewall Jackson around. At that point Jackson seemed, as far as the Federals were concerned, to disappear from the face of the earth. Feinting at Banks with cavalry, Jackson took the bulk of his forces east, crossed the Massanutten Mountains in the middle of the Valley, joined Ewell (making a total then of 16,000 men) and, after marching up to 30 miles a day with his "foot cavalry,"

Opposite: *The beautiful Shenandoah Valley, where Jackson pinned down a large Federal force that might otherwise have supported McClellan at Richmond.*

Left: *Belle Boyd served as a Confederate spy, reporting Union intentions in the Valley to General Jackson.*

Overleaf: *Harpers Ferry, Virginia, at the confluence of the Shenandoah and Potomac rivers. Here Jackson briefly threatened an invasion of Maryland.*

pounced on a Federal garrison of 1000 at Front Royal on 23 May.

Confederate General Richard Taylor remembered the approach to Front Royal:

> Past midday . . . there rushed out of the wood to meet us a young, rather well-looking woman, afterward widely known as [Southern spy] Belle Boyd. Breathless with speed and agitation, some time elapsed before she found her voice. Then, with much volubility, she said we were near Front Royal, beyond the wood; that the town was filled with Federals, whose camp was on the west side of the river, where they had guns in position . . . that they believed Jackson to be west of Massanutten . . . that General Banks, the Federal commander, was at Winchester . . . where he was slowly concentrating his widely scattered forces to meet Jackson's advance, which was expected some days later.

Shocked by Jackson's surprise attack, the Federals at Front Royal withdrew toward Strasburg; but it was hopeless – by

the end of the day the Union had lost 904 of 1063 men in the garrison, most of them captured. The Confederates had fewer than 50 casualties. Jackson had again concentrated to outnumber an outlying enemy detachment and won the day. Now he had to figure out what Banks was going to do next – stay put in Strasburg, go west to join Frémont, go north to strong positions at Winchester, or retreat east to safety near Washington. Deciding finally that Banks would probably stay put or go east, Jackson began marching to Middletown, near Strasburg.

Banks for once, did not move as expected by his enemy. After learning of the disaster at Front Royal, Banks pulled his army back to Winchester, arriving on 24 May. Hearing word of the Federal move, Jackson saw its potential for trouble – knowing the area as he did, Jackson knew the town had high ground and would be impossible to assault if the Yankees settled in. So once again, he drove his "foot cavalry" hard. At first, the exhausted Confederates dallied, wasting time looting a captured supply train, but then they marched all night and reached Winchester just after midnight.

At dawn on 25 May 1862 the Confederates drove in the Fed-

Above: *A "trooper" in Jackson's famous "foot cavalry," noted for their marching ability.*

Right: *A corps of Confederates fends off an attack from advancing Pennsylvania Bucktails in woods near Harrisonburg on 7 June 1862.*

eral pickets, and the battle of Winchester was on. For a time the Union cavalry and artillery kept the Rebels at bay; then Jackson put men on the Federal right flank, and Ewell worked his division around to the left flank. Jackson thereupon advanced his center and right together, and the Federals broke and ran. Banks withdrew under pursuit across the Potomac and out of the campaign for good. Between the defeats at Front Royal and Winchester, Banks lost some 3000 men of the 8500 in his command; Jackson's losses in the same period were about 400 of 16,000.

With these extraordinary achievements under their belts, the Confederates rested a couple of days before taking the road again. They then marched north to concentrate near

Harpers Ferry. One of Jackson's opponents admiringly summarized Jackson's achievements so far:

As the result of these operations, Milroy and Schenck were now beaten, Banks's army was routed, the fertile Valley of Virginia cleared of Union troops, Harpers Ferry in danger and Maryland . . . threatened. In addition Washington was thrown into alarm and trepidation; McDowell's movement to connect with McClellan was suspended; he was ordered to move 20,000 men into the Valley to cut off Jackson, while Frémont with his whole force was ordered into the Valley at Harrisonburg for the same purpose. The whole plan of Union operations had been completely upset, and confusion reigned from

one end of the line to the other. At no time during the war was there such dismay in the North. . . . General Jackson himself seems to have been the only one who had not lost his head. He kept his army from May 26 to May 30 threatening Harpers Ferry and an invasion of Maryland.

In deciding to devote the efforts of these commands to chasing Jackson instead of reinforcing McClellan near Richmond, the Washington authorities made one of the great blunders of the conflict, quite possibly prolonging the war for three years. All this because of the brooding, brilliant Jackson and his small band of rugged soldiers.

Of course Jackson had planned everything to achieve just

that end. But his problems were by no means over. Now he had simultaneously to keep the Federals in the Valley busy, ship east the enormous quantities of supplies he had captured, and pull back from the Harpers Ferry area to avoid being trapped by the converging advances of Frémont and McDowell. Leaving the Stonewall Brigade to keep Banks in check, Jackson began pulling the rest of his forces south on 30 May. Things quickly came to a head. Jackson was riding on a railway train in front of his troops when a courier stopped the engine to tell Jackson that McDowell had recaptured Front Royal. The two Federal armies were moving in faster than expected, and Confederate forces were spread out around the Valley. Calmly Jackson issued his orders.

Left: *Colonel Turner Ashby, Jackson's cavalry commander, was killed in an engagement near Harrisonburg on 6 June.*

Below: *Virginia infantry encamped in the woods near Leesburg.*

The cavalry under Turner Ashby were sent to stop Federal's advance; an infantry detachment did likewise with McDowell's men at Front Royal. By 1 June, Jackson had pulled 15,000 men, 200 prisoners, and a double wagon-train seven miles long safely out of Strasburg; 50,000 Federals had not been able to corral them. Jackson then moved south up the Shenandoah Valley, burning bridges as he went. On 2 June Federal cavalry hit Jackson's rear guard, but Ashby delayed the Yankees long enough to give the Rebel infantry a day's lead. On 6 June came another Federal strike; this time the gallant Ashby was killed, but the Federal advance came to little – Union reinforcements could not move up because the Confederates had destroyed the bridges.

But by next day Jackson was in the worst spot of the entire campaign, squarely between two converging enemy columns. With customary boldness, he moved out to take the offensive from his position at Port Republic. On 7 June the Confederates tried without luck to draw Frémont out before McDowell arrived. Next morning a Federal detachment got into Port Republic and nearly captured Jackson – this was Shields's advance, part of McDowell's command moving up from the east. Meanwhile, Frémont moved to attack from the west. It appeared to be the end for Jackson.

Yet the Federal push became muddled, mostly due, once again, to the bridges Jackson had so carefully burned. On 8 June the Federals moved forward at Cross Keys, but were driven back and pursued; in that action Ewell's division of 6500 bested Frémont's 10,500. On the next day Jackson held Frémont at bay with Ewell and moved to attack Shields's 3000 men at Port Republic.

On the morning of 9 June the Stonewall Brigade hit the Federal right, while others attacked the enemy left. But the Confederate attacks were beaten back, and Ewell was slow to move over in support. Ewell's advance forces were then sent on an envelopment of the Federal left; this failed too, but at last the rest of Ewell's men came up. CSA General Richard Taylor remembered what happened next:

Wheeling to the right, with colors advanced, like a solid wall [the enemy] marched straight upon us. There seemed nothing left but to set our backs to the mountain and die hard. At the instant, crashing through the underwood, came Ewell, outriding staff and escort. He produced the effect of a reinforcement, and was welcomed with cheers. The line before us halted and threw forward skirmishers. A

moment later, a shell came shrieking along it, loud Confederate cheers reached our delighted ears, and Jackson, freed from his toils, rushed up like a whirlwind, the enemy in rapid retreat.

Shields and his outnumbered Federal forces retreated in good order, fighting as they went. Frémont had been unable to help due to yet another burned bridge. In two days of battle Frémont had suffered 684 casualties of 17,000 engaged; at Port Republic the Federals lost 1018. The total Southern casualties were about 1100 of 16,000 engaged. Jackson had once again defeated his enemy in detail, one division at a time. In fact, in a month of campaigning against vastly superior total Federal forces he had outnumbered his enemy in nearly every individual engagement.

With his extraordinary campaign in the Shenandoah Valley completed and the entire Federal war effort in turmoil and confusion, Jackson now marched east to join Lee in the Seven Days Battles and the Second Manassas. In one month Jackson's army had marched more than 250 miles, fought four pitched battles and endless skirmishes and had captured more than 400 prisoners and enormous quantities of arms and supplies. Jackson had brilliantly followed his own maxims of war:

Always mystify, mislead, and surprise the enemy, if possible; and when you strike and overcome him, never let up in the pursuit so long as your men have strength to follow; for an army routed, if hotly pursued, becomes panic-stricken, and can then be destroyed by half their number. The other rule is, never fight against heavy odds, if by any possible maneuvering you can hurl your own force on only a part, and that the weakest part, of your enemy and crush it. Such tactics will win every time, and a small army may thus destroy a large one in detail, and repeated victory will make it invincible.

Stonewall Jackson's tactics of speed and secrecy have been studied by military men ever since (for example, these lessons were not lost on the Nazis in preparing their *Blitzkreig* of World War II). But the immediate effect on Southern fortunes in the Civil War was direct and profound. Jackson had played a remarkable chess game and had checkmated his enemy. Now the impetus of the war in the Eastern Theater was firmly on the Confederate side.

Right: *A Confederate camp in the Shenandoah Valley.*

FREDERICKSBURG

On 3 September 1862 Lee proposed to Jefferson Davis that the Confederacy capitalize on its great victory at Second Manassas by mounting an immediate invasion of Maryland. In theory, there was much to recommend this bold stroke. The Union Army of the Potomac was injured and off balance, and, because a Confederate thrust into Maryland would indirectly threaten Washington, McClellan would be kept fully on the defensive and would be incapable of any meaningful counter-strokes into Virginia. Also, Lee and the South in general had high hopes that a Confederate military presence in Maryland would cause many citizens of that crucial border state to rally to the Confederate cause and perhaps even prompt the whole state to secede. Finally, and perhaps most important, a successful offensive into the North might well clinch the Confederacy's continuing efforts to gain diplomatic recognition from Great Britain and France, thus assuring the South of a badly needed infusion of foreign capital, weapons and supplies.

Attractive as all these strategic objectives were, they were predicated on some large assumptions, and indications that the assumptions may have been too large began appearing almost as soon as the Army of Northern Virginia crossed over into Maryland early in September. Marylanders did *not* hasten to throw in their lot with the CSA; indeed, they gave Lee's

army a generally chilly reception. Worse, McClellan seemed to be pulling his Union forces together remarkably efficiently and to be moving with unaccustomed dispatch toward another major confrontation.

That confrontation took place at Sharpsburg, near Antietam Creek, less than two weeks after the Maryland invasion had begun, so soon, indeed, that Lee barely had time to assemble his scattered forces to receive the shock. (But for McClellan's last-minute dawdling, Lee probably would not have had time; but then, Lee knew his dilatory opponent well.) Hostilities began early in the morning of 17 September and raged confusedly and indecisively throughout a day that would prove to be the single bloodiest in the entire Civil War. When it was over, Lee for the first time had not won a decisive victory in a major encounter. True, his army was still very much intact, but there was no denying that it had been much harmed. The number of dead, wounded and missing on each side was about the same – something over 12,000 apiece – but as a percentage of those engaged, the South's losses were much higher – on the order of 26 percent, as opposed to the Union's 16 percent.

Although the South had consistently displayed superior generalship in the battle, Antietam ended as a tactical stalemate and a strategic reversal for the Confederacy. None of the objectives of the now-stymied invasion had been achieved, and when, in the aftermath of the battle, Lincoln issued his Emancipation Proclamation, thus formally making slavery a war issue, the Confederacy's hopes of receiving foreign diplomatic recognition became even more remote, for now not even the South's best European friends wanted to appear to be on the side of slavery.

After the convulsion of Antietam the two great armies of the East rested, licking their wounds. Nonetheless, the processes of planning, raiding, and reconnaissance continued: in early October, Jeb Stuart and his Southern cavalrymen raided completely around the Army of the Potomac, as they had done before, during the Peninsular Campaign. President Lincoln goaded McClellan to action, and the general reluct-

Left: *The Battle of Antietam, 17 September 1862. Union troops crossing Burnside Bridge are met by withering Rebel fire.*

Above: *A soldier in the uniform of the Maryland Guard.*

Overleaf: *Soldiers and wagons on the bridge at Antietam Creek.*

antly put his army in motion to the south – as always, with maddening caution. Lincoln had seen it before; McClellan, Lincoln had cracked, was chronically infected with "the slows." This time, however, the president had had enough. Lincoln was not fooled into thinking Antietam a victory, as most of the North thought it. Now his general had returned to his inchworm mode of campaigning. On 7 November 1862, Lincoln removed McClellan from command. It was undoubtedly a long overdue change. But as McClellan's replacement Lincoln made a most unfortunate choice – General Ambrose E Burnside, who happened to be one of the most inept generals of all time.

A genial handsome man, Burnside sported an extravagant set of muttonchop whiskers which were perhaps his most enduring legacy – they gave the word "sideburns" to the language. Perhaps the secret of his success was that "Burn," as he was affectionately known, *looked* the way most folks thought a general should look. Favoring the appointment as well, from the president's point of view, was the fact that Burnside had no political ambitions, as McClellan certainly did (McClellan was to challenge Lincoln for the presidency in the next election). As to Burnside's generalship – Grant later wrote that he was "an officer who was generally liked and respected. He was not, however, fitted to command an army. No one knew better than himself."

When Burnside assumed command, his Army of the Potomac was near Warrenton, Virginia, nearly between Jackson's and Longstreet's divisions, Jackson then being in the Shenandoah Valley and Longstreet at Culpeper. Instead of striking

Left: *The Emancipation Proclamation, proposed five days after Antietam.*

Below: *Jeb Stuart crosses the Potomac, October 1862.*

Opposite: *The Battle of Fredericksburg, 13 December 1862. General Burnside wasted his Federal forces in frontal assaults on the entrenched enemy.*

PLAN OF THE BATTLE OF FREDERICKSBURG

DECEMBER 13TH 1862

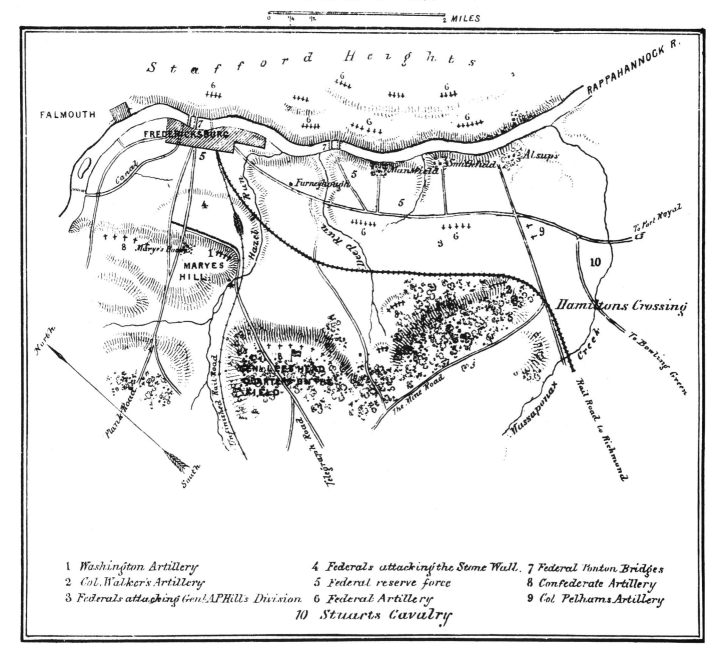

1 Washington Artillery
2 Col. Walker's Artillery
3 Federals attacking Genl. A.P.Hill's Division
4 Federals attacking the Stone Wall
5 Federal reserve force
6 Federal Artillery
7 Federal Ponton Bridges
8 Confederate Artillery
9 Col. Pelhams Artillery
10 Stuarts Cavalry

the two enemy wings in succession, with a fair chance of defeating them in detail, Burnside simply decided to try and make a beeline for Richmond, occupying Fredericksburg on the way. This was his first blunder: his real goal should have been to conquer Lee's army, not the Rebel capital.

On 17 November, Sumner's Federal division arrived across the river from Fredericksburg, which lay on the banks of the Rappahannock. At that point Sumner could have taken the town without resistance; Longstreet's division was alerted and on the way but had not yet arrived. Making his second big mistake, Burnside did not allow Sumner to cross the river but told him to wait for the arrival of a pontoon train with which to build bridges.

Longstreet arrived on 18 November; Jackson's corps did not pull in until the 30th. During this time, when the enemy was quite vulnerable, Burnside sat on the east bank waiting for his pontoons. Arriving on the 20th, Lee sized up his opponent with his usual acumen and decided to dig his army into the heights behind Fredericksburg, and from there to await

the attack. Burnside's pontoons arrived on the 25 of November; nonetheless, he delayed his offensive until 11 December, giving the Confederates time to construct virtually invulnerable positions on high ground.

Lee had wisely picked the heights behind Fredericksburg to defend rather than the town itself. Knowing he could not prevent the Federals from crossing the Rappahannock, he positioned sharpshooters in town to slow the crossing. The Confederates had 78,500 men to Burnside's 122,000 – as always, Lee was vastly outnumbered. For the Southerners, it was a matter of nearly three weeks of waiting.

On 10 December, General Burnside issued some confusing orders, the gist of which was that five pontoon bridges were to be pushed across the river for the crossing of infantry. Longstreet remembered the effectiveness of the sharpshooters Lee had placed in the town:

On the morning of the 11th . . . the Federals came down to the river's edge and began the construction of their

Opposite top: *Union engineers placed these pontoon bridges across the Rappahannock River at Fredericksburg.*

Opposite bottom: *While some Federal troops row across the river, engineers hurry to complete a pontoon bridge.*

Right: *Union soldiers rest briefly in the center of Fredericksburg before attempting to assault the heights above the town.*

bridges, when Barksdale opened fire with such effect that they were forced to retire. Again and again they made an effort to cross, but each time they were met and repulsed by the well-directed bullets of the Mississippians. This contest lasted until 1 o'clock, when the Federals, with angry desperation, turned their whole available force of artillery on the little city, and sent down from the heights of a perfect storm of shot and shell, crushing the houses with a cyclone of fiery metal. . . . But, in the midst of all this fury, the little brigade of Mississippians clung to their work. At last, when I had everything in readiness, I sent a peremptory order to Barksdale to withdraw . . . before the Federals, who had by that time succeeded in landing a number of their troops. The Federals then constructed their pontoons without molestation, and during the night and the following day the grand division of Sumner passed over into Fredericksburg.

About a mile and a half below the town, where the Deep Run empties into the Rappahannock, General Franklin had been allowed without serious opposition to throw two pontoon-bridges on the 11th, and his grand division passed over . . . in front of Stonewall Jackson's corps. The 11th and 12th were thus spent by the Federals in crossing the river and preparing for battle.

During the night of the 12th, 50,000 Federals spent an uneasy bivouac around Fredericksburg, the time enlivened by a considerable amount of looting (though the valuables of the citizens had already been well picked over by the Confederates after the civilians evacuated to the hills and woods). Everyone knew that the next day would see a bloody contest indeed; and many Federals were already in despair at the prospect of assaulting the heights.

Longstreet wrote of the dawn of the 13th, which he observed from his position of command on the left wing of Lee's army:

As the mist rose, the Confederates saw the movement against their right near Hamilton's Crossing. [Artillery]

Major Pelham opened fire upon Franklin's command and gave him lively work, which was kept up until Jackson ordered Pelham to retire. Franklin then advanced rapidly to the hill where Jackson's troops had been stationed, filling the woods with shot as he progressed. Silently Jackson awaited the approach of the Federals until they were within good range, and then he opened a terrific fire which threw the Federals into some confusion. The enemy again massed and advanced, pressing through a gap between Archer and Lane. This broke Jackson's line and threatened very serious trouble. The Federals who had wedged themselves in through that gap came upon Gregg's brigade, and then the severe encounter ensued in which the latter general was mortally wounded. Archer and Lane very soon received reinforcements and, rallying, joined in the counter-attack and recovered their lost ground . . . the counter-attack drove the Federals back to the railroad and beyond the reach of our guns on the left. Some of our troops following up this repulse got too far out, and were in turn much discomfited when left to the enemy's superior numbers, and were obliged to retire in poor condition. A Federal brigade advancing under cover of Deep Run was discovered at this time and attacked by regiments of Pender's and Law's brigades. Jackson's second line advancing, the Federals were forced to retire. This series of demonstrations and attacks, the partial success and final discomfiture of the Federals, constitute the hostile movements between the Confederate right and the Federal left.

This fighting on the right had gone on for some three hours. Having been repulsed, Franklin's division sank into exhaustion. But while the Union assaults of the 13th were breaking on Lee's right, the other half of the Army of the Potomac had been crossing the river and gathering around Fredericksburg for an all-out offensive on Longstreet's position at and below Marye's Height. The first of six major Federal assaults set out about noon, heading straight for the strongest part of the Confederate line. Advancing across open ground, the Federal lines were torn by artillery fire, then came in rifle range of a line of Rebels, the brigade of General Thomas Cobb, posted in a sunken road behind a stone wall at the foot of Marye's Heights.

From Lee's Hill, above the battlefield, Longstreet watched wave after wave of Federal advance as if on parade to be torn to pieces at the foot of Marye's Heights:

> The field in front of Cobb was thickly strewn with the dead and dying Federals, but again they formed with desperate courage and renewed the attack and again were driven off. At each attack the slaughter was so great that by the time the third attack was repulsed, the ground was so thickly strewn with dead that the bodies seriously impeded the approach of the Federals.

And so it went as the long afternoon wore on, assault after hopeless and tragic assault, the Union dead and wounded pil-ing higher before the stone wall. Late in the day, as the Federal efforts were tailing off on the left, Jackson ordered an advance on the right, but he was dissuaded due to extensive Federal artillery covering the open ground in his front. Lee had shifted a number of troops from his right to the center to meet the Union offensive, but they were scarcely necessary. As a Union soldier bitterly commented, "No troops in the world would have won a victory if placed in the position ours were. Few armies . . . would have stood as well as ours did. It can hardly be in human nature for men to show more valor, or generals to manifest less judgment, than were perceptible on our side that day." Another Yankee soldier put it more succinctly: "They may as well have tried to take Hell."

Night fell at last on the scene of carnage, and it was over for those Federals who had made their escape from Marye's Heights. But many were too wounded to move, or were trapped in front of enemy guns and hugging the ground all

Left: *General Humphrey's division charges into heavy fire from the Confederate defenders entrenched at the foot of Marye's Heights.*

Left: *General Edwin Sumner's men launch a fruitless assault on Marye's Heights, 13 December.*

night. Union officer Joshua Chamberlain wrote an unforgettable account of that night of horror:

> Out of that silence [following] the battle's crash and roar rose new sounds more appalling still . . . a strange ventriloquism, of which you could not locate the source . . . a wail so far and deep and wide, as if a thousand discords were flowing together into a key-note weird, unearthly, terrible to hear and bear . . . the writhing concord broken by cries for help pierced by shrieks of paroxysm; some begging for a drop of water; some calling on God for pity; and some on friendly hands to finish what the enemy had so horribly begun; some with delirious, dreamy voices murmuring loved names, as if the dearest were bending over them. . . .

In Burnside's tragic and stupid assaults of 13 December at Fredericksburg the North had lost 12,700 killed and wounded of 106,000 committed. The South's casualties were less than half those – 5300 casualties of 72,500 engaged. During the night a Federal prisoner caught in Confederate lines produced a memorandum from Burnside ordering renewed attacks next day. Lee and Longstreet made ready to meet it. The attack never came; Burnside's staff had dissuaded him. Surveying the field that showed only dead and dying Federals and no attack, Lee joked to Longstreet. "General, I am losing confidence in your friend General Burnside." Perhaps Lee should have ordered a counterattack; but he did not know

Above: *Rebel troops view ruined Fredericksburg Bridge after the battle. The defeated Union troops withdrew across the river unopposed.*

Overleaf: *Union soldiers cross the Rappahannock as engineers rush to complete a span of a pontoon bridge before Fredericksburg.*

how stricken the Federals were, and certainly he had on his mind his army's narrow escape in the Antietam campaign.

But Burnside was not quite done yet. He made one more effort to do his job, this time by marching the Army of the Potomac upstream to cross the Rappahannock in hopes of striking Lee's flank. But this operation began squarely in the middle of the usual January thaw, with its accompanying torrents of rain. During it the entire army nearly disappeared into an apparently bottomless sea of mud. This Mud March as history dubbed it, was soon aborted, and the bedraggled and demoralized Army of the Potomac slogged back to their camps across the river from Lee at Fredericksburg. A compassionate Longstreet wrote perhaps the best epitaph for the Union dead.

> The spectacle that we saw upon the battle-field was one of the most distressing I ever witnessed. The charges had been desperate and bloody, but utterly hopeless. I thought, as I saw the Federals come again and again to their death, that they deserved success if courage and daring could entitle soldiers to victory.

I ntelligence concerning enemies' doings traveled slowly and tenuously in the Civil War compared with later conflicts. But news always seemed to travel faster in the direction of Robert E Lee. The Confederate commander got his information from a variety of sources – above all from Jeb Stuart's cavalry, which were the eyes of the Army of Northern Virginia; from spies in Washington and in Southern towns occupied by the Union; from Northern prisoners and deserters; and, not infrequently, from reading Northern newspapers (there was little organized censorship in Washington, and often the South could find out about enemy operations simply by perusing the daily papers).

At the end of January, 1863, Lee learned that he had a new opponent, that the Union Army of the Potomac had seen the fourth change of command in a year. Following Burnside's debacle at Fredericksburg and his being relieved at his own

request, Washington gave the army to General Joseph Hooker, called "Fighting Joe" by the press. Hooker's friends in Washington had overcome political opposition to the appointment, and Hooker was one of the few generals who genuinely wanted the job – indeed, he had schemed to get it. Lee's response to this Federal change of command is not recorded. It is likely he knew his opponent's strengths and weaknesses as well as usual. If so, Lee knew that there were two Joe Hookers: one of them an experienced, dashing and hard-fighting general; the other was a man fond of criticizing his superiors and scheming for his own benefit, and equally fond of the bottle and the ladies.

But in taking command in the winter of 1863 Hooker suddenly revealed unexpected qualities as an organizer. He repaired the Army of the Potomac from the ground up, improving the food supply, hospital care, and sanitation of his

Opposite: *General "Fighting Joe" Hooker, depicted leading his corps at Antietam, succeeded Burnside as commander of the Army of the Potomac.*

Above: *A well equipped company of Federal troops, Company H of the 36th Pennsylvania Infantry.*

Right: *The 7th New York Cavalry encamped near Washington DC.*

troops, and drilled them incessantly. The intelligence service was reorganized, with the result that there were fewer of the exaggerated estimates of Lee's strength that had plagued McClellan. The pride and morale of the army rose with its physical condition and its numbers: by April there were 122,000 men in the infantry, 12,000 men in a well-trained cavalry, and 400 cannons. Hooker called it the greatest army on the planet and crowed, "May God have mercy on General Lee, for I will have none!"

In April, Lee's Army of Northern Virginia still lay along the Rappahannock at Fredericksburg. To dislodge them, Hooker devised a plan that was sound and imaginative: leaving a force to hold Lee in position, Hooker would march the bulk of his infantry around Fredericksburg in a wide strategic envelopment, crossing the river and coming in behind Lee from the west. In theory, the Confederates then had the choice of sitting and being destroyed or retreating and thus exposing their flank to the Federals.

Opposite: *Jeb Stuart's cavalry gave Lee a reconnaissance advantage at Chancellorsville.*

Right: *The Army of the Potomac marching in force along the Rappahannock on the way to Chancellorsville.*

Below: *Hooker's troops camped between rows of breastworks in the Wilderness.*

Hooker was sure his revitalized cavalry could take on Jeb Stuart now. Thus he prepared his campaign by sending 12,000 horsemen on a raid to cut Southern supply lines in the rear. Leaving on 13 April, the Union riders soon ran into floods on the rivers that held them up for two weeks, after which they ranged around to little purpose. Lee sent Stuart and his scouts to investigate this floundering maneuver, and after receiving the report simply ignored the Federal cavalry.

On 27 April Hooker struck camp, leaving 40,000 men under General John Sedgwick to hold Lee in place at Fredericksburg, and moved the rest of his army northwest and then south across fords on the Rappahannock and Rapidan. By 30 April these forces were gathered around Chancellorsville, which was simply a wide clearing with a mansion near to a road crossing. Surrounding the clearing was the virtually impenetrable forest of the Virginia Wilderness. On the 30th the Federals began marching towards Fredericksburg, ready to take the Rebels by surprise.

However, Robert E Lee had no intention of playing his assigned role in Hooker's little game. Lee and his generals had divined what Joe Hooker was going to do almost as soon as Hooker did. A Federal general recounts the information he found in a captured officer's diary:

In March a council of war had been held at General Stuart's headquarters, which had been attended by Generals Jackson, A P Hill, Ewell, and Stuart. They were in conference over five hours, and came to the decision that the next battle would be at or near Chancellorsville, and that the position must be prepared.

On 30 April Jeb Stuart notified Lee that Hooker was moving his army from Chancellorsville toward the Confederate rear. At that time Lee had available some 60,000 men, less than half his enemy's strength (Longstreet and Hood had gone foraging in Virginia with a large detachment). Nonetheless, Lee once again boldly split his army to meet the Federal threat. A screen force of 10,000 men under General Jubal Early was left to hold Sedgwick at Fredericksburg and was ordered to build many fires to fool the Yankees. Lee and Stonewall Jackson marched northwest on 1 May to deal with Hooker's main body.

Hooker had seen the necessity of pushing past the dense woods of the Wilderness to meet Lee on open ground, where superior Federal artillery could have room to function and the army room to maneuver. On May Day morning the Federals pulled into open country, exactly where Hooker wanted to meet the enemy. Everything was going according to Hooker's plan; Fredericksburg lay less than a dozen miles away. Then, on high ground some two miles from Chancellorsville, around ten-thirty in the morning, Federal skirmishers ran into a line of Confederate skirmishers from Anderson's and McLaws' forces. As one Union soldier recalled, "There they stood facing each other, steady and silent, gazing, the one in apparent wonderment, the other in real surprise at the unexpected situation." Soon Federal units began moving up and easily forced the Rebel skirmishers back. All that seemed necessary for the North was to form line of battle and sweep the Rebels back toward Fredericksburg.

For every Federal general confronting Robert E Lee, there came a moment of truth: when the full realization of just how

dangerous Lee was, combined with the awful responsibility of holding in his hands the future of the American nation, came down on the Union commanding officer with the force of doom itself. On 1 May, with the Wilderness at his back and commanding vastly superior forces, Hooker began to act like a beaten man at the first brush with Lee that had not been part of his pretty plan. After several hours of inactivity he fled back to the reassuring safety of the forest, overruling the furious protests of his staff and ordering all his forces back towards Chancellorsville to dig into the Wilderness. The significance of this retreat was not lost on the Union troops.

During the afternoon of 1 May Jeb Stuart's cavalry had moved freely around the Union army, and late in the day Stuart reported to Lee that the Federal right was vulnerable, "in the air," with no real protection on the flank. A Confederate officer, Robert's nephew "Fitz" Lee, recalled Lee's response:

> On May 1 General Lee wished to cut Hooker off from the United States Ford, preventing his communication with Sedgwick, and rode down himself and examined the lands all the way to the river, but found no place where he could execute this movement. Returning at night, he found Jackson and asked him if he knew of any place to attack. Jackson said he had been inquiring about roads and soon returned with the Reverend Doctor B T Lacey, who said a circuit could be made around by the Wilderness Tavern. A young man living in the country, and then in the cavalry, was sent for to act as guide. Lee and Jackson took their seats on a log to the north side of the Plank Road and a little distant from the wood. "General," Lee said, "we must get ready to attack the enemy, and you must make arrangements to move around his right flank."

The Confederates slept on the field that night. Waking in the early morning, one of Lee's staff saw an historic meeting: Jackson and Lee, finalizing their plans for yet another un-

Above: *At Chancellorsville on 3 May 1863 Hooker's Union Army briefly stems a Rebel breakthrough.*

Opposite: *The last meeting of Robert E Lee with Stonewall Jackson at Chancellorsville.*

pleasant surprise for Joe Hooker. It was to fall on that luckless Union right flank, O O Howard's XI Corps. Lee would divide forces again, holding Hooker's line of some 80,000 men in place with only 12,900 Confederates while Jackson marched 30,000 around to the west to strike the exposed Federal flank.

On the morning of 2 May 1863 the Union army was well fortified and easily handled probing attacks by the Rebels. The Federals little expected that these were feints to hold them in place; still less did they realize how thin Lee's line was in their front. Meanwhile, Jackson pulled his detachment out for the march across the front of the Union army, protected by the screen of the thick woods.

The XI Corps on the Union right was ill prepared to receive Jackson, though there had actually been fair warning of his maneuver. About noon Union general Dan Sickles had noticed Jackson's force moving to his right beyond the thick woods. Hooker, wondering at first if they were in fact headed for his right flank sent a cautionary note to Howard. But then Hooker began to convince himself that Lee must be retreating; in response to all further questions Hooker spent the afternoon insisting that the Rebels were hightailing it. When Sickles asked permission to move against the enemy column in his front, Hooker agreed, apparently figuring it would hasten the enemy in their retreat. Sickles cut his way through the brush with great difficulty and made contact with the end of the Confederate column. During the ensuing skirmish he captured some 500 men of a Georgia regiment. As these prisoners were being led to the rear, some were heard to jeer the Yanks. "You'll catch hell before night," and, "You wait until Jackson gets around to your right." (By then Jackson's column had apparently divined what their secretive commander was up to.) The Federals ignored these threats.

Below: *Generals Lee and Jackson conferring on the eye of the Battle of Chancellorsville.*

Meanwhile Hooker stripped his right flank of Barlow's division and sent them to help Sickles pursue the supposedly retreating rebels. As Sickles pulled away he left the rest of the XI Corps isolated and even more vulnerable than before.

At six o'clock in the afternoon the advance positions of the XI Corps were startled to see a mass of rabbits and deer scampering out of the woods towards them. The men whooped and laughed as the animals bolted towards the rear. There were scattered shots, and cannon suddenly appeared on the front. And then arose from thousands of throats the bone-chilling screech of the Rebel yell, and 26,000 of Stonewall Jackson's men came crashing through the Federal flank in a front a mile wide and four divisions deep, all of them shooting and screaming like demons.

Jackson's men moved straight down the enemy trenches, the 9000 men on the XI Corps fleeing in panic before them. Amidst the rout was General O O Howard, "in the middle of the roads and mounted, his maimed arm embracing a stand of colors . . . while with his sound arm he was gesticulating to the men to make a stand by their flag. With bared head he was pleading with his soldiers, literally weeping as he entreated the unheeding horde." Hooker knew nothing of the rout until he heard an aide screaming, "My God here they come!" A Union colonel remembered the appearance of the panic-stricken mob at Chancellorsville and the successful rally that followed:

> It was a complete Bull Run rout. Men, horses, mules, rebel prisoners, wagons, guns, etc. etc. were coming down the road in terrible confusion, behind them an unceasing roar or musketry. We rode until we got into a mighty hot fire, and found that no one was attempting to make a stand, but every one running for his life. . . .
>
> I found General Hooker sitting alone on his horse in front of the Chancellor House, and delivered my message; he merely said, "Very good, sir." I rode back and found the Eleventh Corps still surging up the road and still this terrible roar behind them. The rebels had received no check, but now troops began to march out on the plank road and form across it.

These troops were a division of the I Corps, whom Hooker had led forward and ordered, "Receive 'em on your bayo-

nets!" This infantry and the XII Corps artillery shoved through the fleeing men and hit the charging Rebels obliquely, slowing their advance on the left and center. Seeing a stand of Union artillery was in danger of being overrun on the right, General Alfred Pleasonton ordered Major Peter Keenan to charge his 8th Pennsylvania Cavalry into the Rebels, to buy time to turn the guns around. Keenan cheerfully accepted the order hardly knowing it was virtually suicidal. The cavalrymen, many of them scraped up from a poker game with no idea what was happening, rode directly into the middle of the oncoming enemy.

Though scores of Union saddles were emptied, the cavalry charge gave Pleasonton time to get 22 pieces aimed into the Rebels, and eventually the Federals had 36 more guns pelting the enemy from Fairview Cemetary. The Rebel advance halted before the cannonade, the troops becoming disorganized in the growing dark. Over in Hazel Grove, the 15,000 men of Sickles's III Corps had been cut off by Jackson's charge, and as night fell they began fighting their way back to

Left: *Panicked men of the Union XI Corps retreat before the onrushing Stonewall Brigade.*

Below: *Perched high in a tree, a Confederate sharpshooter takes careful aim.*

Overleaf: *Depiction of the fighting on 2 May and the wounding of Stonewall Jackson.*

their lines. After a hot and confused struggle in the gloom, with men falling from their own side's fire, part of the III Corps made it back while the rest settled into an uneasy bivouac in Hazel Grove.

Then at nine o'clock, amid the confusion of nighttime action, came the accident that was to temper this, Lee's greatest victory, with the most irreplaceable loss he had ever sustained. Stonewall Jackson had ridden out scouting from his lines just west of Chancellorsville. An officer of his staff recalled the tragedy that resulted:

From the order Jackson sent to General Stuart it was evident that his intention was to storm the enemy's works as soon as the lines were formed. While these orders were issued, Jackson started slowly along the pike toward the enemy. When we had ridden only a few rods, our little party was fired upon [by a group of Union infantry], the balls passing diagonally across the pike. . . . At the firing our horses wheeled suddenly to the left, and General Jackson galloped away into the woods to get out of range of the bullets, but had not gone over twenty steps ere the brigade to the left of the turnpike fired a volley. It was by this fire that Jackson was wounded [by three bullets, the most serious in the left arm]. We could distinctly hear General Hill calling, at the top of his voice, to his troops to cease firing. I was alongside Jackson and saw his arm fall at his side, loosing the rein. The limb of a tree took off his cap and threw him flat on the back of his horse. I rode after him, but Jackson soon regained his seat, caught the bridle in his right hand, and turning his horse toward our men, somewhat checked his speed. I caught his horse as he reached the pike. . . .

I dismounted, and seeing that he was faint, I asked the General what I could do for him, or if he felt able to ride as far as into our lines. He answered, "You had best take me down," leaning as he spoke toward me and then falling, partially fainting from loss of blood. I caught him in my arms and held him until Captain Wynn could get his feet out of the stirrups, then we carried him a few steps and laid him on the ground.

Jackson was placed on a litter, and with his bearers came under heavy artillery fire before they could reach an ambulance. That night Jackson's left arm was amputated and he began slowly to sink. Hearing the news that Jackson had been wounded by his own troops, Lee responded prophetically, "Jackson has lost his left arm but I have lost my right arm."

Left: *At Chancellorsville the brilliance of Lee's tactics stunned Hooker and so demoralized him that he virtually forfeited the option of counterattack.*

Also during the night, Federals bivouacking near Chancellorsville heard a strange, muffled firing. It was soon discovered, to the men's horror, that the Wilderness was burning and the woods were full of wounded; the sound was that of of exploding muskets and cartridge cases. Soldiers dashed into the woods and removed the few wounded they could reach. And then the survivors sat and listened: "Curses and yells of pain, piteous appeals and spasmodic prayers could be distinguished . . . the flames roared more fiercely, the cries grew fainter, until at last they were hushed."

Taking over Jackson's corps, Jeb Stuart rallied the men with the name of their stricken leader and led a savage attack at five in the morning of 3 May. Stuart caught the Federal III Corps in motion back toward their lines and pushed them out of high ground at Hazel Grove, whence 30 Rebel cannons were brought to bear on the heart of the Federal position at Chancellorsville. The clearing around Hooker's headquarters quickly became a maelstrom of shot and shell. Then the Rebels began shoving the Federals back toward the Rappahannock River.

That morning, 3 May, as the Confederate attack was tearing into the Union lines, Sedgwick mounted a series of assaults on Jubal Early's men outside Fredericksburg at Marye's Heights, where Burnside had been so tragically repulsed in December, and finally stormed the position with heavy losses by eleven in the morning. Sedgwick then moved toward Chancellorsville, hoping to catch Lee in a vise.

On the front porch of the Chancellor mansion, his headquarters, General Hooker seemed paralyzed amidst the furious enemy fire that was destroying his batteries one by one, smashing into the house, exploding in the upper rooms and sending showers of brick fragments flying in every direction. As he stood on the front porch leaning on a pillar, straining for the sound of Sedgwick's approach, Hooker was thrown to the ground by a shell that splintered the pillar. Dazed, he gave Couch temporary command and ordered a withdrawal to entrenchments already prepared in an arc between the Rapidan and Rappahannock. The Rebels pursued this withdrawal, their cannons firing everything they could lay their hands on – including old railroad iron, chains and tools. The woods burned again, consuming the dead and wounded of both sides.

Then Lee put the finishing touch on his masterpiece. Leaving Stuart with 25,000 men to hold Hooker's dug-in 80,000,

Lee marched with 20,000 men to confront Sedgwick's advance on his rear. Sedgwick ran into General Lafayette McLaws's troops around Salem Church on that afternoon of 3 May. By next morning Lee had surrounded Sedgwick on three sides with McLaws, R H Anderson, and Early, while also reoccupying Marye's Heights with William Barksdale's men. Sedgwick was driven back to Bank's Ford on the Rappahannock, where the Rebels harassed him strongly. The Federal division withdrew across the ford on the night of 4 May.

Lee began planning an all-out offensive against Hooker's remaining division for 6 May, an offensive that might well have been a disaster for the South given the strength of the Federal entrenchments. Concerning this plan, Confederate

General Edward P Alexander circumspectly but wryly commented, "It must be conceded that Lee never in his life took a more audacious resolve than when he determined to assault Hooker's entrenchments."

But Hooker had already had enough. Over the objections of most of his staff he withdrew across the Rappahannock during the miserably wet and muddy night of 5 May. He had gone into battle with a better than two to one advantage and had nonetheless let his forces be outnumbered in every encounter; indeed, some 30,000 Union troops had never been committed at all.

Years later, Hooker was to make a simple confession about himself at Chancellorsville, when he confronted the battlefield genius of Lee and his army: "To tell the truth, I just lost confidence in Joe Hooker."

In contrast, the morale of the Army of Northern Virginia was never so exultant, their confidence in themselves and their leaders never more unshakable. But such confidence is dangerous in armies and in leaders, as the Army of Northern Virginia was about to learn. And glorious as Lee's victory at Chancellorsville was, it was a Pyrrhic one. Casualty figures are uncertain; Lee had about 12,821 in killed, missing and wounded to Union's 17,278. But while the Federals had lost 13 percent of their army, Lee had lost 22 percent of his. Numbers were beginning to count in the war; the South's supply of manpower was limited and becoming more critical with every battle won or lost.

On 10 May Stonewall Jackson cried out in delirium from his bed, "Order A P Hill to prepare for action – pass the infantry to the front rapidly – tell Major Hawks . . ." And then, after a silence, "No, let us cross over the river and rest under the shade of the trees." On that enigmatic word of peace the great warrior died.

Left: *Southern artillery: crucial to the victory at Chancellorsville.*

Below: *Stonewall Jackson's death from wounds on 10 May saddened the South.*

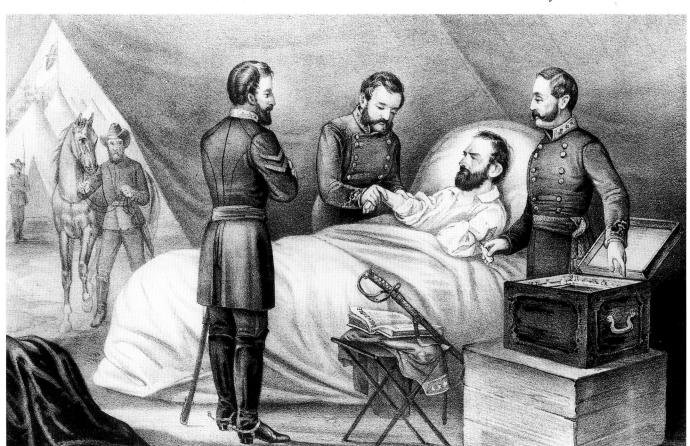

CHICKAMAUGA

As he had done in 1862 after his victory at Second Manassas, Lee proposed to follow up his triumph at Chancellorsville with a second invasion of the North. This time his target was different – Pennsylvania rather than Maryland – and his army was considerably larger and stronger than before, but the strategic considerations that suggested this move were less sanguine than those of 1862. Although the war had so far been going well for the Confederacy in the East, it was going badly in the West: the Mississippi was all but lost, and once Union General Ulysses S Grant succeeded in capturing Vicksburg, he would be free to turn his full attention on Tennessee, perhaps slashing across that state, bursting into Georgia and cutting the South in half. At the same time, the Confederacy was also not faring well on the home front. All Southern hope of foreign recognition was now dead, and the Union's ever-tightening blockade was causing mounting public privation and financial chaos.

Thus Lee's proposed second invasion of the North was as much a product of desperation as of optimism. What Lee wanted was one final, truly decisive victory in the East, one that would either win the war at a stroke or at least be so crushing as to leave his armies free to deal with the threat from the West. Some other Southern commanders, notably Longstreet, disagreed, arguing that the time to deal with the Western problem was now, and that any offensive actions that might be taken by the Union Army of the Potomac in the interim could probably be frustrated by relatively light defending forces in Virginia. How much merit Longstreet's view had is impossible to say, for it was Lee's strategy that was adopted.

The result of this great gamble was the Civil War's most famous battle and the South's most shocking defeat. In the first three days of July 1863, on and around the low hills that lie just south of the small town of Gettysburg, Pennsylvania, Lee lost a third of his army – 28,063 killed, wounded or missing. The North had not fared much better – 23,049 total casualties – but the crucial difference was that the Union could make good such losses and the Confederacy now could not. After the catastrophe of Gettysburg the South would be incapable of mounting any more important offensive operations in the Eastern Theater.

And there was good reason to suppose that the same would be true of the Western Theater as well. So far, the South had lost every major engagement fought deep within

Opposite: *Dead soldiers on the field after Gettysburg, the South's most shocking defeat.*

Right: *By the end of the third day of fighting Gettysburg was the war's costliest battle.*

Below: *Southerners attempt to breach the Union defenses at Cemetery Hill during the Battle of Gettysburg.*

its own territory, and most of these defeats had been at the hands of the tight-lipped, hard-fighting Ulysses S Grant. In a string of brilliant victories rivalling Lee's, Grant had risen from utter obscurity to fame with his operations at Shiloh, Forts Henry and Donelson, and, most of all, in the year-long campaign, extraordinary for its boldness and innovation, around the vital Mississippi River city of Vicksburg, which fell to the Union the same day as the Battle of Gettysburg concluded, 3 July 1863.

Those two Northern victories, Gettysburg and Vicksburg, were the decisive ones of the conflict, when the fortunes of war turned the corner that would lead inexorably to victory for the North. Ironically, the decisive year of 1863 had been was ushered in by the indecisive battle of Stone's River, near Murfreesboro, Tennessee. There, in three days of fighting between the Federal Army of the Cumberland and the Confederate Army of Tennessee, 20,000 men had fallen to no advantage to either side. For nearly six months thereafter those two armies sat some 40 miles apart, waiting for their next great confrontation.

Commanding the Southern forces was General Braxton Bragg, a veteran of the Mexican War and a trusted friend of President Jefferson Davis. That friendship was not to bode well for the Confederacy. Bragg was an intelligent man but a poor leader, a great maker of plans who could not bring them to fruition.

Bragg's Federal counterpart, General William S Rosecrans, had earned his command by demonstrating a considerable talent for strategy. Early in the war Rosecrans had driven the Confederates from West Virginia, and later and been of great service to Grant in Mississippi. Rosecrans was meticulous in planning campaigns down to the last wagonwheel; he was also maddeningly slow to move. After the standoff at Stone's River, the obvious goal of his Army of the Cumberland was what was perhaps the last remaining truly vital city of the Confederacy – Chattanooga.

The city lay in the southeastern corner of Tennessee, near

Above: *General Braxton Bragg commanded the Confederate Army of Tennessee at the Battle of Chickamauga.*

Right: *The city of Chattanooga in wartime. It was an important strategic center for the South.*

the corners of Alabama and Georgia on the banks of the Tennessee River. Railroads converged on it from all over the South. For the Confederacy, Chattanooga was the best base for operations in Tennessee and Kentucky; for the North, it was the gateway to Atlanta and all of Georgia. For these reasons, Chattanooga was the real strategic center of the Confederacy. If it were to be conquered by the Union, much of the Southern war effort would be hamstrung.

In the first six months of 1863 Bragg's Confederate Army of Tennessee lay in Tullahoma, on the road between Rosecrans's army (near Murfreesboro) and Chattanooga. In May the Federal high command began to pressure Rosecrans to move against Bragg; this would not only threaten Chattanooga but would keep Bragg from sending men to reinforce Vicksburg, which was now besieged by Grant. Rosecrans waffled and Bragg did send some troops to Mississippi.

In mid-June Rosecrans finally got his army moving and at once demonstrated his strategic skills. He threatened the Rebel left flank with cavalry, and when Bragg attempted to meet this threat he discovered that two Union corps, those of George H Thomas and Thomas L Crittenden, had gotten behind the Confederate right. Confused and helpless, Bragg was forced after 30 June to pull back to his nearest stronghold – Chattanooga.

Rosecrans had made a brilliant tactical move, but then he stopped again, asking for reinforcements. These were soon available, after the fall of Vicksburg in early July. But then Washington decided to occupy conquered territory rather than reinforce Rosecrans. Meanwhile, Bragg was heavily reinforced, most notably in mid-July by General Daniel H Hill, formerly of Lee's army. Also on the way were two divisions under Longstreet, which were now available after Gettysburg. (Longstreet had suggested a move much like this well before Gettysburg).

On 5 August Rosecrans was imperatively ordered to move against Bragg. Now he faced the problem of getting the Confederates out of heavily-fortified Chattanooga. Bragg had reorganized his army to defend the city – there were two divi-

B-7043

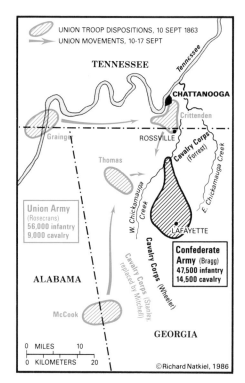

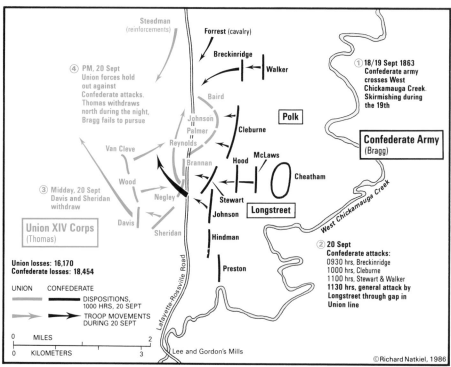

Above: *Operations in the Western Theater during September 1863.*

Below: *Union commander William S Rosecrans was a careful strategist but slow to move.*

Right: *General George Thomas (left), afterward known as the "Rock of Chickamauga," held against the Southern attack and prevented a Union rout.*

Below: *Confederate troops charge a Union line.*

sions each under Leonidas Polk, D H Hill, Simon B Buckner and W H T Walker, with cavalry under Joseph Wheeler and the brilliant Nathan Bedford Forrest (though Forrest only worked well in independent commands).

Rosecrans tried another strategic gambit, and it worked handsomely, abetted by Bragg's poor intelligence-gathering: Federal columns appeared along the Tennessee River at several widely-spaced points; as Bragg hesitated, worrying about his supply line to the rear, the Federal army crossed the river unopposed west of the city and Crittenden marched on Chattanooga.

Confronted by an enemy seeming to appear all over the map, Bragg evacuated Chattanooga on 6 September and headed south into Georgia. It was actually a wise move on Bragg's part – he was getting out of town with his army while the getting was good. Certain that they had the enemy forces on the run, the Federals made haste to pursue them into Georgia. Rosecrans boasted he would chase the Rebels to Atlanta, if not clear to the sea.

But in fact, Rosecrans was marching his army into a trap. Bragg was not fleeing; instead, he was concentrating his forces near Lafayette, Georgia, and preparing to turn and destroy the Federal army. Whether Bragg had actually planned the trap in advance is debatable. D H Hill later wrote about Bragg at that time, "The truth is, General Bragg was bewildered by 'the popping out of the rats from so many holes.' The wide dispersion of the Federal forces, and their confronting him at so many points, perplexed him, instead of being a source of congratulation that such grand opportunities were offered for crushing them one by one."

The wide dispersion Hill mentions refers to Rosecrans's deployments as he moved into Georgia – the three Union corps were spread out over 50 miles of rugged country, moving through three narrow gaps in the long ridge called Lookout Mountain. Bragg had merely to bring his superior numbers to bear and crush them in detail, one corps at a time. The Federal army was ripe for the picking.

Deliberate trap or not, Bragg and his generals proceeded to spring it ineptly. The forces of General Leonidas Polk were ordered to attack Thomas on 10 September. Though Polk's men appeared in Thomas's path, nothing happened. Another attack failed to materialize on the 11th. Two days later Bragg

arrived at Chickamauga Creek, expecting Polk to have anni-
hilated Crittenden's corps there. Polk had not budged.

The continuing presence of parties of Confederates in his
front, all of whom seemed to be withdrawing towards
Lafayette, finally tipped off Rosecrans that he was in serious
trouble. On 12 September he urgently ordered his wings to
converge toward the center and concentrate on the west side
of Chickamauga Creek, near Lafayette. Bragg, meanwhile,
was also concentrating his forces near the creek and was im-
patiently awaiting the arrival of Longstreet's divisions. When
they arrived Bragg would have over 65,000 men to Rosecrans's less than 60,000.

Rosecrans had divined what Bragg's strategy would be in
the battle, which was to move around the Union left and cut
off their line of retreat – road to Chattanooga. The Federal
commander thus paid special attention to his left, placing
General George H Thomas in command there. The positioning of the indomitable Thomas was to prove a decision
most fortunate indeed for the fate of the Union army.

On the night of the 18th both sides prepared for battle,
Rosecrans building a strong defensive position. Because of
the thick woods in the area, neither general knew where his
enemy was – or, indeed, where his own forces were. Bragg
thought the Union left was at Lee's and Gordon's Mill, and
planned his attack to flank that position and gain the road to
Chattanooga. Since Rosecrans had anticipated that, he had
strung his lines out north from the mill and along the road. By
daybreak on 19 September Thomas had formed his line of
battle above the steep sides of Horseshoe Ridge.

As dawn came on the 19th, both armies were poised for
battle at Chickamauga Creek. Prophetically, the creek's name

came from an old Cherokee Indian word meaning "River of
Death."

The battle began by accident. Unsure whether there were
Confederates north of the creek, Thomas sent cavalry to
scout his front. Soon these men stumbled on some of Forrest's cavalrymen, who were dismounted on the Reed's
Bridge road. The Southerners retreated under fire back to
their infantry, who then pushed forward. Slowly the battle
spread outward until both armies were firing all along the
line. There followed a confused but nonetheless bloody day
of fighting. As Hill later wrote, "it was the sparring of the
amateur boxer, and not the crushing blows of the trained
pugilist." All morning there was a gap of some two miles in
the Federal lines, but it was hours before Bragg found the gap
and tried to exploit. Finally, an attempt was made by the
forces of John B Hood, whose division of Longstreet's command had just arrived ahead of the others. Hood smashed the
right center of the Union line and got on to the Chattanooga
road, but a wave of Federals charged in to drive them back.

After a day of heavy but indecisive fighting on 19 September the guns fell silent in the late afternoon. By then Longstreet had arrived by rail with the rest of his forces. It took
him until eleven at night to find Bragg, who got out of bed for
a conference. Dividing his army into two wings, Bragg gave
the right to Polk and the left to Longstreet. Polk was to begin
at dawn with a strong assault on Thomas; after Polk's attack
there were to be successive attacks down the line to the
south. As the Confederate general spoke they heard the
sound of axes from the Federal lines – the Army of the Cumberland was building a strong defensive line of log breastworks through the thick woods.

At dawn on the 20th visibility was negligible due to the woods and a thick blanket of fog. Bragg sat in his head-quarters straining to hear the sound of Polk's dawn attack. After an hour of inactivity a messenger was dispatched to find Polk. The general was discovered reading a newspaper on a farmhouse porch while waiting for his breakfast. When que-ried about his attack, Polk grandly responded, "Do tell General Bragg that my heart is overflowing with anxiety for the attack – overflowing with anxiety, sir!" When this was re-ported at about nine-thirty to Bragg, he swore, "in a manner that would have powerfully assisted a mule team in getting up a mountain," and ordered Polk to begin the attack on Thomas immediately.

By this time the front stretched some two miles, north to south, Polk's men fell with a will onto Thomas, who held on to his breastworks in the Horseshoe Ridge but soon found his more vulnerable left flank being pushed across the vital road to Chattanooga. Again and again Thomas called for re-inforcements from Rosecrans, to whom he had a direct tele-graph wire (one of the first of these on any battlefield). Con-fusion began to creep into Union deployments due to the thick woods. At eleven in the morning this confusion created a strange and catastrophic turn in the battle. An aide, who had been riding behind the Union position, reported to Rose-crans that there was a gap in the Federal line between T J Wood's and J J Reynolds's divisions. Intending to seal that gap, Rosecrans hurriedly sent an order to Wood to move left, to "close up on and support" Reynolds (both these divisions lay near the Federal right flank, which was so far inactive).

But the aide had made a disastrous mistake: there was no gap in the Union line. Between Wood and Reynolds was John Brannan's division, exactly where they were supposed to be, but so hidden by the woods that the aide had not seen them.

Wood received Rosecrans's order and puzzled over it. How was he to "close up on and support" Reynolds when Brannan was between them? Finally Wood decided that "support" was the operative idea and ordered his division to pull out of line and march behind Brannan towards Reynolds. His men formed line of march and headed for the rear, leaving a gap-ing hole in the Union right wing.

At just that moment, hardly a stone's throw away but still hidden in the woods, Longstreet was massing eight brigades for the attack. (That the attack was gathering then and there was apparently sheer coincidence.) At the head of the column rode hard-fighting John B Hood. About eleven-thirty

Opposite: *A Rebel attempt to take a Union battery at Chickamauga is foiled by Lieutenant Van Pelt and his men.*

Right: *Confederate General John Bell Hood.*

Below: *Southern marksmen in the Chickamauga woods.*

in the morning the Confederates headed for the Union lines and found to their astonishment that no one was there.

The results were immediate and dramatic. A solid column of screaming Rebels flooded straight through the Union line, crashed on to the end of Wood's departing column, and scatted the divisions of Federal generals Philip Sheridan and Jefferson C Davis, who had begun moving into the gap from the right. Hood, having lost the use of an arm at Gettysburg, was wounded seriously in the leg, but his men pushed on.

During this rout the Federals lost thousands in casualties and captured; Hill later wrote that he had never seen Federal dead so thickly blanketing the ground except after the suicidal charge at Fredericksburg. Among the fleeing were a panicky and demoralized Rosecrans and most of his staff. Assuming his whole army was routed, Rosecrans ordered everyone to retreat to Chattanooga.

Fortunately for the Union, not everyone obeyed that order, because Rosecrans was wrong about his forces being totally beaten. Along Horseshoe Ridge, to the left, Thomas was holding on like grim death, with thousands of enemy swarming

Left: *The fight at Orchard Knob, one of a number of battles near Chattanooga in November 1863.*

Above: *Ulysses Grant, the new Union commander, views the fighting at Chattanooga.*

danger. Yet not all the routed Federal divisions had continued on to Chattanooga. Wood, Brannan and Reynolds fell into position on Thomas's right, Wood meeting the first appearance of Longstreet's men with a determined bayonet charge that stopped the Rebels in their tracks. As Thomas's line on the right stabilized a little, Rebel assaults swarmed on to his left flank. D H Hill later wrote admiringly of Thomas's stand, "that indomitable Virginia soldier, George H Thomas, was there and was destined to save the Union army from total rout and ruin, by confronting with invincible pluck the forces of his friend and captain [Bragg] in the Mexican War."

As the afternoon wore on Thomas's Federals were running out of ammunition, their front and flanks were staggering under heavy assaults, and the enemy was moving around the right flank to the rear. Rebel cannons were moving into position to enfilade the Union right, and there were no men left to do anything about it. And then, at three-thirty, Thomas noticed a column of dust approaching in his rear. If the troops that were making that dust were foe, his men were doomed. An officer was dispatched to take a look. They proved to be friends, part of two divisions of reserves commanded by General Gordon Granger, who had just committed a serious and most salutary breach of orders. Placed in reserve by Rosecrans, with strict orders to guard the road to Chattanooga, Granger had listened with increasing anxiety to the sound of battle growing steadily on the Federal left. Finally, he made his own decision – "I am going to Thomas, orders or no orders." By four o'clock Granger was shaking hands with an overjoyed Thomas, men and ammunition arriving rapidly behind them. Granger's men cleared the enemy from a valley in the rear, and a path of retreat was at last open.

The South had won the field at Chickamauga, one of the greatest victories of the war in the Western Theater. But General George Thomas had saved the Federal army to fight another day, becoming in the process one of the immortal heroes of the Union cause. To history, Thomas is forever "The Rock of Chickamauga."

Casualties in the battle were among the worst of the war: of 66,326 Southerners engaged, there were 2312 killed, 14,674 wounded, 1468 missing, a total of 18,454 casualties; for the North, of 58,222 engaged, there were 1657 killed, 9756 wounded, 4757 missing, a total of 16,170. Altogether, nearly 35,000 men fell; both sides had lost 28 percent of their forces.

Back in his headquarters, Bragg could not seem to get it

around the steep sides of the ridge. At Confederate headquarters Longstreet was begging General Bragg to give him all his remaining troops to surround Thomas's position. Bragg, seemingly of the opinion that his army was losing, replied that the rest of the men had "no fight left in them." Having fought at the side of Lee most of the war, Longstreet's frustration with the obtuse Bragg must have been titanic.

By mid-afternoon Thomas was watching enemy forces moving towards his right. He knew his front along the precipitous slopes was strong, but his flanks were in great

into his head that he had won. His generals pressed him to pursue, the impetuous Forrest screaming at his commander, "You are a coward and a damned scoundrel!" By next morning, 21 September, Bragg was finally willing to admit victory. He sent a force to Missionary Ridge in Chattanooga with orders to attack; but Bragg's men found the Federals "ready to receive and entertain us."

Yet Bragg had one more chance to reclaim Chattanooga. He put his army in strong position on the ridges and settled in to starve the Yankees out. The Federal army was now besieged deep in enemy territory. And starve the Yankees did, while both Bragg and Rosecrans spent their time writing elaborate reports blaming their subordinates for everything.

On 23 October 1863 General Ulysses S Grant arrived in Chattanooga. He had been appointed to command of most Union forces west of the Alleghenies. His first act was to replace the spent Rosecrans with Thomas as commander of the Army of the Cumberland. Gaining reinforcements, Grant soon had food and supplies flowing into the city. And on 25

November the vindictive Federals, shouting "Chickamauga!" as they charged, swarmed up and over the slopes of Missionary Ridge and chased the Confederate Army of Tennessee back to Georgia in one of the worst routs the Confederacy ever suffered. Chattanooga, the strategic center of the South, was secure for the Union. Now the way was prepared for William Tecumseh Sherman's devastating march across Georgia to the sea.

Contemplating this last golden opportunity lost, General D H Hill later concluded:

It seems to me that the *élan* of the Southern soldier was never seen after Chickamauga – that brilliant dash which had distinguished him was gone forever. He was too intelligent not to know that the cutting in two of Georgia meant death to all his hopes . . . He fought stoutly to the last, but, after Chickamauga, with the sullenness of despair and without the enthusiasm of hope. That "barren victory" sealed the fate of the Southern Confederacy.

EPILOGUE: THE END OF THE CONFEDERACY

When, at the end of 1863, Ulysses S Grant lifted the siege of Chattanooga, the Union was at last in a position to begin its invasion of the Deep South. But the anticipated lunge into Georgia did not start immediately. Early in the new year Grant was recalled to Washington, where he was created lieutenant general (a rank held previously only by George Washington), placed in charge of all the Union armies and given the task of devising a strategy for winning the war. When it emerged, that strategy, in essence, involved not one invasion but two: the thrust into Georgia, to be commanded by Sherman, would be coordinated with a simultaneous drive south from Washington aimed at Richmond – this latter operation to be conducted by General George Meade under Grant's personal supervision.

Both offensives began on the night of 3-4 May 1864. Within two days, Grant's part of the operation had become embroiled in savage fighting with Lee's Army of Northern Virginia, and this continued almost unabated for the next six weeks. Time and again – in The Wilderness, at Spotsylvania, at North Anna and at Cold Harbor – Lee attempted to block Grant's advance, and each time, after a bloody confrontation, Grant would disengage, swing around to the east and continue his relentless drive southward. By 18 June Grant was actually south of Richmond, facing Lee's strongly fortified position at Petersburg. At this point Grant abandoned maneuver and settled in for a long siege, reasoning that since Petersburg was the most important rail junction supplying Richmond, it was as good a place as any to begin starving the Rebel capital into submission. It was also a good – perhaps necessary – place to pause and try to recover from the rigors of the campaign thus far. The casualties on both sides had been appalling: 50,000 (41 percent) for the Union and 32,000 (46 percent) for the Confederacy. Given Lee's lack of reserve manpower, the figures were more ominous for the South than even the numbers and percentages might suggest.

Meanwhile, Sherman, fighting all the way, slowly made his

Above: *Remains of a Confederate battle flag. Many Southern units refused to surrender their banners but burned, buried, or hid them.*

Left: *Richmond, burned by Rebel soldiers as they prepared to abandon the Southern capital.*

Opposite: *A Union mortar battery prepares its position. Such siege weapons represent the North's overwhelming military strength.*

way towards Atlanta. He invested the Georgia capital in July, finally captured it in September and, after burning much of it, left it on 15 November to begin his infamous march to Savannah and the sea. Leaving a 60-mile-wide swath of calculated destruction in his wake, he reached and took Savannah on 21 December. A few days earlier, Union General George Thomas, the "Rock of Chickamauga," had, on Sherman's orders, engaged and all but destroyed the army of Confederate General John Bell Hood in Tennessee. There was now hardly any major military organization left in the Confederacy that might be sent to reinforce Lee at Petersburg.

By early 1865 it was obvious to all that the end was near. Sherman had wheeled north into the Carolina, and there seemed little hope that a hastily-improvised Confederate force under Joseph E Johnston could long deter Sherman from his ultimate objective: junction with Grant outside Petersburg. There were no great battles left to the Confederacy now, only the slow agony of failing strength and hope in the trenches of Petersburg. On 2 April 1865, after six months of devastating siege, Lee and the remains of his army bolted from Petersburg. Lee was making a last desperate effort to join forces with Johnston's army in South Carolina, but his leaving doomed Richmond. Lee was run to ground by Grant and General Philip Sheridan, who circled and harried the pathetic remains of the Army of Northern Virginia until that 9 April at Appomattox when Lee's men made their last charge, breaking through the center of Sheridan's line as it blocked their path. For a brief moment there was open country in front of the Army of Northern Virginia. Then from over a hill appeared Union infantry, line after line of blue, marching to fill that last gateway to freedom. Soon from within Confederate lines came a rider carrying a white flag into the ranks of the enemy.

The war was over. Lee's surrender to Grant at Appomattox on 9 April 1865 largely ended the hostilities (Johnston surrendered to Sherman on the 8th). Now the country was one again, the glorious exploits of the men in gray a matter of history and proud memory.

Throughout the long days of the war a volunteer nurse in Union military hospitals had put into impassioned words this thoughts about the struggle. He was Walt Whitman, later to be recognized as the great poet of the reborn nation. At the war's conclusion, Whitman wrote this benediction:

The dead in this war – there they lie, strewing the fields and woods and valleys and battlefields of the South: Virginia, the Peninsula, Malvern Hill and Fair Oaks, the banks of the Chickahominy, the terraces of Fredericksburg, Antietam bridge, the grisly ravines of Manassas, the bloody promenade of the Wilderness.

The dead, the dead, the dead . . . somewhere they crawled to die, alone, in bushes, low gullies, or on the sides of hills . . . Our young men once so handsome and so joyous, taken from us . . . the clusters of camp graves . . . the single graves left in the woods or by the roadside . . . the general million, and the special cemeteries in almost all the states.

The infinite dead, the land entire saturated, perfumed with their impalpable ashes' exhalation in Nature's chemistry distilled; and shall be so forever in every future grain of wheat and ear of corn, and every flower that grows, and every breath we draw.

Opposite: *A Union soldier surveys a ruined Richmond and its still-standing Southern capitol.*

Right: *Union soldiers at Appomattox Court House pose after the surrender ceremony.*

Below: *Grant and others (Sheridan between Grant and Lee, Meade at Grant's left) with General Lee at the McLean house at Appomattox Court House on 9 April 1865.*

Northern Victories

THE NORTH GOES TO WAR

The Civil War arose from a complex of problems – political, philosophical, economic and moral – that had haunted the United States from the beginning, implicitly from their first days as colonies and explicitly from their inception as a nation. These problems rolled through the years of the nineteenth century, gaining momentum, swelling until they had grown beyond the control of even the wisest of people.

Chief among these problems – or at least the one that proved to be breaking point – was the institution of human slavery imposed upon black people (which endured in America longer than in any other Western nation). By the mid-nineteenth century, slavery had been eliminated throughout the North, but was maintained in the South with a

tenacity that was only partially explainable by slavery's support of the cotton economy. The other major problem festering over the years was that of federalism versus states' rights: federalism, strongest in the North, proclaimed the primacy of the Federal Government; states' rights doctrine, dominant in the South, upheld the primacy of each state's government.

These and related problems had tended increasingly to split the country along sectional lines. So it was that in the early spring of 1861 the volatile spirit of sectionalism came to its long-feared explosion point: when the wisest of people cannot solve a nation's problems, they must often be solved by the strongest, and great suffering results.

In the midst of this crisis, the most serious in the nation's

Left: *Lincoln as portrayed by Alexander Gardner, an associate of Mathew Brady. Lincoln's first priority in conducting the Civil War was restoration of the Union. Emancipation of the slaves came second.*

Previous page: *The Battle of Gettysburg.*

Opposite top: *Philadelphia Zouaves parade past Independence Hall. Anticipating a short war, Northern volunteers flocked to join locally-raised army companies.*

Opposite bottom: *Lincoln's call for the raising of a militia to suppress the insurrection in South Carolina impelled thousands to volunteer for the fight. Northern enthusiasm was typified by this fanciful painting of joyful Uncle Sams marching into Dixie.*

PHILADELPHIA ZOUAVE CORPS.

history, the man whose election helped to precipitate it was inaugurated president. Elected by less than 50 percent of the voters, Abraham Lincoln came to the White House largely untried in national politics – an unknown quantity. Even before he arrived in Washington in February 1861, Lincoln faced the prospect of dealing with a rival government that was already claiming all Federal property within the boundaries of seven Southern states – South Carolina, Mississippi, Florida, Alabama, Georgia, Louisiana and Texas. After the November 1860 election these states had seceded from the Union and now called themselves the Confederate States of America. They had assembled their own representatives, who drew up a Constitution and selected a president – Jefferson Davis, a former secretary of war in Washington. In his first inaugural address Lincoln repudiated the Confederate claim, vowing to "hold, occupy, and possess" all Federal property. He made it clear that secession would not be tolerated.

Most significant among the Federal properties claimed by the Confederates were symbols of Federal power: four garrisons – three in Florida, far from the centers of government, and one in South Carolina. By the end of 1860, the attention of the entire country was riveted on the last garrison – Fort Sumter, in Charleston Harbor. As early as 26 December 1860 the Federal commander there, Major Robert Anderson, had withdrawn troops from the even more vulnerable Fort Moultrie, also in the harbor, and moved them to Sumter. At the beginning of 1861 this garrison, a pentagonal fort occupying an artificial island just off-shore, was unfinished, poorly

armed, understaffed and running low on food. In January a provision boat sent by then President Buchanan had been fired on and turned back. Since then the Confederates had erected a semicircle of batteries on the mainland and islands around the fort. The Federals inside had done what they could to prepare for battle.

Both Secretary of State Seward and aging general-in-chief Winfield Scott pressed Lincoln to evacuate Sumter. The President decided on 29 March 1861 neither to evacuate nor to reinforce the garrison, but to send a ship with provisions for the soldiers. On April 6 Lincoln advised South Carolina's governor of this order; he was making sure that the next critical step, an act of aggression, would have to be taken by the South.

On the next day the Confederate commander in Charleston, General P G T Beauregard, cut off communications between Charleston and Sumter. Events accelerated, pulled on by the seemingly irresistible magnet of war. On 8 April the Confederacy organized its forces in the harbor. Two days later Beauregard was instructed by the Confederate Government to demand the fort's surrender and evacuation; the demand was presented to Major Anderson on 11 April. Anderson replied that he would evacuate on 15 April unless he were attacked or received further orders from Washington. This last stipulation did not satisfy the Confederates.

At 3:20 in the morning on 12 April, Anderson received a note from Beauregard's messengers: "We have the honor to notify you that we will open the fire . . . in one hour from this time." Sumter's commander notified Captain Abner Doubleday (later to become incorrectly known as the founder of modern baseball) that the attack would begin at first light and that to conserve ammunition, fire should not be returned until broad daylight. After giving his final notice to Major Anderson, General Beauregard sent firing orders to Captain G S James in Fort Johnson, on James Island. Captain James

offered a friend the "honor" of discharging the opening shot; the friend agitated, replied, "I could not fire the first gun of the war." At 4:30 AM, 12 April, Captain James himself pulled the lanyard.

Fort Sumter, indefensible at the outset, endured 34 hours of bombardment and some 4000 shells: there was clearly little point in continued resistance. It was agreed that the Federals would evacuate the fort on 14 April, and that they might salute their flag with 100 guns before leaving. During this salute some sparks from the smoldering fires accidentally ignited a cannon cartridge as it was being loaded; the resulting explosion killed Private Daniel Hough instantly and seriously wounded five others, one of whom died. In this pointless accident fell the first soldiers of the war.

After their salute the Federals marched out, banners flying, the band playing "Yankee Doodle," and sailed off on the steamer *Baltic* to a heroes' welcome in New York. Confederate forces marched into the fort with equal ceremony. Maybe that's how it will be, many Southerners thought: we shell them a little and they go away. Maybe it would all be this easy: the North would soon be compelled to recognize the military superiority of the South and, lacking the South's will to fight, would sue for peace. Thus, without too much pain, would the South win its independence.

But the South did not yet know the resolve of Abraham Lincoln. On 15 April the president declared a state of "insurrection" and called for 75,000 volunteers to join the regular army in suppressing it. Northern States were immediately suppor-

Below left: *US recruiting poster. As the war drew on, ever more volunteers were needed.*

Below: *Wives and children bid farewell to the men of the Union garrison at Fort Sumter.*

tive, Border States resistant. On 19 April Lincoln declared a blockade of all Confederate ports. In the wake of Sumter four more states seceded – Virginia, Arkansas, Tennessee and North Carolina – but the Border States – Delaware, Maryland, Kentucky and Missouri – stayed loyal. Six days after Sumter fell, US Army General Robert E Lee declined an offer to command Union forces, resigned his commission and proclaimed his duty to defend his home state of Virginia.

Thus the war began. Everywhere citizens rallied to the colors, galvanised by romantic visions of a noble cause, of heroic battle. But a few, above all Abraham Lincoln, already understood that the coming conflict would be long and bitter. On paper, the North seemed to have some obvious advantages: it was more than twice as populous as the South, had built an industrial plant five times as large, and possessed a much superior system of communications, a far more flexible agricultural base, and considerably more ready cash. But the South had one unquantifiable advantage that would, during the first half of the war, prove nearly decisive: a seemingly inexhaustible reservoir of great commanders – Lee, Jackson, Stuart, Longstreet, Forrest, the two Johnstons, and many more. Against such men, the Northern mediocrities of early years of the war, generals such as McDowell, McClellan, Pope, Hooker, and Burnside, could only come to grief.

Yet even as the furnace of war was slowly hardening the rank and file of the Union armies, so it was also burning away the dross in the Federal officer corps, revealing hitherto-unrecognized talent. When the new breed of Northern commanders finally emerged – men such as Grant, Sherman, Sheridan, Thomas, and Meade – they differed from their Southern counterparts in important ways. They were less interested in (and propably less adept at) classical tactics, but they displayed a truly formidable grasp of strategy. They seemed to understand that this was a new kind of conflict, a Total War, and they were perhaps psychologically better prepared than their enemies to do whatever was necessary to win it. Their great victories – Gettysburg, Vicksburg, Atlanta, Petersburg, and the rest – were sometimes appallingly costly and seldom elegant, but in sum they were devastating.

Above: *Rebel batteries shelling Fort Sumter on 13 April 1861. The fort was evacuated the next day.*

Below: *Southern dignitaries view the defenses at Fort Sumter a few days after it fell to Rebel bombardment.*

SHILOH

In April of 1862 the war was a year old, and the original optimistic hopes on both sides for a short conflict, resolved in one or two decisive battles, were fading. After the fall of Fort Sumter, Lincoln had called for three-month volunteers to put down the rebellion. That was expected to be time enough. But the initial major battle of the war, the First Bull Run (Virginia) in July 1861, had been a humiliation for the Union, as had the action as Ball's Bluff, Virginia, in October.

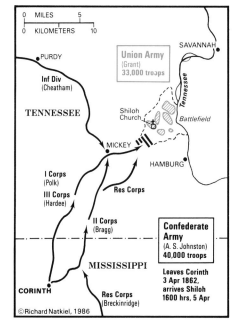

Far left: *General William Tecumseh Sherman distinguished himself at Shiloh, the first battle in the Western Hemisphere to involve more than 100,000 men.*

Left: *Disposition of the forces at Shiloh on 5 April 1861.*

Below: *The engagements on the first and second days.*

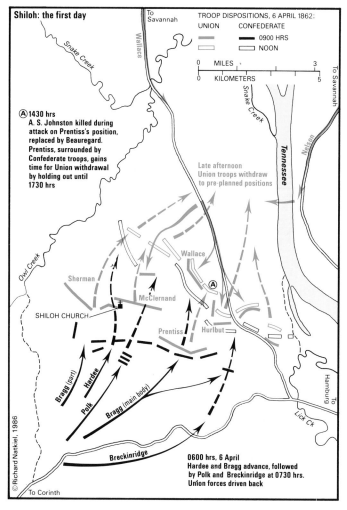

Shiloh: the first day

TROOP DISPOSITIONS, 6 APRIL 1862:
UNION   CONFEDERATE
0900 HRS
NOON

Ⓐ 1430 hrs
A. S. Johnston killed during attack on Prentiss's position, replaced by Beauregard. Prentiss, surrounded by Confederate troops, gains time for Union withdrawal by holding out until 1730 hrs

Late afternoon Union troops withdraw to pre-planned positions

0600 hrs, 6 April
Hardee and Bragg advance, followed by Polk and Breckinridge at 0730 hrs. Union forces driven back

© Richard Natkiel, 1986

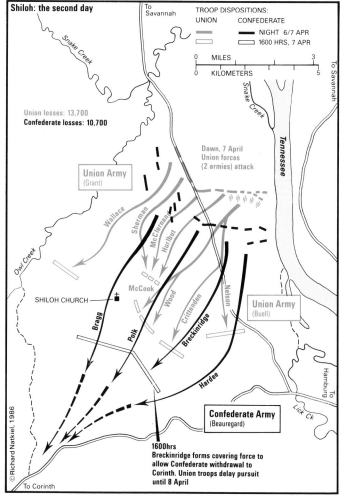

Shiloh: the second day

TROOP DISPOSITIONS:
UNION   CONFEDERATE
NIGHT 6/7 APR
1600 HRS, 7 APR

Union losses: 13,700
Confederate losses: 10,700

Dawn, 7 April
Union forces (2 armies) attack

1600hrs
Breckinridge forms covering force to allow Confederate withdrawal to Corinth. Union troops delay pursuit until 8 April

© Richard Natkiel, 1986

It began to be clear that in order to defeat the South, the North had to invade and occupy it. If the North could be said at this stage to have a strategy to achieve that gargantuan task, it was to split the Confederacy on a north-south line along the Mississippi River, then east-west somewhere through the middle of the south; then it would deal with the fragments. To achieve the north-south sundering, Federal forces early in 1862 began moving south into Rebel territory from Kentucky, along the Cumberland and Tennessee rivers.

The district commander of these forces was an up-and-coming Union general named Ulysses S Grant. In February 1862 Grant had leaped from obscurity into national prominence with his dramatic campaigns to capture Forts Henry and Donelson. His surrender note to the latter – "No terms except for immediate and unconditional surrender can be accepted" – had earned him the nickname "Unconditional Surrender" Grant.

But no one really knew yet what Grant was capable of. He was an unkempt and not particularly soldierly looking man whose gait was a sort of controlled stumble. His habitual expression was once described in the words "He looked as if he had decided to drive his head through a brick wall and was about to do it." There was talk, perhaps more than rumor, about his past – failures in business, a near-court-martial in his first military command some years before and a fondness for the bottle abnormal even for an officer. And after his recent victories Grant had somehow displeased his superiors enough to get himself relieved of command and virtually under arrest for a week. He was no one's image of a great commander.

Right: *The notoriously unkempt General Ulysses S Grant, the Union's finest commander.*

Overleaf: *Scouts and guides of the Union army. Poor Northern intelligence-gathering led to Grant's inadequate preparation against the first Confederate attack at Shiloh.*

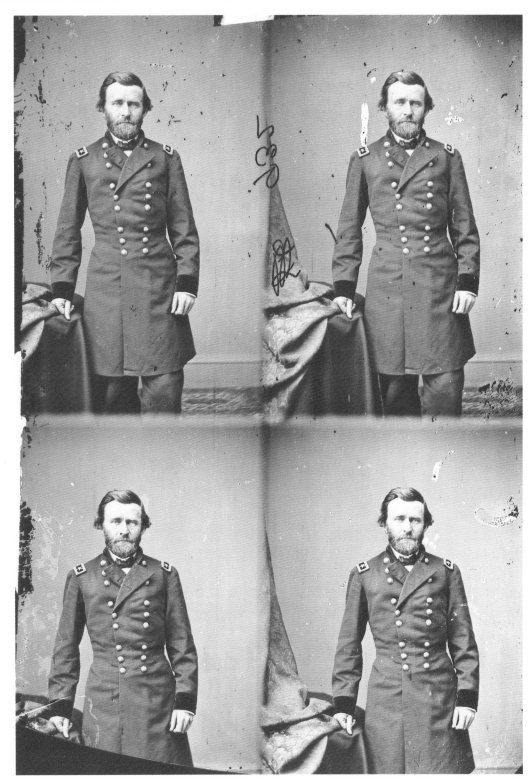

Left: *A Union cavalryman would usually be better equipped than this Rebel horseman.*

Above: *General Henry W Halleck, Grant's commander in 1862.*

Opposite: *Federal forces, almost overwhelmed by the Rebel advance on their position atop the high bluffs on the Tennessee, are rescued by fire from Union artillery and the gunboats* Lexington *and* Tyler.

When Grant got back his district command on 13 March, he found his army on the Tennessee River, part at the small town of Savannah, Tennessee, and part nine miles above, on the western bank of the river near Pittsburg Landing, Tennessee. His plan was to concentrate these forces, called the Union Army of the Mississippi, with those of General Don Carlos Buell's Army of the Ohio; the latter were ordered to move southwest from Nashville. When finally combined, the two armies were to move on Corinth, Mississippi, an important Confederate rail center (all these towns were near the conjoined corners of Tennessee, Mississippi and Alabama). Buell began promptly to move his forces, but then was held up for ten days by floods.

Grant knew there were enemy forces near his camps and a large Rebel force in Corinth. He did not know, however, that they were preparing an offensive designed to smash his army before Buell could reach him. (As was often the case during the war, Southern intelligence-gathering was more accurate than that of the North.) For the purpose of dealing with Grant's forces, General P G T Beauregard, the hero of Sumter and Bull Run, had assembled in Corinth a new Confederate Army of 40,000 men, consisting of corps under Generals Leonidas Polk, Braxton Bragg, William J Hardee, and John C Breckenridge. In overall command of this new Confederate Army of the Mississippi was General Albert Sidney Johnston, considered among the greatest hopes of the southern cause.

Johnston developed a bold offensive strategy, overruling Beauregard's insistence on a defensive approach. According to the plan, the Confederate Army was to move out of Corinth, envelop the Union left flank by the river – thus cutting off reinforcements from Buell in the east – and push the Federals back to Owl Creek to the northeast, thereby forcing a surrender.

On 6 April Grant had six divisions – those of John A McClernand, William H Wallace, Lew Wallace (later the writer of *Ben Hur*), Steven A Hurlbut, William Tecumseh Sherman and Benjamin M Prentiss – encamped on the west side of the Tennessee River in the vicinity of Pittsburg Landing and the little log meetinghouse called Shiloh Church. A considerable portion of these 33,000 troops were quite green; indeed, many scarcely knew how to load their rifles, and some of the officers were little more experienced.

Though there had been continuous skirmishing along his front for some days, Grant wrote his superior Halleck on 5 April, "I scarcely have the faintest idea of an attack . . . being made on us." Grant's close associate, Sherman, concurred with this supposition: they reasoned that Corinth was a good defensive position and that the Confederates would not venture out of it. The Union camps were therefore chosen for their comfort rather than for their defensive strength; guarding was desultory, and there were no entrenchments.

On the morning of 6 April Grant confidently left his camp

well before dawn to have breakfast in Savannah and meet with Buell, who had arrived there the day before. Grant was on crutches, lamed by a riding accident. Most of his troops were beginning a normal day, having a leisurely breakfast and polishing up for the usual Sunday inspection.

Then, still before dawn, the Rebel attack swarmed into the Union camps with overpowering suddenness and strength. Companies of the 16th Wisconsin and 21st Missouri were sent to reinforce the slim Union forces in the front, but these were soon driven back. The majority of the 25th Missouri (on the left middle of the Union lines) were standing at rest in their camp when they were astonished to see a huge body of Confederates, line after line, unpreceded by skirmishers, coming down a slope toward them within easy range. Both sides simply stood and fired away, with devastating effect – at this point in the war, many considered it cowardly to dig a hole or even to take cover.

Meanwhile, at six o'clock that morning, Hildebrand's hastily-formed brigade of Sherman's division, on the right of the Union lines, received the full force of the Confederate attack. Green troops of the 53rd Ohio immediately broke and ran, followed by two other regiments. The rest of Sherman's division fell back from their camps after some resistance, and by eight in the morning Prentiss's whole division had done likewise, pursued through their camps and across a ravine.

About that same hour, Confederate General Johnston's designs on the left flank of the Federal army – the original focal point of his strategy of envelopment – began to take shape. On the extreme Union left was a small brigade of Sherman's division, without artillery, led by Colonel David Stuart. His small force met a strong charge by the Rebels and, after some initial panic, was formed into line and mounted a furious resistance some 500 yards behind their original position. This Union stand, coming as it did after a frightened stampede,

was so determined that it convinced the enemy it must be a trap: as one Rebel officer observed, "No such little body of men could ever stand up and fight like that without something back of them." Stuart's brigade would hold on until after two o'clock that afternoon, withdrawing only when its ammunition was exhausted. The wary Confederates, still suspecting a trap and not realizing how small a force had stayed them, did not immediately press their advantage.

By midmorning the fighting was furious all along the line. The battle clearly had the appearance of a major Confederate victory. Most of the Union forces had pulled back from their camps with heavy losses. There was a serious gap in the center of the Federal line, and hordes of Union stragglers were collecting along the river to the rear. The raw volunteers of the Northern armies had experienced their baptism of fire.

Things were indeed going well enough for the Confederacy on the morning of 6 April, but not so well as they seemed to the Rebels. Johnston's attack was in fact poorly organized: his units had intermingled, the commands becoming confused; men were thrown into attack by columns as they arrived on the roads, and no reserves were left at all; the main thrust of Johnston's original attack plan, the left of the Union line, had bogged down. Instead of the intended envelopment, there was a disorderly advance all along the front.

Furthermore, Union forces were withdrawing not in disarray but in rather good order, the stragglers notwithstanding. Having heard the onset of hostilities that morning, Grant rushed to Pittsburg Landing from Savannah, arriving about eight o'clock. Not having had time to see Buell in Savannah, Grant sent a note to hurry him along. Lew Wallace was ordered to rush his 5000 troops south from Crump's Landing (confusion about the orders delayed Wallace until after dark). Guards were placed in the rear to stop stragglers at

Left: *Three months after Shiloh, Henry Halleck became general-in-chief of the Union armies. He assigned Grant a relatively minor mission. Later proven a poor field commander, he would be replaced by Grant.*

Opposite: *General Grant at the head of a Union charge on the afternoon of 7 April.*

Opposite below: *The death of the highly regarded Confederate General Albert Sidney Johnston at Shiloh effectively slowed the Rebel advance and cost the South one of its greatest generals.*

gunpoint. Hearing that General "Bull" Nelson's division, the closest part of Buell's army, had arrived at Savannah, Grant ordered them to move to the east bank of the Tennessee opposite Pittsburg Landing. Determined Federal resistance remained on the left (Stuart) and also in a densely wooded area on the left center, dubbed by the Confederate attackers "The Hornet's Nest." Grant asked Prentiss to hold the Hornet's Nest, the key to the middle of his line, at all costs.

At half past two in the afternoon came a crushing blow both to Southern fortunes in the battle and to hopes for the Confederate cause itself. General Johnston had ridden over to the right of his lines to deal with what was intended as his main thrust, on the Federal left. He found his men still bogged down in the face of galling Union fire. Johnston ordered a charge and personally led his men in pushing the Federals back some three-quarters of a mile. While dressing their lines in the new position, the Confederates found themselves subject to enfilade fire from the left. Johnston had just ordered one regiment to wheel and meet this fire when he was struck by a stray shot and sagged on his horse. I G Harris, the Governor of Tennessee, righted the general and led his horse behind the lines. Johnston had previously dispatched his chief surgeon to the rear, to deal with Federal wounded. This act of charity probably cost him his life. The shot had cut an

artery, but the wound could easily have been treated had the surgeon been available. Without help, Johnston bled to death in a few minutes. The South thereby lost one of its greatest generals and the Confederate attack began to lose momentum. Beauregard, who had strenuously opposed the offensive tactic and was also quite ill at the time, was now in command of the Southern forces.

But the Confederate advance by no means came to an immediate halt. The Federal left was at length pushed back almost to Pittsburg Landing, threatening the arrival of Buell's reinforcements as Johnston had intended. On the Union left center, the Hornet's Nest held on with divisions commanded by Hurlbut and W H L Wallace, along with the remnants of Prentiss's division.

In all, the Rebels mounted 11 unsuccessful charges on the Hornet's Nest. But at length the Federal defenders grew exhausted, and the retreat of their own forces around them slowly exposed their flanks. Finally, Confederate General Ruggles massed 62 cannon on the position and encircled it. Federal General W H L Wallace was killed leading his division to safety out of the area. At half past five in the afternoon General Prentiss and 2200 men surrendered after some eight hours of fighting.

But the Federal's stand in the Hornet's Nest had been more

It was therefore some time before Confederate forces were gathered again for what was intended to be the decisive move on the Union Army. At Pittsburg Landing the Federals had fallen back as far as the ground permitted; one more strong Rebel push would send them into the river. At that most critical moment, artillery came to the rescue of the North. Grant's artillery chief, Colonel J D Webster, opened up from a battery on high ground near the landing; the Union iron-clad gunboats *Lexington* and *Tyler*, just arrived from Savannah, opened up with long-range 64-pounders on the Rebel positions. In the face of this bombardment, the enemy advance ground to a halt. Soon came yet another moment to cheer the Federals: troops of Nelson's division of Buell's army, the desperately awaited reinforcements, were seen gathering on the east shore. In short order they were being ferried across the Tennessee.

At about six that evening, just before a final Rebel attack was to be made on Pittsburg Landing, Beauregard suspended operations to the dismay of several of his commanders. He did so partly because night was coming, partly because he was ignorant of Buell's impending arrival. His intelligence reported that Buell could not be expected to arrive in time to aid Grant, and therefore the Southerners could take time to rest and regroup.

The Confederates that night assumed they had won. Back in the captured Union camps, the Rebels celebrated with the enemy's provisions and liquor, enjoying the shelter of the tents when a storm blew in; Union troops had to bivouac outside in the torrential rain. True, the Rebels were harried by the Union gunboats, which continued to shell their positions all night, but neither that nor the rain could dampen the Southerners' sense of impending victory.

During that wet and miserable night Grant hobbled about, kept awake by the pain of his riding injury and sickened by

than empty heroics. The number of men and the time it took to take the position had slowed the whole Confederate thrust. It took yet more valuable time to disarm the Federal prisoners, gather them and send them to the rear, where other Southern soldiers, thinking the bulk of the Federal Army had been taken, left their positions to go peer curiously at the "captured Yanks."

the suffering of his wounded men. Nonetheless, he thought coolly and clearly. He saw that the next day's victory would go to whoever attacked first, and made his plans accordingly. All night, while the Confederates were celebrating, Buell's men were being transported across the Tennessee – divisions led by Crittenden, McCook and Nelson, totaling 25,000 men, all of them fresh. Lew Wallace's division of 5000 finally arrived after dark. This was entirely unknown to Beauregard, who expected the imminent arrival of 20,000 reinforcements under General Van Dorn, moving up from Arkansas.

On 7 April, at 7:30 AM, Grant's supposedly beaten Federals unleashed a well-co-ordinated counterattack on both enemy flanks, led by Lew Wallace on the Union right and Nelson, of Buell's army, on the left. Wallace began with his artillery, dueling with the enemy cannon, and sent his soldiers across a ravine on to the Southern flank; the enemy hastily withdrew with their own guns. Nelson pressed forward with equal success on the left. By 10:30 the fighting was general all along the line, and the Federals had regained much of the ground lost the previous day.

A Southern offensive developed around a peach orchard on the Union right; the Federals, having outrun their artillery, gave way for a time. At length Union artillery was moved up, and General Buell directed the assault; after a seesaw contest the Rebel lines were again driven away. By early afternoon the Confederate right had been pushed back and the Federals had reoccupied their original camps, recapturing weapons and materiel they had abandoned the day before. Beauregard mounted a strong resistance in front of the crossroads by Shiloh Church, now his headquarters; the roads there were Van Dorn's best route to reinforce Beauregard, and also the best route on which to retreat, if it came to that. Beauregard had only 20,000 men left fighting. Without Van Dorn, he saw that it would indeed come to retreat. He held on to the crossroads grimly for a time; the insignificant meetinghouse became the focal point of the battle that would bear its name.

By 2:30 that afternoon Beauregard had learned that Van Dorn had been halted by the swollen Mississippi. The Federals were pushing back his forces all along the line, casualties were mounting and straggling was becoming uncontrollable – troops fell out by the hundreds and streamed to the rear. There was only one option left: Beauregard issued orders to retreat. The Confederates withdrew toward Corinth in good order, the retreat covered by infantry and artillery under General Nathan Bedford Forrest. At three o'clock Grant personally directed a last Union charge along the road to Corinth. By five o'clock, the Rebels had retired from the field. The exhausted Federals sank into their recaptured camps and did not pursue.

In the ensuing days both sides claimed victory, and in fact, Union casualties were greater. But it was unquestionably a Union victory, if an incomplete one. The South had begun with a tactical surprise – much disputed by Grant in his memoirs, but a suprise all the same – and had fought gallantly and with great initial effect. But the Rebel attack had been poorly co-ordinated and overextended; those facts, combined with the disaster of Johnston's death, had allowed the Federals to regroup and finally to take the initiative. As is usually the case, the side that in the end held the initiative gained the victory.

Shiloh was the first battle in the Western Hemisphere to involve over 100,000 men. Casualties were appalling on both sides: of 62,682 Union effectives (by the second day), 1754 were killed, 8408 wounded and 2885 missing, for a total of 13,047 casualties; of the South's 40,335 effectives, 1723 were killed, 8012 wounded, 959 missing, for a total of 10,694.

Beauregard's defeat was to damage his prestige for some time during the war. As for Grant, he had been surprised, and the brilliance of his holding on and striking back did not erase that fact. But Lincoln, seeing things clearly from distant Washington, was soon to reply to demands for Grant's dismissal with eloquent simplicity: "I can't spare this man. He fights."

Left: *The Union resistance at the Hornet's Nest withstood eleven Rebel charges, slowing the Confederate thrust.*

Opposite top: *Wisconsin volunteers charge a New Orleans battery at Shiloh.*

Opposite bottom: *P G T Beauregard (right) succeeded Confederate General A S Johnston but was no match for Grant. Nathan Bedford Forrest (left) directed troops covering Beauregard's retreat toward Corinth.*

VICKSBURG

A little more than three weeks after the Battle of Shiloh ended, the commander for the Confederate Army in Virginia, Joseph E Johnston, was replaced by a man who would soon be recognized the world over as one of history's greatest generals. If Union fortunes in the Eastern Military Theater had been low before the advent of Robert E Lee, they were about to sink to their nadir. Within two months of his accession to the command of the newly named Army of Northern Virginia, Lee had utterly defeated Union General George B McClellan's massive, clumsy offensive against Richmond via the Virginia Peninsula, and a month later Lee routed McClellan's Army of the Potomac at the Second Battle of Bull Run (Second Manassas). In mid-September the two armies clashed again in the bloody, inconclusive Battle of Antietam. Some in the North professed to believe that Antietam was a Northern victory (presumably on the grounds that Lee had not actually won it), but whatever comfort Northerners drew from such fancies evaporated when Lee again smashed the advancing Army of the Potomac (now under McClellan's successor, Ambrose Burnside) at the dismal Battle of Fredericksburg in mid-December.

The high-water mark of Lee's remarkable string of victories occurred when serious campaigning resumed in the spring of 1863. Late in April, General Joseph Hooker, the hapless Burnside's successor, attempted to pin Lee's army at Fredericksburg between a combined frontal assault and right-wing envelopment. Lee repelled the frontal assault as easily as he had Burnside's, while at the same time moving the bulk of his forces so adroitly that in short order he had not only stymied the envelopment but placed it on the defensive at Chancellorsville, about ten miles west of Fredericksburg.

Opposite top: *Ambrose E Burnside commanded the Union Army of the Potomac at Fredericksburg.*

Opposite bottom: *Lincoln visits McClellan (facing him) in October 1862.*

Above: *Mississippi riverboats at Vicksburg, the principal supply center for the Southern war effort and the focus of an eight-month-long campaign by General Grant to split the entire Confederacy.*

Lee then mounted an attack on Hooker's right flank at Chancellorsville, an attack that proved so successful that by 5 May the whole 90,000-man Army of the Potomac was again in full retreat. Only the death of Lee's great lieutenant, Stonewall Jackson, marred this otherwise brilliant victory. Hardly pausing for breath, Lee next hurled the Army of Northern Virginia northwest in an invasion of Pennsylvania, a bold stroke that would shortly culminate in the most famous battle in American history.

But while Robert E Lee was dominating the Eastern Theater of the war with his tactical genius, a different kind of military genius was demonstrating his brilliance in long-range strategic planning in the Western Theater. The man was Ulysses S Grant. The complex and historic Vicksburg Campaign of 1862-63 would be remembered as Grant's masterpiece, as Chancellorsville was Lee's.

The town of Vicksburg, Mississippi, lies atop high bluffs on the banks of the Mississippi River. It occupies the first high land on the eastern bank of the river below Memphis, some 400 miles to the north. Throughout the winter of 1862-63 the Mississippi was swollen by heavy rains, and Vicksburg overlooked hundreds of miles of flooded and swampy land and river bottom. The town was approachable by land only from the east, from Confederate territory. And the water route was impassable to most Union shipping: the bluffs before Vicksburg were bristling with fortifications and batteries that dominated the river below.

Strategically, Vicksburg was one of the two most vital towns of the Confederacy, the other being the rail center of Chattanooga. To the east through Vicksburg came food, supplies and cotton necessary to the Southern war effort. Could the North conquer the city, those supplies would be cut off and Union armies and supplies could pass unmolested through the very center of the Confederacy. It was essential to the North's grand strategy to accomplish that task.

On 25 October 1862 Ulysses S Grant was given command of the Federal Department of the Tennessee. A week after his

Left: *Union troops confront Lee's soldiers at Burnside Bridge in the Battle of Antietam. The battle put the South on the defensive and set the scene for the failed Union assault on Fredericksburg.*

Below: *In the Western Theater of the war, General Grant mounted his Vicksburg Campaign in the winter of 1862. By mid-May 1863 he had begun his siege of Vicksburg.*

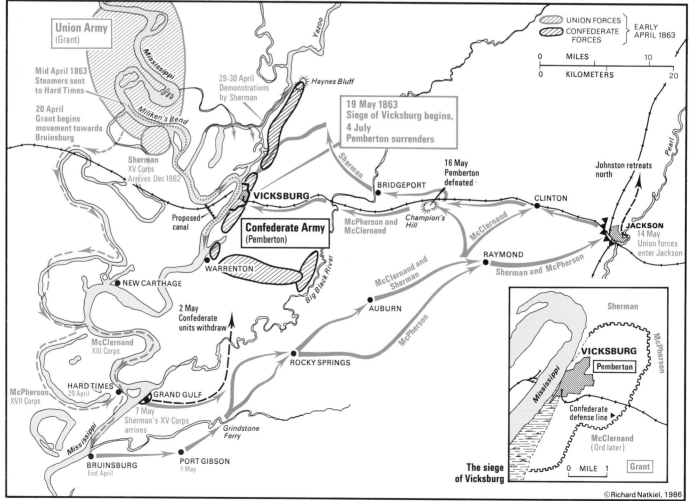

UNION FORCES
CONFEDERATE FORCES

EARLY APRIL 1863

0   MILES   10
0   KILOMETERS   20

Union Army (Grant)

Mid April 1863 Steamers sent to Hard Times

20 April Grant begins movement towards Bruinsburg

Mississippi

Milliken's Bend

29-30 April Demonstrations by Sherman

Yazoo

Haynes Bluff

19 May 1863 Siege of Vicksburg begins, 4 July Pemberton surrenders

Sherman

16 May Pemberton defeated

BRIDGEPORT

Pearl

Johnston retreats north

Sherman XV Corps Arrives Dec 1862

Proposed canal

VICKSBURG

Confederate Army (Pemberton)

McPherson and McClernand

Champion's Hill

McClernand

CLINTON

McClernand

JACKSON
14 May Union forces enter Jackson

WARRENTON

Big Black River

RAYMOND

Sherman and McPherson

2 May Confederate units withdraw

McClernand and Sherman

NEW CARTHAGE

McClernand XIII Corps

AUBURN

McPherson

Sherman

VICKSBURG

Pemberton

McPherson

ROCKY SPRINGS

McPherson XVII Corps

HARD TIMES
29 April

GRAND GULF

7 May Sherman's XV Corps arrives

Mississippi

Grindstone Ferry

BRUINSBURG
End April

PORT GIBSON
1 May

Confederate defense line

McClernand (Ord later)

Grant

0   MILE   1

The siege of Vicksburg

©Richard Natkiel, 1986

Right: *For many months the Union tried to dig a canal across a bend of the Mississippi River opposite Vicksburg to allow Federal gunboats to avoid the defending Rebel batteries. The attempt was thwarted by rising waters.*

Below: *General John Pemberton, the Confederate commander in Mississippi, was forced by Grant's siege to formally surrender Vicksburg on 4 July 1863. It is considered by many to be the turning point of the war.*

appointment he began to move overland on Vicksburg. Much of the Mississippi already lay in Union hands – Admiral Farragut had conquered New Orleans in the spring of 1862 and had cleared the river up to Baton Rouge, Louisiana. Soon after, a Federal flotilla had all but destroyed a Confederate fleet on the Mississippi at Memphis and taken that city.

In November Grant moved his 40,000 men out of Jackson, Tennessee, marching south on the east side of the Mississippi toward Vicksburg. This campaign soon came to grief: on 20 December a Confederate cavalry force under General Earl van Dorn swept into the Federal base at Holly Springs, Mississippi, just south of the Tennessee border, and destroyed most of Grant's supplies. At the same time, cavalry under Nathan Bedford Forrest raided Union communication lines in western Tennessee, destroying 60 miles of railroad. The Union advance ground to a halt just as further misfortunes developed to the south.

William T Sherman, Grant's closest subordinate, had been dispatched down the Yazoo River to take possession of the landings at Vicksburg, in support of Grant's campaign. But just north of the city at Chickasaw Bluffs, Sherman's forces were severely repulsed on 27-29 December; in that action the Union suffered 1776 casualties to the South's 207. It became clear to Federal leaders that Vicksburg was going to be a tough nut indeed to crack.

Thus at the beginning of 1863 the North's war effort was stalled all over the map: Grant was apparently going nowhere, and neither were Hooker in the East or Rosecrans in Tennessee. Grant proceeded to size up his situation. An over-

Above: *Admiral David Dixon Porter commanded the Union Mississippi Squadron in the Vicksburg Campaign.*

Right: *Admiral Porter's fleet of transports, escorted by six gunboats (including his flagship* Benton*), run the Rebel blockade at Vicksburg on 16 April 1863.*

Opposite: *Confederate General Joseph E Johnston's defense of Vicksburg was thwarted both by Grant and by the enmity of Jefferson Davis, who countermanded his orders.*

land advance on Vicksburg had just been proven impossible, and the high waters made all land operations difficult, but public and political pressure from the North obliged him to do *something* – or else. Accordingly, Grant shifted his base to Young's Point, nearly opposite Vicksburg on the western (Louisiana) bank of the river, and in the first months of 1863 indulged in a series of experiments that he privately doubted would work.

The first experiment was to cut a canal across Young's Point, in hopes of moving Union boats through it and down the Mississippi. But the canal when finished could not be filled to a depth sufficient to float the ships. While the canal was in progress Grant dispatched General James B McPherson's XVII Corps to try to open a passage from Lake Providence south through the soggy landscape in order to come out on the Red River south of Vicksburg, whence steamers could move back upstream. This scheme was abandoned in March for a more promising one in the Yazoo Pass, 325 miles north of Vicksburg. There the Federals cut through a levee and the fleet steamed into the Tallahatchie River, moving south toward the Yazoo and Vicksburg. This expedition ran afoul of a hastily constructed Rebel work named Fort Pemberton in honor of Vicksburg's commander, General John C

Pemberton. For six days in mid-March the little fort turned back the best efforts of the Federal fleet to pass. Grant then moved on to his fourth and final experiment, an attempt to push Federal ships north through a tangled mass of streams and backwaters called Steel's Bayou. Trying to move up through the tiny waterways to the Yazoo, Admiral David D Porter's boats were obstructed by trees, some of them felled by the Confederates, who then attacked the Union boats on 19 March. Porter had to be rescued by Sherman's corps. There ended Grant's experiments, all of them fantastically difficult and round-about ways to traverse the few miles that separated Vicksburg from the Union base, which was now at Millikin's Bend just across the river from Vicksburg.

Grant had tried every possible water route to Vicksburg: now he had to go overland, and do it soon. The whole progress of the war in the West was on his shoulders, and the West was where the Confederacy must ultimately be beaten – in its own territory. So Grant devised a new plan. The high water had receded enough so that he could march his men south on the Louisiana side of the river. Once south of Vicksburg, they had somehow to cross the Mississipi, which could be done only by running the Federal fleet directly past the fearsome Vicksburg batteries; the ships would meet the army

McClernand's considerable chagrin. On 29 March Grant sent McClernand's XIII Corps to forge a trail from Millikin's Bend south to New Carthage. The men set about tearing down plantation homes, and anything else handy, to build bridges across the tangled waterways on the Louisiana side. Admiral Porter stood by to provide troop transport and supplies.

By 16 April it was time for the first critical gamble of the campaign – running Union ships past Vicksburg. The ships, six gunboats and several transports of Admiral Porter's fleet, were manned by a few volunteers; in the holds waited men with boards, cotton and gunny sacks to patch up holes made by enemy fire. The vulnerable transport ships were padded with cotton bales and had barges of coal and forage lashed alongside. Around 11:00 PM the ships began floating silently downstream. An hour later they were opposite Vicksburg, where they were spotted by the Confederate defenders. The Rebel batteries opened up, turning the bluffs into a sheet of flame, and the ships put on steam.

Remarkably, Porter succeeded in running the batteries, losing only one ship and a few barges, and the battered flotilla came to rest at Hard Times, where Grant's army was gathering. On 22 April more transports and barges ran the gauntlet. Meanwhile, Sherman made a feint at Haines's Bluff, moving his corps up and down the river and the shore until Pemberton, in Vicksburg, was convinced a major attack was coming there. Once the Confederates were properly distracted, Sherman marched to join Grant below Vicksburg.

Much as Pemberton was confused by the feint at Haines's Bluff, however, he was more concerned by the other Federal diversion designed to screen Grant's crossing of the Mississippi. General Benjamin H Grierson and 1700 cavalrymen left LaGrange, Tennessee, on 17 April, riding south through Mississippi. A worried Pemberton sent cavalry in pursuit (at the same time marching men to meet Sherman's imaginary offensive at Haines's Bluff). After two weeks of hard riding, evading pursuers, raiding and skirmishing, Grierson arrived at Federally-held Baton Rouge on 2 May. His men had ridden 600 miles in 16 days, accounted for 100 Rebel casualties,

downriver and ferry the troops across. (Admiral Farragut had moved ships past the batteries in the summer of 1862, so perhaps it was possible.) If this could be done, Grant would then move his men northwest across Mississippi, cut communications between Vicksburg and the Confederacy and lay siege to the city. Meanwhile, to screen the operation, Sherman and Colonel R H Grierson would pursue diversionary operations, Sherman on Haines's Bluff near Vicksburg and Grierson moving his cavalry south from Tennessee through Mississippi. Thus Grant planned four carefully co-ordinated operations – his army, Porter's fleet, Sherman's corps and Grierson's cavalry – involving many thousands of men and horses, a fleet of ships and thousands of square miles of land. To take Vicksburg, many things had to work perfectly in concert, and Washington had to co-operate as well.

This latter element of Grant's requirements was as undependable as any. He had already run afoul of a secret river expedition on Vicksburg planned in Washington by a politically appointed Volunteer general, John A McClernand: this expedition was in effect competing with Grant's for the same prize. Having kept Grant in the dark for some time about McClernand, General-in-Chief Halleck finally scotched that expedition and put McClernand's forces under Grant – to

Right: *Shirley House, headquarters of General Grant during the siege of Vicksburg.*

Below: *General John A McClernand had been put in charge of a secretly planned expedition to Vicksburg before coming under Grant's command.*

taken 500 prisoners, destroyed 50 miles of railroad and much enemy weaponry, captured 1000 horses and mules – and suffered only 24 casualties. It was to be remembered as one of the most brilliant cavalry exploits of the war.

Grant, meanwhile, had run into resistance trying to cross his troops at Grand Gulf, where on 29 April 17 gunboats failed to reduce a Confederate garrison. Moving a little farther south, Grant crossed his army unopposed at Bruinsburg the next day. The Confederates then pulled out of Grand Gulf and met Grant's overland advance at Port Gibson on 1 May. In a day of fighting amid hills and deep ravines, Grant flanked the 8000 Confederates and brushed them out of the way before their reinforcements could arrive. The Northern forces – the corps of Sherman (XV), McPherson (XVII) and McClernand (XIII) – then pushed northeast across Mississippi, skirmishing constantly with Rebel forces in the rear.

Grant was planning so far to march south and join General Nathaniel P Banks (another politically appointed general of volunteers, who at the outbreak of the war was Governor of Massachusetts) in moving on Confederate-held Port Hudson, on the Mississippi to the south. Learning that Banks was busy with what was to become the extensive – and ill-fated – Red River Campaign, Grant made a bold change in plans that was destined to elevate him to the ranks of the great generals in history. Against the advice of his staff, he decided to cut away from his supply and communications lines and move into the rear of Vicksburg, first taking Jackson, the capital of the state, in the east. Then, having taken care of any potential enemy reinforcements to Vicksburg, he would besiege the city. In military terms, he would *defeat the enemy in detail* before they had the chance to concentrate superior forces against him. His army would march with all the supplies it could carry and would forage in the countryside; now Southern civilians would have to bear directly the cost of war.

Grant's opponent in Jackson was one of the best generals in the Confederacy – Joseph E Johnston. He had only somewhat recovered from wounds he had received during the Peninsular Campaign and was desperately trying to accumulate enough forces to oppose Grant. Arriving in Jackson the evening of the 13th, Johnston was so ill that he did much of his work in bed.

As Grant moved toward Jackson he sent a detachment to feint toward Vicksburg, where Pemberton was still trying to figure out what the Federals were up to. Sherman crossed his corps at Grand Gulf on 6 May, and by the 12th Grant was approaching Jackson with 44,000 men. That day McPherson's corps routed a Rebel detachment at Raymond, Mississippi; leaving McClernand in that town to protect his rear, Grant arrived before Jackson on the 13th. That night Johnston wrote to Pemberton in Vicksburg, ordering him to move on Grant's rear.

Johnston had only 6000 men to oppose the Federals' two corps; Confederate reinforcements were on the way, but Grant had no intention of waiting for their arrival, or for Pemberton to move. On 14 May, McPherson and Sherman easily stormed Jackson: that night Grant slept in the room Johnston had occupied the night before. Johnston moved his troops north, writing the recalcitrant Pemberton to cut Grant's supply line and then join forces.

But Pemberton had two problems with this order: one, Grant in fact had no supply line, and two, Confederate President Davis had ordered Pemberton to stay in Vicksburg. Thus Pemberton, already perplexed, was caught between contradictory orders from his government and from his superior, Johnston. He managed to satisfy neither very well.

Having first spent a fruitless 15 May looking for the non-existent Union supply line to the south, Pemberton turned his troops around and went east to join Johnston. The Confederate troops were exhausted, having marched in every direction for days without finding the enemy. Grant had already foreseen the Confederate move and had gone with McClernand and McPherson to meet Pemberton. (Sherman was left in Jackson to destroy manufacturing centers and railroads, a task which, as always, he performed with a vengeance.) At Champion's Hill, a small knoll in the countryside between Vicksburg and Jackson, the forces of Grant and Pemberton collided on 16 May.

Champion's Hill saw the hardest day's fighting of the campaign. The forces engaged were not radically unequal: Grant had 29,000 men of McPherson's and McLernand's corps, and Pemberton had some 22,000. (Sherman, ordered out of Jackson in the morning, arrived after the battle.) McClernand made contact with the Rebel left flank about 9:30 AM; however, he waited over four hours to make what should have been the initial attack. This gave Pemberton time to shift troops to meet McPherson's assault on his right flank at about eleven. Had McClernand attacked promptly in the morning, the Federals could probably have overwhelmed Pemberton's army and marched unopposed into Vicksburg. The fighting surged back and forth indecisively for hours, Champion's Hill changing hands repeatedly. At one point Logan's division of McPherson's corps moved on the rear of the Confederate right, cutting off Pemberton's only road of retreat; Grant, not knowing this, uncovered the road again by moving these troops to reinforce his center. Pemberton soon made use of the road, pulling his forces back just after three in the afternoon. The Confederates withdrew, bedraggled but in fair order, to the Big Black River, closely pursued by Grant's men. The casualties in the day's fighting at Champion's Hill were 2441 for the Union, 3851 for the South. Grant points out in his memoirs that Pemberton should then have evacuated Vicks-

Below: *US Signal Corps headquarters at Vicksburg. The static front made the use of telegraphy practical.*

burg and marched north to join Johnston; this in fact was what Johnston, knowing Vicksburg was now doomed in any case, wanted Pemberton to do. Instead, Pemberton pulled back toward the city, leaving a rear guard before the Big Black River. On 17 May Grant's forces attacked this position, Sherman's corps overwhelming the enemy center. Many Confederates were forced into the river to swim across or drown. The remaining Southerners soon noticed that a Federal force was heading for the only bridge. Something of a footrace ensued, the Confederates reaching the bridge first, while their artillery remained behind, slowing the Northerners until they were captured. As the Confederates withdrew they burned the bridge and Federal pursuit came to a halt while engineers constructed a new one.

The action at Big Black River produced one of those fortuitous moments that can affect profoundly the course of wars and of nations. As Grant was observing the battle, a messenger appeared with an order from General-in-Chief Halleck. Dated several days previous, the order directed Grant to retire without delay to Grand Gulf and then to move in support of Banks at Port Hudson. Grant and the messenger began to debate whether or not the order was still relevant: at that moment Grant heard a cheer denoting a successful charge. Exclaiming "See that charge! I think it is too late to abandon this campaign," he leaped on to his horse and rode toward the action. The messenger was never seen again. Had he had time to convince Grant to obey the order, Vicksburg might never have fallen.

That night the beaten Rebels marched back into town. One of the soldiers remembered: "By nightfall the fugitive and disheveled troops were pouring into the streets of Vicksburg, and the citizens beheld with dismay the army that had gone out to fight for their safety returning to them in the character of a wild, tumultuous and mutinous mob." On 18 May Johnston notified Richmond that defense of the city was hopeless. Grant, meanwhile, sent a detachment to keep Johnston at bay. Thus Pemberton was bottled up, and Johnston had been rendered helpless.

While his army moved across the new bridge on 18 May, Grant and Sherman stood surveying the defenses of Vicksburg, the goal of so many months of complex and frustrating campaigning. Sherman observed that up to this moment he

Left: *On 25 June Federal mines were exploded under the Rebel defenses. Union soldiers who rushed through the crater were slaughtered by defenders firing down on them.*

Below: *A view of Confederate defenses behind Vicksburg.*

Overleaf: *A depiction of General Pemberton's surrender to Grant at Vicksburg.*

IMPORTANT FROM AMERICA!!

Awful Slaughter at Vicksburg,

And Elsewhere,

The Bloody Conflict between the North & South

CONTINUED!

We regret to say that this unnatural war seems still to rush upon the unhappy Yanky with fearful impetuosity, so as to stun the entire population and saturate the States of America with blood, by sacrificing the lives of hundreds of thousands of honest men, at the whim or caprice of a few noxious individuals. Federal accounts state that the siege still continues, —and, that the incredible number of 3,600 bombs were thrown into the city of Vicksburg in an hour! The streets are ploughed up with shot and shell, and that the inhabitants dwell in caves which they have excavated in the sides of the Bluff!

In the force under Banks and Sheridan there was a battalion of Negroes, who are said to have fought well. They suffered terribly, for out of a regiment of 900, 600 were killed or wounded in an hour!

The Prize Court at Key West has laid down the law of confiscation so as to insure the condemnation of every British Ship a Federal vessel may seize,—'Any vessel bound to Nassau, with the intention of sailing from thence to a blockaded port, is liable to condemnation." As the prize court constitutes inself sole judge of the intention, and as Matamoras has been, de facto blockaded, all British vessels bound for that port will, of course, be at once condemned. The Key west correspondent of the New-York Herald has good reason to say that " nowhere else is prise law rigidly enforced, vessels being condemned at the rate of two each week."

Although 49,688 emigrants had arrived in New York from Ireland since the first of January, 1863, and though the negroes are said to be the " best hope of restoring the Union." the enrollment is being enforced.

Queenstown, Saturday.—The following is the latest " correspondence " from Vicksburg. One regiment only, the 22nd Iowa Volunteers, commanded by Colonel William M. Stone, by a'most superhuman efforts, and after immense loss, planted its colours on the rebel rampart. There it remained all day long, the colonel hourly demanding aid, until at nightfall, after having been exposed all day to a destructive fire, the lieutenant-colonel and 15 men only remained and they were taken in great triumph to Vicksburg. Every man who entered the fort in the morning was kill. d or wounded except those sixteen. Colonel Stone was struck in the arm whilst on the bastion, loudly calling for reinforcements. It was a stupid blunder, or worse, to storm the works at all. It needs not a military eye to discover that it is impossible to lead men over an abrupt embankment twenty feet high, with ditches from ten to twelve feet deep. It was doubtless, necessary that the experiment should be tried. It has proven a costly one. Twenty-five hundred killed and wounded is a fearful loss.

The northerns are evidently constructing a new line of works between the onter line opposed to us and the city. While the charge was being made on the 22nd some of our sharp-shooters, po-ted in the trees overlooking the fortifications, could plainly see contrabands and white men digging for dear life.

OUR LOSSES

I regret to learn that Colonel Abbet, of the 30th Iowa, was killed on the 22nd instant. He was a brave officer, and his loss is universally regretted. In the battle of Champion's Hill, on the 16th instant, the tenth Iowa lost, killed, wounded, and missing, one hundred and sixty-one men. Among the killed were three commissioned officers and 7 wounded. In the centre charge on the fortifications the twenty-second Iowa, lost two hundred and fifty men ; General Stevenson's Brigade, two hundred and sixty; General Ransom's Brigade, three hundred and fifty-eight ; General Carr's division, five hundred ; General Blair's division, five hundred and fifty ; General Steele's division, heavily, estimated six hundred ; General Osterhaus' division two hundred, estimated ; and General Smith's three hundred and fifty, estimated. This is rather under than over the estimate.

CANNONADING.

To-day there has been vigorous cannonading at intervals from batteries on the right and left of the railroad. A misdirected shot fell in our own ranks killing three soldiers of the thirty-second Ohio, and seriously wounding as many more.

Over one hundred women and children have been killed by our bombardment.

New-York, June 14—General Banks filiocially reports that the conduct of the Negro troops has been most praiseworthy, and there is no longer any doubt that the Government will find in the Negroes effective supporters

General Banks' loss from the 28rd to the 30th, ult., was 1,000 men, including many of his ablest officers.

General Sherman has died of his wounds.

General Neal Dow is also dangerously wounded.

ANOTHER BATTLE.

Three brigades of Federal Cavalry, and 2,000 infantry crossed the Rappahannock on Tuesday at Beverley Ford, and had a severe engagement with General Stuart's cavalry, lasting all day, when the Confederates received heavy infantry reinforcements, and the Federals recrossed the river bringing away their dead and wounded. Sharp firing was kept up from the confederate rifle pits during the crossing, and 40 of the Federals were killed or wounded. A portion of Federal land and naval forces at Yorktown, made an incursion into King William Country, Virginia, via the Mattapony River. On the 4th inst. a Foundry at Ayltes, with all its machinery, several mi ls, and large quantities of grain, were destroyed, and many horses, mules, and cattle were captured. The expedition returned to Yorktown the following day.

The agricultural resources of the Yazoo country are described as being most abundant

John F. Nugent and Co., Steam-Machine Printers, 35, New-Row West, Dublin. N.B.—No connection with any other person of the name.

Left: *European interest in the Civil War was intense. An Irish newspaper reports on the siege at Vicksburg.*

Above: *Drawing by a field artist of Grant receiving Pemberton's 3 July request for surrender negotiations.*

had been unsure of their ultimate success, and added generously that it was the end of one of the greatest campaigns in military history. Sherman was right enough, except for the fact that Vicksburg itself was not yet conquered. To be sure, it would take a miracle to save it – but the South had been known to produce miracles. The fortifications around Vicksburg had been seven months in the making. They included a line nine miles long, with nine forts as strong points. The works took advantage of the broken ground around the city, which made it an excellent place to defend and a dangerous one to attack. Restless at the idea of a protracted siege, Grant attempted an assault on 19 May, resulting only in a few yards' gain toward the city. Another assault was mounted on the afternoon of the 22nd: it proved a costly failure. The 13,000 Confederate defenders turned back 35,000 Federals and inflicted 3200 casualties; Southern casualties were around 500. (Grant was later to write that he regretted this assault, as well as a later and more disastrous one at Cold Harbor in 1864). Within Vicksburg, the spirits of Pemberton's men revived in the aftermath of their success.

Grant then settled into a siege, gradually extending his lines over fifteen miles in a bear-hug around Vicksburg. Federal supplies and reinforcements arrived steadily until the Northerners numbered some 71,000. Washington co-operated fully: as Halleck wrote to Lincoln, "To open the Mississippi River would be better than the capture of forty Richmonds."

The opposing lines were at times only a few yards apart; soldiers of the two sides regularly exchanged news and gibes. Sharpshooters picked off anyone careless enough to poke his head above the ramparts. On 25 June and 1 July Federal mines under the defenses were blown up, but the planned attacks did not develop.

Within the city the civilians dug into the hills to escape incessant shelling from Union batteries and gunboats. Citizens

and soldiers starved together: by late June most of the army's mules had been consumed. One soldier recalled that he and his companions came positively to enjoy a hearty helping of fried rat for breakfast.

A major Federal assault on the starving garrison was planned for 6 July, but on the 3rd, as Southern fortunes in the East were foundering in distant Gettysburg, white flags appeared on the ramparts of Vicksburg. Union troops danced, cheered and set off cannon. Soon Pemberton, an old army acquaintance of Grant, appeared, and Grant asked of him the same unconditional surrender he had demanded at Fort Donelson. When Pemberton curtly declined these terms, Grant hastened to negotiate. While the generals of the opposing staffs discussed terms, Grant and Pemberton sat on a hillside frostily passing the time of day. After some discussion Pemberton agreed to surrender the garrison on 4 July, Independence Day, and Grant agreed to parole the Confederates rather than imprison them. (To this point in the war, prisoners of both sides were often paroled until exchanged.)

At three o'clock in the afternoon of 4 July 1863, 30,000 ragged and hungry Confederates filed out of Vicksburg to stack their arms. Union troops watched in silence: as he would in future victories, Grant forbade any demonstration of triumph by his troops (though one unit was heard to cheer the valor of the Confederates). Federals were seen reaching into their supplies to give food to the Rebels. In the northeast at Gettysburg, the South had just lost a great battle. But here in Vicksburg the Confederacy had, in effect, already lost the war. Port Hudson, the last Confederate stronghold on the river, fell to Banks on 8 July. The South was cut in two, for the Mississippi lay open to the North. In Washington a jubilant Lincoln wrote "The Father of Waters runs unvexed to the sea."

Grant had carried off one of the greatest campaigns in history, showing a gift for wide-ranging strategic planning that took advantage of the North's superiority in materiel and manpower and that was based more on maneuver than on fighting. Grant was soon to pit his strategic brilliance against the tactical genius on the battlefield of Robert E Lee: then the war would become a duel of strategy versus tactics.

GETTYSBURG

In June of 1863 the two great armies of the East were on the march, moving inexorably toward the convulsion that everyone knew had to come some time, and which both sides fervently prayed would settle everything once and for all.

The Confederate Army of Northern Virginia had whipped the Yankees three times in the past 12 months – at the Second Bull Run, Fredericksburg and Chancellorsville, with Antietam more or less a draw – and they were led by a man they considered the greatest general in the world. If ever an army felt invincible, the Army of Northern Virginia did that summer. And now they were headed toward Washington.

But things were not so good as they seemed for the South. Lee's decision to invade the North for the second time was made partly in desperation. The situation in the Confederacy was critical: the Mississippi was all but lost; badly needed European recognition had not come; the Union blockade was tightening; anti-war sentiment in the North was fading; Southern finances were collapsing. The only hope for the Confederacy now, Lee reasoned, was a decisive victory that would win the war in one stroke. On the desk of Jefferson Davis was a letter to be given to Lincoln after that victory: a letter from the victor to the vanquished, proposing terms for peace.

But Lee's convictions were not shared by his second in command, James Longstreet, whom Lee affectionately called "my old war horse." Longstreet objected to the invasion from

Right: *General Robert E Lee in the uniform he preferred – that of a colonel of cavalry. For three days at Gettysburg he ordered repeated attacks on the Union lines.*

Opposite: *General Joseph ("Fighting Joe") Hooker, depicted leading a Union charge at Antietam, was relieved as commander of the Army of the Potomac only a few days before the onset of fighting at Gettysburg.*

the beginning, proposing instead a plan to hold Hooker and his Union Army of the Potomac with two divisions while sending the rest to Tennessee, where they would join Bragg and Johnston in fighting Rosecrans. This move would probably force Grant away from his siege of Vicksburg, paralyze the North and threaten Kentucky and Ohio.

It was a good plan and might very well have worked, but Lee rejected it. His sights, as always, were fixed above all on his beloved Virginia: he wanted to end the Union threat to his exhausted state and find food for his army in the farms of Pennsylvania. The most Longstreet could get from Lee was agreement that the campaign should be offensive in strategy but defensive in tactics. And in the end Lee would not abide by that notion either.

Lee's first move was to reorganize his army into three corps with integral artillery: those led by Longstreet, A P Hill and the brilliant and eccentric Richard S Ewell. Added to this was an oversize cavalry division under Jeb Stuart – in all, some 89,000 men.

The Confederate Army pulled out of its old field of triumph, Fredericksburg, Virginia, on 3 June, leaving Hill behind to fool Hooker and the Army of the Potomac. But Joe Hooker was not be fooled this time. Union reconnaissance parties skirmished with the Rebels at Franklin's Crossing (5 June) and Brandy

Above: *An engraving shows Rebel cavalry crossing the Potomac into Maryland on 11 June 1863.*

Left: *Inhabitants and Union guards flee Wrightsville, Pennsylvania, as it is occupied by General Ewell's forces on 28 June.*

Station (8 June) and established that Lee was on the march. Concentrating around Culpeper, Virginia, Lee sent Ewell to clear away R H Milroy's Federals in the Shenandoah Valley, which was accomplished easily enough. It was hoped this operation would keep Hooker away from Richmond and put him in a defensive posture. It did just that. The state militias of Maryland and Pennsylvania hastened to organize against Lee, but their resistance was pathetically inadequate. So far, things were not going badly for the campaign.

By mid-June Hill had left Fredericksburg, and the whole Army of Northern Virginia was on the move through Maryland to the northwest, circling Washington. Paralleling them to the east like a shadow were Hooker and the Army of the Potomac, 122,000 strong, staying between the Rebel Army and Washington. Hooker had entreated his superiors to let

him march on Richmond, but General-in-Chief Henry Halleck insisted on maintaining a defensive posture. Meanwhile, Halleck was trying to find some way to get around Hooker's political supporters and give the army to someone else – Hooker's humiliation at Chancellorsville was not to be overlooked.

As the South's and North's main forces marched northwest, the two cavalries, both on reconnaissance, fought a running series of skirmishes. Now the Federal horsemen (under General Alfred Pleasonton) had enough confidence and experience to challenge Jeb Stuart. Though largely indecisive, these skirmishes served to keep the Rebel cavalry at a distance from the Federal infantry: as a result, Stuart was not at all sure where the bulk of the enemy was.

This problem was soon compounded when Stuart proposed to Lee that his men repeat an old ploy of theirs – riding completely around the Federal Army. Lee agreed to the plan. Stuart set out on what seemed like a good bit of fun, but soon found he was getting more than he had bargained for. The Federals were spread out far more widely than expected; to avoid them Stuart had to detour farther and farther east. He was ultimately to be out of touch with Lee for ten days and did not rejoin the army until the second night of the battle. The effect on Lee's campaign was devastating – the Confederate Army was in effect marching blindfolded into extremely dangerous enemy territory.

Thus Lee moved into Pennsylvania, his forces widely separated, not knowing that Hooker had crossed the Potomac (15-16 June), and that the Federal Army was squarely on the Confederate flank and the shortest road to Richmond. Finally, on 28 June, a spy revealed to Lee that the Federals were concentrating around Frederick, Maryland. Moreover, the Army of the Potomac had a new commander. In late June, Hooker had ordered the XII Corps to join the Federal garrison at Harpers Ferry and operate on the rear of Lee's army. Halleck countermanded the order and, as was hoped, this blow to his authority was too much for Hooker. He resigned on 28 June and was replaced by General George G Meade, who, despite his protests, was chosen over his superior John Reynolds and ordered to command virtually on the eve of battle.

It was the fifth change of command in ten months for the Army of the Potomac, and a good sign of how desperate the authorities in Washington were. By now the soldiers scarcely cared any more: they had long since lost enthusiasm for the whole race of generals, and most of them knew little of Meade. He was a drawn and gloomy man, still suffering from the effects of a wound at White Oak Swamp, and his foul temper was legendary among his subordinates. The terrible burden of responsibility that dropped on him so unexpectedly served only to make Meade still more gloomy and irascible.

Above: *General George G Meade replaced Hooker on 28 June 1863.*

Below: *Alarmed by Lee's advance, Baltimore prepared its defenses.*

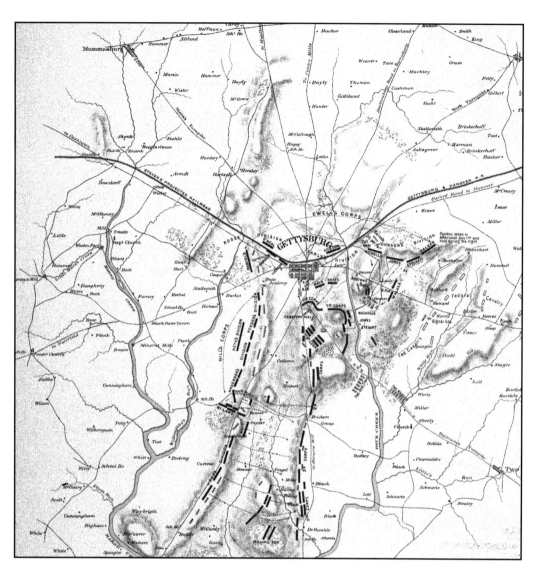

But if not truly brilliant, Meade was still a tough and competent general. Hearing the news, Lee prophesied accurately "General Meade will make no blunder on my front." Meade's army consisted by now of seasoned, hardened soldiers. Cynical as they had become about commanders, they were ready to do as they were told. They had seen victory elude their grasp time and time again and knew it was not their fault; they were ready to win if only they could find a leader who would let them.

Realizing the enemy was on his flank, Lee decided to concentrate at the nearest place handy, which happened to be Gettysburg, Pennsylvania, a little town with a great many road crossings. Lee was by no means planning a battle there: he could not in any case, for with Stuart gone he was still unsure just where the Army of the Potomac was. He was concentrating simply in order to discourage operations on the rear of his army. If it came to battle, his intended position was to be nearby Cashtown, which would be ideal for defense.

Meade, however, had made the same decision – to concentrate at Gettysburg – and for the same reason: convenience. Like Lee, he was not entirely certain where his enemy was. His real goal was to settle into a defensive position at Pipe Creek, 15 miles southeast of Gettysburg. Thus the most terrible battle ever fought on American soil was about to break out by accident. The course of the battle would also be significantly determined by happenstance – the Confederate Army was by then fairly tightly concentrated, the Union Army spread out. Jeb Stuart was still skylarking, Lee was still blindfolded and A P Hill's men had heard they might find some shoes in town.

On 1 July John Buford's Federal cavalry division was scouting in Gettysburg. Buford, a tough old cavalry soldier, had felt a premonition they would run into trouble. Watching from a ridge just west of town that morning, Buford saw the trouble coming: a column of enemy troops, preceded by skirmishers, slogging toward town. They were Harry Heth's division of Hill's corps, and they were looking for shoes not Yankees.

The 2500 Federal cavalry dismounted, formed a thin line of battle from McPherson's Ridge north to Seminary Ridge and began firing away with their new Spencer repeating carbines. The Rebels spread out and returned fire. By ten in the morning the fighting was hot, and Confederates seemed to be pouring in from everywhere. General William D Pender had arrived to support Heth, and the Federal cavalrymen were now badly outnumbered, but still they held on. Buford had sent a plea for help to John Reynolds and the I Corps. About ten o'clock in the morning Reynolds arrived just in front of his corps, expertly surveyed the situation and rushed to position his arriving infantry. They included John Gibbon's old bunch, the black-hatted Iron Brigade, a legendary outfit since their first battle at the Second Bull Run. (They were now under Solomon J Merideth.) As they fell into line the men of the Iron Brigade could hear the Rebels observing "Here are those damned black-hat fellers agin. . . .'Tain't no militia - that's the Army of the Potomac!"

Hill's Confederates were now falling into line in waves. The I Corps took over from the exhausted cavalrymen and began to stabilize the Union position a little. The Federals were slowly pushed back from McPherson's Ridge to Seminary Ridge, but they were not in retreat. Hundreds of Southerners were captured after vicious fighting in a railroad cut to the South. General Reynolds rode behind his lines, strengthening the position. He was considered by many the best soldier in the Union Army, the man who should have been commander of the Army of the Potomac all along. But a sharpshooter's bullet knocked Reynolds dead from his saddle early in the action. Without a commander now, his men held the line.

At noon there was an ominous lull. Heth formed his Confederates south of the Cashtown road. Federal Generals Abner Doubleday and James Wadsworth dressed their lines along and in front of Seminary Ridge as the rest of the I Corps arrived and fell into line. About 1:00 PM Oliver O Howard's XI Corps, called forward urgently, began arriving; the divisions of Carl Shurz and Francis Barlow took position to the north, on the Federal right. Howard decided to leave an artillery reserve on Cemetery Hill, just south of town. His placement of the battery on Cemetery Hill turned out to be one of those small decisions that win battles.

Lee by early afternoon had decided to throw everything he had at the Federals. Ewell, leading Jackson's old corps, descended from the north on to the Federal right. The luckless XI Corps were flanked and finally caved in, with Barlow critically wounded. Frantic calls went back to the nearest Union corps,

Daniel E Sickles's (III) and Henry W Slocum's (XII). The XI Corps fled through Gettysburg and there, in the streets, ran into large masses of Rebels.

The collapse of the XI Corps in the north made the position of Doubleday, now commanding the I Corps to the south, untenable. Finally, I Corps was pulled back.

On the left of the Union line the Iron Brigade had been ordered to hold out to the last extremity. This they did as Rebels swarmed on to them from three sides. Time and again they requested General Wadsworth to let them retreat; time and again Wadsworth refused. One stand of colors had five color-bearers shot from under the same flag, the last being the commanding general. Finally, the devastated Iron Brigade pulled back to barricades at the Seminary and made another stand before Hill pushed them back again.

The Confederates pressed on relentlessly, scattering the I Corps before them. It was an all-too-familiar story for the Army of the Potomac: Lee had massed his troops to gain local superiority and was crushing his enemy piece by piece. But there remained Howard's Union artillery reserve to the south on Cemetery Hill. As evening descended, General Winfield Scott Hancock arrived at that position. He had been sent by Meade to take charge and to survey the situation.

Right: *General John J Reynolds, considered one of the Union's best commanders, was killed in the first day's fighting.*

At first sight it was very bad. From the hill Hancock saw the Federals in confused rout. The I Corps had only 2400 men left of its original 10,000. The Iron Brigade was virtually ruined; its 24th Michigan Regiment had lost 399 of 496 men. The XI Corps had 4000 captured in the wild melee as they fled through Gettysburg. There were at most only 5000 men left available out of two corps.

Shouting and cursing, Hancock slowly rallied the stragglers around Howard's battery on Cemetery Hill. As dark came on he had a serviceable position; somehow the I and XI Corps were in line of battle again. Hancock saw that this hill was not a bad place to be, in fact might be a very good position indeed. Noticing that Culp's Hill, just to the west, might be vulnerable, Hancock sent some of the I Corps survivors over to occupy it. Another serviceable position, maybe.

Across the way, Ewell was taking a good look at Cemetery Hill. Lee had asked him to assault it "if possible." That courteous proviso would have inspired Stonewall Jackson to move mountains. But Ewell was no Jackson, and he was plagued with an odd paralysis of will in these days. He decided not to try to take Cemetery Hill. Had he tried, American history might have been different. That position, so vulnerable that night, was to become the foundation of the Union line.

Nonetheless, the South had clearly won the day on the first

of July. It had pushed the enemy back and inflicted a terrible toll on the Union Army. A confident Lee made plans for an all-out attack as early as possible next morning; his men would walk right over the enemy, just as they had so many times before. Yet things were, again, less good than they seemed for the South. Lee had been drawn into battle at a time and on ground not of his own choosing. With Stuart still away, Lee did not know exactly where Meade's forces were. Jackson was gone, and Longstreet recalcitrant. The enemy was in its own territory, fighting for its own soil. And though the Union Army had been forced back, it had been driven on to positons that were stronger than anyone, North or South, seemed to realize that night – except perhaps for Hancock, who surveyed the area with increasing satisfaction.

This time there were to be no uncommitted corps in the Union Army, as there had been at Antietam and Chancellorsville. Meade was cautious, too much so in the long run, but this time he was going to give it everything he had. All night and next morning he moved troops into position on high ground, the lines spreading out from Cemetery Hill. He was most worried about his right flank to the north, which Ewell had smashed before. To protect this flank the Unions lines bent around the hills to the north, Slocum's XII Corps from Culp's Hill south, Howard and the XI Corps bending from the side of Culp's Hill to Cemetery Hill. Below that, the I Corps

Opening engagement

Retiring with prolonge.

Shelled out.

Position on the 3rd and 4th July.

Leaving the field, July 5th.

Above: *Drawings of experiences of the 9th Massachusetts battery at Gettysburg.*

Right: *General George Meade's headquarters on Cemetery Ridge. The photograph is by Alexander Gardner, one of Mathew Brady's associates.*

Opposite: *A Union encampment at Gettysburg.*

(now under General John Newton since Reynolds's death) and Hancock's II Corps stretched south along Cemetery Ridge; Daniel E Sickles's III Corps was on the left flank, from the end of Cemetery Ridge to the Round Tops. George G Sykes's V Corps was to the rear in reserve; John Sedgwick's Corps was still moving up. Meade established his headquarters in a shabby farmhouse on the Taneytown Road, behind the center of his line.

Good as his ground was, however, Meade's concern for the right flank – he feared the enemy could get around it to his rear – led him to build up the right and stint the left flank, especially the Round Tops, which thus became his weak points. It was just that left flank that Lee was planning to strike on the second day of battle. Once again, Longstreet had demurred – it seemed to him impossible to assault the enemy on those heights. Instead he proposed a strategic envelopment on the right, moving around behind the Federals and coming between them and Washington; then the Union Army would have to come down from those hills and fight it out where the Confederates wanted them.

Lee would have none of this: he would strike the Union left, around the Round Tops. If he could overrun these positions he would roll up the Federal line like a rug. The Confederate Army was then stretched around the fishhook shape of Meade's lines: Ewell on the left with the divisions of Johnson, Early and Rodes; Hill in the center with Pender and Anderson's divisions (Heth's in reserve); Longstreet on the left, leading the attack with Hood and McLaws. The attack was to sweep obliquely from left to right; Ewell was instructed to begin a strong diversion on the right when he heard Longstreet's guns.

A workable enough plan, but on 2 July it was bungled by everybody – though there was enough of a blunder on the Union side to give Lee's plan a good chance of working. To begin with, Ewell balked at attacking entrenched Union positions on Culp's and Cemetery hills; he made only a few ineffectual efforts during the day, far less than the major diversion intended. In any case, Ewell never got his signal from the right during the morning. Longstreet, supposed to attack on the Confederate right at dawn, delayed through the morning and into the afternoon, saying he was waiting for Pickett's fresh division, which had not yet arrived. Jackson was sorely missed indeed.

Longstreet's delay nearly gave the Federals enough rope to hang themselves. The blunder was accomplished by Union General Daniel E Sickles, who felt the ground occupied by his III Corps on the left flank, along the southern part of Cemetery Ridge, was not high enough; besides, there were Rebels out there moving toward his left. Itching for a fight, Sickles moved the III Corps forward without orders to slightly higher ground on a line from the Peach Orchard through the Wheat Field to Devil's Den. Watching from the heights, Generals Hancock and Gibbon saw Sickles's salient forming and accurately prophesied the outcome. About four o'clock in the afternoon a furious Meade rode over and ordered Sickles to pull the line back. As they argued, an earsplitting cannonade erupted square on Sickles's left flank – 46 of Longstreet's guns. Meade curtly observed that it was too late to pull back now: the III Corps would have to fight it out as best they could.

While part of the II Corps was ordered by Meade into Sickles's original position on Cemetery Ridge, Confederate infantry under John B Hood and Lafayette McLaws struck Sickles's salient at about five o'clock. The rest of the Union Army looked on helplessly as Hood's men, despite the wounding of Hood himself, routed the Union position in Devil's Den and swarmed around the left flank and up Round Top. By six, Sickles had been carried from the field minus a leg and General David B Birney had taken command, his left already giving way.

As Meade desperately shifted troops from his center and

Left: *Lee's headquarters (Mrs. Thompson's house) on the Chambersburg Pike.*

Below: *Southerners attempt to break the Union defensive line at Cemetery Hill.*

Above: *Fighting at the Peach Orchard, where Union General Daniel E Sickles advanced his III Corps without orders, thereby creating a salient in the Union line. Sickles lost a leg in the ensuing battle.*

right toward the beleaguered left, the Rebels began moving north down Round Top toward Little Round Top. It was a disastrous prospect for the Army of the Potomac: if Little Round Top were to be taken, the Union left would crumble and Cemetery Ridge would no longer be defensible.

Now the fate of a great battle and of a nation concentrated on a small hill and on the actions of a very few men. One of these men, for a few critical moments the bearer of his nation's destiny, was General Gouverneur K Warren, Meade's chief engineer, who arrived at Little Round Top about this time. To his dismay, Warren saw that this place was the linchpin of the Union position and that there were no troops on it at all, only a signal station. He sent an imperative note to Meade and awaited results while watching Hood's forces – 500 men of the 15th Alabama – climbing toward him.

As bullets began to fly around Warren, a few Federal cannon arrived and began sending canister into the enemy. Then at a run came 350 men of the 20th Maine commanded by young Colonel Joshua Chamberlain, who just one year before had left his position as Professor of Rhetoric at Bowdoin College to realize his dream of becoming a soldier. Now it was up to Chamberlain and the men of Maine to save or lose the Army of the Potomac.

Chamberlain's brigade commander, Colonel Strong Vincent, took him to the southern end of the hill, pointed to the advancing enemy and told Chamberlain to hold the ground at all costs. The 20th Maine spread out in a pitifully thin line, the sparse growth providing little cover. The charging Confederates crashed into the line and began pushing it back. The men of Maine fell in dozens, pulled back, but would not run: the exasperated Confederates could not dislodge

them, even when their guns were in Federal faces. Then Chamberlain saw that his brigade's ammunition was nearly gone. What in God's name was left to do? Dazed and desperate, he ordered the only thing he could think of: "Fix bayonets! Charge bayonets, charge!"

Their bayonets fixed, the men hesitated before this suicidal prospect. Suddenly Lieutenant H S Melcher ran out between the lines, into a hail of bullets, and shouted "Come on! Come on, boys!" Here was another single man on whom the fulcrum of battle swung: the 20th Maine rose from their positions and with a scream of anguish ran right into the Rebels.

The enemy had never seen anything like it (bayonet fighting was in fact rare in the war). In sheer shock, the Confederate line hesitated, then crumbled and ran back downhill. Their confusion was such that one Confederate officer was seen offering his sword in surrender with one hand while firing his pistol with the other. Heading for cover behind a stone wall below, the fleeing Southerners ran head-on into the rifles of the 20th Maine's skirmishers, who had been presumed killed.

For the moment the heroic men of the 20th Maine had saved the Federal left, but General Warren, still on the summit of Little Round Top, saw that the right of Strong Vincent's brigade was caving in. Trying to rally the men, Vincent himself was killed. Warren rode for help and grabbed the first troops he could find, the 140th New York, of Sykes's V Corps, which was now moving up from the rear. Coming up over Little Round Top at a dead run with unloaded guns and no bayonets, the New Yorkers simply charged straight at the enemy, their bodies their only weapons. Somehow this bizarre counterattack worked – the surprised Confederates pulled back. Little Round Top was safe, and Federal soldiers began piling in to reinforce it.

But no one could save the rest of the devastated III Corps. Surrounded by McLaws's men on three sides, Sickles's salient caved in, and McLaws made for the gap that opened

Right: *An attack by Longstreet on the Federal left center.*

Below: *View of Little Round Top, the anchor of the Union left on 2 July*

Above: *At a site called Trostle's Farm, artist C W Reed sketched a Union captain and his men hauling an artillery piece into position by hand.*

up between the fleeing III Corps and Hancock's II Corps. From all over his line, Hancock, ordered by Meade to stop the rout, feverishly rushed troops to plug this gap. Again the battle came down to a few men, this time Union artillerymen around Trostle's Farm. There, just after seven o'clock, Artillery Captain John Bigelow held back William Barksdale's Mississippians long enough for a stronger battery to be mounted to the rear. Fighting surged into the artillery positions, the cannoneers beating back the Rebels with rammers, handspikes and fists; men rolled on the ground slugging away like barroom rowdies. At last Barksdale was killed, and his Mississippians could not get through the gap.

It had been a day of almosts for the Confederacy, but Lee was by no means finished. Southern efforts were shifting steadily northward; the next blow came in the Federal Center on Cemetery Ridge. Hancock, commanding that part of the field, saw a flag moving toward him, apparently from his own lines. He asked angrily why his men were retreating: a volley showed him that it was a Rebel column, some 50 yards away. Hancock rode back and found Colonel Colville of the 1st Minnesota. "Do you see those colours?" Hancock demanded. Colville did. "Well, capture them!" he shouted. Still in marching column, the 1st Minnesota charged the Confederates, who fell back and then rallied, getting the Federals into a pocket. The Minnesotans' line held on somehow, and when the Confederates finally fell back, the 1st Minnesota had 47 men left of the 262 who had charged so gallantly - 82 percent casualties, the worst of the war.

As the fighting began to die down on the center and left, the Confederates settled into position at the base of the Round Tops, in Devil's Den and along the base of Cemetery Ridge. About six in the evening there had been a threat to the Federal right. After an artillery barrage Ewell finally made a move on Culp's Hill, held by Howard's XI Corps. Federal strength there was depleted due to troops being sent south. Edward Johnson's brigade, on the Confederate right, advanced up the hill toward strong but sparsely manned Union breastworks. Again Federal reinforcements arrived in time to stop the attack, and after eight o'clock Johnson's men settled into position on the slopes.

An hour later, in the last fighting of 2 July, Jubal Early's Confederates made it into XI Corps batteries on Cemetery Hill. For the second time that day, Union cannoneers and Rebel infantry fought hand-to-hand, the Union's so-called Dutchmen cursing vigorously in German. After an hour of bitter fighting, Early called it quits when Federal reinforcements arrived for a countercharge. Except for a few confused attempts on Culp's Hill by Ewell's men during the night, the second day's fighting was finally done.

In the middle of the night General Meade took the unusual step of assembling his staff for a council of war. They met in the small shabby farmhouse that was his headquarters. The youngest man attending was General Howard, age 35; Meade, at 45, was the oldest. The Army of the Potomac had lost some 20,000 men in two days of fighting. Now Meade wanted a consensus on what to do next: should they retreat, attack or wait for Lee to attack? The decision was quick and nearly unanimous: they would wait for the Confederate attack. As the generals left, Meade took aside John Gibbon, former commander of the Iron Brigade, who had three brothers in the Southern Army and was to command troops in every remaining major battle of the east. "If Lee attacks tomorrow," Meade told Gibbon, "it will be in your front."

Dawn broke and the Union Army looked out from the heights and waited. Over on the right, at Culp's Hill, there was soon some action. Ewell opened up a cannonade and then sent his men up the hill. But the Federals, in good log-reinforced trenches, turned back the attack with impunity. Then an order from some Union commander went out to scout the Rebel lines a bit; for some reason this reached the 2nd Massachusetts and 27th Indiana as an order for a counterattack. Colonel Charles R Mudge, in command, shrugged "It is murder, but that's the order." He led his two regiments down into the enemy line, and they were cut to pieces, losing a colonel, four color bearers and 250 men, including Colonel Mudge. Following this pointless tragedy another Confederate charge was mounted and broke apart with heavy losses. Ewell finally realized that he had been right, that he could not take Culp's Hill. About 10:30 a silence spread once again over the battlefield.

Again the Union Army waited, resting on their arms. As the morning haze burned off, the day became clear and oppressively hot. Meade tinkered with his dispositions. His lines were still in the shape of a fishhook, Slocum behind in the east and curving to Culp's Hill, Howard from there over to Cemetery Hill, then Gibbon. Hancock (now commanding the III Corps after Sickles's injury), Sykes on the ridge to the

Below: *A painting by Edwin Forbes shows Ewell's Confederates moving toward the sparsely manned Federal position on Culp's Hill on the evening of 2 July.*

Round Tops, Sedgwick and cavalry commander Judson Kilpatrick protecting the left flank.

In the Union middle stood 6000 men of the Second and Third Divisions of the II Corps under Gibbon. The two divisions lay mostly along a stone fence so low the men had to lie or kneel behind it to gain cover. Near the middle of the fence was a little clump of trees, at which point the fence made a dogleg. Behind it were artillery and infantry positioned to fire over the heads of the men in front. It was perhaps the weakest part of the entire Union line.

As the fighting on the right died down, the waiting Federals began to see enemy activity on Seminary Ridge, across the way. Many cannon were being moved into position – a wall of cannon in clear view, their empty muzzles glinting in the late-morning sun as they pointed toward the Union Army. Finally there was a line nearly two miles long, some 150 guns. Opposing them on the Federal side were less than a hundred cannon.

The silence prevailed as noon approached: Hancock opined that the batteries were covering a Confederate retreat. Gibbon was not at all sure about that, but he was sure that he was getting hungry. He invited Meade, Hancock and some other officers to join him behind the II Corps line to reconnoiter a bit of stewed chicken. During lunch Meade shifted Hancock back to his II Corps command and Gibbon to the Second Division. About 12:30 PM Meade excused himself; the others wandered off or lay lolling in the sun.

On the front line dozing Federals sat up and looked across: a puff of smoke was drifting up from one of the Rebel guns. It was one o'clock. Then, pandemonium: all 150 Rebel guns roared at once. The Federal position erupted in a hail of fire and iron. Men died while lighting cigars, with food halfway to their mouths; wagons, trees, horses, men and the very earth itself exploded into the air.

Above: *On 3 July, the last day of fighting at the Battle of Gettysburg, Confederate prisoners are led from the field. Lee had gambled all on a frontal assault.*

Below: *General George E Pickett led his Confederate troops straight into the Union center.*

Right: *"Pickett's Charge."*

The Union guns opened in reply, commanders cautioning their gunners to conserve ammunition. For now it was certain what was happening: this was the prelude to a major assault that would fall where the cannonade was hottest – the II Corps, just as Meade had predicted. Despite the indescribable confusion of men, horses and wagons behind the Federal lines, it became clear that the Confederate gunners were making a fatal mistake – they were firing just a shade too high. As a result, the Union front line, where the coming attack would fall, was scarcely touched.

It went on for an hour and a half, the worst cannonade ever on American soil, and perhaps on any soil to that time. Then slowly it slackened, fell away, died; by three o'clock in the afternoon there was ominous silence again. The men of the II Corps rose to their feet and looked out over the open fields of grain in their front for several minutes. Then they saw something that took their breaths away, something they would never forget: 15,000 of their enemy dressed immaculately on a front half a mile wide and three ranks deep, colors flying, sunlight flashing on musket barrels and drawn swords, officers galloping up and down, the men's steps firm and determined. Silently, the Union men watched their enemy approach. For the last time in the war, perhaps for the last

time in history, it was to be a grand charge in the old Napoleonic style, and it was a terrible and magnificent thing to behold.

That morning Longstreet had struggled for the last time to convince Lee of the necessity for a defensive strategy – a strategic envelopment on the Union right. In reply Lee had pointed imperiously with his fist to Cemetery Hill, saying "The enemy is there, and I am going to strike him." Greatly agitated, Longstreet argued "General, I have been a soldier all my life. It is my opinion that no 15,000 men ever arrayed for battle can take that position." Lee, calm as always, proceeded to give his orders.

While the guns were firing Longstreet had arranged the lines. In front were two divisions, J Johnston Pettigrew on the left and the fresh troops of George E Pickett on the right. To the middle rear was the division of Isaac R Trimble (a mistake in placement, for Trimble was supposed to be in echelon to the left, supporting that flank where fire would be heaviest). Hill and Ewell had been ordered to support the charge, but they did almost nothing.

For some reason history decided to call this action 'Pickett's Charge,' although Longstreet was actually in command. But General George Pickett was certainly one of the

most enthusiastic soldiers on the field. A perfumed dandy, Pickett had been last in his class at West Point, and indeed would probably not have gotten in at all without the influence of his good friend Abraham Lincoln – whose name Pickett would not allow to be slandered in his presence.

On Cemetery Ridge the men of the II Corps watched in awe for a while. Then they got down to business – guns loaded and cocked, thumbs checking the percussion caps, cartridges lined up to hand on the ground. With a running rattle, thousands of muskets stretched out over the stone wall. Lieutenant Alonzo Cushing of Battery 4A, wounded three times in the Rebel cannonade, was being propped by a sergeant amid the wreckage of his battery; his two remaining guns awaited his orders. The Confederate lines marched across half a mile of open fields, the grain parting gently before them; they moved over the plank fences of the Emmitsburg Road, closing in toward the little clump of trees at the angle of the stone wall on Cemetery Ridge. The Federal artillery watched, poised: There, in range! "Fire!"

Now a storm of shell opens into the Rebels. Holes appear in their lines, colors fall and are retrieved. Still the men march steadily forward. They come into shrapnel range, into canister range. Southerners fall in tens, in hundreds; great gaps are torn in the lines. Across the way the Rebel batteries have few shells to fire in reply. The Confederate right flank brushes past some concealed Vermont regiments, who open up a blistering musket fire.

A hundred yards away now. Soon the left side of the Federal line is firing; the Confederates on that flank begin drifting to their left, toward the angle at the little clump of trees. The 8th Ohio, posted forward as skirmishers, enfilades the Confederate left; the flank disappears in smoke. Both Rebel flanks begin to falter, then the left gives way. But the center moves forward still. Pettigrew is down, Generals Garnett and Kemper of Pickett's corps are mortally wounded.

Alonzo Cushing has one gun left; he orders it wheeled down to the stone wall to fire point-blank with triple-shotted canister into the oncoming mass of Rebels. He fires his last charge just as a fatal bullet finds him. The Rebel spearheard is at the wall now, and some have leaped over it. They are led by General Lewis Armistead, holding his hat on his sword to show his men the way. Armistead is headed for a strange rendezvous with one of his oldest and dearest friends, Winfield Scott Hancock.

Armistead and a handful of men are over the wall; the Rebel colors are arriving one after another; the Rebels are among Cushing's wrecked battery. Armistead himself grasps one of the guns. Gibbon and Hancock are wounded, and Pennsylvanians are retreating from the overrun angle. In this small place and time, the issue is to be decided.

Things happen fast now. The Pennsylvanians rally and surge forward. Reinforcements come from somewhere. A leaderless horde of Federals swarms around the enemy spearhead, while Union cannons continue tearing apart the Rebels in front. Armistead is down, gasping out his life.

All at once, it is finished. The Confederate spearhead seems to dissolve. Some Southerners fall back; others throw down their muskets, raising their hands in surrender. The irresistible charge of a few minutes before becomes a rabble of survivors pouring back down the slope to their own lines.

Meade rides up from the rear, his face very white, and inquires of Lieutenant Franklin Haskell "How is it going here?" "I believe, General, the enemy is repulsed," Haskell replies. "Thank God," Meade says, and adds a choked cheer.

Lying on a stretcher dictating orders, Hancock is interrupted by an aide, who hands him a watch and a few personal effects. They are from Armistead, whose last words were a message to his old friend: "Tell Hancock I have done him and my country a great injustice which I shall never cease to regret." But all regrets are over for Armistead.

Strewn with thousands of dead and wounded, the battleground looked, as one soldier remarked like "a square mile of Tophet." Across the way the beaten Confedeates sank exhausted into their lines, to be visited by Lee who said, and meant it, "All this has been my fault." Even Stuart, finally arrived the previous night, had been repulsed today by Fed-

Left: *Union soldiers relax behind their breastworks on Culp's Hill on 4 July.*

Below: *View from the summit of Little Round Top at 7:30 in the evening of 3 July, as defending Pennsylvania reserves repulse part of Longstreet's corps.*

Opposite: *A Union 12-pounder gun crew, one of the units that helped to repel "Pickett's Charge."*

Overleaf: *A Currier & Ives print depicts Union General Meade (on white horse) commanding at Gettysburg on 3 July.*

Above: *The aftermath of Pickett's Charge.*

Left: *Three Confederate soldiers captured at Gettysburg.*

Below: *Dead Federal soldiers at Gettysburg. Battle casualties were the worst of the war. Lee now withdrew his army slowly back to Virginia.*

eral cavalry on the north flank. For the Army of Northern Virginia it was complte and unmitigated defeat that third of July. A prostrated Pickett wrote to his sweetheart: "My brave boys were so full of hope and confident of victory as I led them forth! Well, it's all over now."

But there was still work to be done. The Confederates next day formed their lines and waited for the counterattack that never came – the Army of the Potomac was too hurt and exhausted for that. In the afternoon of 4 July a downpour began, washing the blood from the grass. Maintaining his lines, Lee buried his dead and evacuated his wounded on a long dismal wagon train that headed back to Virginia. The casualties were the worst of the war: of 88,289 Federals engaged, 3155 were killed, 14,529 wounded - many mortally – and 5365 missing, a total of 23,049 casualties. For the South, of 75,000 engaged, 3903 were killed, 18,735 wounded, 5425 missing, a total of 28,063. Lee had lost over a third of his army.

Reaching the Potomac, the Confederates found the waters swollen and halted on the banks to wait. Meade and his army pursued cautiously, paused before the entrenched enemy but did not attack. Lee's army withdrew across the receding Potomac the night of 13-14 July. Next day there was a rearguard skirmish at Falling Waters, in which Heth lost 500 captured and Pettigrew was killed.

Robert E Lee was a man unaccumstomed to losing, but at Gettysburg he had made the mistake of Napoleon at Wagram and of Burnside at Fredericksburg – throwing a frontal attack against impregnable positions. He had overestimated his army and underestimated his enemy. Now Lee had no choice but to do what Longstreet had begged him to do at the outset – go on the defensive. But first he submitted his resignation to President Davis, assuming full responsibility for the defeat. Davis refused the resignation, knowing that if the South had any hopes at all now, they were in Lee's hands.

Lee had escaped with his army, and thus there was to be more killing, no one knew for how long. Hearing the news of Lee's escape, an anguished Lincoln asked Secretary Welles, "What does it mean? Great God! What does it mean?" A few months later, in his unforgettable words of dedication for the dead at Gettysburg, Lincoln would begin to try and find that meaning.

TOTAL WAR

After the fall of Vicksburg and Lee's calamitous defeat at Gettysburg, the focus of the war shifted to Tennessee, where Union General William S Rosecrans was slowly advancing on the crucial Southern rail center of Chattanooga. By 6 September 1863 Rosecrans had forced his opponent, General Braxton Bragg, to evacuate the city, but Bragg's army was far from finished and, indeed, was planning a deadly surprise for the pursuing Federals. Bragg had established himself in an excellent defensive position a few miles south of Chattanooga, just over the Georgia border, and was rapidly being reinforced. By 19 September, Bragg had achieved numerical superiority and went over to the offense, striking Rosecrans a crushing blow in a wooded area near Chickamauga Creek. Only a dogged delaying action fought on the Union left by General George H Thomas (for which he earned the sobriquet "The Rock of Chickamauga") saved Rosecrans's army from rout, but as it was, Rosecrans was obliged to withdraw into Chattanooga and remain there in a humiliating state of siege until his army was relieved by Grant.

It took Grant a full month of campaigning to repair the damage done at Chickamauga, but he finally did so, the climax coming on 25 November when, in the freakisn Battle of Missionary Ridge, the Confederate line was finally cracked, and Bragg was forced to retire to Dalton, Georgia. The Union was at last in position to mount its long-anticipated offensive into the Deep South.

To be sure, that offensive did not take place until the resumption of campaigning in the spring of 1864, and by then it had become simply one facet of a larger strategic enterprise. Early in 1864 Lincoln had recalled Grant to Washington, had promoted him to lieutenant general (a rank theretofore held only by George Washington) and had placed him in command of all Union armies. In the following weeks Grant had evolved a massive, potentially war-winning strategy involving simultaneous advances on five separate fronts. William Tecumseh Sherman, who now had Grant's old job of com-

manding the Western armies, would strike into Georgia. George Meade and the Army of the Potomac, under Grant's personal supervision, would at the same time drive due south towards Richmond. To these major offensives would be added three lesser ones in the Virginia Peninsula, the Shenandoah Valley and Alabama. In the event, all three of the small offensives would fail, and the entire burden would be carried by Sherman and Grant alone.

The multiple Union offensive began on 4 May 1864, and Grant's part of it was quickly embroiled in savage fighting with Lee's Army of Northern Virginia. Time and again Lee tried to break Grant's momentum – in The Wilderness, at Spotsylvania, at North Anna and at Cold Harbor – and each time, after a bloody confrontation, Grant would disengage, slide around to the right and continue his relentless advance. By 18 June he was actually south of Richmond, facing Lee's heavily fortified positions at Petersburg, the major rail junction supplying the Confederate capital. At this point Grant abandoned maneuver and settled in for a long siege. Thus far, casualties on both sides in the Eastern Theater had been appalling: 50,000 (41 percent) for the Union and 32,000 (46 percent) for the Confederacy.

At the same time U S Grant was setting out to challenge Robert E Lee in the East, the other part of the Union's grand strategy was rolling into motion in the South. Grant's closest associate in the army, William Tecumseh Sherman, had been ordered "to move against Johnston's army, to break it up, and to get into the interior of the enemy's country as far as you can, inflicting all the damage you can against their war resources."

Sherman's forces, now consisting of three entire armies, lay in Chattanooga. They were the Army of the Cumberland under "Rock of Chickamauga" George H Thomas; the Army of the Tennessee under James B McPherson; and the Army of the Ohio under John M Schofield – in all, over 100,000 men. Their immediate goal was the critical supply, manufacturing

Left: *Union troops move against massed Confederates in the Wilderness on 5 May 1864.*

and communications center of Atlanta, Georgia, some 140 miles to the southwest.

Sherman's opponent would be General Joseph E Johnston, whose Confederate Army of Tennessee lay south of Chattanooga in Dalton, Georgia. President Jefferson Davis had reluctantly given that command to Johnston after a public clamor following the defeat at Chattanooga had forced the removal of Davis's friend, the incompetent Braxton Bragg. Despite his differences with Davis, Johnston was one of the best generals the South had, and he defined his present goals clearly. He had only 62,000 men and therefore could not immediately take the offensive, especially when the Federals were led by one as able as Sherman. Thus Johnston's tactics must be defensive, resisting Sherman on every foot of ground, forcing him to overextend his supply line and reduce his forces to protect it. When they were reduced, it would be time to take the offensive. Finally, *Atlanta must not fall before*

the presidential election. In sum, Johnston realized his strategy must be Fabian – a fighting retirement over successive positions. This would weaken Sherman for the kill and make it likely that a more accommodating Union president could be elected.

There were two major problems with implementing Johnston's strategy. One was Jefferson Davis, the other a member of his own staff – General John B Hood, who hated defensive strategy of any kind. The army's other generals – William J Hardee, Leonidas Polk and cavalry leader Joseph Wheeler – would wait and see. As for the Army of Tennessee itself, it was

Below: *Sherman's March to the Sea from Atlanta split the Confederacy in two along an east-west axis.*

Bottom: *Sherman's Atlanta Campaign, beginning with his departure from Chattanooga 4 May.*

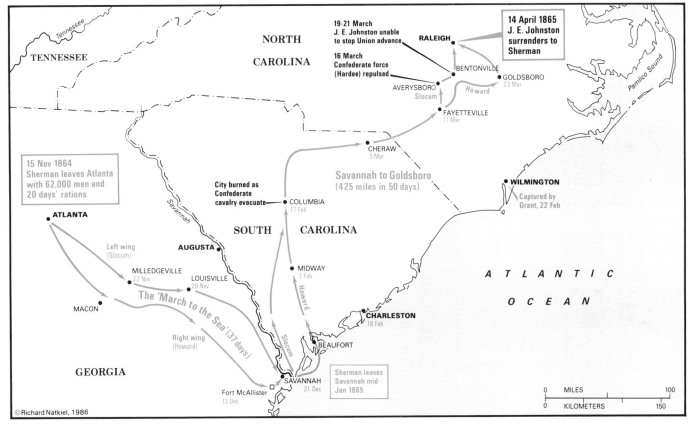

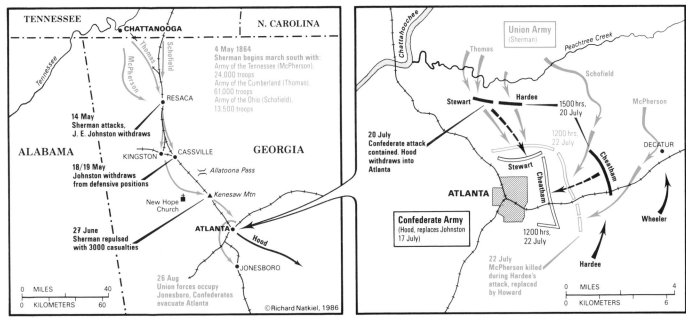

Left: *William Tecumseh Sherman surrounded by commanders of the Union armies in the West.*

Left: *William Tecumseh Sherman surrounded by commanders of the Union armies in the West.*

Opposite top: *Battlefield at Resaca, Georgia, one of nine successive defensive positions Johnston would yield as his forces fell back toward Atlanta.*

Opposite bottom: *The wreckage of a train derailed by Confederate irregulars is examined by Union engineers.*

in splendid condition, its equipment and spirit restored by Johnston after the humiliation at Chattanooga.

On 7 May 1864 Sherman's great offensive got under way, his troops probing Confederate positions around Dalton. That morning, as Union troops clashed with the enemy near Ringgold, Georgia, a Federal officer observed "The ball is opened." The ensuing campaign to Atlanta was indeed to be like a formal dance, Sherman sweeping to the side of his opposite, Johnston gracefully withdrawing.

On 9 May McPherson's Federal Army flanked Johnston and gained his rear at Snake Creek Gap, threatening Confederate communications at Resaca. On 12 May the Confederates pulled back to strong entrenchments around Resaca, where

Sherman mounted three futile attacks against the Rebel lines. At the same time he sent other forces around Johnston's left flank. This dislodged the Confederates three days later. Retiring without haste, the Confederate Army of Tennessee came to a halt farther south at Cassville.

So the dance progressed, sashaying southeast around the fulcrum of the Western and Atlantic Railroad toward Atlanta. The Rebels would break up the railroad as they withdrew, the Yankees would repair it as they advanced. From positions at Cassville, Johnston prepared to mount an attack but was dissuaded by Hood and Polk, who claimed they were flanked. The Confederates then withdrew briefly to Allatoona but found Sherman brushing by their left. Sending Wheeler's

cavalry to raid Sherman's ever-lengthening supply line, Johnston moved west to positions near Dallas, where beginning on 25 May there was a sharp fight that lasted four days. On the first and third days Sherman assaulted the Confederate entrenchments and lost heavily. On 4 June, however, Johnston realized Sherman was again flanking his left and pulled back to prepared positions at Kennesaw Mountain, near Marietta. Sherman followed and the dance continued; thus far it had accounted for some 9000 casualties on each side.

Sherman knew well that every step he took made his supply line more tenuous. In early June his cavalry moved east and again secured the railroad, which improved his prospects. (The Civil War was the first in history wherein railroads were essential in moving men and supplies.) But there were threats to Federal supply lines farther back, in Tennessee and Mississippi, centered in the person of Confederate cavalryman Nathan Bedford Forrest, an almost illiterate former slave-trader who had become one of the most brilliant and aggressive generals of the war.

Sherman declared, with his customary ferocity, "That devil Forrest . . . must be hunted down and killed if it costs ten thousand lives and bankrupts the Federal Treasury." In early June Federal cavalry under General S D Sturgis were dispatched to deal with Forrest. In his finest action, commanding less than half Sturgis's numbers, Forrest completely routed the Federals and inflicted enormous losses at Brice's Crossroads, Mississippi (10 May). Union efforts to hunt down "that devil" were to continue, and to fail, right to the war's end. Nonetheless, Sherman's supplies were never seriously disrupted.

By 14 June Sherman's men were in sight of Johnston's positions on Kennesaw Mountain. That day a Federal artillery bat-

Below: *The start of General Sherman's doomed frontal assault on Johnston's Rebels well-entrenched on Kennesaw Mountain near Marietta, Georgia.*

tery lobbed a few cannonballs at a Confederate staff conference on Pine Mountain, one of which squarely caught General Polk, killing him instantly. Sherman had only to flank Johnston again to destroy the position. But for some reason, perhaps partly in order to vary his tactics, Sherman decided on an assault. He sent his men sharply uphill into strong works fronted by abatis and swept by crossfire. The result, on 27 June, was a debacle. "All that was necessary," one Rebel defender wrote, "was to load and shoot." The Federals suffered over 2000 casualties to the South's 442. Yet Sherman scarcely paused to lick his wounds. In a few days he sent McPherson east around Johnston's right flank toward the Chattahoochie River, just northwest of Atlanta.

Failing to anticipate this move was Johnston's first mistake in the campaign. As a result, he was forced to withdraw to the banks of the Chattahoochie, knowing he could not remain there long and that the next stop was Atlanta. This was not his only problem – an increasingly frustrated Davis was pressing him to take the offensive: Johnston was caught between a still impregnable enemy on one side and an implacable commander-in-chief on the other.

On 17 July a telegram arrived from Davis relieving Johnston and giving command of the Army of Tennessee to General John B. Hood. It was in essence an order to attack, which was what Hood would certainly do. Sherman was delighted.

Sherman's three armies converged on Atlanta. Lulled by token resistance, Sherman speculated that Hood, contrary to form, might be evacuating the city. He sent McPherson's army away on a wide envelopment to the east, heading for Hood's rail line. The Federals became careless. On the afternoon of 20 July, Thomas was moving his army slowly across Peachtree Creek; there was a gap of several miles between his army and those of Schofield and McPherson. It was a serious oversight, but after all, the enemy was supposed to be retreating. In the afternoon the men were resting on the banks of the creek.

Above: *Pencil sketch by A R Waud of Sherman (astride the horse facing right) at Kennesaw Mountain.*

Right: *Wash drawing by A R Waud of the Federal artillery bombarding Kennesaw Mountain.*

Then Hood struck and struck hard, his forces swarming on to the surprised Federals. There was a fierce four-hour fight at close quarters; the Rebels moved around Thomas's right flank, into the gap in the Federal line. For the Federals there was no time to hope for reinforcements. Across the creek, "Rock of Chickamauga" Thomas found some reserve batteries and began shelling the Confederates along the opposite bank. In Thomas's phrase, that cannonade "relieved the hitch"; the Rebels fell back. Thomas's men had proved as good as their leader. Both sides had had about 20,000 engaged; Confederate losses were some 4800 to about 1800 for the Union. Hood's aggressive strategy thus had a most inauspicious beginning. But the Rebel general was by no means ready to relinquish the initiative, such as it was. Hearing that McPherson's left flank was exposed east of Atlanta and a Federal wagon train vulnerable at Decatur, Hood moved to attack again. While the main body of the Confederates fell back to fortifications around Atlanta, Wheeler was ordered to take his cavalry to Decatur and Hardee to march 15 miles to attack McPherson's flank at dawn. Thus came about the Battle of Atlanta on 22 July.

That morning Hood waited anxiously for the sounds of Hardee's attack. Finally, at about 11:00 AM, he heard skirmishers open up on the Union left – but apparently in front of McPherson's line, not on the flank as ordered. Hood was furious at this apparent blunder. When Hardee's attack began, Sherman and McPherson were conferring in the middle of the Federal position. Puzzled by the unexpected sound of firing on his front, McPherson leaped on to his horse

to investigate. Sherman paced nervously, waiting for news. Shortly an aide dashed up and reported that McPherson's horse had returned bleeding and riderless. McPherson had found Hardee's attack hitting hard, but their attempt to flank him had run afoul of Grenville Dodge's XVI Corps, which was moving into position on the left when the Rebels charged. Thus Hardee had moved as ordered on the enemy flank, but when he got there it was no longer a flank. Dodge's men were pushed back in furious fighting, but put up enough resistance to blunt the attack. McPherson had arrived just in time to see a successful countercharge by Ohio regiments. He then dressed his lines and headed to the right to see how the XVII Corps was faring.

McPherson rode right into a group of Confederate skirmishers, who signaled him to surrender. In response, he politely tipped his hat and bolted; immediately he was shot

dead from his horse. When his body was brought to Sherman, the general wept openly; at 35 McPherson had been one of the brightest and most promising generals in the army. Command of the Army of the Tennessee was given to General Oliver O Howard, a one-armed veteran of Chancellorsville and Gettysburg.

The battle on the Union left was to rage furiously into the evening, but Hardee's men made no headway after their first assault. The Yankees were as determined as their attackers, sometimes meeting and repelling simultaneous attacks on front and rear. Farther to the east, Wheeler had no better luck in his assault on Decatur.

Bitterly disappointed by the lack of success on the Federal left, Hood sent General Benjamin Cheatham's corps to attack the center of the Union line at three o'clock in the afternoon. The Confederates charged to the east along a railroad and

Left: *A Union cavalryman examines recently taken fortifications at Atlanta.*

Above: *John B Hood replaced Johnston on 17 July 1864.*

punched clear through the Union center, capturing two batteries. But in the end, they too were driven back by Union artillery.

For the second time Hood had failed. His casualties were some 8000 of nearly 37,000 engaged, to the North's 3722 of 30,000 engaged. The Confederates had fought the best they knew how, with superior numbers, and failed. It would take as good a general as Sherman to whip the Federals, but Hood knew only how to fight, not how to make plans.

After the battle Atlanta was besieged. On 28 July Sherman ordered Howard's army to cut the railroad to the south. Hood sent the corps of S D Lee against Howard at Ezra Church; six Rebel assault waves could not rout them but did succeed in keeping the railroad open to Atlanta. Sherman steadily tightened his grip around the city, meanwhile sending more futile sorties against Forrest in Mississippi. He now had command of all the rail lines into Atlanta except the Macon line to the south. In late July 10,000 cavalry under Edward McCook and George Stoneman were sent to raid Macon and cut the railroad. Sherman learned thereby that Hood was still dangerous: McCook's division was routed and dispersed, Stoneman's all but wiped out. For the moment, the Confederates' lifeline stayed open.

In mid-August Hood took the offensive again, making one of the most serious in the chain of blunders that had shattered and demoralized his army. Wheeler's cavalry was ordered to raid Sherman's supply line to the north. The raid lasted a month, but Sherman had already collected all the supplies he needed, and the absence of cavalry fatally weakened Confederate defenses in Atlanta. That fact was not lost on Sherman, who had been waiting for Hood to make the ultimate mistake. This was it.

Leaving a small force before the city, Sherman pulled the armies of Schofield and Thomas from their trenches on 26 August and made a wide sweep around the west of Atlanta, heading for the Macon rail line to the south. Hood concluded the enemy was giving up. Telegrams went out all over the Confederacy: "The Yankees are gone!" Several railway cars full of ladies arrived in town to assist in the celebration. Hood sent troops south to Jonesboro to hasten his enemy's retreat, but by the end of the 31st the Federals had easily repelled that force and cut the railroad in two places.

Obtuse as he was, Hood knew the game was up. On 1 September he evacuated Atlanta, blowing up the munitions and stores he could not carry away and heading for entrenchments to the southwest at Lovejoy. On the next day the Federals roared into the city, and Sherman telegraphed Lincoln "Atlanta is ours, and fairly won." The overjoyed president declared a national day of celebration for the victories at Atlanta and Mobile Bay. Privately, he celebrated his own suddenly improved prospects for re-election.

Above: *A postwar depiction of the death of Union General James B McPherson at the Battle of Atlanta on 22 July. He actually was killed in an encounter with Rebel skirmishers.*

Sherman now decided on a course of action that would make him simultaneously one of the great generals of history and the most hated personage in the long memory of the South. He decreed that the full weight of war was to fall on the civilians of the Confederacy. Atlanta was to become a military camp, its population forcibly evacuated, all buildings of possible military importance destroyed. (Ultimately, only half the civilians were evacuated, and his men were ordered not to burn private dwellings, but they often got a little careless with matches: no one was likely to stop them.) Sherman wrote to Halleck, "If the people raise a howl against my barbarity and cruelty, I will answer that war is war, and not popularity seeking. If they want peace, they and their relations must stop the war."

Hood was soon on the road again with his army, heading north to operate against Sherman's supply line in a desperate gamble to force a Federal retreat. First sending Thomas's army to Nashville on 3 October, Sherman set out in pursuit of Hood, following him back north along his old route. Again Kennesaw Mountain, Allatoona, Resaca and Chattanooga echoed to the sound of gunfire. Then Sherman came to rest in Kingston, Georgia, and made an historic change of plans. He decided to let Hood go, to let Schofield and Thomas handle him. Hood could not stop him now: Sherman would set out on a gamble of his own. As he and Grant had done in Mississippi on the way to Jackson, he would cut his supply line and march away from Hood, directly across Georgia to the sea. He would show the South and the world that his 60,000 men could go anywhere in enemy territory with impunity. On

the way he would take what food his army needed from the people. He would destroy the South's will to resist, would "make Georgia howl."

"War," Shermon wrote, "like the thunderbolt, follows its own laws and turns not aside even if the beautiful, the virtuous and the charitable stand in its path." At the time, this was considered barbarism; future generations would call it Total War.

Thus Sherman left Hood to his desperate and ineffectual raids and moved back to Atlanta to complete the work of destruction. On 16 November he set out to the east across the South toward Savannah and the sea. As far as the world was concerned he marched into a hole: there would be no communication. His army was ordered not only to forage off the land but to "enforce a devastation more or less relentless." With the air of a holiday rather than a campaign, his army made about ten miles a day and spread aross a front some 50 miles wide. That front cut through the South like a scythe, leaving a burning and ravaged swath across the rich landscape. On the periphery, like a swarm of locusts, ranged a rabble of deserters – both Yankees and Rebels bonded by a common rapacity. These "bummers," as they were called, robbed and burned at random. Opposing Sherman's march was a motley collection of state militias and Wheeler's cavalry – some 13,000 in all. Though they forced the Federals to contend with almost constant skirmishing, they could not begin to halt their progress.

Meanwhile, Hood continued haplessly on his way north in Tennessee, battering his army to pieces on the Federal juggernaut. On 30 November he lost 6000 men in attacking Schofield at Franklin. He continued somehow to Nashville, where in mid-December Thomas finally wrecked what little was left of the Confederate Army of Tennessee, which had been

Right: *S D Lee's Rebels attacking General Oliver Howard's army at Ezra Church on 28 July. Six assaults failed to dislodge the Federal troops.*

Below: *An Atlanta railroad station after occupation by Federal troops. It is being used as a staging area; note the troops atop the boxcars and the tents in the background.*

Left: *General Sherman ordered total war as his Federal army marched through Georgia, but their depredations were mostly against property, not people.*

Right top: *A Thomas Nast drawing of Union soldiers halted for rest on the march to Savannah.*

Right bottom: *A Federal wagon train leaves Atlanta for the March to the Sea.*

hounded to death by President Davis's almost unerring facility for firing good generals and promoting bad ones.

On December 10 the world learned that Sherman had emerged unscathed at Savannah. Three days later the Rebel fort outside the city fell; Hardee, in command, evacuated the city on the 21st. Sherman facetiously wired to Lincoln, "I beg to present you, as a Christmas gift, the city of Savannah." The March to the Sea was accomplished. Sherman prepared to turn north through the Carolinas to join Grant's Army; together they would finish off Lee. The march through the Carolinas was to be another campaign of destruction.

William Tecumseh Sherman had fulfilled his task, had mortally wounded the Confederacy's potential for war, had earned the unbridled admiration of the North and the undying hatred of the South. Was his ruthlessness justifiable? History has debated that issue ever since.

On paper, Sherman was ferocious – his letters bristle with threats: "I shall then feel justified in resorting to the harshest measures, and shall make little effort to restrain my army"; "Until we can re-populate Georgia, it is useless to occupy it, but the utter destruction of its roads, homes, and people will cripple their military resources"; "I almost tremble for her [South Carolina's] fate." Yet none of these threats came fully to pass. By modern standards, his campaign was scarcely a reign of terror at all, since most of the violence and looting fell on property, not persons. There was none of the indiscriminate slaughter of modern guerrilla war and terrorism.

In the end it could be argued that Sherman was not the real culprit in the March to the Sea, that the true blame lies in the fact put forth succinctly by Sherman himself in the statement: "War is hell." From the Civil War onward, that judgment would resonate ever more deeply.

PETERSBURG

By the summer of 1864, the Confederacy was sinking into defeat. It had lost most of its vital cities and ports, a substantial number of its men and its grip on the oppressive slave-labor system that had supported its economy. Already there was serious talk of enlisting freed slaves in the Confederate Army, which was a manifestly desperate course. (In the North the Thirteenth Amendment, abolishing slavery as an institution, was in preparation.)

Yet the Rebels fought on. The Union Army of the Potomac had been hard hit in the Wilderness, at Spotsylvania and at Cold Harbor. When U S Grant changed his tactics in June, ordering his army south, away from Richmond, it was partly an admission of short-term frustration and partly an assumption of victory in the long run. He would besiege Petersburg, a rail center through which flowed the food and supplies Lee's army lived and fought on. When Petersburg fell, both Richmond and Lee would be finished, and so would the last hope of the Confederacy.

As at Vicksburg, Grant had begun by trying to avoid a siege, but was forced to settle for the inevitable. The main Confederate entrenchments surrounded Petersburg in a large east-west arc, both ends resting on the Appomattox River, which was protected against Union ships by cannon. Grant's lines took shape to the east, and over the next months slowly crept to the west around the city. On 22-23 July the Federals made a sortie against the Weldon Railroad south of Petersburg, but A P Hill's men pushed them back. Meanwhile, Confederate General Jubal Early had mounted a raid toward Washington that threw the capital into a panic and brought his forces to the very gates of the city before he fell back on 11 July. Early's purpose, of course, was to draw away Grant's men from Petersburg. Knowing, or at least hoping, that Washington was strong enough, Grant did not take the bait. Lee was his only objective.

There was another Federal offensive around Petersburg during July, one that would cap the military career of the

Left: *A lithograph entitled "Come and Join Us Brothers" published by the Supervisory Committee for Recruiting Colored Regiments in Philadelphia. About 186,000 blacks served on both sides.*

Below: *Confederate soldiers at Petersburg prepare for the Union siege.*

Opposite: *A pencil drawing by Edwin Forbes shows the Union 18th Corps storming the first line of fortifications outside of Petersburg on 14 June 1864.*

genial and inept Ambrose E Burnside. Burnside's fancy had been caught by one Colonel Henry Pleasants, who had been a mining engineer before the war. Pleasants had formulated a plan to dig a 510-foot tunnel under the Confederate trenches at Elliot's Salient, just east of the city. Grant and Meade were distinctly cool to the notion, but approved it mainly to keep Burnside and his men out of trouble. On 25 June, 400 former Pennsylvania coal miners went to work. By 23 July the tunnel, of unprecedented length in military history, was completed, and workers began placing hundreds of barrels of black powder in magazines dug under the Confederate parapets. Burnside had not neglected to prepare troops for this unusual duty. The division of General Edward Ferrero had spent a month training for the attack. They had been picked supposedly because they were the freshest troops in the army. They also happened to be a black division.

Black troops had been actively recruited in the North since 1863; by the end of the war they numbered about 300,000, many of them former slaves. Their progress in the Union Army had been attended by all the racism then prevalent in the North as well as the South. Their fighting ability had been maligned, until they had repeatedly proved they could fight as well as whites (their officers were almost entirely white). In the army they remained a touchy subject, a problem close to the core of the entire American dilemma.

On 30 July the show was ready to begin. However, on the day before, Meade, with Grant's approval, had ordered a change in plans: the black division was not to lead the attack – if it failed, public opinion might accuse the Union of callously misusing its black soldiers (which, given the experimental nature of the operation, was very possibly the case). After this rebuff, Burnside seemed listless and indifferent, simply drawing straws to see whose division would lead the attack. James H Ledlie, commanding the I Division, lost. Burnside must have known this was the weakest division in the army and Ledlie the least experienced general, but it did not seem to bother him. Furthermore, Burnside was vague in giving his final instructions: Ledlie rounded up his men with only a very hazy idea of what they were supposed to do.

The explosion was planned for 3:30 in the morning on the 30th. At that moment all eyes strained toward the Rebel parapet. Ledlie's division waited in the trenches, but nothing happened. It was discovered that the long fuse had fizzled, and it was relit. At 4:45 AM one of the largest explosions ever seen on the American continent sent flames, earth, cannons, Confederates and parts of Confederates a hundred feet into the air in the midst of a mushroom-shaped cloud. When it had all settled, there was a gigantic crater 170 feet long, 60 to 80 feet wide and 30 feet deep stretching well into the Southern position, the outer defenses of which had been breached.

For the time being, the surviving Rebel defenders had fled the area. Terrified by the blast, so had Ledlie's division. It took ten minutes to get them back in position to advance, at

Below: *Drawing by Alfred R Waud for* Harper's Weekly *showing the explosion of the mine at Petersburg on 30 July. The stratagem proved disastrous for the Union soldiers.*

which point it was discovered that no provision at all had been made to get them out of the trenches, which were quite deep. They scrambled up as best they could, already considerably disorganized, and then stopped around the crater to gawk at the appalling mess within. With some prodding, the I Division began jumping and sliding into the hole. Finding themselves in a morass of pits and house-high blocks of clay, they stumbled in confusion toward the other end. Meanwhile Ledlie, their commander, cowered in a bombproof shelter behind Union lines, consoled by a jug of rum.

Soon the Southerners collected their wits and began to train their artillery and muskets into the hole. Finding themselves relatively sheltered in the crater, the ostensible attackers were even less disposed to climb out of it. By the time 15,000 men had been herded into the crater, the enemy fire had become truly murderous and the Federals were interested solely in hiding. The Union Army was now literally at the feet of the enemy.

Finally, in desperation, Burnside ordered in the black division originally slated to lead the attack. After dispatching them, their commander, Ferrero, joined Ledlie in the bombproof shelter. The black soldiers advanced resolutely and alone and were cut to pieces on the other end, though not before somehow taking 250 prisoners. Firing into the huddled masses of Federals, the Confederates screamed, "Take the white man – kill the nigger!" The whole inglorious affair ended with a confused melee of surviving Federals rushing devil-take-the-hindmost back to their own lines. The North suffered 3748 casualties of 20,708 engaged – about a third of them from the black division; the South lost about 1500 of 11,466.

Grant called the Petersburg mine assault a "stupendous failure," while admitting that if the black troops had led the attack as planned it would probably have succeeded. Lincoln's reported reaction was an historic epitaph to the unique military career of Ambrose E Burnside: "Only Burn-

Above: *Artillery battery of the Union 18th Corps at a captured fort on the outer line at Petersburg on 15 June, 1864.*

Left: *Officers and men of the 114th Pennsylvania Infantry relax in front of Petersburg in August 1864.*

Overleaf: *The "Dictator," a 13-inch siege mortar used in the bombardment of Richmond and Petersburg.*

side could have managed such a coup, wringing one last spectacular defeat from the jaws of victory."

The siege of Petersburg continued, day on day, month on month. In its first weeks there had been no rain, and a choking cloud of dust hung everywhere. Later weeks brought too much rain; the men in the trenches stood all day in waist-high water. Snipers waited in readiness for those careless enough to show their heads. Every day a battle raged somewhere; cannon and mortars roared incessantly (the soldiers hated the mortars most – they could drop shells unexpectedly straight into the trenches). The Federals gradually inched around the city, moving steadily toward the Confederate life-lines of the railroads.

The Army of the Potomac was hardly the same force that had set out in May. Subjected to three months of the hardest and most deadly fighting in American history, it had lost well over half its veterans in casualties over the summer of 1864. Many famous units, like the Iron Brigade, had virtually ceased to exist. The fabled II Corps, which began the summer with 6799 men, had suffered 7970 casualties, including 40 regimental commanders. Yet that corps and the whole army stayed more or less at strength, thanks largely to the draft and to enlistment bounties that kept personnel in the trenches but by no means guaranteed good soldiers. And the sullen waiting and ducking of trench warfare was poor training for an army of recruits.

The rigors of the campaign and the siege had their effect on the Northern command structure as well. Meade was more irascible than ever, and his relations with Grant – which so far had been surprisingly good – began to deteriorate to the extent that Grant considered relieving him. Hancock, the best fighting general in the army, was troubled and demoralized by his old Gettysburg wound and by the strain of constant fighting; he quarreled with John Gibbon, his best division commander.

Lee's troops were also devastated, and hungrier and shabbier than ever. They were nearly all veterans, for the simple

reason that there were few recruits to be found. For all their experience, however, hunger, exhaustion, disease and desertion had taken their toll. The army was by no means capable of the heroics of its recent past; indeed, it was hardly capable of taking the offensive at all. The weight of the North was slowly squeezing the life out of the Army of Northern Virginia, the South's only remaining viable army.

In August of 1864, Grant sent General Gouverneur K Warren to try again to seize the Weldon Railroad south of Petersburg. The Federals occupied the line on the 18th, and two attacks by A P Hill could not dislodge them, though the North had 4455 casualties to the South's 1600. Now only one Confederate lifeline was left – the South Side Railroad on the west.

In September Grant sent "Phil" Sheridan with infantry and cavalry on a campaign into the Shenandoah Valley of Virginia, which would become nearly as famous as Stonewall Jackson's operations there in 1862. Sheridan had two goals. First, he was to drive out Jubal Early, whose army had retired there after the raid on Washington. Second, he was to make quite sure the valley would send no more food and forage to Confederate Armies. Grant's instructions were ruthless: devastation was to be so complete that a crow flying over the valley would have to carry its own provisions.

Sheridan proceeded to turn the fertile, beautiful Shenandoah Valley into a smouldering ruin. In the process he dealt harshly with Jubal Early, defeating him at Winchester and Fisher's Hill in mid-September. On 19 October Early's men suddenly attacked and routed the Federals at Cedar Creek while Sheridan was away. Arriving and riding furiously through his fleeing troops, Sheridan turned them around and swamped Early's army. It was the last significant Rebel resistance in the valley, which had been the breadbasket of the Confederacy.

Sheridan then pursued his course through the Shenandoah Valley like an avenging angel. A small but volatile man of manic ferocity in battle, Sheridan drove his men and officers almost as hard as he drove the enemy. An admiring sub-

Opposite: *Surgeons'*
quarters at the camp of the
50th New York Engineers in
front of Petersburg in
November, 1864.

Right: *Abandoned*
Confederate field defenses of
earth and timber around
Petersburg.

Below: *Part of the Union*
lines outside Petersburg.

ordinate called him "that form of condensed energies"; to the Rebels, he was "Sheridan the Inevitable."

On 8 November Abraham Lincoln was re-elected to a second term as president by a substantial majority over his opponent, General George B McClellan. Significantly, for all their affection for "Little Mac," the military vote went overwhelmingly to Lincoln. The doubts felt by many civilians in the North about the president's war policy were clearly not shared by the army.

In mid-January 1865, after a bungled attempt by Ben Butler that got him fired, Admiral David Dixon Porter took Fort Fisher on the coast of North Carolina, the last port held by the Confederacy for its blockade-runners and virtually its last link to the outside world. Now the South was alone.

In February Grant extended his lines to Hatcher's Run, south of Petersburg. Sherman, meanwhile, was fighting and burning his way north through the Carolinas toward union with the Army of the Potomac. If Sherman effected that union, Lee's army had not a chance in the world. Shattered and tired as the Confederates were, they had to try something; the only choices left were those of desperation.

At length Lee decided to try and get part of his army to Carolina to join forces with Joe Johnston, who was incapable of resisting Sherman alone. Perhaps together they could deal with Sherman and then turn to defeat Grant.

The Southern attempt to break out of Petersburg came on 25 March at Ford Stedman, east of the city. Lying 150 yards from the Confederate position, it was the weakest part of the Federal line. Lee hoped to break through here and strike the Federal communications, thereby forcing Grant to pull troops from farther south and leave an opening in his line through which Lee could send forces south to Johnston. In the early morning, Federals at Fort Stedman were surprised and quickly overwhelmed by the Confederates; the Rebel infantry was swarming down the Union trenches and into the Federal rear before any resistance was mounted. For an hour or so it seemed like old times. But then a counterattack by six new Pennsylvania regiments, commanded by General John Hartranft, brought the Confederate advance to a halt. At eight o'clock Lee called off the attack. It was the last great offensive of the Army of Northern Virginia. The next day Lee notified President Davis that his position in Petersburg was no longer

Opposite: *General Philip Sheridan and his staff.*

Right: *In the Western Theater, at Franklin, Tennessee, a Union force under John M Schofield repelled several Confederate assaults on 30 November.*

Below: *Pencil sketch of General Sheridan's famous ride to rally his men at Cedar Creek on 19 October. Sheridan's defeat of Jubal Early's army ended Confederate resistance in the Shenandoah Valley.*

tenable, given the approach of Sherman, and that the Confederate Government had best consider pulling out of Richmond. Simultaneously, Sheridan's Federal forces arrived back from their devastation of the Shenandoah Valley, ready to join in the last battle.

For Robert E Lee, for the Army of Northern Virginia, for the Confederate States of America, the incredible was about to happen. After all the glorious speeches, the fatuous defenses of slavery, the gallant fighting and the victories, the unforeseen and terrible suffering and dying – after all this, the gaunt and humiliating specter of final defeat was at their

door. Robert E Lee was far from a loser, but he had lost. His ranks and his command structure were decimated: Jackson, Stuart, dozens of other generals were dead. The Army of Northern Virginia had been one of the most remarkable fighting forces in history, but it had lost. Now it had only to play out its role to the final curtain.

The curtain came down with bewildering speed. On 29 March Grant sent cavalry and infantry under Sheridan and Warren southwest to envelop the Confederate right flank. Lee dispatched 10,000 men under George Pickett to stop them. The Federal operation was slowed by heavy rains and Rebel resistance, but Sheridan was implacable: vowing the rain would not stop his cavalry, he shouted, "I'm ready to strike out tomorrow and go to smashing things!"

On 31 March, Sheridan assaulted Pickett around Dinwiddie Court House; outnumbered five to one, Pickett's force fought for hours before pulling back to Five Forks. Lee sent a desperate message to Pickett to hold that position "at all costs"; if it fell, the South Side Railroad, the last lifeline, was doomed. But on 1 April Sheridan, seemingly everywhere on the field at once with his battle flag, overpowered the Confederates at Five Forks and captured nearly half of them. Many of the rest fled the war back to their homes.

Now Lee had to get out. He notified Davis on 2 April that he would evacuate Petersburg. Grant, determined above all else not to let Lee escape again, unleashed a stupendous artillery barrage on the whole length of the Confederate line, and followed it with an attack by the VI Corps, who broke through the Rebel right. In the fighting, A P Hill, who had saved the Confederacy at Antietam and had been at Lee's side through all the victories, was killed. The news visibly staggered Lee.

During the day the Confederate Government fled Richmond. Warehouses and arsenals were set afire, the flames spreading into the city. Lee pulled out that night and marched his exhausted and starving army west toward Amelia Court House, hoping to put them on the Danville Railroad to the Carolinas. On 3 April Federal soldiers occupied Petersburg and Richmond. The next day the Confederate capital saw the lanky form of Abraham Lincoln, surrounded by cheering slaves, striding through the streets. At last Lincoln sat pondering at the desk of Jefferson Davis.

If defeat seemed incredible to the Confederate Army, the

Left: *An attempt to take the defenses outside Petersburg. The city was finally occupied by Union troops on 3 April 1865.*

Below: *Sketch of railroad cars and workshops burned by the Rebels evacuating Petersburg.*

prospect of victory after so many disappointments was equally incredible to Union soldiers. News of the fall of Richmond was received by Union troops at first with derision: they had heard that one before. No sooner had they absorbed the reality than they were on the road in the final race with the enemy. Sheridan had anticipated Lee's march to Amelia Court House and rode to cut off the Danville Railroad. Lee's army was now surrounded – Meade's infantry was on the east and Sheridan on the south and west. Escape to the north was impossible. Lee the fox was being run to earth by Sheridan the hound. Rebel soldiers were deserting in hundreds. "My God!," cried Lee, "Is the army dissolved?"

Denied the railroad by Sheridan, Lee marched again on 5 April. By the next day his army was divided by accident into two segments. Led by Sheridan's dismounted cavalry, the Federals fell on one of the wings at Saylor's Creek and captured 8000, one-third of the remaining Rebel strength. The pathetic remains of the Army of Northern Virginia limped on to the west, harried incessantly by Federal cavalry. Then on 9 April Lee found sheridan the Inevitable blocking his path at Appomattox Court House. It was the end.

But still the shadow of that great army could not die without a fight. Lee sent cavalry around the Federal right flank, and infantry and artillery under John B Gordon broke through the center of Sheridan's line. For a brief moment there was open country in front of the Army of Northern Virginia. Then from over the hill appeared Union infantry, line after line of blue.

The firing died down. For the last time the two armies surveyed one another across the battlefield. Then Sheridan sounded his bugles for the charge. But before the Federals could fall upon the ragged Confederates, a horseman appeared, galloping furiously from behind Southern lines. He carried a white flag.

The war was over, and it was not over. Lee's surrender to Grant at Appomattox on 9 April almost ended the hostilities (Johnston surrendered to Sherman on the 18th). But the assassination of Lincoln on 14 April was only the first of the aftershocks that would shake American society: the Civil War would never leave the consciousness of the nation.

Lincoln above all had tried to see beyond the immediate business and horror of the war to the deeper questions: What good could come out of this suffering? What did it all mean?

Above: *A Mathew Brady photo of the ruins of Richmond, burned by its defenders on 2 April 1865.*

Below: *Commemorative illustration of Robert E Lee's surrender to Ulysses S Grant at Appomattox Court House.*

In the Gettysburg Address he had dealt with the first question. The "honored dead," "those who gave their lives that this nation might live," were the dead of both sides: Lincoln prophesied that the nation that would arise from the war, purged by great suffering of slavery and sectionalism, would be stronger and greater than ever before. In this prophecy he was to prove right.

The second question, the meaning of the war, the meaning of great wars themselves, Lincoln spoke of in his Second Inaugural Address. There he was obliged to admit that the question defeated him, that the causes and meaning of such gigantic scourges are beyond human comprehension.

Clockwise from top: *Stonewall Jackson and his home; Ulysses S. Grant; Robert E. Lee; and William T. Sherman.*

LEADING FIGURES OF THE CIVIL WAR

Preface

There are probably many good reasons for America's seemingly insatiable interest in the Civil War, but surely one of the most important has to do with the war's intense *personality*. Personality, that is, in the literal sense, for the many actors who played central roles in this greatest of our national epic dramas were nothing if not individually fascinating. They ran the gamut of human types – from the noble to the venal, from the brilliant to the ludicrously incompetent, from the brave to the cowardly. Many of them were animated by passions so extreme that they were at times driven to extremes of behavior, some to atrocity, others to something approaching saintliness.

Yet – and this may be what truly makes them fascinating – they were all far more complex and multidimensional than sentimental mythology would have us believe. Like all real human enterprises, the Civil War was no theatre of humours: it was fought by living, flesh-and-blood people, men and women whose characters were filled with all the quirks and contradictions that the human estate entails.

Thus the courtly, sedate Robert E. Lee had in his nature at least some elements of bloodthirsty rashness that would not have seemed out of place in a Western gunslinger. The wise and visionary Lincoln was also a sly politician and a somewhat meddlesome armchair strategist. W. T. Sherman, whose name is to many Southerners still a synonym of military barbarity, was a man who detested war, had more sympathy for the Southern cause than most of his Union colleagues, and offered his defeated foe, J. E. Johnston, such generous surrender terms that they were repudiated by Congress. Heroic battlefield nurses Clara Barton and Dorothea Dix both had difficult personalities and questionable administrative skills. The war's most legendary bungler, Ambrose Burnside, was also famous among his contemporaries for his unfailing charm and engaging humility. The flamboyant Jeb Stuart, that "gay knight-errant of the elder time," was in private the most sobersided and conventional of husbands. Whether the brilliant Stonewall Jackson was altogether sane was a question that bemused at least a

few of those who knew him well. Such examples could be multiplied almost indefinitely.

Knowing human details about the men and women who played important roles in the Civil War in no way diminishes our regard for them. On the contrary, it both heightens our admiration for their accomplishments and serves to make us more sympathetic towards their failures and shortcomings. At the same time, it vastly increases our understanding both of them and of the war itself.

Yet the very fact that our understanding of the war is so heavily rooted in our sense of its personalities also has its penalties. Our histories of the war, even the most summary and general, fairly bristle with names, many of which keep reappearing in confusingly various contexts. It is no wonder that casual readers sometimes have difficulty in keeping track of all the players. And the problem is compounded in all those formal military histories which observe the hallowed – if inexplicable – martial convention of almost always providing the exact rank of every army and navy officer mentioned and almost never giving their first names (thereby leaving it to the reader to puzzle out just which Lee, Porter, Johnston, Davis, Anderson, Reynolds, Smith, Hill, Cooke, etc. the author might have in mind).

This section of this two-part book has been designed to assist non-expert readers in negotiating the sometimes complex shoals of Civil War biography. It contains approximately 520 profiles – many illustrated – of the period's most prominent figures, men and women, military and civilian. The entries vary in length

according to the importance of the subject. The longest entries run to more than 1,000 words; the shortest, brief entries, are sometimes less than 50. The criteria for judging the relative importance of a subject almost always have to do with the subject's relationship to the war itself. Thus, for example, James Garfield and Benjamin Harrison receive rather brief entries, not because these future presidents were unimportant in other contexts, but because their roles in the Civil War were comparatively minor. On the other hand, in a few cases where individuals' future lives and works were largely determined by their Civil War experiences, their postwar careers are dealt with in more detail: Clara Barton, whose battlefield experiences ministering to sick and wounded soldiers led to her founding of the American Red Cross, is a case in point.

It is worth adding that readers of this section should bear in mind that although it can be read separately, it is meant to be used in conjunction with both the first section on the battles as well as with other historical works. Although it is true that the reader will find the broad outlines of Civil War history presented piecemeal in various key biographies – mainly those of Lincoln, Jefferson Davis, Lee, Grant, and Sherman – this section was not intended to double as a general history of the period. Thus, while it takes pains to try to identify the major campaigns and battles in which all its military subjects participated, it rarely attempts to give more than cursory descriptions of any of the actions so noted. And the same is true of its treatment of political, economic, and social events. In short, its purpose is to serve as a useful supplement to general histories, to do precisely what most of them, by their very nature, cannot hope to do as well. If it succeeds in this aim, its authors and its editor will be well pleased.

OPPOSITE: Robert Shaw at Fort Wagner.

BELOW: Abraham Lincoln.

legislator in the 1840s he helped to confirm Massachusetts's opposition to slavery. He founded the *Boston Whig* (1846) and ran as a Free-Soiler as Martin Van Buren's vice presidential candidate (1848). In the U.S. Congress (1859-1861) he skilfully headed the House Committee on the State of the Union. In the crucial post of U.S. minister to Great Britain (1861-1868), he successfully maintained England's (and thus Europe's) neutrality, a feat regarded as the diplomatic equivalent of winning a major military victory at home. He helped to arbitrate the U.S. government's *Alabama* Claims against Great Britain for war damages (1871-1872) and eventually retired to Massachusetts.

Edward Porter Alexander

Abercrombie, John Joseph
(1798-1877) Union general

Tennessee-born Abercrombie was graduated from West Point in 1822 and fought in the infantry in the Seminole and Mexican wars. Commissioned at Union colonel in 1861, he commanded a brigade in the Peninsular Campaign. As a brigadier general he led Abercrombie's Division in the defense of Washington and defended the Fredericksburg depots. After retiring from the regular army in June 1865 he served on courts martial.

Adams, Charles Francis
(1807-1886) U.S. diplomat

The son of President John Quincy Adams, he was educated at Harvard and became a writer on politics and history. As a state

Charles Francis Adams

Daniel Weisiger Adams

Adams, Daniel Weisiger
(1821-1872) Confederate general

A Kentucky-born lawyer-politician, he settled in Natchez, Mississippi, and later in New Orleans. Weisinger commanded the 1st Louisiana Regulars at Shiloh, then led a brigade at Perryville, Murfreesboro and Chickamauga. Wounded and captured at Chickamauga, he was exchanged in 1864. He commanded the District of Central Alabama during the final months of the war. After a brief postwar exile in England, he returned to New Orleans to practice law.

Alexander, Edward Porter
(1835-1910) Confederate general

A Georgia-born graduate of West Point, he taught at the academy, helped develop the army's "wig-wag" system of flag signals and served in the Pacific Northwest before resigning during the secession crisis. Commissioned a captain in the Confederate

army in May 1861, Alexander developed a reputation as one of its most resourceful and energetic officers. First as a staff officer, later as an artillerist, he fought at First Bull Run, Fredericksburg and Gettysburg and commanded James Longstreet's artillery at Knoxville, the Wilderness, Spotsylvania and Cold Harbor. Alexander's influential *Military Memoirs of a Confederate* appeared in 1907.

Allen, Henry Watkins
(1820-1866) Confederate general

A Louisiana planter and legislator, Allen had only recently returned from extensive European travels when the Civil War broke out, whereupon he joined the Confederate army. He was wounded at Shiloh in 1862 and fought at Vicksburg in 1862-63. He led the Louisiana Brigade at Baton Rouge in 1864. His wounds there prevented further field service, but he proved an outstanding governor of Louisiana (1864-1865): he restored the state's shattered economy by establishing trade routes through Mexico to beat the Union blockade and negotiated Confederate General Kirby Smith's surrender. He died in Mexico.

Ames, Adelbert
(1835-1933) Union general

A native of Maine, he was seriously wounded at First Bull Run 10 weeks after his West Point graduation (and earned a Congressional Medal of Honor for gallantry). He fought in the Peninsular and Antietam campaigns and at Fredericksburg and Chancellorsville. As a brigadier general he led divisions at Gettysburg, then in Virginia and North Carolina in 1864-1865). He was Mississippi's governor (1868-1870, 1874-1876) and US Senator (1870-1874. He engaged in milling and manufacturing in the North and, after serving in the Spanish-American War, retired to Massachusetts.

Anderson, "Bloody" Bill
(d. 1864) Confederate guerrilla

His band of near-criminals looted Centralia, Missouri, on September 27, 1864, hijacked a train and murdered 24 unarmed Federals and two civilians on board. Two hours later Anderson's gang ambushed a

ABOVE: Adelbert Ames (seated, l.) served in both the Civil and Spanish-American wars.

RIGHT: Confederate General George B. Anderson, mortally wounded at Antietam.

Union cavalry detachment, killing 124 of 147 troopers in what became known as the Centralia Massacre. Pursuing Federals caught and killed Anderson near Richmond, Missouri, in later October.

Anderson, George Burgwyn
(1831-1862) Confederate general

He was graduated from the University of North Carolina at age 17, then entered West Point, from which he was graduated in 1852. Anderson resigned from the U.S. Army in 1861, entered Confederate service and commanded a North Carolina regiment at First Bull Run. He led a brigade of North Carolina troops during the battles of the Seven Days in 1862. Wounded in the ankle at Antietam in September, he died of the effects of an amputation of his foot on October 16, 1862.

Joseph Reid Anderson

Anderson, Joseph Reid
(1813-1892) **Confederate general**

A Virginia-born West Point graduate, he bought the Tredegar Iron Works (Richmond, Virginia) in 1858 after serving for a time in the Virginia legislature. In August 1861 he was made major of artillery in the Confederate army while still running the ironworks, which were considered vital to the Confederacy's military armaments. In September 1861 he was promoted to brigadier general and given command of the District of Cape Fear. In 1862 he was wounded at Frayser's Farm while leading the 3rd North Carolina Brigade on the Peninsula; no longer fit for field duty, he resigned and returned to the ironworks in 1862.

Anderson, Richard Heron
(1821-1879) **Confederate general**

This West Point graduate and 20-year army veteran resigned from frontier service in March 1861 to join the 1st South Carolina infantry. A brigadier general by July, he fought steadily with the Army of Northern Virginia, distinguishing himself particularly in the Peninsular Campaign and at Chancellorsville and, from May to October 1864, commanding General James Longstreet's corps at Spotsylvania, Cold Harbor, Petersburg and Richmond. After the war he worked for the South Carolina railroad and as a state phosphate inspector.

Anderson, Robert
(1805-1871) **Union general**

An 1825 West Point graduate, the Kentucky-born Anderson fought in the Seminole and Mexican wars and taught artillery tactics at the military academy. He commanded the U.S. garrison in Charleston Harbor, South Carolina, during the secession crisis and became the "hero of Fort Sumter" when Confederate forces bombarded the harbor citadel in April 1861. Promoted to brigadier general in May, he commanded Union forces in Kentucky during the period of that state's so-called neutrality. Anderson retired on a disability in October 1863. He returned to Fort Sumter on April 14, 1865, for the ceremonial raising of the U.S. flag there.

Andrews, John Albion
(1818-1867)
Governor of Massachusetts

Born in Maine and a graduate of Bowdoin College, he became a lawyer in Boston and was outspoken in his opposition to slavery. A Republican, he was elected governor of Massachusetts in 1860, taking office in 1861 and retaining it throughout the Civil War (and until his death in 1867). He was prompt and effective in lending his support to the Union war effort – the Massachu-

Robert Anderson

BELOW: Fort Sumter in April 1861

setts 6th Regiment was the first major armed force to arrive in Washington after President Lincoln's call for volunteers – and Andrews's Massachusetts remained a pillar of Union strength throughout the remainder of the war.

Armistead, Lewis Addison
(1817-1863) Confederate general

Born in North Carolina to a respected military family, he attended West Point and fought in the Mexican War. He resigned his U.S. Army commission in 1861 and entered Confederate service. He led a brigade in "Pickett's Charge" at Gettysburg that is said to have made the deepest penetration in the Federal line; he died in this action. Union General Winfield Scott Hancock, Armistead's close friend, led the defending troops in this part of the line, and later Hancock had the sombre duty of sending Armistead's spurs to his family. On the spot where Armistead fell is a monument marking what has come to be called "the high tide" of the Confederacy.

Armstrong, Frank Crawford
(1835-1909) Confederate general

Born in Indian Territory, he joined the regular army and fought on the western frontier, taking part in the Utah Expedition with the 2nd U. S. Dragoons. In August 1861 he resigned from the United States Army and joined the Confederate forces, fighting at Wilson's Creek, Missouri. Promoted to brigadier general in April 1863, he fought at Stones River, Tullahoma, Chickamauga, Knoxville and in the Franklin and Nashville Campaign. Following the war, he served as a U.S. Indian inspector (1885-1889) and commissioner of Indian affairs (1893-1895).

Armstrong, Samuel Chapman
(1839-1892) Union officer

Born in Hawaii, where his parents had gone as missionaries, he was attending Williams College when the Civil War

LEFT: Frank Crawford Armstrong

broke out. He volunteered for Union service and was commissioned a captain in August 1862. In 1864 he was made a colonel with the 9th Regiment, made up of African-Americans, and was breveted a brigadier general in November 1864. Because of his experiences with the black troops, he was made an agent of the Freedmen's Bureau after the war. This led him to found the Hampton Institute (1868), and he spent the rest of his life working to educate African-Americans.

Ashby, Turner
(1828-1862) Confederate general

The grandson of a Revolutionary War officer, he was born in Fauquier County, Virginia, where he became a planter and grain dealer in the Shenandoah Valley. An influential local politician, Turner favored slavery but opposed secession, and in 1859 he raised a volunteer company and led it to Harpers Ferry to defend Virginia against John Brown. When Virginia seceded, he again raised and led a mounted troop to Harpers Ferry, staying to scout. As part of the 7th Virginia Cavalry after June 1861, his men defended the upper Potomac border, participating in First Bull Run. A daring intelligence-gathering expedition to Chambersburg, Pennsylvania, undertaken in disguise in the spring of 1862 cemented his growing reputation for courage and resourcefulness. As Stonewall Jackson's cavalry commander, he played an important role in the Jackson's Shenandoah Val-

OPPOSITE: William W. Averell (seated).

BELOW: Turner Ashby.

ley Campaign in 1862. Joining Jackson at Front Royal, he displayed exceptional leadership on picket and scouting duty and fought at Winchester. He was promoted to brigadier general in May of that year. He was killed in a rearguard action protecting Jackson's retreat from the Valley on June 6.

Augur, Christopher Colon
(1821-1898) Union general

A New York native, Augur saw Mexican War and frontier service after graduation from West Point. Appointed a brigadier general in the Union army, he fought on the Rappahannock (capturing Fredericksburg in April 1862) and was wounded at Cedar Mountain. As a major general he was second-in-command in Nathaniel Banks's 1862 New Orleans Campaign. He later commanded the District of Baton Rouge, the Department of Washington and XXII Corps. In his 20-year postwar army career he directed operations against the Indians and was Reconstruction commander of the Department of the Gulf.

Averell, William Wood
(1832-1900) Union general

This New York-born West Point graduate was a pre-war Indian fighter. In the Civil War he was one of the Army of the Potomac's more accomplished young cavalry leaders, bringing the Union cavalry its first taste of success in the engagement at Kelly's Ford in March 1863. He was one of General George Stoneman's lieutenants at Chancellorsville (May 1863), but General Joseph Hooker relieved him of command for apparent lack of aggressiveness. He served in the Shenandoah Valley Campaign of Philip Sheridan (1864), who also relieved Averell of command for the same reason. After the war he served as U.S. consul general in Canada (1866-69), then became wealthy as a manufacturer and inventor of industrial products.

Ayres, Romeyn Beck
(1825-1888) Union general

This New York-born West Point graduate, having served in the Mexican War and on the frontier, was promoted to captain in the U.S. Army in May 1861. He fought at First Bull Run, Yorktown, Lee's Mill, Williamsburg, Gaines's Mill, South Mountain, Antietam, Fredericksburg, Chancellorsville, Gettysburg and the Wilderness. He was wounded at Petersburg and breveted a major general for war service. He remained in the army after the war.

Babcock, Orville
(1835-1884) Union officer

Born and raised in a small Vermont town, he entered West Point in 1857 and was graduated third in his class four years later. He saw action with a Union engineer unit on the Virginia Peninsula in the spring of 1862 and won appointment as chief engineer of the Left Grand Division of the Army of the Potomac later in the year.

Babcock joined Ulysses S. Grant's staff in 1864 as an aide-de-camp and took part in the Wilderness, Spotsylvania and Cold Harbor battles and in the siege of Petersburg. Grant had great confidence in his abilities, employing him as a courier, to collect information and to survey positions, and it was Babcock whom Grant sent

Orville Babcock (right), a longtime associate of Ulysses S. Grant

to conduct Robert E. Lee to the McLean house for the surrender on April 9, 1865.

Babcock served as Grant's private secretary for several years after the war. In the 1870s he became associated with the group of corrupt government officials known as the "Whiskey Ring" and accepted costly presents from one of the ring leaders, John McDonald, the Internal Revenue Service supervisor in St. Louis. In December 1875 a grand jury indicted Babcock for conspiracy to defraud the IRS. Grant stood by him, insisting he could not be guilty. Swayed by Grant's defense, the court returned a verdict of not guilty in February 1876.

Babcock re-entered public service briefly, then retired to Florida. He was accidentally drowned at Mosquito Inlet, Florida, on June 2, 1884.

Bagby, Arthur Pendleton
(1832-1921) Confederate officer

He was graduated from West Point in 1852 and served on the frontier before quitting the army to practice law in Texas. Commissioned a major in the 7th Texas in 1861, Bagby participated in the New Mexico Campaign and in the defense of Galveston. He commanded a brigade during the Red River Campaign of 1864 and saw action at Mansfield and Pleasant Hill. He returned to his Texas law practice after the war.

Bailey, Joseph
(1825-1867) Union general

This Ohio-born lumberman became a captain in the Union's 4th Wisconsin Cavalry in July 1861 and became an engineer of defense at New Orleans in December 1862. He was breveted a brigadier general in June 1864 for his successful efforts to save Nathaniel Bank's fleet in the Red River Campaign and won the Thanks of Congress. Promoted to brigadier general in November 1864, he held various posts as an engineer before resigning in July 1865. He was sheriff of Newton County, Missouri, when he was killed in 1867.

Bailey, Theodorus
(1805-1877) Union admiral

This New Yorker became a midshipman in 1818 and earned his first independent command during the Mexican War. He commanded U.S.S. *Colorado* in the blockade of Pensacola; in the sloop-of-war *Cayuga* he was second-in-command under Admiral David Farragut at New Orleans in April-May 1862 and accepted the city's surren-

Theodorus Bailey (above) and (right) Alpheus Baker

der. From November 1862 he led the East Gulf blockading squadron in intercepting 150 blockade runners. Ill health forced him to a shore command in September 1864. He retired as a rear admiral in 1866.

Baker, Alpheus
(1828-1891) Confederate general

Born in South Carolina, Baker was a delegate to Alabama's secession convention. He entered Confederate service and in March 1862 fought at New Madrid and Island No. 10. He was captured in this latter action and was exchanged in September 1862. He was wounded during the Vicksburg Campaign. Promoted to brigadier general in March 1864, he fought in the Atlanta Campaign at Resaca and at Ezra Church. In January 1865 he was sent to Mobile and then fought at Bentonville. He practiced law after the war.

Baker, Edward Dickinson
(1811-1861) Union officer

A childhood immigrant from England, he settled in Illinois and in 1835 established a law practice in Springfield. There he became an intimate of Abraham Lincoln. He became a state legislator and U.S. Representative (1845-1846, 1849-1851). He moved to San Francisco (1852) and achieved such a political reputation on the West Coast that Oregon Republicans solicited him for a U.S. Senate seat (1860-1861). A skilled orator, he helped to deliver both of these states in the election of 1860 to Lincoln, to whom he was now an advisor. Baker at first declined a brigadier general's commission in 1861 to remain in the Senate, but it was as a colonel of the 71st Pennsylvania that he was killed at Ball's Bluff in October 1861.

Baker, LaFayette Curry
(1826-1868) U.S. secret service chief

This New Yorker, a San Francisco Vigilante and State Department detective, was a Union special agent throughout the war, reaching the rank of brigadier general. His intelligence-gathering against Confederates, conspirators and bounty-jumpers often involved unconstitutional searches and arrests, in addition to spectacular work behind enemy lines. Baker organized the pursuit and capture of John Wilkes Booth.

LaFayette Curry Baker

Baker, Laurence Simmons
(1830-1907) Confederate general

This West Point graduate left frontier Indian fighting to join the cavalry of his home state, North Carolina, in May 1861. He fought in the Army of Northern Virginia in the Peninsular, Antietam and Fredericksburg campaigns of 1862 and the Gettysburg Campaign of 1863. He assumed a North Carolina territorial command in 1864 as a brigadier general. Paroled soon after his surrender in 1865, he farmed in Virginia and, after 1878, worked as a railroad agent.

Banks, Nathaniel Prentiss
(1816-1894) Union general

Massachusetts-born Banks was a career politician: he would represent no less than five political parties in 10 Congresses (1853-1891) and was an able governor of Massachusetts (1858-1860). Commissioned a major general in May 1961, he commanded the Department of Annapolis, led V Corps during the Shenandoah Valley Campaign of 1862 and, leading II Corps, made a controversial and unsuccessful attack at Cedar Mountain in August of that year. Replacing B.F. Butler as commander of the Gulf Department late in 1862, he assisted Ulysses S. Grant in opening the Mississippi: his leading role in the capture of Port Hudson (July 1863) earned him the Thanks of Congress. He resigned after leading the ill-fated Red River Campaign of 1863-1864, though his superiors, notably Henry Halleck, were probably even more responsible for the operation's failure.

Barker, Mrs. Stephen
Sanitary Commission worker

She accompanied her husband, a Massachusetts regimental chaplain, to the war. A nurse attached to the 1st Heavy Artillery at Fort Albany for two years, she became the Sanitary Commission superintendent of several Washington hospitals in 1864 and in the last years of the war lectured widely to raise funds for the commission. After the war she was active in veterans' relief.

Mrs. Stephen Barker, one of the most noted Sanitary Commission workers

William Barksdale

Barksdale, William
(1821-1863) **Confederate general**

This Tennessee-born lawyer served in the Mexican War and ran a pro-slavery newspaper. He was a Democratic Congressman in 1861, but he resigned in January and subsequently joined the Confederate army. He served at First Bull Run and in the Peninsular Campaign, at Antietam, Fredericksburg, Chancellorsville and Gettysburg. He commanded a brigade in Lafayette McLaws's division of James Longstreet's Corps; the brigade saw particularly heavy fighting and became known as "Barksdale's Mississippi Brigade." He was both wounded and captured at Peach Orchard, Virginia, and died the following day from his wounds.

Barlow, Francis Channing
(1834-1896) **Union general**

He was a Harvard-educated New York lawyer and writer. Despite several serious wounds requiring long recuperations, Barlow fought in many major eastern theater battles and campaigns between 1862 and 1865: the siege of Yorktown, Fair Oaks, Antietam, Chancellorsville, Gettysburg, the Wilderness, Spotsylvania, Cold Harbor, Petersburg and Sayler's Creek. He was appointed a brigadier general in September 1862. Resuming his law career after the war, Barlow was a prominent anti-corruption reformer; as New York attorney general (1871-1873) he prosecuted William "Boss" Tweed.

Barnard, John Gross
(1815-1882) **Union general**

A Massachusetts native and West Point graduate, he was a career army engineer and coastal defence specialist who superintended the fortification of New York, Mobile and San Francisco, among other ports. During the Civil War, as chief engineer of Washington, D.C., and the Union armies, he designed Washington's defenses, supervised Union positioning at First Bull Run and in the Peninsular Campaign of 1862 and briefed General W.T. Sherman for the Carolinas Campaign of 1865. He retired from the army in 1881. Barnard published many works on engineering and science.

Barnum, Henry A.
(1833-1892) **Union general**

This New York-born teacher and lawyer was commissioned a captain in the Union army on the same day in May 1861 that he attempted to enlist as a private. He fought at First Bull Run and Blackburn's Ford before being wounded and captured at Malvern Hill. Released in June 1862, he was made a colonel in September 1862. He fought at Gettysburg, was wounded at Lookout Mountain and was the first Union officer to enter Savannah in December 1864. He was awarded the Medal of Honor

John Gross Barnard, the Federal army's chief engineer

in 1865 and was breveted a major general. He served as New York inspector of prisons after his resignation from the army in 1866.

Barringer, Rufus
(1821-1895) Confederate general

A North Carolina-born legislator in the Whig Party, Barringer was against secession, but he went with his state and was commissioned a captain in the Confederate army in May 1861. He fought on the Peninsula, at Second Bull Run, Antietam, Fredericksburg and Chancellorsville, and was wounded at Brandy Station. Promoted to brigadier general in June 1864, he was captured at Sayler's Creek on April 3, 1865, but was released in July. He practiced law and ran a plantation after the war. Both Stonewall Jackson and D. H. Hill were his brothers-in-law.

Barry, John Decatur
(1839-1867) Confederate officer

A native of North Carolina, he enlisted in the home state regiment that later became the 18th North Carolina. Elected captain in that regiment in April 1862, he fought throughout the Seven Days' Battles of late June and early July, in the Second Bull Run Campaign in August and at Antietam in September.

E.P. Alexander, in his *Military Memoirs of a Confederate* (1907) identified Barry, by then a major, as the officer who gave the fatal order to fire on Stonewall Jackson and his retinue at dusk on May 2, 1863, during the Battle of Chancellorsville. Jackson had just completed the rout of the Federal right wing and meant to press on that night for a junction with R.E. Lee that might have led to a decisive defeat for the Army of the Potomac. Seriously wounded in the fusillade, he died eight days later.

Barry commanded the 18th North Carolina on the Gettysburg Campaign and participated in Pickett's Charge on the third day of the battle. He briefly commanded a brigade at Cold Harbor in June 1864 and again for a short time during the closing days of the war.

He edited a newspaper in Wilmington, North Carolina, during the two years that remained to him after the war.

Barry, William Farquhar
(1818-1879) Union general

Born in New York, this West Point graduate served on the frontier, in the Mexican War and in the Seminole War. He fought at

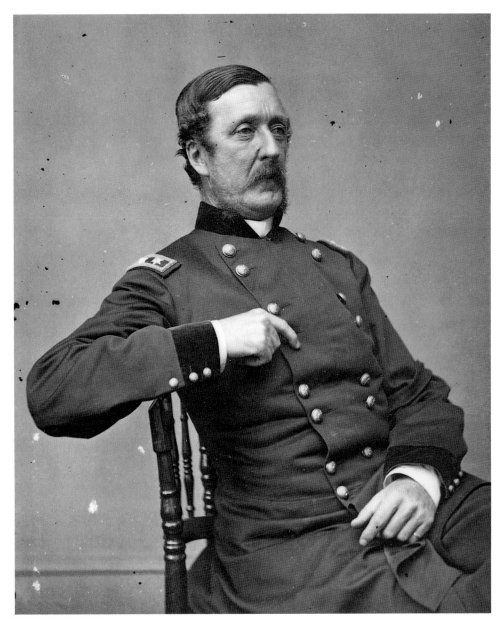

First Bull Run and was appointed a brigadier general in August 1861. He served as chief of artillery in the Peninsular Campaign and fought at Yorktown, Gaines's Mill, Mechanicsville, Charles City Crossroads, Malvern Hill and Harrison's Landing. He was chief of artillery of the defenses of Washington (1862-1864) and became W.T. Sherman's chief of artillery in March 1864. He remained in the regular army after the war and headed the army's artillery school at Fort Monroe for 10 years, dying a colonel on active duty.

Barton, Clara
(1821-1912) Humanitarian

A farmer's daughter, born near Oxford, Mass., Clara (Clarissa Harlow) Barton grew up as virtually an only child, for her next elder sibling was seven years her senior. Her public-spirited father, Stephen Barton, a veteran of Anthony Wayne's Indian campaigns, served as a selectman

William Farquhar Barry (above) and (below) John Decatur Barry

and state legislator. Her mother, Sarah Stone, and her older brothers and sisters attended to her primary education. As partial repayment, she skillfully nursed her brother David through a two-year illness, tending him day and night, almost without respite, with a toughness and stamina that would see her through many hard times on Civil War battlefields.

Independent and willful even as a girl, Barton went to work as a schoolteacher at the age of 15. For a decade she superintended a school for the children of North Oxford millhands. She studied at the Liberal Institute in Clinton, N.Y., in 1851 and, after a period of recuperation from a nervous ailment, accepted an unusual teaching position in Bordentown, N.J., for Barton offered to teach without salary for three months if the town agreed to provide, in return, a free education for all its children. The Bordentown school flourished under the Barton system. Indeed, it expanded so rapidly that the town officials decided it could no longer be entrusted to a woman's management, and when they

LEFT: Clara Barton.

BELOW: Clara Barton tended Union troops wounded in the 1861 Baltimore riots.

Washington's Armory Square Hospital was far better equipped than most of those in which Clara Barton served.

hired a male principal to supervise Barton's activities she angrily resigned.

Moving to Washington, D.C., in 1854, Barton obtained a clerkship in the U.S. Patent Office and settled in the capital. On the outbreak of Civil War in April 1861 she became one of the first volunteers to minister to the Union sick and wounded, collecting medical supplies and providing nursing care for the casualties of the 6th Massachusetts, a militia regiment caught in a riot in Baltimore as it made its way to Washington.

After the Union defeat at the First Battle of Bull Run/Manassas in July, Barton advertized in a Massachusetts newspaper for provisions for the sick and wounded, and she received such enormous quantities that she set up her own distribution agency. By July 1862 she had obtained the surgeon general's permission to work in the front lines.

Only five feet tall, frail and slightly built, with prominent features and a mass of thick brown hair, she became a familiar figure in Army of the Potomac camps and field hospitals, handing out medicines and comforts and providing nursing care. The troops soon came to call her "the angel of the battlefield."

She operated almost entirely on her own, a free lance with no connection with the private aid agencies such as the Sanitary Commission or with the army itself, though for one period she bore the semi-official title of supervisor of nurses for the Army of the James. She carried her work to Charleston, S.C., during siege operations there in 1863 and set up in Fredericksburg during Ulysses S. Grant's Wilderness and Spotsylvania campaigns in 1864.

At President Lincoln's request, Barton organized a postwar search for missing soldiers. She also lectured widely on her wartime experiences. In 1869, her health again failing, she went abroad, only to find herself caught up in the Franco-Prussian war of 1870-71. She collected and distributed supplies throughout the battle zone under the auspices of the International Red Cross of Geneva and won acclaim from both sides in the conflict.

Returning home in 1873, she launched an eight-year campaign to establish an American branch of the Red Cross. In its isolationist way, the U.S. had refused to sign the Geneva Convention, impeding efforts to establish an American branch. Barton worked tirelessly to overcome political and bureaucratic difficulties. She saw the organization into formal existence in May 1881, became its first director and remained at the head of the American Red Cross for the next 23 years.

As she always had done, Barton kept the levers of control firmly in her own hands and expended much of her considerable energy in the field, insisting on visiting the scenes of calamity herself and seeing personally to the distribution of Red Cross assistance. She went to Turkey after the Armenian massacres of 1896. She delivered supplies to Cuban war zones in 1898. At the age of 79 she spent six weeks tending the ill and homeless in Galveston, Texas, after a devastating flood there. She disliked delegating authority, still less sharing it, and earned a well-deserved reputation as a poor manager. As a result, the American Red Cross failed to grow as an organization, membership and fundraising both lagging significantly during the last years of Barton's leadership.

After a long struggle, largely over control of finances, the board of the American Red Cross finally forced Barton aside, though she fought for her perquisites almost to the last. In the end, it took an act of Congress to bring about the reorganization and reform that left her powerless and allowed the Red Cross to expand. She resigned the directorship in June 1904 and spent the last eight years of her life in Glen Echo (outside Washington), where she died, in her 91st year, on April 12, 1912.

Edward Bates (far right) attends the 1862 cabinet meeting at which Lincoln announces his Emancipation Proclamation.

Bate, William Brimage
(1826-1905) Confederate general, governor of Tennessee.

Bate, a Mexican War veteran, ardent secessionist and public servant in his native Tennessee, rose from private in the Confederate army's 2nd Tennessee to major general in four years. He was wounded three times during a career that included fighting at Shiloh, Stones River, Chattanooga and Missionary Ridge and in both the Atlanta and Franklin and Nashville campaigns. He was later a powerful Tennessee Democrat, serving as governor (1882-1886) and U.S. Senator (1886-1905).

Bates, Edward
(1793-1869) Union attorney general

Virginia-born Bates moved to St. Louis in 1814 and there became a lawyer and moderate Republican. He gained a national reputation presiding over the River and Harbor Improvement Convention in Chicago (1847) and continued thereafter at the forefront of national politics as a Free-Soil Whig; he was considered as a Republican presidential nominee in 1860. As Abraham Lincoln's attorney general (1861-1864), he proposed establishing the Mississippi naval fleet, but he eventually lost his initial influence by opposing West Virginia statehood, Union military policies and what he considered to be the erosion of constitutional rights. He resigned in November 1864 and spent his last years opposing radicals in Missouri.

Baxter, Henry
(1821-1873) Union general

Born in New York, Baxter was commissioned a captain in the Union army in August 1861 and was promoted to brigadier general in March 1863. At Fredericksburg he led a regiment that crossed the river to try to eliminate the Confederate sharpshooters and was wounded. He went on to fight at the Wilderness, Dabney's Mills and Five Forks and was wounded two more times. After the war he served as U.S. minister to Honduras (1866-1869).

Beale, Richard Lee Turberville
(1819-1893) Confederate general

A Virginia lawyer, legislator and Congressman (1847-1849), Beale joined the Confederacy's "Lee's Light Horse" in 1861 and won rapid promotions fighting in every Army of Northern Virginia campaign – including the Peninsular Campaign, Second Bull Run, Fredericksburg and Gettysburg. His repeated resignations in 1862-1863 were refused. In March 1864 his troops intercepted Ulric Dahlgren, a Union officer carrying evidence of an assassination plot against Jefferson Davis. He returned to his Virginia law practice and political career after the war.

Richard Lee Turberville Beale

Beauregard, Pierre Gustave Toutant
(1818-1893) Confederate general

Born into a prosperous old Creole family in St. Bernard Parish, Louisiana, he attended school in New Orleans, obtained a West Point cadetship and was graduated from the military academy in 1838, second in his class. Commissioned into the engineer corps, he worked on fortifications, primarily in the New Orleans area, in the early years of his career. In 1846 he went to Mexico as an engineer on General Winfield Scott's staff and was wounded at Chapultepec the following year.

Beauregard returned to engineering duties after the Mexican War, overseeing drainage works around New Orleans, navigation improvements to the mouths of the Mississippi River and the construction of the New Orleans custom house. Appointed superintendent of West Point, he served just five days (early in 1861) before his outspoken secessionist sympathies led to his recall. He resigned his U.S. commission on February 20, 1861, and accepted an appointment as a brigadier general in the Confederate army, with command of the defenses of Charleston, South Carolina.

Small, animated, of soldierly bearing and courtly manner, he became the new Confederacy's first hero as the result of his role in the assault on Fort Sumter. Before dawn, April 12, at the expiration of a surrender ultimatum, he opened the bombardment on the Federal harbor fort, forcing the garrison's capitulation some 34 hours and 4,000 shells later. The Sumter success gained him command of one of the two field armies forming in northern Virginia. On June 1 he took charge of the army assembling at Manassas, 30 miles from Washington. Beauregard received much of the credit for the Confederate victory at the Battle of First Manassas/Bull Run, leading from the front while Joseph E. Johnston, who outranked him, fed reinforcements from his own Shenandoah army into the battle. This victory of July 21 raised Beauregard higher than ever in public esteem. Jefferson Davis soon approved his promotion to full general.

Transferred to the western theater early in 1862, he served as A. S. Johnston's second in command at the Battle of Shiloh, succeeding Johnston when he fell mortally wounded on the afternoon of April 6. Beauregard actually wired news of a decisive victory to Richmond that evening, but the Federal forces under Ulysses S. Grant rallied the next day, counterattacked and

turned an apparent Confederate victory into a serious setback. Beauregard retreated to Cornith, Mississippi., where he fell victim to a siege and then to the collapse of his health. When he returned from a long sick leave, Davis removed him from the western command and reassigned him to the coastal defenses of Georgia and the Carolinas. There, his forces checked Union attacks on Charleston in 1863.

Beauregard's military reputation rested on his ability to defend static positions. Critics found him lacking in the qualities of

Pierre Gustave Toutant Beauregard

coolness, enterprise and vision necessary for success on a fluid battlefield. Nevertheless, he led his small command to an open-field victory over the Federal Army of the James at Drewry's Bluff, Virginia, in May 1864 and kept the James army bottled up in Bermuda Hundred while Grant moved down from the Rapidan. After Grant's crossing of the James in June, Beauregard conducted a successful initial defense of the strategic communications center of Peters-

burg, repulsing repeated attacks until Lee finally recognized the threat and sent the Army of Northern Virginia to his assistance. When Grant's Petersburg initiative ended in a siege, Lee absorbed Beauregard's command. Toward the war's end Beauregard returned to the West, where he became Johnston's second-in-command, serving through the Carolinas Campaign. He surrendered with Johnston in late April 1865.

After the war Beauregard turned down offers of senior commands in the Rumanian and Egyptian armies. He headed the New Orleans, Jackson & Mississippi Railway for five years, managed the Louisiana lottery and, in 1888, became commissioner of public works in New Orleans. Among his extensive writings on military affairs were *Report on the Defense of Charleston* (1864) and *A Commentary on the Campaign and Battle of Manassas* (1891).

Bee, Bernard Elliott
(1824-1861) Confederate general

Born in South Carolina, he moved with his family to Texas and obtained a West Point cadetship in 1841. Bee was graduated in 1845, fought in the Mexican War and served on the frontier throughout the 1850s. Resigning in March 1861, he entered Confederate service and took command of a brigade in Joseph E. Johnston's army in June. It was Bee who gave Thomas J. Jackson his *nom de guerre* during the First Battle of Bull Run, July 21, 1861. "Look at Jackson's brigade," he cried, "it stands like a stone wall! Rally behind the Virginians!" Wounded shortly thereafter, he died the next day.

Beecher, Henry Ward
(1813-1887) Clergyman and reformer

Brother of Harriet Beecher Stowe and himself an outspoken opponent of slavery (although he advocated allowing it to wither away in the slave states), he was probably the best-known Protestant minister of his day. During the violence that overran Kansas in 1854-59, carbines were shipped to the anti-slavery proponents in boxes marked "Bibles" to disguise their true contents. These weapons came to be known as "Beecher's Bibles" because Beecher had publicly declared that there was "more moral power in one of these in-

ABOVE: The First Battle of Bull Run.

BELOW: Henry Ward Beecher, with his sister, Harriet Beecher Stowe, the author of the novel *Uncle Tom's Cabin*.

struments so far as the slaveholders were concerned than in a hundred Bibles." Pastor of the Plymouth Congregational Church in Brooklyn, N.Y., since 1847, he became editor of the *Independent* in 1861. A series of lectures he delivered in England in 1863 is credited with doing much to gain British sympathy for the Union cause.

William Worth Bellknap

Belknap, William Worth
(1829-1890) Union general

A New York native, he was graduated from Princeton, practiced law and served in the Iowa legislature. Belknap obtained a U.S. commission in the 15th Iowa in December 1861 and fought at Shiloh, Corinth and Vicksburg. He commanded a brigade during W. T. Sherman's Atlanta Campaign. Charged with corruption as President Ulysses S. Grant's secretary of war (1869-1876), he resigned before he could be brought to trial. The charges eventually were dropped.

Bell, John
(1797-1869) Southern statesman

He was born in Nashville and became a prominent lawyer there. As a U.S. Representative (1827-1841) he at first supported Andrew Jackson; after a subsequent rift, he led the Tennessee Whigs for 20 years. He was briefly President William Henry Harrison's secretary of war (March-September 1841). His moderation alienated Southerners during his U.S. Senate career (1847-1859) and doomed his presidential candidacy on the Constitutional Union ticket in 1860. He worked to keep Tennessee in the Union, but was finally forced to recommend a Confederate alliance.

Benham, Henry Washington
(1813-1884) Union general

This Connecticut-born West Point graduate served as an army engineer in the Mexican War. In the Civil War he commanded a Union brigade in the occupation of western Virginia and later (April 1862) played a role in the capture of Fort Pulaski, Georgia. Charged with disobedience for ordering a disastrous attack at Secessionville (June 1862), he was relieved of command and his brigadier general's rank. Reappointed brigadier general (February 1863), he worked as an army engineer, and redeemed his reputation by constructing pontoon bridges during the Chancellorsville Campaign and at Franklin's Crossing. He is perhaps best remembered for building the famed James River bridge in 1864. He remained in the regular army until 1882.

Benjamin, Judah Philip
(1811-1884) Confederate statesman

Born in St. Thomas, British West Indies, the son of Jewish parents, he moved with his family to Charleston, where he attended a local academy before going north to Yale at the age of 14. He left after two years without taking a degree. Returning to the South in 1828, he accepted a job with a merchant in New Orleans. He meanwhile studied law, opened a practice and began to rise rapidly in the profession.

Benjamin's participation in the case of the brig *Creole* solidified his growing reputation. His brief, which reviewed the status of slavery under U.S. and international

The first Confederate cabinet, 1861: Judah Benjamin (4 o'clock position) was the Confederate attorney general.

law, was reprinted and widely read. For a time he ran a sugar plantation but encountered financial difficulties and soon returned to law and its near relation, politics. He served in the Louisiana legislature and in 1852 won election to the U.S. Senate as a Whig. The political crisis over slavery turned him gradually toward the Democratic party, which he formally joined in 1856.

Upon Abraham Lincoln's election to the presidency in 1860 Benjamin became one of the strongest supporters of secession. He resigned from the Senate in early February 1861 after Louisiana left the Union, and within a few weeks he accepted Jefferson Davis's offer of the Confederate States' attorney generalship. He got on well with Davis from the start, and in September 1861 Davis appointed him secretary of war, succeeding the ineffectual Leroy P. Walker. Within a few months, Benjamin had become one of the most unpopular men in the South, blamed for the Confederacy's first defeats, at Roanoke Island, North Carolina, and forts Henry and Donelson in the Kentucky-Tennessee theater.

A congressional investigating committee, in search of a scapegoat, found Benjamin responsible for the loss of Roanoke Island. Davis stood by him staunchly, easing the pressure on him slightly in early March 1862 by naming him secretary of state. Benjamin seemed to lack political in-

Judah Philip Benjamin

William Plummer Benton saw most of his Union army service in the West.

stincts, and some of his political problems were of his own making. In one famously clumsy instance he quipped that Confederate soldiers were barefoot not because the army failed to supply them with shoes but because they traded their footwear for whiskey.

Benjamin did not appear to mind being the object of almost universal dislike. He was, and remained, one of the most clear-sighted of Confederate leaders. He became one of the first to discard the hallowed Southern political principle of states' rights, recognizing that it served as a brake on the central authority's ability to wage war. States' rights policies on conscription and taxation, he argued, would lead to the Confederacy's ruin. He had no particular interest in preserving the institution of slavery: in 1864 he campaigned in favor of educating slaves, drafting them into the Confederate military forces and sending them into combat. In return, slave veterans would be granted their freedom.

The proposal outraged most Southerners. "If we didn't go to war to save our slaves what did we go to war for?" Senator Robert Hunter asked. In January 1865 Benjamin sent a diplomatic emissary to England to offer general emancipation in return for British intervention and the raising of the Federal blockade. But the offer came too late, and the Confederacy's last diplomatic gambit ended in failure. As for Benjamin, he narrowly survived censure by congress, the Confederate senate dividing evenly in February on the resolution that he had not been "a wise and prudent Secretary of State."

It hardly mattered by then. Benjamin lasted in office as long as Robert E. Lee did, fleeing south with Davis in April 1865. He took leave of the presidential party in Charlotte, North Carolina, and made good his escape to England. Penniless, he studied for the English bar and supported himself with journalism, specializing in articles on international relations. His Lincoln's Inn colleagues waived the three-year rule and admitted him to practice in June 1866, after only five months of study. He gradually built a successful practice, which he continued until failing health forced his retirement in 1883. He died in Paris the following year.

Benning, Henry Lewis
(1814-1875) Confederate general

A Georgian, Benning was for 40 years a Columbus, Georgia, lawyer and legislator. An early and extreme secessionist, he attended the Nashville Convention in 1850 and his state's secession convention; on the Georgia supreme court (1853-1859) he ruled the state and federal supreme courts to be "coordinate and co-equal." In his Civil War career he fought with distinction, if not brilliance, throughout the war, after April 1863 as a brigadier general. "Old Rock" led a brigade at Antietam, Fredericksburg, Gettysburg, Chickamauga and the Wilderness, where he was seriously wounded. He recovered to fight at Petersburg and Appomattox. Fort Benning, Georgia, is named after him.

Benton, William Plummer
(1828-1867) Union general

Maryland-born, he was a judge and lawyer when he was commissioned a colonel in the Union army and fought from April until August 1861. Mustered out, he re-enlisted in September 1861 and fought under General John Frémont in Missouri and Kansas. He was appointed a brigadier general in April 1862 and fought at Pea Ridge and Vicksburg. He went on to serve in Tennessee, the Gulf, southeast Missouri and Baton Rouge. He was breveted a major general March 1865.

Berdan, Hiram
(?1823-1893) Union officer

This New York-born mechanical engineer was known as the best rifle shot in the country long before the Civil War. He also invented a repeating rifle. Commissioned a colonel of the 1st U.S. Sharpshooters in November 1861, he was breveted a brigadier general after Chancellorsville and a major general after Gettysburg. Having antagonized many who had dealings with him – he was regarded as "unscrupulous" – he resigned January 2, 1864. He went on to develop much new military technology.

Bickerdyke, Mary Ann Ball
(1817-1901)
Sanitary Commission worker

As an Illinois widow supporting three children, she began to practice "botanic" medicine in 1859. At the onset of the war she began ministering to Illinois volunteers. "Mother" Bickerdyke worked throughout the war, evacuating the wounded from Fort Donelson, then running field hospitals with Ulysses S. Grant's army in Tennessee and Mississippi and with W. T. Sherman's in the Chattanooga and Atlanta campaigns. Resourceful and efficient, she set up army laundries and tirelessly nursed, foraged and cooked through 19 battles. Her colorful personality and Northern fundraising tours made her the most famous Sanitary Commission worker of the war. She later engaged in charitable ventures in San Francisco before retiring to Kansas with a Congressional pension in 1887.

Mary Ann Ball Bickerdyke

Birney, David Bell
(1825-1864) Union general

Son of a prominent abolitionist, he became a Philadelphia lawyer. In response to the looming crisis, in 1860 he studied military manuals and joined the militia; in 1861 he raised a Pennsylvania regiment. He led a brigade in the Peninsular and Second Bull Run campaigns. Succeeding Philip Kearny's division command, he then fought at Fredericksburg and Chancellorsville. At Gettysburg he assumed command of III Corps after General Daniel Sickles was wounded. He died from the effects of malaria the following year.

Birney, James Gillespie
(1792-1857) Abolitionist leader

Born in Kentucky, he practiced law there and in Alabama and began working to restrict slavery and the slave trade. Back in Kentucky in 1832 he became ever more outspoken in his opposition to slavery, and in 1836 he founded an abolitionist newspaper, the *Philanthropist*. In 1840 and 1844 he was the presidential candidate for the abolitionist Liberty Party.

William Birney

Birney, William
(1819-1907) Union general

Born in Alabama, he was active in the revolution of 1848 while in France and was made a professor at Bourges. Like his father, James G. Birney, he was fervently opposed to slavery. Commissioned a captain in the Union army in May 1861, he fought at First and Second Bull Run, Chantilly and Fredericksburg, and he helped the Union to regain parts of Florida in 1864. He also helped to raise seven African-American regiments that went to the field. Breveted a major general and mustered out in August 1865, he served as attorney for the District of Columbia after the war.

Blackwell, Elizabeth
(1821-1910) Physician

The first-ever woman medical school graduate (Geneva College, New York, 1849), this Englishwoman helped to found a women's infirmary (1857) and medical college (1868) in New York. Her initiative in organizing women's relief work in 1861 led to the establishment of the Sanitary Commission; she trained Union nurses throughout the Civil War. She lived in England after 1869, retiring in 1876. Her promotion of sanitation and preventive medicine were important contributions to public health.

Elizabeth Blackwell

Blair, Francis Preston Jr.
(1821-1875)
Union statesman and general

Kentucky-born Blair organized the Free-Soil (1848) and Republican parties in Missouri and achieved national prominence as a Unionist orator, as a state legislator and as a U.S. Congressman in the 1850s. He saved Missouri and Kentucky for the Union by seizing the St. Louis arsenal in May 1861.

Blair participated in the Yazoo expedition, Vicksburg and, as a major general and corps commander, the Chattanooga and Atlanta campaigns. He turned Democrat after opposing Reconstruction policies and was a U.S. Senator (Missouri, 1871-1873).

Blair, Montgomery
(1813-1883)
Lawyer, Union postmaster general

Son of a prominent political leader, Francis P. Blair, he was graduated from West Point (1835) but resigned his commission in 1836 to become a lawyer. A moderate on the slavery question, he represented Dred Scott in the Supreme Court. Having become a Republican, he was named postmaster general by President Lincoln and organized the army's postal system during the Civil War. Suspect because of his Southern and Democratic past, he was forced out of office in 1864 by more radical Republicans; after the war he went back to the Democratic Party. The Blair family home, across from the White House, was purchased by the U.S. government in 1942 and is now used to house high-ranking foreign visitors.

Blenker, Louis
(1812-1863) **Union general**

Born in Germany, Blenker participated in the 1848 revolution and was forced to leave Germany, coming to the United States in 1849. He was commissioned a colonel in the Union Army in 1861, and his regiment covered the Union retreat at First Bull Run. He was appointed a brigadier general in 1861, and in March 1862 he led a division of German brigades in a difficult six-week march from George McClellan's Army of the Potomac command to join John Frémont in West Virginia, subsequently

ABOVE: Louis Blenker (left center), leader of German-American Troops.

BELOW: Francis Preston Blair, Jr., has been credited with saving Missouri and Kentucky for the Union.

taking part in several battles in the Shenandoah Campaign of 1862. Discharged on March 31, 1863, he died on October 31, 1863, of injuries he sustained from an earlier fall from his horse.

Blunt, James Gilpatrick
(1826-1881) Union general

This Maine-born doctor practiced in Ohio and then moved on to a political career in Kansas, where he was a supporter of John Brown. Appointed a lieutenant colonel in the Union army in July 1861, he was promoted to major general in November 1862. He fought successfully with the Army of the Frontier at Cane Hill and Prairie Grove, captured Fort Van Buren and then suffered a sharp defeat at Baxter Springs. He beat back Sterling Price's Raid in Missouri, ending the Confederate threat in the West. He was mustered out in July 1865.

Bonham, Milledge Luke
(1813-1890) Confederate general

Born in South Carolina, Bonham fought in the Seminole War and in the Mexican War. A lawyer by training, he was named to Congress as a states-rights Democrat to finish out the term of his cousin, Preston Brooks. He chose to serve under General P. G. T. Beauregard in the initial firing at Fort Sumter, was appointed a brigadier general in the Confederate army in April

Milledge Luke Bonham

1861 and fought at Fairfax, Centreville, Vienna and First Bull Run. He resigned in January 1862 to serve as governor of South Carolina (1862-1864). He was reappointed brigadier general on February 20, 1865, to serve under General Joseph Johnston until the surrender. After the war he was a Democratic politician, legislator and railroad commissioner.

Bonneville, Benjamin Louis Eulalie de
(1796-1878) Union officer, explorer

French-born, he was brought to the U.S.A. as a child. He was a West Point graduate (1815) and became publicly known for his western exploratory expedition (1831-1836); his journal was later used by Washington Irving to write *The Adventures of Captain Bonneville* (1843). He fought in the Mexican War, retired from active duty in September 1861 due to disabilities but continued to command recruiting and mustering activities in Missouri throughout the war. He was a breveted brigadier general and served until 1866.

Booth, John Wilkes
(1838-1865) Lincoln's assassin

He was born and raised on a farm near Bel Air, Maryland, one of a large family. An active child, good-looking, athletic and adventurous, Booth received an irregular

Benjamin Louis Bonneville

John Wilkes Booth

From the outbreak of the Civil War, Booth was a zealous Southern sympathizer and a great supporter of slavery, though he made no effort to enlist in the Confederate army and fight for his beliefs. He viewed the war as a simple struggle between freedom and tyranny; Edwin Booth thought him "insane" on the subject. By 1864 Booth had hatched a plot to kidnap President Lincoln and carry him away to Richmond, where he could be held hostage to force a successful end to the war.

His acting now took second place to conspiracy. He recruited two former Confederate soldiers and a onetime Roman Catholic seminarian, John Surratt, who had been a dispatch rider for the Confederacy. Surratt's mother, Mary, kept a boarding house in Washington, and it provided an occasional meeting place for the conspirators. By early 1865 he had recruited three more men, including Lewis T. Powell, also known as Payne, a near-destitute Confederate veteran of the Battle of Gettysburg.

The conspirators planned a March 20 abduction of Lincoln as he drove to the Soldier's Home on Washington's outskirts, but the president failed to turn up. Fearing the authorities had found them out, the group separated. In early April, Robert E. Lee surrendered the Army of Northern Virginia, effectively ending the war and making the notion of kidnapping Lincoln irrelevant. Booth decided instead to kill him.

He learned at midday on April 14 that Lincoln was to attend a performance of the English farce *Our American Cousin* at Ford's Theatre that evening. He assigned two remaining members of his band the tasks of killing Vice President Andrew Johnson and Secretary of State William Seward. Booth himself entered the presidential box shortly after 10 p.m., raised his pistol and shot Lincoln in the head. He leaped down from the box on to the stage, shouting "*Sic temper tyrannis!* The South is avenged!" He broke his left leg in the fall but managed to escape the theater and flee the city. Johnson was not attacked, but Powell (a.k.a. Payne) assaulted and seriously injured Seward. Lincoln died on the morning of April 15.

Booth evaded capture for nearly two weeks. Dr. Samuel Mudd, a Maryland physician, set his broken leg. He crossed into Virginia on April 23. Early on the 26th his pursuers trapped him in a barn. When he refused to surrender they set the barn on fire. A shot rang out. Pulled mortally wounded from the burning barn, Booth died a few hours later.

education and preferred passing the day with Chesapeake Bay watermen to going to school. Stage-struck like others in his family, he made his acting debut at age 17 at the St. Charles Theater in Baltimore.

In 1857-58 Booth played minor roles at the Arch Street Theater in Philadelphia, where his failure to learn his parts adequately made him unpopular with audiences. He soon achieved distinction, however, especially in Shakespearean roles. In 1860, on tours of the South, the Southwest and finally the North, he became an acknowledged star.

He acted in Boston and Washington, D.C., in 1862-63, and his reputation rose steadily. Even his brother, Edwin Booth, a much more famous actor, saluted him as one of America's great young stage talents. His repertoire included *Richard III*, in which he played a realistic and widely admired royal death scene, *Hamlet*, *Romeo and Juliet* and popular favorites such as *The Robbers* and *The Corsican Brothers*.

John Wilkes Booth murders Lincoln in Fords' Theatre, April 14, 1865

His accomplices were quickly rounded up. Four of them, including Mary Surratt, were convicted of conspiracy by a military tribunal and hanged. Mudd received a sentence of life imprisonment. (He was later pardoned.) Though the government claimed Booth had been in conspiracy with Jefferson Davis and the Confederate government, no evidence of such a link was ever found.

A poster offering rewards for the capture of Booth and two others

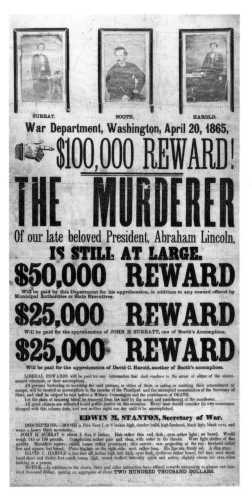

Boyd, Belle
(1844-1900) Confederate spy

Born Isabelle Boyd in Martinsburg, Virginia (now West Virginia), she attended Mount Washington Female College in Baltimore and was in due course formally presented to Washington, D.C. society. Returning to Martinsburg at the outbreak of the war, she traded on her considerable presence to elicit military information from occupying Union soldiers and pass it to the Confederates. Her charm was such that when she shot and killed an abusive Union soldier there was no question of her being punished for the act. As a courier to P. G. T. Beauregard and T. J. Jackson after autumn 1861, she was especially useful for her equestrian skill and intimate knowledge of the local terrain. She became a Confederate heroine in May 1862 by signalling Jackson's troops to accelerate their advance to save the bridges at Front Royal. Three times arrested, she escaped to England carrying Confederate dispatches in 1864 and was again captured. She subsequently married her captor, Union Lieutenant Samuel Wylde Hardinge, Jr., in London. He died soon afterward, and to support herself she wrote a dramatic (and unreliable) account of her espionage career (1865) and became an actress. Making her stage debut in Manchester, England, in 1866, she then toured the U.S. until she remarried in 1869. She took to the stage again after her third marriage in 1886, when, once again in financial straits, she began presenting popular dramatic recitals of her wartime adventures. She died while on tour.

Bradley, Amy Morris
(1823-1904)
Educator, Sanitary Commission worker

A New England teacher, she joined the 5th Maine as a nurse at First Bull Run, then

supervised Sanitary Commission hospital ships throughout the Peninsular Campaign. After December 1862 she transformed Camp Distribution, a squalid convalescent camp near Alexandria, Virginia, into a clean, efficient operation and edited the *Soldiers' Journal*, which disseminated practical information to Federal troops. She later established schools for the poor in Wilmington, North Carolina, and retired in 1891.

ABOVE: Mathew B. Brady, the world's first great war photographer.

OPPOSITE TOP: Belle Boyd, perhaps the most famous Southern spy.

OPPOSITE BOTTOM: Mathew Brady in the field (wearing straw hat).

Brady, Mathew B.
(1823-1896) Photographer

Established as a New York portrait photographer by 1843, he early worked in daguerreotype, publishing the *Gallery of Illustrious Americans* (1850) and winning numerous international prizes. He adopted the new photographic wetplate technology in the mid-1850s and opened a successful Washington, D.C., studio in 1858. Early in the Civil War he sought Lincoln's authorization to photograph camp and battle scenes. Accompanying Federal troops with cumbersome wetplate cameras, often at great personal risk, Brady and his assistants compiled a documentary record of 3500 photographs that preserves some of our most enduring and valuable images of the conflict. His career collapsed after the war, and he died in poverty.

Braxton Bragg

Bragg, Braxton
(1817-1876) Confederate general

Bragg, a North Carolinian, was graduated from West Point in 1837, fought in the Seminole War and saw distinguished service in Mexico, where he won acclaim for the performance of his battery at Buena Vista in February 1847. He resigned from the army in 1856 to become a planter in Louisiana.

Appointed a brigadier general in the Confederate army in February 1861, he commanded the coastal defenses between Mobile and Pensacola. He helped Albert Sidney Johnston reoranize the Army of Tennessee in northern Mississippi in the early spring of 1862 and led Johnston's right wing at Shiloh in April. Promoted to full general shortly after the battle, he took charge of the Army of Tennessee in June. In late August, Bragg launched his invasion of Kentucky, with the political aim of drawing the state into the Confederacy. After the drawn battles of Perryville (October 1862) and Stones River (December 1862-January 1863) he withdrew to Tullahoma, the campaign a failure.

Federal forces under William J. Rosecrans maneuvered Bragg out of Tullahoma, and then out of Chattanooga, in the summer of 1863. Bragg attacked Rosecrans along Chickamauga Creek on September 19 and 20, driving the Federals back to Chattanooga with heavy losses. This was potentially a great victory, but Bragg failed to exploit his initial advantage. Instead of pressing the attack, he drew his army up into the hills above Chattanooga and besieged the city.

U.S. Grant reopened a supply line into Chattanooga in October and launched a breakout attempt on November 23. Two days later the Confederate center on Missionary Ridge collapsed, forcing Bragg to retreat into north Georgia. Joseph E. Johnston relieved him of command of the Army of Tennessee on December 2.

Bragg's difficult personality compounded his lack of battlefield success. Irritable, disputatious, dyspeptic, he made many enemies among the senior officers and inspired little affection in the ranks. Senior subordinates such as James Longstreet, D. H. Hill and William Hardee had no confidence in him. "The tone of the army among its higher officers toward the commander was the worst conceivable," Longstreet's aide, G. Moxley Sorrel, wrote of the period after Chickamauga. "Bragg was the subject of hatred and contempt, and it was almost openly so expressed."

Bragg served as an adviser to President Jefferson Davis through most of 1864. He returned to the field toward the war's end and fought his last battle against W. T. Sherman's forces in North Carolina in March 1865. He joined Davis in his attempt to escape Union forces; taken prisoner on May 9, he was paroled shortly thereafter.

He worked as a civil engineer in Texas and Alabama after the war, served a four-year term as Alabama's commissioner of public works and supervised a harbor improvement scheme at Mobile. He died in Galveston, Texas.

Branch, Lawrence O'Bryan
(1820-1862) Confederate general

Born into a well-to-do family in North Carolina, of which state his uncle was the governor, he became a journalist, lawyer and Democratic Congressman before the war. He had initially been an advocate of moderation in the South, but he joined the secessionists and enlisted in the Confederate army. He served as quartermaster and paymaster of the North Carolina troops and was made a brigadier general in November 1861. He fought at Hanover Courthouse, in the Seven Days' Battles and at Second Bull Run and Harpers Ferry. He was killed at Antietam.

Brannan, John Milton
(1819-1892) Union general

Born in Washington, D.C., Brannan was a West Point graduate who served on the frontier and in the Mexican and Seminole wars. Appointed a Union brigadier general in September 1861, he fought at Pocotaligo, Hoover's Gap and Chickamauga; led the St. John's River expedition; was chief of artillery for the Army of the Cumberland; and was at Mission Ridge, Dalton, Resaca, Dalls, Kenesaw Mountain, Chattahoochee, Peach Tree Creek, Atlanta and Jonesboro. He remained in the regular army until his retirement in 1888.

Breckinridge, John Cabell
(1821-1875) Confederate general and secretary of war.

He was born near Lexington, Kentucky, into a politically powerful Deomcratic family. After graduation from Centre College and studying law at Transylvania University, he practiced law in Iowa and Kentucky. He joined the 3rd Kentucky Volunteers too late to fight in the Mexican war and returned to Kentucky to begin a political career. As a U.S. representative (1851-1855), he established a national reputation with his funeral oration for Henry Clay (1852). He was President James Buchanan's vice president (1857-18610 and ran against Abraham Lincoln in 1860 as the candidate of the breakaway Southern Democrats. In the U.S. Senate (March-September 1861) he unsuccessfully promoted compromise, then helped to organize Kentucky's provisional Confederate government. He joined the Confederate army as a brigadier general in November 1861. Natural leadership outweighing his inexperience, Breckinridge commanded the reserve corps with distinction at Shiloh and, promoted to major general, led a division at Stones River. He fought in the Vicksburg Campaign, unsuccessfully attacked Baton Rouge and fortified Port Hudson. He later commanded divisions at Chickamauga and Missionary

John Cabell Breckenridge

Ridge. Summoned to the Shenandoah Valley, he fought at Cold Harbor. In Jubal Early's Washington Raid in the summer of 1864 he fought at Martinsburg and Monocacy. He served as the Confederate secretary of war after February 1865 and advised J. E. Johnston during surrender negotiations. He returned from foreign exile in 1868 and resumed his Lexington law practice and developed railroads.

Breckinridge, Margaret E.
(?1832-1864)
Sanitary Commission worker

Born in New Jersey, she came from a family divided between Confederate and Union sympathies, her most notable relation being to her cousin, Confederate General John Breckinridge. She was an agent with the Sanitary Commission and a nurse from 1862, serving under Ulysses S. Grant. She also ran a boat carrying aid between St. Louis and Vicksburg. She died in July 1864 from exhaustion and typhoid fever.

Margaret E. Breckenridge

Brooke, John Mercer
(1826-1904) **Confederate naval officer**

This Florida-born Annapolis graduate became the Navy's chief of ordnance and hydrography; he invented a deep-sea sounding device used to map the topography of the ocean's bottom. Joining the Confederate navy, he helped in the reconstruction of the USS *Merrimack* into the ironclad vessel CSS *Virginia*. He was also known for his invention of the Brooke Gun, a rifled cannon shaped like the Parrott gun but differing in its reinforcing band of iron rings. After the war Brooke taught at the Virginia Military Institute.

Brooke, John Rutter
(1838-1926) **Union general**

He joined the Union's infamous 4th Pennsylvania Infantry in 1861, which claimed its discharge and returned home rather than fight at First Bull Run. Brooke re-enlisted and fought in the Peninsular Campaign, Antietam, Fredericksburg, Chancellorsville, Gettysburg, the Wilderness, Spotsylvania and Cold Harbor, there sustaining

wounds that ended his field career. In the regular army, after 1866, he served in the Spanish-American war, commanded the Department of the east and retired as a major general in 1902.

Preston Brooks

Brooks, Preston
(1819-1857)
South Carolina Representative

He was a Democratic member of the House of Representatives (1853-57) when, in 1856, Senator Charles Sumner of Massachusetts, an impassioned anti-slavery proponent, delivered a speech in the Senate that criticized Brooks's uncle, Senator Andrew P. Butler of South Carolina. Two days later (May 22) Brooks came upon Sumner seated at his desk in the Senate and beat him severely with his cane. Sumner was so seriously injured that it was over three years before he could return to take his seat in the Senate.

Brooks, William Thomas Harbaugh
(1821-1870) **Union general**

An Ohio-born West Point graduate, Brooks fought in the Indian wars and under Robert E. Lee in the Mexican War. He fought with the Army of the Potomac in the Peninsular, Antietam and Rappahannock campaigns, commanded the District of the Monongahela (June 1863-April 1864), led a division at Cold Harbor and Drewry's Bluff and X Corps at Petersburg, before resigning in ill-health in June 1864. He farmed in Alabama after the war.

Brown, John
(1800-1859) Abolitionist

He was born in Torrington, Connecticut, into a family with a history of mental instability: Brown's mother died insane when he was only 8 years old. His father, an itinerant handyman and jack of several trades, supported the abolition cause and worked for a time on the underground railroad. He moved often in John's early years, finally settling in Hudson, Ohio.

Brown absorbed a little learning in the Hudson school, took up the trade of tanner and married Dianthe Lusk in 1820; the couple had seven children before she died in 1831. Less than a year later he married again, a 16-year-old named Mary Anne

John Brown (below) and (opposite) *en route* to his execution

Day. They produced 13 more children over the following 21 years.

He set up a tannery in Richmond, Pennsylvania, in 1825 but could not settle down. He moved some 10 times over the next three decades, pursuing various vocations, including shepherd, land speculator and farmer. He failed at everything he tried. Beset by lawsuits, he turned away from his own affairs to ponder larger issues, especially, and obsessively, slavery.

By the early 1850s he was indulging in visions of slave insurrections. Long an abolitionist like his father, he now began to dream of setting up a mountain base from which runaway slaves and their white sympathizers could sortie for terror raids against the slaveowners. In May 1855, responding to calls from several of his sons who had emigrated to Kansas, he went west to join the fight for free soil.

Brown arrived with a wagonload of weapons and settled in Osawatomie, Kansas, where, in the spring of 1856, he planned retaliation for the sacking of Lawrence by pro-slavery bands. In May, Brown and his sons carried out the cold-blooded murder of five Kansan settlers thought to be pro-slavery.

He returned east in the autumn of 1856. Old acquaintances thought he looked old, won, slightly deranged; the found him monomaniacal on the subject of slavery., "With an eye like a snake, he looks like a demon," the widow of one of the murdered men said of him. Nevertheless, respectable abolition circles embraced Brown. Emerson called him "a pure idealist of artless goodness," Several prominent Massachusetts abolitionists, the so-called "Secret Six," supplied him with money, arms and moral support, and he began recruiting men to join him in fomenting a slave uprising.

"One man and God can overturn the universe," Brown said. He chose the U.S. arsenal at Harpers Ferry, Virginia, as his first target. Renting a farm a few miles away, he laid final plans for the raid and assembled a band of 21 accomplices. He set out on the evening of October 16. The first casualty was the bridge watchman on the Baltimore & Ohio railroad – a free black, as it happened. Brown's little army took possession of the Harpers Ferry arsenal and seized several hostages, including one slaveholder.

Word of the raid spread quickly, and by midday of October 17 militia forces arrived and drove Brown's guerrillas into the shelter of the armory buildings. A detachment of U.S. Marines under Army Lt. Col. Robert E. Lee marched into Harpers Ferry that night and stormed the arsenal the next morning. Ten of the raiders were killed; Brown, slightly wounded, was captured and taken to Charles Town, Virginia, to be tried for treason.

"I believe that to have interfered as I have done, in behalf of His despised poor, is no wrong, but right," Brown told the Virginia court. He was convicted anyway, and sentenced to be hanged. On December 2, 1859, he rode in a wagon atop his own oak coffin to the scaffold outside Charles Town. He seemed to welcome his martyrdom. "I John Brown am now quite certain that the crimes of this guilty land will never be purged away but with blood," he wrote in a note to his jailer. Upon his death he became a saint to many Northern abolitionists and a demon to almost all Southerners. The blood purge he had foretold began at Fort Sumter, 17 months later.

Brown, Joseph Emerson
(1821-1894)
Confederate governor of Georgia

Born in South Carolina and educated at the Yale Law School, Brown was a Georgia legislator and judge. As a secessionist governor of Georgia (1857-1865) he reformed the militia and seized forts Pulaski and Jackson (January 1861) and the Augusta arsenal. A strong states' rights advocate, he opposed Jefferson Davis's centralization of the Confederate government. Georgians denounced his short-lived Republicanism during Reconstruction as opportunistic but later elected him U.S. Senator (Democrat, 1880-1891).

Brownell, Kady
(b.1842) Vivandière

The daughter of a British soldier, she was born in South Africa. She accompanied her American husband to war carrying the regimental colors and, wearing trousers under her skirts, fighting alongside the men. She fought with her husband's Rhode Island regiments at First Bull Run and New Bern. General Ambrose Burnside signed her discharge, and she received an army pension. Her last years were spent in poverty and obscurity.

Brownlow, William Gannaway
(1805-1877)
Tennessee Unionist and governor

A Virginia-born itinerant preacher, Brownlow became an influential Tennessee newspaperman, eventually editing the state's premier Whig journal, *Knoxville Whig* (1849-61). He supported slavery but joined the eastern Tennessee Unionists in 1861. Briefly imprisoned by the Confederates for treason in 1861-1862, he was a vocal Unionist lecturer, throughout the war. He was later Tennessee's Republican governor (1865-1869) and U.S. Senator (1869-1875).

Buchanan, Franklin
(1800-1874) Confederate admiral

Born in Maryland, Buchanan served in the U.S. Navy and helped to plan the U.S. Naval Academy under Navy Secretary George Bancroft in 1845. He served in the Mexican War, and went with Commodore Matthew Perry's expedition to China and Japan (1852-1855). He headed the Washington Navy Yard from 1859 to 1861. He resigned from the U.S. Navy in 1861 and accepted a commission as a captain in the Confederate navy, taking command of

the Chesapeake Bay Station in 1862. He was in command of the CSS *Virginia* – the rebuilt USS *Merrimac* – and was wounded in the course of capturing the USS *Congress*. In the Battle of Mobile Bay in August 1864 he was in command of the Confederate squadron that was defeated by Admiral Farragut: he was wounded in the action. He became president of Maryland State Agricultural College after the war.

Buchanan, James
(1791-1868)
15th president of the United States

After graduation from Dickinson College, he established a successful law practice in his native Pennsylvania and launched a Democratic political career. He sat in the U.S. House (1821-1831) and Senate (1834-1845) and served as U.S. secretary of state

Kady Brownell

James Buchanan

(1844-1849, negotiating the treaty ending the Mexican War); he was minister to Russia (1831-1834) and Great Britain (1852-1856). A states' rights advocate who nevertheless opposed secession, he was elected U.S. president in 1856 on a platform of conciliation. His indecisiveness when Fort Sumter was threatened and Southern states seceded left his successor, Abraham Lincoln, facing imminent war upon his inauguration in 1861. Buchanan was, however, a vocal Union advocate throughout the war.

Buckner, Simon Bolivar
(1823-1914) Confederate general

A farmer's son, born in Kentucky, he was graduated from West Point in 1844, taught at the academy, and fought in Mexico in 1846 and 1847. He saw frontier duty in the Minnesota and Arkansas territories before resigning from the army in 1855 to go into business.

Buckner did well in real estate and construction in Chicago. He moved to Louisville in 1858, where he continued to build the small fortune he had started in the North. Though he was not politically active, he drafted a militia bill which the Kentucky legislature adopted in March 1860. At the same time, the legislators appointed Buckner inspector general of state forces with the rank of major general.

By early 1861 he had raised, trained and

armed a militia of 61 companies. In May the state issued a declaration of neutrality in the Civil War, and Buckner negotiated a sort of non-belligerent agreement with George McClellan, who commanded Federal troops north of the Ohio River. The agreement fell apart after a few weeks. Buckner resigned his militia command in July, though at first he declined a commission in the Confederate army. When Confederate forces occupied Columbus, Kentucky, he urged the Confederates to withdraw; he also opposed the Kentucky legislature's decision to abandon the state's policy of neutrality.

With Kentucky drawn into the war, Buckner moved to obtain a brigadier general's appointment in the Confederate army. Sent to Fort Donelson in Tennessee early in 1862, he succeeded to command there when the two ranking officers fled their posts after being brought under siege by Ulysses S. Grant. When Grant called on Buckner to surrender, he asked for terms. He and Grant had been friends in the old army and Buckner expected favorable treatment. But Grant demanded unconditional surrender. Though this surprised and angered Buckner, he had no choice in the matter. The Federals held him prisoner until August, when he was exchanged.

He led an infantry division during Braxton Bragg's invasion of Kentucky and saw action at Perryville in October. At the year's end Jefferson Davis sent him to Mobile to strengthen that port city's defenses. He returned to Bragg's army in time to command a corps at Chickamauga. He afterward commanded the Department of Louisiana, and he helped negotiate the surrender of the transmississippi armies in May 1865.

Buckner settled in New Orleans after the war and became head of an insurance company there in 1866. Returning to Kentucky in 1868, he edited the Louisville *Courier* and became active in Democratic politics, serving as governor of the state from 1887 to 1891.

Buckner kept up a long friendship with Grant, despite their unhappy encounter at Fort Donelson: he was a pallbearer at Grant's funeral. He died in January 1914, the last of the high-ranking Confederate generals. His son Simon Bolivar Buckner Jr. was killed commanding the 10th Army at Okinawa in 1945.

Buell, Don Carlos
(1818-1898 Union general

Born in Ohio and raised in Indiana, Buell was graduated from West Point in 1841 and reported to the 3rd Infantry as a second lieutenant. He saw service in the Seminole War in Florida and fought in Mexico – at Monterey, Contreras and Churubusco – in 1846 and 1847.

Appointed a brigadier general of volunteers in May 1861, Buell helped organize the Army of the Potomac and commanded an infantry division under George McClellan. In November, succeeding William T. Sherman, he took command of the Department of the Ohio, with responsibility for organizing and training a new field army.

Buell's task was to advance into east Tennessee, a stronghold of Union sentiment and therefore of particular political interest to President Lincoln. As Ulysses S. Grant moved on forts Henry and Donelson, Buell advanced with the 50,000-man Army of the Ohio to Bowling Green, Kentucky, and then into central Tennessee. He occupied Nashville without a battle on February 24, 1862.

Buell received orders in March to advance south to Savannah, on the Ten-

Don Carlos Buell

Simon Bolivar Buckner

ABOVE: Buell took Nashville in 1862.

RIGHT: Abraham Buford.

nessee River, and his leading division arrived in time to save Grant from a possible defeat during the first day of the Battle of Shiloh, April 6. His reinforcements on the second day forced the Confederate retreat south to Corninth.

He marched east in July and August, repairing the railroad as he went, but could not reach Chattanooga before Braxton Bragg's Army of Tennessee occupied the place. He responded to the Confederate invasion of eastern Kentucky by falling back all the way to Louisville. On October 8, at Perryville, he engaged Bragg's army and fought a drawn battle. Buell was relieved of command when he failed to pursue the retreating Confederates aggressively. William Rosecrans replaced him on October 30.

A military commission investigated Buell's conduct but made no recommendations. He remained in limbo for more than a year, "awaiting orders" in Indianapolis, before the government discharged him as a major general of volunteers in May 1864. He resigned his regular army commission the following month.

Buell, whose reputation as a good military organizer survived the wreck of his career, may have been a victim of his association with McClellan. He was viewed as opposed to the Lincoln administration, and even Grant's recommendation could not convince the government to restore him to duty.

Buell settled in Kentucky after the war. He headed a mining concern and worked as a pension agent in Louisville in the 1880s. He died at Rockport, Kentucky.

Buford, Abraham
(1826-1894) Confederate general

A Kentucky native, Buford was graduated from West Point in 1841. He served on the frontier and fought in Mexico. He resigned in 1854 to raise cattle and horses in Kentucky. Entering the Confederate army in September 1862, he fought at Stones River and commanded a cavalry brigade under N. B. Forrest. He returned to horsebreeding after the war. The death of his wife and his son, coupled with a series of financial setbacks, led Buford to take his own life.

John Buford

Buford, John
(1826-1863) Union general

A Kentucky native, he was graduated from West Point in 1848 and saw extensive service on the frontier during the 1850s. Buford took charge of a Union cavalry brigade at the outset of the Second Bull Run Campaign in August 1862 and proved a first-rate cavalry commander. He led the cavalry screen that intercepted Confederate forces moving toward Gettysburg on July 1, 1863. Buford's decision to hold McPherson Ridge until Federal infantry could arrive both precipitated the great Gettysburg battle of July 1-3 and helped to secure its favorable outcome for the Union. He came down with typhoid fever in the autumn on 1863 and died from its effects on December 16.

Bulloch, James Dunwoody
(1823-1901) Confederate naval officer

This Georgian served in the U.S. Navy from 1839 to 1854, resigning to command a mail service steamer. As a wartime Confederate naval agent, he served in England and France outfitting such raiders as the *Alabama*, *Florida*, *Shenandoah* and *Stonewall*. After the war he stayed in Liverpool, England, as a cotton merchant. In later years he wrote a book about the Confederacy's secret foreign service (1894).

Burnett, Henry Lawrence
(1838-1916) Union officer

This Ohio lawyer enlisted in the Union army in 1861 and fought in Missouri and Kentucky. In 1863 he became judge advo-cate of the Department of the Ohio. He prosecuted the white-supremacist Knights of the Golden Circle in Indiana, Chicago conspirators to free Confederate prisoners at Camp Douglas and Abraham Lincoln's assassins. In later life he was a prominent Republican strategist, a Cincinnati and New York lawyer and a federal district attorney.

Burns, John Lawrence
(1793-1872)
"The Old Hero of Gettysburg"

An ageing veteran of the War of 1812 and the Seminole and Mexican wars. Burns persistently tried to enlist with the Federals at the beginning of the Civil War. Repeatedly rejected, he doggedly accompanied the army as a teamster until he was sent home to Gettysburg, Pennsylvania, and appointed to the local constabulary. He joined in the fighting as a sharpshooter on all three days of the Battle of Gettysburg and was wounded three times. He became a folk hero, and Congress eventually voted him a pension.

Burnside, Ambrose Everett
(1824-1881) Union general

Born in Liberty, Indiana, and raised there in modest circumstances, he received an adequate education in the village seminary but could not afford to go on to college. He was working as a tailor's apprentice when his father won election to the Indiana senate and, through political influence, obtained a West Point appointment for him. He was graduated in 1847, 18th in a class of 38 cadets.

Burnside saw routine duty on the frontier and served in the garrison of Fort Adams, Rhode Island, before resigning in 1853 to open a factory for the production of a breechloading carbine he had invented. He drove the venture into bankruptcy in 1857. His friend George McClellan found a place for him on the Illinois Central Railroad, and he rose quickly to become its treasurer. When war came in April 1861 Burnside organized the 1st Rhode Island

John Lawrence Burns, "The Old Hero of Gettysburg"

ABOVE: Ambrose Burnside and his staff.

BELOW: Ambrose Everett Burnside.

regiment. He commanded a brigade at the First Battle of Bull Run in July.

His genial nature and agreeable manners made him many friends, including President Lincoln, and his connections brought him rapid advancement in the army. In February 1862 he commanded the land forces in the capture of Roanoke Island, North Carolina, then went on to take New Bern in March and Beaufort in April. Recalled to Virginia in midsummer, he led McClellan's right wing at Antietam in September. His inept performance before what became known as "Burnside's Bridge" may have cost McClellan a decisive victory at Antietam.

In November, Lincoln relieved McClellan and put Burnside in his place as commander of the Army of the Potomac. Burnside had protested that he was not qualified for the assignment, and events proved him all too correct. He was in turn relieved after the disastrously mismanaged Battle of Fredericksburg on December 11-15 and its low comedy aftermath, the famous "Mud March" of mid-January 1863, in which his whole army became so enmired in rain-sodden ground that it could not get back across the Rappahannock to resume the fight with the Rebels.

Burnside, six feet tall, handsome, famous for his flamboyant whiskers (he gave the word "sideburns" to the language), was unlucky as well as inept. The government bought more than 55,000 of his carbines during the war, but all the profits went to the creditors who had taken over his patents. He was ill-served by his subordinates at Fredericksburg, some of whom were conspiring to see him removed from command. Yet, unlike many other failed commanders, he took full responsibility for his operations and refused to blame anyone but himself for the Fredericksburg debacle.

In March 1863 he took charge of the Department of the Ohio and launched offensive operations against the enemy behind the fighting line. In May, Burnside arrested former Congressman Clement Vallandigham, a prominent Democratic critic of the war effort, and saw him into exile with scant regard for his civil rights. He also suppressed the Chicago *Times* newspaper, an action Lincoln soon repudiated.

On the other hand, Burnside did attain a measure of success with military operations in the department. He led the little Army of the Ohio to Knoxville, Tennessee,

in early September, withstood a siege there, repulsed a general assault on November 29 and saw the Confederates withdraw early in December.

In early 1864 he returned to the Virginia theater to serve as a corps commander under Grant and Meade. He led the IX Corps in the battles of the Wilderness, Spotsylvania and Cold Harbor in May and June. At Petersburg, in late June, a Pennsylvania officer sold him on the notion or mining the Confederate stronghold at Elliott's Salient. The 511-foot-long main shaft ended with two lateral galleries filled with 8,000 pounds of black powder. The mine worked beautifully, the detonation burying parts of two enemy regiments in a crater 170 feet long, 80 feet wide and 30 feet deep. But the follow-up assault was bungled in the classic Burnside manner. The IX Corps reported 4,000 casualties, and Burnside left the army on leave. He was not recalled.

Burnside enjoyed considerable postwar success. He accepted the presidencies of two railroads, became a director of a steamship company and won election as governor of Rhode Island in 1866, 1867 and 1868. He served in the U.S. Senate from 1875 until his death on September 13, 1881.

Butler, Benjamin Franklin
(1818-1893) Union general

He was born in Deerfield, New Hampshire. Dramatic and effective as a speaker, Butler became a nationally influential Massachusetts criminal lawyer and Democratic politician. Always a figure of controversy, he supported Jefferson Davis, then the

Southern candidate, J. C. Breckinridge, in the 1860 presidential campaign. Following the outbreak of the war, his 8th Massachusetts helped to garrison Washington after the fall of Fort Sumter. Commanding the District of Annapolis, he peacefully occupied Baltimore in May 1861, soon thereafter being promoted to major general. He was then disastrously engaged at Big Bethel before turning south, taking forts Hatteras and Clark and, in May 1862, New Orleans. He was an arbitrary and corrupt military governor there: he confiscated Southerners' bullion on deposit with the French consul, hanged a man for taking down a

Burnside commanding his brigade at the First Battle of Bull Run

Union flag and issued the notorious "Woman Order" declaring that any woman insulting a Federal soldier would be treated as a prostitute. Removed from his New Orleans command in December 1862 after international protests, Butler took over the Army of the James, but his incompetence at Petersburg and Fort Fisher finally cost him that command as

Burnside at Fredericksburg, his first great military disaster

Benjamin Franklin Butler (seated, left center) and his staff

Butterfield, Daniel
(1831-1901) Union general

Cabell, William Lewis
(1827-1911) Confederate general

well. Butler is considered typical of the politically appointed generals who made such a dubious military contribution to the Union. As a Radical Republican Congressman (1867-1875, 1877-1879) he was instrumental in impeaching President Andrew Johnson. He became governor of Massachusetts (1883) after numerous unsuccessful campaigns, and in 1884 he was the National Party's unsuccessful presidential candidate.

Daniel Buttlerfield

A New York merchant, Butterfield led the first Union regiment to reach Virginia. He fought with distinction in the eastern theater: a brigadier general by September 1861, he earned a Medal of Honor for action at Gaines's Mill. He was chief of staff to generals Joseph Hooker and George Meade in 1863-1864, and led a division in W. T. Sherman's March to the Sea in 1864. He wrote the music for the war's most haunting melody: "Taps." After the war his extensive business interests encompassed shipping, railroads and banks.

This Virginian West Point graduate served in the quartermaster corps on the frontier and participated in the Utah Expedition (1858-1860). He organized the Confederate quartermaster, commissary and ordnance departments and was quartermaster to P. G. T. Beauregard and both Albert and Joseph Johnston. He fought at Iuka and was wounded at Corinth and Hatcher's Ridge. As a brigadier general commanding northwest Arkansas troops, he organized outstanding cavalry brigades. Captured at Marais des Cygnes in October 1864, he was imprisoned for the duration of the war. After 1872 he was a lawyer and railroad executive in Dallas, where he served four terms as mayor.

Calhoun, John Caldwell
(1782-1850) Southern statesman

He grew up in upcountry South Carolina, the son of a modestly prosperous homesteader and small slaveholder. His father, a state legislator, held strong states' rights views and opposed ratification of the federal Constitution. Young Calhoun ran the family farm for a time after his father died in 1796, then went on to study at Yale. He was graduated in 1804, read law in Connecticut and South Carolina and was admitted to the bar in 1807.

Calhoun built a successful law practice and, in 1811, married into a wealthy lowland South Carolina planter family. His wife's property, added to his own small holdings, made him financially independent and enabled him to enter public life full time. He launched his political career in 1807 with a speech denouncing British violations of American maritime rights. Cal-

John Caldwell Calhoun

houn won election to the South Carolina legislature in 1808 and to the U.S. Congress two years later. There he joined the "War Hawks" faction that agitated for war with Britain in defense of American maritime rights.

Though a supporter of the treaty of Ghent that ended the war in 1815, Calhoun lobbied for the development of a navy that would be strong enough to protect American maritime interests. He also called for a larger standing army, government support of industry, taxpayer funding on internal improvements and a national bank – positions associated with politicians who favored strong national power at the expense of states' rights. He became secretary of war in the James Monroe administration in 1817 and served in that office for more than seven years.

A powerful debater, Calhoun developed a reputation as an eloquent and persuasive public speaker, He gradually turned his talents toward a defense of states' rights against what he took to be encroachments of the federal government. He won election to the vice presidency in 1824, even though his views had begun to diverge from those of the president, John Quincy Adams. He was elected to a second term in 1828, this time with Andrew Jackson at the top of the ticket.

He and Jackson soon quarrelled, both on political and personal grounds. At the same time, South Carolina stepped up its opposition to tariffs aimed at protecting Northern manufacturers. Tariffs, the South's argument ran, caused further damage to the region's cotton economy, already in decline after several years of low prices. Calhoun argued that the federal government had overstepped its constitutional bounds in imposing high tariffs on foreign factory goods.

This view led eventually to his theory of nullification, which held that the constitutional compact gave a state the right to declare null and void any federal law it deemed unconstitutional. "It is the Constitution that annuls an unconstitutional act," Calhoun wrote. "Such an act is itself void and has no effect." Calhoun resigned from the vice presidency in a flareup over the tariff dispute in 1832 and returned to the Senate, where he began a 20-year defense of his nullification theory.

A compromise averted a national crisis over tariffs, but Calhoun's nullification doctrine formed the theoretical underpinning for the secessionist arguments of the following political generation. The issue of slavery because the next great states' rights battleground, and Southerners turned to Calhoun to defend that "Peculiar Institution." Abolition "strikes directly and fatally, not only at our prosperity, but our existence as a people," he said in 1836.

Calhoun served in the Senate until 1843, when he resigned to take up direct management of his plantation. He returned to Washington as President John Tyler's secretary of state in 1844 and regained his Senate seat the following year. His last Senate speech argued that Henry Clay's conciliatory bill regulating slavery in the territories (the measure became the Compromise of 1850) offered insufficient guarantees to the South. He died March 31, 1850, 11 years before nullification evolved into secession. More than any man of his time, Calhoun articulated the constitutional, political and moral assumptions that led the South out of the Union, and the nation into civil war.

Cameron, Simon
(1799-1889) Union secretary of war

Born in Lancaster County, Pennsylvania, he was early apprenticed to a printer, became a newspaper editor and, by 1824, was the publisher of the influential Harrisburg *Republican*. Various other business interests made him rich and paved the way for his entry into politics. His corrupt dealings as a commissioner for settling Winnebago claims in 1838 led to his being satirically called "The Great Winnebago Chief." He won James Buchanan's old

Simon Cameron

Senate seat as a coalition candidate in 1845. As U.S Senator (1845-1849, 1857-1861, 1867-1877) and as the organizer and highly effective party boss of his state's Republican Party (1855-1877), he dominated Pennsylvania politics for 30 years. He traded his support for Abraham Lincoln in 1860 for a cabinet post: Lincoln reluctantly honored this ill-advised promise (made by his subordinates) and named Cameron as his first secretary of war. In office Cameron presided over massive fraud and corruption in appointments and procurement, attracting widespread complaints. Equally embarrassing to the administration, he publicly advocated freeing and arming the slaves. He received a Congressional censure, and, probably to get him our of Washington, Lincoln appointed him minister to Russia in January 1862. Cameron resumed his Senate career after the war as a Radical Republican. A consummate politician dedicated to patronage rather than issues, he was particularly powerful during President Ulysses S. Grant's administration. Cameron delivered his Senate seat and state political empire to his son, James Donald Cameron, in 1877 and retired to his Pennsylvania farm.

Campbell, John Archibald
(1811-1889)
Jurist and Confederate statesman

In 1861 Campbell, a Georgian, resigned after an eight-year term on the U.S. Supreme Court, during which he had actively sought to avert the war. He was subsequently the Confederate assistant secretary of war and administrator of the conscription law (1862-1865). He was a commissioner at the Hampton Roads Peace Conference (January 1865). In later years he was one of the nation's leading lawyers, practicing in New Orleans.

Canby, Edward Sprigg
(1817-1873) **Union general**

He was graduated from West Point in 1839 and fought in the Seminole war in Florida and in Mexico. Canby held New Mexico for the Union in 1861, even though he lost the only battle of the campaign. He commanded troops in New York City in the wake of the 1863 draft riots there. Forces under Canby captured Mobile, Alabama, in April 1865; he received the surrender of the last two Confederate field armies in May. Canby later commanded U.S, forces in the Pacific Northwest. Modoc Indians murdered him during a parley in 1873.

Capron, Horace
(1804-1885) **Union officer**

Capron was born in Massachusetts. He hoped to go to West Point but failed to obtain an appointment, so he turned to scientific and large-scale farming. President Millard Fillmore appointed him a special Indian agent. He obtained a commission as a lieutenant colonel in the Union cavalry in December 1862 and served in many posts, ending as commander of a regiment in VI Cavalry Corps and breveted a brigadier general. After the war he resumed his career in farming and cattle-breeding. In 1867 he was named U.S. commissioner of agriculture. He was esteemed for his progressive farming techniques and served as an advisor to the Japanese on the development of agriculture on Hokkaido Island (1871-1875).

Horace Capron (right) and (below) Edward Sprigg Canby

Carleton, James Henry
(1814-1873) Union general

A Maine native, Carleton fought in the Aroostook War and began a long army career by joining the dragoons in 1839. His frontier and western service continued through the Civil War. In spring 1862 he raised the "Californian column" and led it to New Mexico, and as a brigadier general (April 1862) he commanded the Department of New Mexico (1862-1865). He died while on active duty in 1873.

Carr, Eugene Asa
(1830-1910)
Indian fighter and Union general

Carr was a New Yorker and West Point graduate whose 40-year career as an Indian fighter was interrupted by the Civil War. He fought for the Union with distinction at

Eugene Asa Carr

Wilson's Creek, Pea Ridge (winning a Medal of Honor), Port Gibson and Champion's Hill. He also led divisions in the Vicksburg Campaign and Mobile Campaign and commanded the District of Little Rock. His later cavalry operations against the Indians, who dubbed him "War Eagle," made him famous.

Carrington, Henry Beebee
(1824-1912) Union general

This prominent Ohio lawyer and abolitionist reorganized the state militia in 1857. In 1861 nine Ohio militia regiments saved western Virginia for the Union before volunteers could be organized. During the war he recruited 100,000 troops in Indiana and directed the controversial trials of the Sons of Liberty and the Louisville guerillas. He retired from the army in 1870. He thereafter wrote *Battle of the American Revolution* (1876) and other military and historical works.

Carroll, Anna Ella
(1815-1893) Union pamphleteer

She was the daughter of a leading Maryland Democrat. By the 1850s she had emerged as a leading polemicist of the Know-Nothing Party, lecturing widely and writing for Millard Fillmore's 1856 presidential campaign. She moved to Washington D.C., at the outbreak of the war to support Maryland's Unionists. Encouraged by a war department official, she published several substantial pamphlets and justifying Lincoln's wartime assumption of executive prerogative. She spent the rest of her life unsuccessfully demanding payment for that service and for military strategy she claimed to have supplied the government, notably for Ulysses S. Grant's Tennessee River naval operations.

Christopher (Kit) Carson

Carson, Christopher
(1809-1868)
Union officer and Indian fighter

In 1826 "Kit" Carson ran away from his native Kentucky and, in New Mexico and on southwestern expeditions, learned trapping and Indian fighting. He became famous as John C. Frémont's guide on his first expedition of exploration in 1842 and, after accompanying Frémont's second and third expeditions, became a national hero for his exploits fighting under Frémont and Philip Kearny in the Mexican War. He was later a Taos, New Mexico, Indian agent (1853-1860). In 1861 he organized a New Mexico regiment and spent the Civil War fighting Indians in New Mexico and Texas. Breveted a brigadier general in 1865, he resigned from the army in 1867.

Carter, Samuel Powhatan
(1819-1891) Union general

A Tennessee native and Princeton College graduate, Carter became a midshipman in 1840 and was graduated from Annapolis in 1846. Seconded to the war department in 1861, he served the Union throughout the war in the army and eventually held the unique double rank of major general and rear admiral. He organized the first eastern Tennessee Union volunteers and, as a brigadier general (May 1862), held a series of field commands in the Ohio and Cumberland Armies, finally commanding XXIII Corps. He is perhaps best remembered for leading the first successful Union cavalry raids of the war in the upper Tennessee Valley in December 1862. He returned to the navy after the war, served as Annapolis commandant of cadets (1877-1880) and retired in 1881.

Casey, Silas
(1807-1882) Union general

A Rhode Island-born career infantryman, he was graduated from West Point and participated the Seminole and Mexican wars and fought on the frontier. His *Casey's Tactics* (1862) was long a standard infantry manual. He was wounded in the Peninsular Campaign, then commanded the defense of Washington, D.C. (1862-1865) and trained troops. From 1863 to 1865 he superintended examinations of prospective officers of black troops. He retired in 1868.

Silas Casey

Cass, Lewis
(1782-1866) Statesman

A veteran of the War of 1812, he was an Ohio lawyer and legislator who rose to national prominence negotiating Indian treaties as governor of Michigan Territory (1813-1831). Cass served as U.S. secretary of war (1831-1836) and U.S. Senator (Michigan, 1845-1848). He ran for president in 1848. A strong Unionist, he was secretary of state (1857-60). His diplomatic successes were clouded by his resignation over President James Buchanan's failure to reinforce the Charleston forts, despite the impending war.

Chamberlain, Joshua Lawrence
(1828-1914) Union general

Born in Brewer, Maine, and educated at Bowdoin College and Bangor Theological Seminary, he was professor of rhetoric at Bowdoin when the Civil War broke out. In August 1862 he obtained a commission as a lieutenant colonel in the Union army's 20th Maine.

Joshua Lawrence Chamberlain

Chamberlain fought at Shepherdstown Ford immediately after Antietam and at Fredericksburg in December 1862. He took command of the 20th Maine in May 1863 and led it on the Gettysburg Campaign. In a decisive action, Chamberlain's regiment held the extreme Union left on Little Round Top against repeated Confederate assaults on the second day of Gettysburg, July 2, 1863.

He led the 20th Maine at Spotsylvania in May 1864 and commanded a brigade in the June 18, 1864, assault on Petersburg. Severely wounded in that battle, he returned to the army in the autumn of 1864 and fought at Five Forks on April 1, 1865, and throughout the Appomattox Campaign. Ulysses S. Grant chose Chamberlain to receive the formal surrender of the Confederate infantry at Appomattox on April 12, 1865.

After the war, Chamberlain was four times elected governor of Maine. From 1871-83 he was president of Bowdoin College, and in 1900 he obtained the patronage appointment of surveyor of the port of Portland, Maine.

Chamberlain's memoir of the last campaign, *The Passing of the Armies*, appeared in 1915, the year after his death. He died from complications of the wound he had received at Petersburg in 1864.

Chase, Salmon Portland
(1808-1873)
Union secretary of the treasury

This New Hampshire native and Dartmouth College graduate made his name as a Cincinnati lawyer who defended escaped slaves. He helped to found the Free-Soil (1848) and Republican parties (1854), served as U.S. Senator (1849-1855, 1860) and state governor (1855-1859) and attended the Washington Peace Convention (1861). As Lincoln's secretary of the treasury (1861-1864), Chase successfully financed the war with the help of private financiers, though he was forced to issue unsecured "greenback" paper currency. He also created the national banking system (1863). Dissatisfied with what he considered to be Lincoln's administrative incompetence and undue moderation in prosecuting the war, Chase became the center of a disloyal anti-Lincoln cabinet faction. Nevertheless, after Chase resigned, Lincoln appointed him to the U.S. Supreme Court (1864-1873).

Salmon Portland Chase

Chesnuts, Mary and James
Confederate notables

Mary Boykin Miller Chesnut

Born into the fourth generation of a family of Camden, South Carolina, planters, James Chesnut, Jr. (1815-1885), earned a degree at Princeton, studied law and returned home to enter politics. Sitting in the state legislature almost continuously from 1841 to 1858, he became an ardent secessionist. As a U.S. Senator (1858-November 1860) he was renowned as a fine orator and defender of slavery. He helped to draft South Carolina's secession ordinance and the permanent Confederate constitution and sat in the Confederate provisional congress (1861). He was an aide-de-camp to P. G. T. Beauregard at Fort Sumter and First Bull Run, and was later an aide-de-camp and a trusted adviser to Jefferson Davis (1862-1864). Requesting field service and appointed a brigadier general, he commanded the South Carolina reserves. He returned to state politics after the war.

James Chesnut, Jr.

Meriwether Lewis Clark (above) and (below) Thomas James Churchill

As a brigadier general in the Confederate army in May 1861. He was wounded at Shiloh and again at Baton Rouge; he was also captured at the latter battle and was held prisoner until October 1863. Unable to walk properly because of his wounds, he resigned after being exchanged as a prisoner. He became governor of Mississippi (1863-1865). After the war he returned to his law practice and to resume the farming of his plantation.

Clark, Meriwether Lewis
(1809-1881) Confederate colonel

Named for the Meriwether Lewis who had made the famous expedition with his father, William Clark, he was graduated from West Point (1830) and served in the Black Hawk and Mexican wars. A civilian

As the daughter of a South Carolina governor and U.S. Senator, Mary Boykin Miller Chesnut (1823-1886) was immersed in politics from childhood. She met James Chesnut, Jr., when she was a 13-year-old Charleston schoolgirl and married him four years later. The Chesnuts were at the center of Southern political life, and throughout the Civil War Mary Chesnut kept a detailed diary of the history unfolding around her. Cultured, intelligent, and compassionate, she created one of the most sensitive chronicles of the wartime Confederacy. It was published as *Diary from Dixie* (1905).

Churchill, Thomas James
(1824-1905) Confederate general, governor of Arkansas

This Kentucky native and Mexican War veteran was an Arkansas planter and postmaster. In 1861 he raised the 1st Arkansas Mounted Riflemen and fought at Wilson's Creek: he surrendered his outnumbered and poorly equipped force at Arkansas Post. He fought in the Red River Campaign of 1864 and at Jenkins's Ferry. He surrendered reluctantly in Texas in 1865. Churchill was later Arkansas's state treasurer (1874-1880) and governor (1881-1883)

Clark, Charles
(1810-1877) Confederate general, governor of Mississippi

Born in Cincinnati, Ohio, Clark moved to Mississippi in about 1830 and served in that state's legislature. He fought in the Mexican War. He accepted an appointment

engineer when the Civil War broke out, he accepted a commission as a major in the Confederate army in March 1862. He held staff positions in charge of artillery under generals Sterling Price and Braxton Bragg and ended the war as an inspector for the Confederate Ordnance Department. After the war he was both the commandant of cadets and a professor at Kentucky Military Institute.

Clark, William Thomas
(1831-1905) Union general

A Connecticut-born Iowa lawyer, he raised an Iowa regiment and fought at Shiloh, Corinth, Port Gibson and Champion's Hill. He was General James

Cassius Marcellus Clay

McPherson's adjutant general during the Vicksburg and Atlanta campaigns and ended the war commanding a division in Texas. He was "the last of the carpetbaggers" in Texas (1868-1872), then was expelled from Congress for vote-rigging. He achieved more lasting success as a Galveston banker and federal tax agent.

Clay, Cassius Marcellus
(1810-1903) Union diplomat

The son of slave-owning Kentucky planters, Clay became a staunch abolitionist while a student at Yale. Back in Kentucky, he founded a crusading abolitionist journal, *True American* (1845), served with distinction in the Mexican War and established a strong emancipation party in his state. He was a confidant of Abraham Lin-

coln. On his way to a ministerial posting in Russia (1862-1863) he briefly suspended his diplomatic appointment to consider an army commission but refused to fight until slavery was abolished. In Russia (1863-1869) he helped to negotiate the purchase of Alaska. He lived as a recluse in Kentucky in his later years.

Clay, Henry
(1777-1852) Statesman

He had three years of education in a frontier school before moving with his family from his native Hanover County, Virginia, to Richmond. He worked there as a store clerk, then in more congenial surroundings as a clerk in the chancery court. Taking up the study of law in 1796, he gained a license to practice within a year and, having moved to Lexington, Kentucky, soon built a successful practice, specializing in criminal law.

Clay entered public life in 1798 with a speech against the Sedition Act. He served in the Kentucky legislature from 1803-06 before shifting his base to the new national capital at Washington, D.C., in 1806 to serve out an unexpired U.S. Senate term. After a brief return to Kentucky, he re-entered the Senate in 1809. There he took up issues of trade and internal improvements and became a forceful advocate for the protection of American maritime rights.

Leaving the Senate again, he entered the House of Representatives and won election

Henry Clay

TYRANTS PROSTRATE   LIBERTY TRIUMPHANT.

A pro-Democratic election cartoon of 1844 portrays Whig Henry Clay as an anglophilic aristocrat.

as House speaker in 1811. As an influential member of the "War Hawk" faction in Congress, he helped push the James Madison administration into war with Britain in 1812. Later in the decade he declined an offer to be secretary of war and began to fix his ambitions on the presidency.

Clay helped push through the Missouri Compromise in 1820, a temporary solution to the first great Congressional impasse over slavery. The compromise, simple enough in theory, maintained the sectional balance by admitting Maine as a free state and Missouri as a slave state, leaving 12 states in each column. The Compromise of 1820, as the measure was alternatively known, stilled – but did not dismiss – the slavery debate for a full political generation.

Clay retired briefly from politics, then returned to Congress in 1823 and again became House speaker. He made the first of his three unsuccessful bids for the presidency in 1824. When that disputed election went to the House of Representatives, Clay threw his vote to John Quincy

Adams. He joined Adams's cabinet as secretary of state, leading to charges he had sold his support in a "corrupt bargain." Clay served four rather quiet years in the Adams cabinet. In 1833 he re-entered the Senate and became a bitter opponent of Adams's successor in the White House, the Tennessee Democrat Andrew Jackson.

Despite his frequent criticisms of those in power and his long-term feud with Jackson, Clay retained an ability to forge compromise agreements on complex issues. In 1824, for example, in the House, he had pushed through the highest tariff in America's short history. Yet eight years later, in alliance with John Calhoun, he headed off the Nullification crisis by securing passage of a compromise tariff measure that managed to appease both extremes.

The Mexican War of 1846-47 set off the slavery debate anew. Vast new western territories were America's spoils of victory over Mexico. In 1849-50 Clay, now known as "The Great Compromiser," worked to resolve the dispute that flared over the bid of one of these new territories, California, to enter the Union as a free state.

To assuage Northern opinion, Clay proposed the gradual emancipation of slaves, and he warned Southerners of the perils of

secession. The Compromise of 1850 provided for California to be admitted as a free state and for the Utah and New Mexico territories to decide their future status by local vote. Slavery would be abolished in the District of Columbia. The federal government would rigorously enforce the Fugitive Slave Law – meaning federal agents would aggressively seek out runaway slaves and return them to their owners.

In its way, the compromise was a remarkable achievement. But it soon fell apart under the extraordinary stresses of the sectional conflict. The agreement could satisfy nobody for long: the Kansas-Nebraska Act of 1854 and the U.S. Supreme Court ruling in the Dred Scott case in 1857 wrecked Clay's handiwork and strengthened radicals on both sides of the Mason-Dixon line. But before these events, Clay had died (1852), still doing his best to reconcile the irreconcilable.

Clayton, Powell
(1833-1914) Union general

This Pennsylvania-born civil engineer was commissioned a captain in the Union cavalry in May 1861. He repulsed General

Powell Clayton

John Marmaduke at the Post of Pine Bluff, Arkansas. After being mustered out in August 1865, he settled in Arkansas and became a "carpetbag" politician. He was a Republican governor of that state (1868-71) and then became its U.S. Senator (1871-77), amidst charges of faulty election procedures. The charges were eventually dropped, and from 1879 to 1905 he was the U.S. ambassador to Mexico.

Cleburne, Patrick Ronayne
(1828-1864) Confederate general

This Irishman served in the British army before emigrating to the U.S. in 1849. Established as a Little Rock, Arkansas, druggist and lawyer, he helped to muster

Patrick Ronayne Clayburn

volunteers before the Civil War, He organized the Yell Rifles for the Confederacy in 1861 and seized the Little Rock arsenal. This "Stonewall Jackson of the West" performed impressively at Shiloh (promoted to brigadier general), Richmond, Kentucky (wounded) and Perryville. As a major general (December 1862), he led divisions at Stones River, Chickamauga and Chattanooga, fighting W. T. Sherman at Missionary Ridge. He commanded William Hardee's Corps in the Atlanta Campaign. He was killed in action at Franklin, Tennessee, in November 1864.

Cobb, Howell
(1815-1868) Confederate general)

He was born on a plantation in Jefferson County, Georgia, into a wealthy and socially prominent family. After attending Franklin College (later the University of Georgia), he was solicitor general of the western circuit (1837-1841). As a Democratic U.S. Representative (1843-1851, 1855-1857) he urged the extension of the Missouri Compromise line to the Pacific. His famous "Southern Address" (January 1849) and energetic campaigning incurred the implacable emnity of Southern Rights Democrats by leading Georgia to support the Union, but his moderation also won him Northern support, and he was elected speaker of the House (1849-1851). In this office he presided over the compromise debates of 1850. He served as governor of Georgia (1851-1853) and as his friend James Buchanan's secretary of the treasury (1857-1860). After Lincoln's election he became a secessionist. He chaired the Montgomery Convention in February 1861 and was president of the provisional Confederate congress. He organized the 16th Georgia and, despite his lack of military training,

Howell Cobb

had a distinguished war career. As a brigadier general he fought at Shiloh, Seven Pines, the Seven Days' Battles, Second Bull Run and Antietam; he commanded Georgia's reserve forces and, promoted to major general, the District of Georgia. His troops accepted the surrender of George Stoneman in Macon in 1864. He himself surrendered at Macon, where he established himself as a lawyer, planter and opponent of radical Reconstruction after the war. His brother, lawyer and author Thomas Reade Rootes Cobb (1823-1862), was killed at Fredericksburg.

Philip St. George Cocke

Cocke, Philip St. George
(1809-1861) Confederate general

This Virginia-born West Point graduate managed his many plantations in Mississippi and Virginia before the war. He was commissioned a brigadier general in the Virginia militia in April 1861 and then was mustered into the Confederate army as a colonel. He fought at First Bull Run and Blackburn's Ford and was named a brigadier general in October 1861. Forced to resign from the army in ill health, he committed suicide in December 1861.

Colquitt, Alfred Holt
(1824-1894) Confederate general

The son of a Georgia Senator and secessionist, Colquitt was graduated from Princeton College and settled in Monroe, Georgia, as a lawyer, planter and extreme states' rights politician. He served as a staff officer during the Mexican War. He led the Confederate army's 6th Georgia in the Peninsular Campaign and, promoted to brigadier general (September 1862), led Colquitt's brigade at Antietam, Fredericksburg, Chancellorsville, the Wilderness, Spotsylvania and Petersburg, where he surrendered. His greatest victory was at Olustee (February 1864), where he stopped the Union incursion into Florida. After the war he returned to his plantation: he was Georgia's governor (1876-1882) and U.S. Senator (1882-1894).

Colston, Raleigh Edward
(1825-1896) Confederate general

Born and educated in Paris, France, he came to America in 1842. He left the French faculty of Virginia Military Institute in 1861 to join the 16th Virginia Infantry. He fought in the Peninsular Campaign, led a division at Chancellorsville and took part in the defense of Petersburg. He was commanding at Lynchburg when the war ended. He was paralyzed on a Sudanese expedition after six years in the Egyptian army and returned to a desk job in the U.S. War Department.

Connor, James
(1829-1883) Confederate general

A successful Charleston, South Carolina, lawyer, he served as a U.S. district attorney and wrote several legal works in the 1850s. He prompted the convening of the state's secession convention. He fought for the Confederacy with distinction at First Bull Run and joined the 22nd North Carolina in fighting on the Peninsula (he was seriously wounded at Gaines's Mill) and at Chancellorsville and Gettysburg. He was promoted to brigadier general (June 1864) and commanded brigades during the Peters-

Alfred Holt Colquitt

A. H. Colquitt

ABOVE: John Esten Cooke

James Connor

burg Campaign and the Shenandoah Valley Campaign of Sheridan: the loss of a leg ended his field service. He resumed his law career after the war. As South Carolina's attorney general (1876-1877) he established the legality of the Wade Hampton's right to be governor, despite the protests of the carpetbagger incumbent.

Cook, Philip
(1817-1894) Confederate general

A graduate of the University of Virginia law school, he was a Georgia lawyer and state senator. Cook fought for the Confederacy with the 4th Georgia in the Seven Days' Battles and at Antietam, Fredericks-

burg and Chancellorsville, earning steady promotions. After returning briefly to the state legislature (1863-1864), he fought with Jubal Early in the Shenandoah Valley in 1864. Several times wounded, he was finally captured by Union forces at Petersburg in April 1865. Resuming his law practice after the war, he served as U.S. Representative (1873-1883) and as Georgia's secretary of state (1890-1894)

Cooke, John Esten
(1830-1886) Confederate general

This Virginian became a nationally known writer in the 1950s for his poems, essays and fiction (particularly *The Virginia Comedians*, 1854), much of his work treating colonial Virginia themes. An ardent

secessionist, he served in the army throughout the war. He was J. E. B. Stuart's ordnance officer and Robert E. Lee's inspector general of the horse artillery. He surrendered with Lee at Appomattox, and later returned to his farm to write. Cooke published biographies of Stonewall Jackson (1863) and Lee (1871), among other books about the war.

Cooke, John Rogers
(1833-1891) Confederate general

A Missouri-born, Harvard-educated engineer, he resigned after six years of U.S. Army frontier duty in 1861 to raise a Confederate light artillery company. Cooke fought at First Bull Run, Seven Pines, Fredericksburg, Bristoe Station and the Wilderness, suffering several wounds. His father, Philip St. George Cooke (1809-1895), was a Union general. Cooke was a Richmond merchant and powerful Virginia Democrat after the war.

Cooke, Philip St. George
(1809-1895) Union general

This Virgina-born West Point graduate was involved in Indian fighting and served on the frontier, in the Mexican war and on the Utah Expedition before he was appointed brigadier general in the Union army in November 1861. He led a number of cavalry divisions in combat until June 1862, then served on court martial duty service until August 1863. He was in charge of

Philip St. George Cooke

the army's recruiting service after 1864. He retired a major general in 1873. His son (John R. Cooke), nephew (John Esten Cooke) and son-in-law (Jeb Stuart) all fought for the Confederacy.

Cooper, Joseph Alexander
(1823-1910) Union general

An uneducated Tennessee farmer, this Mexican War veteran vigorously opposed secession at the Knoxville Convention in 1861. His military abilities were revealed by

Joseph Alexander Cooper

the war: he recruited and trained Union troops in eastern Tennessee: earned rapid promotions (brigadier general, July 1864) fighting at Stones River, Chickamauga and Chattanooga; led a division at Atlanta; and participated in eastern Tennessee operations toward the war's end. He became a Knoxville tax collector (1969-1879) and later farmed in Kansas.

Cooper, Samuel
(1798-1876) Confederate general

A New Jersey-born West Point graduate, Cooper was a Washington, D.C., staff officer for much of his long military career. He became adjutant general of the army in 1852. His administrative experience proved invaluable when his Southern ties and sympathies led him to become the Confederate army's highest ranking officer in 1861. He served as adjutant- and inspector-general throughout the war. He saved and surrendered the historically valuable Confederate War Department records. After the war he retired to his Virginia estate.

Corcoran, Michael
(1827-1863) Union general

Irish-born, Corcoran served with the Irish Constabulary in 1845 and then came to the U.S. in 1849. He entered the New York militia, and, soon after the Civil War began, he narrowly avoided a court martial for his refusal to serve in the guard honoring Britain's Prince Albert when he came to the U.S. on a state visit. He was captured and imprisoned for a year after First Bull Run and, after his exchange (August 1862), was promoted to brigadier general. He is known for raising a brigade called the Corcoran Legion. He was killed in December 1863 when his horse accidentally fell on him.

Corse, Montgomery Dent
(1816-1895) Confederate general

A veteran of the Mexican War and the Gold Rush, this Virginian banker enlisted in the

Samuel Cooper

ABOVE: Fort Corcoran, one of the fixed defenses of Washington, D.C., was named in honor of Michael Corcoran. Shown here: one of the fort's heavy batteries.

LEFT: Montgomery Dent Corse.

Confederate army's 17th Virginia. He fought at First Bull Run, on the Peninsula and at Second Bull Run and Antietam. Promoted to brigadier general (November 1862), he took over George Pickett's brigade and fought in the battles of Fredericksburg, Gettysburg, Chickamauga and the Wilderness and in the Appomattox Campaign. He was captured at Sayler's Creek and briefly imprisoned, returning to his Alexandria bank after his release.

Cox, Jacob Dolson
(1828-1900)
Union general, governor of Ohio

He was a Canadian-born Ohio lawyer, legislator and radical antislavery activist before the war. Cox fought for the Union in the Kanawha Valley and Antietam campaigns. As major general (October 1862) his commands included divisions in the Atlanta and Franklin and Nashville campaigns. He was later a single-term Ohio governor (1866-1867), Congressman (1876-1878) and dean of the Cincinnati Law School (1881-1897). A prolific author, he wrote extensively and authoritatively about the Civil War.

Crawford, Samuel Wylie
(1829-1892) Union general

After medical training at the University of Pennsylvania, he enlisted as an army surgeon (1851) and served in the Southwest. He fought for the Union as a commissioned officer throughout the Civil War. He led a battery at Fort Sumter and, as a brigadier general (April 1862), fought at Winchester, Cedar Mountain, South Mountain and Antietam, where he was badly wounded. He led the Pennsylvania Reserves division at Gettysburg, fought in

Samuel Wylie Crawford (fourth from right) fought almost continuously from Fort Sumter to Appomattox.

all the Potomac Army operations of 1864-1865 and witnessed the Appomattox surrender. He retired from active duty in the regular army in 1873.

Crittenden, John Jordon
(1787-1863) Southern statesman

A Kentucky lawyer and politician, he was a U.S. Senator most years between 1835 and 1861. He achieved national prominence in the 1840s; he served as U.S. attorney general (1841. 1850-1853) and strongly opposed the Mexican war and the Kansas-Nebraska Act (1854). An anti-secessionist, he supported Lincoln and worked to keep Kentucky in the Union. In December 1860 he offered the Senate the Crittenden Compromise, proposing the extension of the

Missouri Compromise line to the Pacific, but this peace-keeping measure was rejected by both sides. He returned to Kentucky to promote that state's neutrality, and sat in the U.S. Congress until his death.

Crook, George
(1829-1890) Union general

Crook was a West Point graduate from Ohio who interrupted his outstanding career as a northwest explorer and Indian fighter to serve the Union with distinction in the Civil War. He fought at South Mountain and Antietam; promoted to brigadier general (August 1863) he led a cavalry division at Chickamauga. He engaged in operations against Confederate bridges and railroads in West Virginia early in 1864, then joined the Shenandoah Valley Campaign of Sheridan, fighting at Winchester, Fisher's Hill and Cedar Creek. As a major general, he led a cavalry division in

the Appomattox Campaign. His later Indian fighting included the Sioux War (1876) and operations against Geronimo in the Sierra Madre. He was celebrated (and sometimes criticized) for the fairness with which he dealt with Indians.

Cullum, George Washington
(1809-1892) Union general

A New Yorker, this West Point graduate and career army engineer (1833-1874) specialized in harbor fortifications. During the Civil War he held Union staff positions under Winfield Scott (1861) and Henry Halleck (1861-1864) and was chief engineer of the Departments of the Missouri and Mississippi. He was long associated with West Point (as superintendent, 1864-1866) and wrote a monumental biographical register of academy graduates from 1802 to 1889. He published many other works on engineering and military history.

Cumming, Alfred
(1829-1910) Confederate general

A Georgia-born West Point graduate and career officer, Cumming participated in the Utah Expedition (1858-1860), resigning from frontier duty in January 1861 to join the Confederate army. He commanded a Georgia arsenal, then joined the 10th Georgia. Wounded at Malvern Hill and Antietam, he was promoted to brigadier general and led the Alabama Brigade at Mobile before helping in the attempt to relieve the Vicksburg siege. Captured and exchanged, he led his reorganized brigade at Missionary Ridge and in J. B. Hood's corps in the Atlanta Campaign. He was wounded at Jonesboro and discharged. After the war he farmed in Georgia.

RIGHT: Alfred Cumming.

BELOW: The harbor fortification expert George Washington Cullum served as a superintendent of West Point.

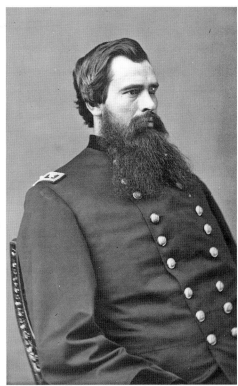

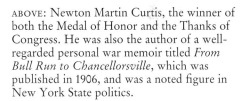

ABOVE: Newton Martin Curtis, the winner of both the Medal of Honor and the Thanks of Congress. He was also the author of a well-regarded personal war memoir titled *From Bull Run to Chancellorsville*, which was published in 1906, and was a noted figure in New York State politics.

Curtis, Newton Martin
(1835-1910) Union general

Curtis was a New York farmer who fought as a Union captain at First Bull Run. Steadily promoted, he fought at Cold Harbor, Petersburg and Fort Fisher, where he was badly wounded. He eventually earned a brigadier generalship, a Medal of Honor and the Thanks of Congress. Later a noted social reformer, he was a New York assemblyman, Congressman (1891-1897), customs inspector, and treasury agent. He wrote *From Bull Run to Chancellorsville* (1906).

Curtis, Samuel Ryan
(1805-1866) Union general

This West Point graduate and civil engineer worked on major road and river projects in the 1830s and raised Ohio volunteers for the Mexican War. He resigned his Iowa Congressional seat (1856-1861) to join a state regiment at the outbreak of the Civil War. As commander of the Union's Army of the Southwest in 1862, he fought at Pea Ridge, then commanded successively the Departments of the Missouri, Kansas and the Northwest. He stopped Sterling Price's Missouri raid (September-October 1864).

William Barker Cushing, who single-handedly destroyed the big Confederate ironclad ram *Albemarle*

George Armstrong Custer

Cushing, William Barker
(1842-1874) Union naval officer

He resigned while still a senior at Annapolis but was reinstated in the U.S. Navy in October 1861. Commanding the USS *Ellis* (1862) and USS *Monticello* (1863-1865), he performed brilliantly in Florida and the Carolinas. He destroyed the formidable Confederate ram *Albemarle* in a daring night torpedo attack made in a small boat in October 1864, and he led an heroic but doomed assault by sailors on Fort Fisher in January 1865.

Cushman, Pauline
(1835-1893) Union spy

Born in New Orleans and raised in Michigan, she became an actress in New York at age 17. She was fired from a Kentucky theatrical production in March 1863 after toasting the South onstage at the behest of Confederate sympathizers in the audience. The Federals soon sent her south to gather military intelligence. She was arrested in possession of military maps near Braxton Bragg's Tullahoma headquarters and sentenced to death; spared by the Confederates' retreat from Shelbyville, she passed valuable information to W. S. Rosecrans. Notoriety had ended her usefulness as a spy, but she capitalized on her adventures by lecturing (wearing Federal uniform) in the North. Her later years were troubled, and she committed suicide.

Custer, George Armstrong
(1839-1876) Union general

Custer's grandfather, a Hessian mercenary officer named Kuster, settled in Pennsylvania after the Revolutionary war. His may have been the example that fired Custer's childhood ambition to be a solider. Custer's father, a blacksmith and farmer who migrated westward to Ohio, did nothing to discourage his hopes and saw to

Pauline Cushman

it that he received sufficient education to qualify for a West Point cadetship.

Never much of a hand with the books, Custer was graduated 34th in the 34-man class of 1861 and proceeded directly to the battlefield. He fought with the Union's 5th Cavalry at Bull Run and later served on the staffs of Philip Kearney, William F. Smith and George McClellan. During the Peninsular Campaign of 1862 one of his staff assignments involved supervision of balloon reconnaissances. Promotion came extraordinarily swiftly, and Custer won his brigadier's star after leading a spirited cavalry charge at Aldie in June 1863. He commanded the Michigan Brigade of the 3rd Cavalry Division at Gettysburg, taking part in a sharp encounter with Wade Hampton's Confederate cavalry on the second day of the battle.

Tall, lithe, with ringletted yellow hair, he was always something of an exhibitionist, cutting a figure that some found dashing and others absurd: in his elaborate uniform he looked "like a circus rider gone mad," Theodore Lyman thought. Yet he was undeniably courageous, excelling in such hell-for-leather operations as Philip Sheridan's raid toward Richmond in May 1864, during which he advanced to within four miles of the Confederate capital.

Custer accompanied Sheridan to the Shenandoah Valley in September 1864 and took part in the battles of Winchester and Fisher's Hill. Promoted to command of the 4,600-man 3rd Cavalry Division, he routed the Confederates on October 9 in what became known as the Woodstock Races: he

Custer with fellow officers during the
Peninsular Campaign.

forced the pursuit of the beaten enemy for more than 25 miles. Ten days later, at Cedar Creek, Custer's division, along with that of Wesley Merritt, held off Jubal Early's infantry long enough for the disorganized Federals to reform and for Sheridan to complete his famous ride and lead them to victory (a feat dramatized in Thomas Buchanan's poem "Sheridan's Ride").

Custer returned, along with Sheridan, to the Army of the Potomac in early 1865 and fought at Dinwiddie Courthouse and Five Forks at the beginning of the Appomattox Campaign. In his greatest triumph, he led the advance in Sheridan's relentless final pursuit of Lee's army westward to Appomattox and received the first flag of truce from the Army of Northern Virginia. In a farewell order to his division shortly after

Lee's surrender, he claimed his command had captured 111 pieces of artillery, 65 battle flags and 10,000 prisoners.

Custer served in Texas in the immediate aftermath of the war and later became lieutenant colonel of the 7th Cavalry. His first experience fighting Indians came against the Cheyenne in the spring of 1867. On November 27, 1868, Custer attacked and destroyed a large Cheyenne village on the Washita River in the Oklahoma territory, a bitter and bloody defeat that forced the Cheyenne to return to their reservation.

From 1871 to 1873 he served with the regiment in garrison in Elizabethtown, Ky., where he wrote his well-regarded memoir *My Life on the Plains*. It showed another, more thoughtful side of Custer, as did his efforts to reform the Bureau of Indian Affairs, then riddled with corrup-

tion. He returned to the plains with the 7th Cavalry in 1873. The regiment had its first encounters with hostile Sioux guarding the Northern Pacific Railroad.

Custer set out on his last campaign on June 22, 1876, moving up the Rosebud River toward the headwaters of the Little Big Horn. On the morning of June 25 he divided his force into three parts and prepared for offensive operations against Sioux and Cheyenne war parties known to be in the vicinity. He himself led five companies up the right bank of the Little Big Horn and into a trap. A Sioux force of some 2,500 warriors ambushed his command and, after three hours of fighting, killed every man in it.

that revolutionized naval armaments, the best known being the "Dahlgren gun": a cast-metal smoothbore cannon with a distinctive shape – thick at the breech and tapering to the muzzle. When the Civil War broke out he became head of the Washington Navy Yard in April 1861 when Captain Franklin Buchanan resigned that post to join the Confederacy. In 1862 Dahlgren was promoted to captain and named head of the navy's Ordnance Bureau. In July 1863 he was promoted to rear admiral and assigned command of the South Atlantic Blockading Squadron. He helped seal off Charleston, South Carolina, captured Savannah, Georgia, and in February 1865 led the Union fleet that entered Charleston harbor. He remained on active duty with the navy until his death. He was the father of Ulric Dahlgren.

Dahlgren, John Adolphus Bernard
(1809-1870) Inventor, Union admiral

He was born in Philadelphia where his father was serving as the Swedish consul. At 16 he joined the U.S. Navy as a midshipman and after spending many years at sea and working for the coast survey he was assigned in 1847 to the navy's ordnance bureau at Washington, D.C. During his years there he invented several weapons

John Adolphus Dahlgren

Dahlgren, Ulric
(1842-1864) Union officer

An admiral's son, he abandoned his law studies to enter the Union army at the beginning of the war. Dahlgren was Franz Sigel's chief of artillery during the second Bull Run Campaign and later served on the staffs of Ambrose Burnside, Joseph Hooker and George Meade. He lost a leg to amputation after being wounded at Gettysburg in July 1863. Dahlgren was

killed near Richmond on the Kilpatrick-Dahlgren Raid of March 1864, of which he was co-commander. Plans for an assassination attempt on Jefferson Davis and his cabinet were allegedly found on his body. Though Union authorities claimed the papers had been forged, recent research suggests they may have been authentic.

Ulric Dahlgren

Dana, Napoleon Tecumseh Jackson
(1822-1905) Union general

This West Point graduate and Mexican war veteran was a Minnesota banker after 1855. He fought for the Union at Ball's Bluff and led a brigade on the Peninsula and at Antietam, where he was seriously wounded. Promoted to major general, he commanded Philadelphia's defenses during the Gettysburg Campaign and led a successful expedition against the Texas coast late in 1863. He resigned his command of the Department of Mississippi in May 1865. His later business interests included western mining and railroads.

Davidson, John Wynn
(1823-1881) Union general

A West Point graduate and career cavalryman, this Virginian fought on the frontier and sustained severe wounds in Indian

Edmund Jackson Davis

fighting. He declined a Confederate commission in 1861, instead joining the Federals. He fought in the Peninsula, held Missouri field commands and led a cavalry division in the Little Rock expedition, finally serving as chief of cavalry of the Division of the West Mississippi in 1865. He remained in the army after the war and died while still on active service.

Davis, Edmund Jackson
(1827-1883)
Union general, governor of Texas

A Texas judge stung by losing an election for the secessionist convention, Davis organized a Texas Unionist regiment in Mexico. He joined the 1st Texas Cavalry in October 1862 and, although he had spent much of the rest of the war in Louisiana, unsuccessfully attacked Laredo in 1864. Elected governor of Texas (1869-1873), he presided over a notoriously dictatorial and corrupt carpetbag administration. He afterward remained a leading Texas Republican and lawyer.

Davis, George
(1820-1896)
Confederate attorney general

Descended from a distinguished North Carolina family, he was graduated as valedictorian from his state university at 18 and practiced law. Actively anti-secessionist, he participated in the Peace Conference in Washington in February 1861 but afterward denounced its recommendations. He was a Confederate senator (1862-1864), then served as the C.S.A.'s attorney general. He resumed his law practice after the war.

Davis, Jefferson
(1808-1889) Confederate president

Born in Kentucky, the 10th child of a modestly prosperous settler who had led a troop of irregular cavalry during the Revolutionary War, Jefferson Davis grew up on a plantation created out of the canebrakes and deep woods of the Mississippi frontier. He returned to Kentucky for his education, studying at a Roman Catholic seminary (where he came close to renouncing his family's Baptist Protestantism) and later at Transylvania University. His older brother, Joseph, with a better head for business than their father, acquired a fortune as a cotton planter and raised the family to social prominence in Mississippi. His influence gained Davis an appointment to the U.S. Military Academy, from which he was graduated in 1828, a year ahead of Robert E. Lee.

Davis spent the next seven years in remote garrison posts in Wisconsin and Illinois. He saw action (as did Abraham Lincoln, an Illinois militia volunteer) in the Black Hawk War of 1832. In 1835 he married, against her family's wishes, the daughter of one of his garrison commanders, future President Zachary Taylor. Resigning in the face of Taylor's disapproval, he took his bride to Mississippi, to a small plantation he called Brierfield. Three months later she was dead of a fever, and for the next decade Davis lived an obscure, lonely life as a planter.

During these years he read widely in political theory and, on his own and in long discussions with Joseph, formed a political philosophy rooted in a deep attachment to the Southern system of plantation slavery. He met the attacks of the increasingly influential abolitionist movement with pure states' rights arguments of a kind that, ironically, would be turned against him as president of the Southern Confederacy.

He ended his period of retirement

Jefferson Davis, the president of the Confederate States of America

abruptly in 1845, with marriage to Varina Howell, daughter of a prominent Mississippi planter, and an entry into politics. With his brother's encouragement, he ran successfully for Congress in 1845 but resigned after only a few months in Washington to accept command of a regiment of Mississippi volunteers bound for Mexico. He led the regiment in a critical stand that may have won the Battle of Buena Vista (1847) for the Americans. The exploit attracted wide notice and heightened Davis's already high opinion of his own military abilities. He returned to Washington later in 1847 as a Senator. He soon became known as a staunch defender of the "peculiar institution" (slavery) and an advocate of its extension into the new territories seized from Mexico after the war.

Davis served as secretary of war during the Pierce administration (1853-57), then returned to the Senate, where he became something of a force for moderation, though he remained bitterly opposed to any political adjustments that would interfere with slavery in the territories. Davis became a familiar figure on the Senate floor during the slavery debates of the late 1850s,

a tall, slender, impressive figure, though often a frail one (he suffered greatly in the late 1850s from a painful eye disease, neuralgia and other ailments). Opposing secession, Davis urged some form of compromise on radical Southerners right up to the newly-elected Lincoln's declaration that he would not permit any expansion of slavery into the territories.

He resigned his Senate seat on January 21, 1861, and followed Mississippi into the Confederacy. He hoped to be made commander-in-chief of the Confederate armies, Instead, on February 18, he was inaugurated as provisional president of the Confederate States of America, a compromise choice. The new government confirmed him in the presidency the following year.

Davis led a thoroughly unprepared and ill-equipped nation into war. The Southern states lacked the industrial and financial base to sustain a long conflict, and Union blockade gradually choked off supplies from the outside world. Davis's political and diplomatic skills proved to be marginal. At home, states' rights radicals opposed his taxation and conscription initiatives. Abroad, he found himself unable to find allies – particularly European allies – to aid the Southern cause.

Inflexible, hot-tempered, in ill health (his wife described him as "a mere mass of throbbing nerves"), Davis quarrelled with many senior military and political leaders, particularly with General Joseph E. Johnston and his own vice president, Alexander Stephens. He often supported mediocre soldiers such as Braxton Bragg at the expense of Johnston and other more capable men, but he never quarreled with Robert E. Lee: Lee and Davis remained in sympathy to the end. From 1863 on, a majority in the Confederate Congress opposed him, and he never inspired much liking among ordinary Southerners.

BELOW: Davis and his cabinet get a briefing from Robert E. Lee.

OPPOSITE: Davis's inauguration in Montgomery, Alabama, in 1861.

In 1864-65, with the Confederacy crumbling, he proposed to draft 40,000 slaves and free them at the successful conclusion of the war, a suggestion that provoked outrage throughout the South. He resisted any proposal for a negotiated peace that fell short of full independence, and this intransigence ultimately condemned the South to much misery. The end came swiftly in April 1865. Davis left Richmond on April 3 just ahead of Union occupation forces (including black troops) and fled into the Deep South where word of Lee's surrender reached him. A Federal cavalry detachment captured him near Irwinville, Georgia, on May 10.

The U.S. government held him for two years as a state prisoner at Fortress Monroe but never bought him to trial. Released on May 13, 1877, Davis returned to his beloved Mississippi. He gradually recovered his health (though not his fortune; he was an inept businessman) and settled on a friend's estate on the Gulf of Mexico, where he wrote his two-volume *The Rise and Fall of the Confederate Government* (1878-81). He died in New Orleans on December 6, 1889.

Davis, Jefferson Columbus
(1828-1879) Union general

Born in Indiana, he served in the Mexican War as a private and then stayed in the regular army. He was at Fort Sumter during the bombardment in April 1861 that ignited the Civil War. From that time on he fought for the Union in many battles – Wil-

Union General Jefferson Columbus Davis (at desk, left)

son's Creek, Pea Ridge, Corinth – and by May 1862 he was a brigadier general. Upset over a rebuke from his commander, General William Nelson, he killed Nelson with a revolver. Thanks to political pressures, Davis was never punished and was allowed to return to active command. He led forces all the way through the Atlanta Campaign, the March to the Sea and the Carolinas Campaign. After the war he stayed on in the regular army, serving in Alaska and in the war against the Modocs.

Varina Howell Davis and husband

Davis, Varina Howell
(1826-1906) Wife of Jefferson Davis

Born in Mississippi, she married Jefferson Davis in 1845 and forged an intellectual and political partnership with him. She was an ambitious and successful Washington hostess during his years in the federal government in the late 1840s and 1850s. As First Lady of the Confederacy she was controversial because of her Northern ancestry and political influence. She supported herself in later life as a New York-based magazine writer and published a memoir of her husband (1890).

Deas, Zachariah Cantey
(1819-1882) Confederate general

A wealthy South Carolina-born cotton broker, Deas served in the Mexican War. Signing on with the Alabama Volunteers when the Civil war began, he spent $28,000 in gold to arm his men with Enfield rifles (he was paid back in Confederate bonds). He was wounded at Shiloh and served at Stones River, Chickamauga, Missionary Ridge and in the Atlanta Campaign and the Franklin and Nashville Campaign. He tried to stop W. T Sherman's March through Georgia. He went back to selling cotton after the war.

George Washington Deitzler

Deitzler, George Washington
(1826-1884) Union general

Born in Pennsylvania, Deitzler farmed and agitated as a Free-Soiler in Kansas, smuggling guns from the East. Arrested by pro-

Frederick Tracey Dent

slavery forces, he was charged with treason but released. He was commissioned a colonel in a pro-Union Kansas unit in 1861. He served at Wilson's Creek and was promoted to brigadier general in November 1862. He resigned due to ill health in 1863 but returned to command the Kansas State Militia when Sterling Price invaded the state in 1864.

Dent, Frederick Tracy
(1821-1892) Union general

This Missouri-born West Point graduate was a classmate and brother-in-law of Ulysses S. Grant. Dent first served in the Mexican War, then in the West as an Indian fighter. In 1863 he took command of a regiment in the Army of Potomac and in 1864 helped to suppress the Draft Riots in New York. As a lieutenant colonel he served as an aide de camp to Ulysses S. Grant (1864-1865). In 1865 he served as military governor of Richmond, Virginia. He retired as a colonel in the regular army in 1883.

Denver, James William
(1817-1892) Union general

By 1861 Denver had been a midwestern teacher, lawyer and newspaper editor; a California secretary of state and Congressman; and a Kansas Territory governor,

James William Denver

besides fighting in the Mexican War. As a brigadier general he commanded the Federal troops in Kansas, held commands in the Army of the Tennessee and fought at Shiloh and Corinth. He resigned in March 1863 to practice law in Washington, D.C. Denver, Colorado, was named after him.

De Trobriand, Philip Regis Denis de Keredern
(1816-1897) Union general

Born in France into a noble family, he was a poet and writer who married while visiting the U.S. He joined the "Guards Lafayette" and later fought with the Army of the Potomac. He was named a brigadier general in January 1864 and was breveted major general in 1865. He took his father's title (baron) in 1874 but remained with the regular U.S. Army until 1879. He wrote (in French) a oft-cited account of his experiences.

Devens, Charles
(1829-1891) Union general

A Harvard-educated lawyer and Massachusetts public school official and orator, Devens became a commander in the Army of the Potomac in 1861. He was appointed a brigadier general in April 1862. Wounded at Ball's Bluff, Fair Oaks and Chancellorsville, he also fought at Fredericksburg and Cold Harbor and took part in the advance on Richmond in 1864-65. He returned to Massachusetts, where he sat on the state supreme court (1873-1877, 1881-1891). He was U.S. attorney general (1877-1881). Camp Devens, Mass., is named for him.

Charles Devens

Dewey, George
(1837-1917) Union naval officer

This Vermont-born Annapolis graduate was a young naval lieutenant in 1861. During the war he held junior commands on the old side-wheeler USS *Mississippi* at New Orleans and Port Hudson, on David Farragut's lower Mississippi flagship, the steam sloop *Monongahela*, and on the steam frigate *Colorado* at Fort Fisher, and he later served on the Atlantic blockade duty. As a commodore commanding the Asiatic squadron, he achieved international fame for the great victory at Manila Bay in 1898 that established the United States a

George Dewey

major Pacific naval power: his instruction to his flagship captain ("You may fire when you are ready, Gridley") became a household phrase. He returned home a hero, and the rank of admiral was created to honor his achievement.

Dibrell, George Gibbs
(1822-1888) Confederate general

Born in Tennessee, Dibrell was a farmer and merchant before the war. Although he was against secession, he enlisted as a private for the Confederacy, eventually

Dix, Dorothea Lynde
(1802-1887) Social reformer

Born in Hampden, Maine, of parents barely competent to raise a family, she moved into her grandmother's home in Boston at the age of 10. Resourceful and determined, Dix saw to the education of her younger brothers and, at the age of 14, began to earn her own living as a schoolteacher in Worcester, Massachusetts. She returned to Boston in 1821 to establish a girls' school and ran it successfully until 1834, when a tubercular illness forced her to give up the work.

Dix taught for a time in a private home, but ill health drove her to seek treatment abroad. Returning to the U.S. after 18 months in England, she took over a Sunday School class of women inmates in a jail in East Cambridge, Massachusetts. What she found there – filth, overcrowding, no distinction between insane persons and criminals – prompted her to launch what would become a two-year study of conditions of the insane in asylums, prisons and alms houses in Massachusetts. The findings appalled her. Conventional wisdom still held that insanity was a moral defect, deserving of punishment rather

LEFT: Dorothea Lynde Dix.

BELOW: George Gibbs Dibrell.

being promoted to lieutenant colonel under Felix Zollicoffer. When his regiment chose not to re-elect him, he raised his own cavalry regiment to harass the Federals behind their lines. He joined General Nathan B. Forrest in the Stones River Campaign (December 1882-January 1863), and in July 1863 he took command of Forrest's former brigade. He led this unit at Chickamauga, during W. T. Sherman's March to the Sea and in the final days of the Carolinas Campaign. He was a successful businessman after the war and also served in the Congress.

Divers, Bridget
Union army nurse

This vigorous Irishwoman accompanied her husband to war with the 1st Michigan Cavalry. A vivandière, nurse and Sanitary Commission agent, "Michigan Bridget" frequently fought with her regiment, riding a government horse and replacing fallen comrades in battle. At Cedar Creek she rode through enemy lines. After the war she remained with the army as a laundress on the frontier.

than treatment. Dix reported on men and women confined "in cages, closets, cellars, stalls, pens; chained, naked, beaten with rods, and lashed into obedience."

She presented her findings to the Massachusetts legislature in January 1843: they caused a sensation. She convinced influential political leaders to stir public opinion to support the cause of reform, and as a result, Massachusetts thoroughly overhauled its system. Over a three-year period in the mid-1840s Dix traveled more than 10,000 miles to carry on her investigations in some 20 states, beginning with New Jersey, where she founded a state asylum. New asylums were built elsewhere, and others improved; eventually, most states adopted more humane methods of treatment.

Dix took her reform crusade abroad to Canada, Europe and Japan. She helped bring about reform of Scotland's lunacy laws and renovated the Channel Islands' system for treatment of the insane. She went on to tour hospitals and asylums in Holland, Norway, Russia, Greece and Italy.

With the coming of war in America she turned her attention to the army camps, nursing sick and wounded soldiers with her characteristic energy, single-mindedness and attention to details. President Abraham Lincoln appointed her superintendent of women nurses on June 10, 1861, a position she retained until the end of the war, despite considerable criticism of her organizational abilities. She eventually oversaw the recruitment, placement and training of some 2,000 volunteers who cared for the Union war wounded.

Some people found Dix, dour, difficult, cold and distant. "I have no particular love for my species," she once said, "but own to an exhaustless fund of compassion." One of the best known of Civil War nurses, Louisa May Alcott, thought her "a kind old soul, but very queer and arbitrary." She established the strictest of standards for her nurses, though these sometimes had little to do with medicine. She accepted only homely women between the ages of 30 and 45 and required applicants to submit certifications of health and character. "I am plain-looking enough to suit you, and old enough," one prospective volunteer wrote her. "I never had a husband and am not looking for one – will you take me?"

Dix carried on a running battle with hospital administrators, the army medical bureau and the U.S. Sanitary Commission, a volunteer agency that provided a broad

OPPOSITE: Some Sanitary Commission workers at Fredericksburg in 1864

range of services to the troops. The secretary of war finally intervened in October 1863, giving the army surgeon general the power to appoint nurses and subordinating Dix's volunteers to hospital medical officers.

She resumed her work on behalf of the insane after the war, despite recurring tuberculosis and other illnesses. She had "the grasp of intellect, the fertility of resources, and the indomitable force of will that go to the make-up of a great statesman, or a great commander," someone said of her. Toward the end of her life, her health ruined, she moved into the asylum she had founded at Trenton, New Jersey. She died there on July 17, 1887.

Dix, John Adams
(1798-1879) U.S. treasury secretary and Union general

After fighting in the War of 1812 as a boy of 14, he served in the army until 1828. In a meteoric Democratic political career he was New York's secretary of state (1833-1839) and U.S. Senator (1845-1849). As Abraham Lincoln's first secretary of the treasury (January-March 1861), he laid a sound basis for financing the war and issued the famous "American Flag Dispatch": ordering the arrest of a revenue

cutter in New Orleans, he directed, "If anyone attempts to haul down the American flag, shoot him on the spot." As a Union major general, he later held territorial commands, ending the war in command of the Department of the East. He was later U.S. minister to France (1866-1869) and served as governor of New York (1873-1875).

Dodge, Grenville Mellen
(1831-1916) Union general

Born into an old Massachusetts family, he trained as an engineer and, after conducting western railroad surveys, settled in Iowa in 1853. As a Union volunteer, Dodge held a series of commands in the Armies of Southwest Missouri and the Tennessee. He was wounded at Pea Ridge and Atlanta. His most important contribution to the Union army, however, was the construction of bridges and railroads. After the war he became one of the country's major railroad builders. His most notable achievement was the completion of the Union Pacific Railroad while serving as its chief engineer (1866-70). He subsequently built thousands of miles of railroads in the West and Southwest and, after 1900, in Cuba.

John Adams Dix

Donelson, Daniel Smith
(1801-1863) **Confederate general**

A West Point graduate, Donelson was a planter, militiaman and Democratic state legislator in his native Tennessee. An ardent secessionist, he built Fort Donelson while in the provisional army. As a Confederate brigadier general (July 1861), he led brigades in West Virginia, under Robert E. Lee at Charleston and under Braxton Bragg at Perryville, Stones River and Shelbyville. In January 1863 illness forced him to a territorial command, and he commanded the Department of East Tennessee. Sources disagree on the place and circumstances of his death.

Doubleday, Abner
(1819-1893) **Union general**

A native of New York state, he trained as a civil engineer, was graduated from West Point and fought in the Mexican and Seminole wars. On garrison duty, he aimed the Federals' first shot from Fort Sumter. He won successive promotions through the Shenandoah Valley Campaign of 1862. As a brigadier general (February 1862) he fought at Second Bull Run and led divisions at South Mountain, Antietam and Fredericksburg. Promoted to major general, he temporarily led I Corps when

Abner Doubleday

Stephen Arnold Douglas

its commander, John Reynolds, was killed at Gettysburg. He was denied the permanent command, however, and served out the war in administration. He retired from the regular army in 1873. Historians agree that Doubleday had nothing of significance to do with baseball, although he is popularly credited with "inventing" the game in 1839.

Douglas, Stephen Arnold
(1813-1861) **U.S. statesman**

Born in Brandon, Vermont, he settled in Illinois in 1833 and quickly established himself in local politics. Active, acute and articulate, he organized the state's Democratic party and from 1934 to 1842 was a public prosecutor and state legislator, secretary of state, and supreme court judge. In the U.S. Congress (1843-1847) and Senate (1847-1861), his brilliant oratory made "the Little Giant" the nation's foremost advocate of compromise in the prewar years. With Henry Clay, he was instrumental in forging the Compromise of 1850, and his chairmanship of the Committee on Territories put him at the heart of the national debate on slavery. He originated the doctrine of popular sovereignty during the Kansas-Nebraska Act debates (1854) and ensured its incorporation in the acts organizing the territories of Utah and New Mexico. His advocacy of popular sovereignty diminished his Northern support, and his denunciation of the proslavery Lecompton constitution in Kansas (1857) made him unpopular in the South. During his successful Senate race in 1858, his debates with Lincoln propelled Douglas's unknown opponent to national prominence. In 1860 the Northern Democrats nominated Douglas for the presidency after the party split at the Charleston convention. He publicly supported Lincoln after the election and finally abandoned his compromise stance after the attack on Fort Sumter. He died of typhoid fever on a northwestern tour to rally support for the war.

Douglass, Frederick
(c. 1817-1875) **Abolitionist**

Douglass was born into bondage in Talbot County, Maryland, and lived in his grandmother's slave cabin until he was five or six years old, when he went into the home of

his father, a plantation overseer. At the age of eight Douglass was sent to the family of Hugh Auld of Baltimore. There his mistress gave him the rudiments of an education before Auld, hearing of his progress, prohibited any further schooling.

Auld put Douglass to work in the family shipyard in Baltimore but also hired him out to a farm where, working as a field-hand, he endured much abuse. Douglass hatched a plot to escape, but his plans were discovered. He was sent to jail and subsequently put up for auction, but in the end his master decided not to sell him, and he eventually returned to his labors in the Baltimore shipyard.

Douglass made his break from slavery in 1838. He fled the shipyard, safely reached free territory and settled in New Bedford, Massachusetts, with his freedwoman wife, Anna Murray. Though he had learned the caulker's trade in Baltimore, Douglass was barred, because of his race, from working at it in New Bedford. He managed to earn a subsistence as a stevedore and common laborer.

He began his career in public life around this time, speaking out on matters of race at

LEFT: Frederick Douglass.

BELOW: Black Union infantry.

abolition meetings. In 1841 he went to work for the Massachusetts Anti-slavery Society as a lecturer. By 1843, under the auspices of the American Anti-Slavery Society, he was traveling extensively in the Northern states as a lecturer for the abolition cause.

Partly to refute charges that he had invented his slave background, Douglass wrote his famous autobiography in 1844. Published the following year, it contained details such as his master's precise name and address, that exposed him to the possibility of arrest and a return to slavery. He thus went abroad in 1845, continuing his lecturer's work in England, Scotland and Ireland. An English sympathizer purchased his freedom, and he returned in 1847 with sufficient funds to found and edit an antislavery journal, the *North Star*, which he published for 16 years.

Douglass continued to agitate for abolition through the 1850s. In 1859 the authorities accused him of taking part in the John Brown conspiracy. Though he had refused to join the Harpers Ferry venture – "You'll never get out alive," he told Brown – he found it expedient again to go abroad for a time. But he shortly returned, and when war broke out in 1861 he issued an immediate call for the arming of slaves.

From the beginning, Douglass saw the war as a crusade against slavery. He persuaded President Lincoln to allow blacks to fight for the Union. "Give them a chance," he asked. "I don't say they will fight better than other men. All I say is, give them a chance." Douglass saw military service as a means to full acceptance for blacks. "Once let the black man get upon his person the letters U.S.; let him get an eagle on his button, and a musket on his shoulder and bullets in his pocket, and there is no power on earth which can deny he has earned the right to citizenship," he said. Douglass helped to raise the 54th and 55th Massachusetts infantry regiments, and two of his sons were non-commissioned officers in the famous 54th Massachusetts, which lost nearly half its complement in an assault on Fort Wagner, South Carolina, in July 1863.

Douglass remained in demand as a lecturer after the war. He founded another journal, *The New National Era*, and campaigned for full civil rights for the South's freed slaves. In 1877 President Rutherford B. Hayes appointed him U.S. marshal for the District of Columbia; he was the first black to hold that office. From 1889 to 1891 he served as U.S. minister to Haiti. Douglass remained a powerful spokesman for civil rights for blacks until his death.

Drayton, Thomas Fenwick
(1808-1891 Confederate general

A South Carolinian, he was graduated from West Point with Jefferson Davis and spent eight years as an army engineer before returning home to farm. He was a railroad president in 1861. He proved an ineffectual field commander as a Confederate brigadier general at Port Royal and elsewhere. After Antietam and brief court martial duty, he was relegated to inactive field commands in Arkansas and Texas. He failed as a Georgia planter and worked as an insurance agent in later life.

Thomas Fenwick Drayton

Alfred Nattie Duffié

Duffié, Alfred Nattie
(1835-1880) Union general

French-born, Duffié had fought in Senegal, Algiers and the Crimea and had won medals for valor during the French campaign against Austria in 1859. He came to the U.S. in 1861 specifically to join the Union cavalry. Promoted to brigadier general in 1863, Duffié played an important role in cavalry actions throughout the war in the East. He was mustered out in August 1865 and later saw diplomatic service.

Basil Wilson Duke

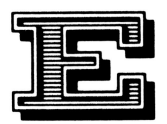

Samual Francis Du Pont

Duke, Basil Wilson
(1838-1916) Confederate general

This Kentucky-born lawyer was an active secessionist in Missouri and was almost hanged by the Union as a spy before he enlisted in his brother-in-law John H. Morgan's "Lexington Rifles." Duke was wounded at Shiloh, was captured in the Ohio raid of 1863 and was promoted to brigadier general in 1864 after his release. In 1865 Duke's cavalry brigade escorted Jefferson Davis from Charlotte, North Carolina, until his capture two weeks later in Georgia. Duke wrote about the Civil War in later years and worked as a lawyer, politician and editor.

Du Pont, Samuel Francis
(1803-1865) Union admiral

Born in Bergen Point, New Jersey, Du Pont began his 50-year navy career in 1815. Commanding the sloop-of-war *Cyane* during the Mexican War, he cleared Mexican forces from the Gulf of California. He helped to organize the naval academy at Annapolis (established 1850),

recommended the navy's adoption of steam power (1851) and in 1855 was prominent on the controversial naval efficiency board that found 201 officers to be incompetent. He headed the Commission of Conference that planned Union naval strategy and operations early in the Civil War (June 1861). As a flag officer, he was appointed (September 1861) the first commander of the South Atlantic Blockading Squadron, at 75 vessels the largest fleet ever commanded by a naval officer at that time. He enforced the blockade in 13 of 14 stations and in a brilliant operation captured Port Royal (November 1861), giving the Federals a southern base and himself earning the Thanks of Congress and a promotion to rear admiral. In coastal operations he seized ships, forts and islands, occupied the Georgia sounds and took Jacksonville and St. Augustine. In April 1863 he suffered a severe setback at Charleston, where the fleet of monitors and ironclads assigned to him suffered much damage in an unsuccessful attempt to take the city. Du Pont thereupon asked to be relieved of his command and spent the rest of the war on boards and commissions. Du Pont Circle in Washington, D.C., is named for him.

Early, Jubal Anderson
(1816-1894) Confederate general

He was born in Franklin County, Virginia. After graduation from West Point he fought in the Seminole War and then resigned to become a Virginia lawyer and Whig state legislator. He volunteered for garrison duty during the Mexican War. Having opposed secession, he nevertheless joined the Confederate army and led the 24th Virginia at First Bull Run. As a brigadier general, he fought in the Peninsular Campaign (wounded at Williamsburg) and Second Bull Run. He commanded a division at Antietam and Fredericksburg and, after being promoted to major general (January 1863), at Chancellorsville, Gettysburg, the Wilderness and Spotsylvania. He led a Corps at Cold Harbor. After

Jubal Anderson Early

May 1864, promoted to lieutenant general, he held an independent command in the Shenandoah Valley, leading raids and other operations as far north as Pennsylvania. He marched on the Union capital in Early's Washington Raid (June-August 1864), but his advance was delayed by the fighting at Monocacy, and when he resumed his advance he found Washington reinforced by two Union corps and was forced to retreat. Defeated by Philip Sheridan at Winchester, Fisher's Hill and Cedar Creek, and routed by George Custer at Waynesboro in March 1865, "Old Jube" was finally relieved of his command in response to mounting public pressure. He resumed his Lynchburg law practice in 1867. He never took the oath of allegiance, but continued to promote the Confederate cause in a war memoir (1866; expanded into an autobiography, 1912) and as president of the Southern Historical Society. He later worked for the Louisiana lottery.

Eaton, John Jr.
(1829-?) Union officer

A New Hampshire native, he entered Union service as chaplain of the 27th Ohio in August 1861. In November of the following year Ulysses S. Grant chose him to

John Echols

direct aid programs for freed slaves in the departments of Tennessee and Arkansas. The War Department used Eton's operation as a model when it established the Freedman's Bureau in 1865; he served as bureau commissioner for Washington, D.C., Maryland and Virginia and ended the war a brevet brigadier general. After the war, Eaton held office briefly as U.S. commissioner of education and later was president of Marietta College in Ohio and Sheldon Jackson College in Utah.

Echols, John
(1823-1896) Confederate general

Echols attended Virginia Military Institute and was graduated from Harvard, returning to Virginia to practice law in 1843. Settling in Monroe (now West Virginia), he became a secessionist and attended the state secession convention. He led the Confederate 27th Virginia at First Bull Run and was wounded at Kernstown. As a brigadier general (April 1862), he fought in the Shenandoah Valley Campaign of Jackson and at New Market and Cold Harbor. He also commanded the West Virginia Department and the District of Southwest Virginia. He surrendered in 1865 after accompanying Jefferson Davis to Augusta. His later business interests included banking and railroads.

Edmonds, Sarah Emma Evelyn
(1841-1898) Union soldier

As a runaway adolescent disguised as "Frank Thompson," she sold Bibles in rural Canada. While living in Michigan she assumed the same identity to join the Union's 2nd Michigan Infantry in 1861. She fought in the 1861-1862 Potomac Army campaigns, deserting in Kentucky in 1863. Her *Nurse and Spy in the Union Army* (1865) made her famous. Pensioned by the army in 1884, she spent her last years as a nurse.

Oliver Edwards

Edwards, Oliver
(1835-1904) Union general

Edwards owned a foundry in Illinois, but he returned home to Massachusetts in 1861 to serve as an adjutant to Union General Darius Couch. He led a regiment on the Peninsula, at Fredericksburg and at Gettysburg. He led a brigade during the New York Draft Riots and fought at the Wilderness and Spotsylvania and in Philip Sheridan's 1864 Valley Campaign. At Sayler's Creek his men captured Confederate generals Richard Ewell and Curtis Lee, their staffs and an entire Confederate brigade. He was promoted to brigadier general in 1865. He was a manufacturer and inventor after the war.

Ellet, Charles, Jr.
(1810-1862)
Engineer, Union naval officer

A native of Pennsylvania, he was a civil engineer famed for designing and building suspension bridges. He also urged the construction of dams and reservoirs to control floods and to foster navigation on the rivers of the American West. In 1855 he published *Coast and Harbour Defences*, in which he proposed construction of "ram boats" – ships with heavy iron prows that could be driven into the hulls of enemy ships. Both the Union and Confederate navies built many of these ram-boats, and in spring 1862 Ellet, by then commissioned an officer in the Union navy, led a fleet of nine ram-boats down the Mississippi River; the operation succeeded in opening the river past Memphis, but Ellet died of wounds received in the action.

Elliott, Washington Lafayette
(1825-1888) Union general

Born in Pennsylvania and the son of a famous naval officer, Elliott failed graduation from West Point and enlisted in the regular army, serving in the Mexican War until he fell ill. He then served on the frontier until appointed a captain in 1861. During the Civil War he fought at Wilson's Creek, New Madrid and Island No. 10 and took part in the siege of Corinth. He was wounded at Second Bull Run. He was breveted a major general for his war services and remained in the regular army until 1879. He later worked in California as a banker.

Ellsworth, Elmer Ephraim
(1837-1861) Union officer

As a young Chicago clerk Ellsworth organized a company of Zouaves, troops known for their exotic Algerian-inspired costumes and flamboyant drill: they performed at the White House in 1860. In May 1861 his New York Zouave regiment helped to take Alexandria, where he was killed in a dispute over a Confederate flag. A friend and election aide of Abraham Lincoln, Ellsworth was the first prominent Union casualty of the war.

Elzey, Arnold
(1816-1871) Confederate general

This Maryland-born West Point graduate served on the frontier, in Seminole War, in the Mexican War and as an Indian fighter. Forced by the Rebels to surrender the U.S.

arsenal in Augusta, Georgia in 1861, he personally brought his troops to Washington, then resigned and accepted a commission with the Confederate forces. He fought at First Bull Run and suffered a head wound at Gaines's Mill (Cold Harbor) in 1862. Although unable to fight, he returned to duty as a major general in December 1862 and commanded the Department of Richmond. He went back into the field as General J. B. Hood's chief of artillery in the Tennessee Campaign. He spent his postwar years peacefully tending to the work on his farm in Maryland.

Ericsson, John
(1803-1889) Marine engineer, inventor

Swedish-born Ericsson joined a corps of mechanical engineers at age 13 and was a Swedish army surveyor before emigrating to England in 1826. There he began his remarkably fertile career as an inventor and engineer, developing, among many other projects, the transmission of power by compressed air, steam boilers, underwater warship engines, screw propellers, a steam

Elmer Ephraim Ellsworth

locomotive (which lost in competition with George Stephenson's Rocket in 1829), and rotary engines. After moving to the U.S. in 1839, he introduced the screw propeller to boats on inland waterways. He designed the steam sloop *Princeton* (1844), the first warship with underwater propellers. In a rare setback, his hot air-powered ship, the *Ericsson*, failed commercially in 1851. In 1861 he revolutionized warship technology with the USS *Monitor*, an ironclad vessel with a revolving gun turret. Based on a design Ericsson had made in 1854, the *Monitor* was built in only 100 days and launched in January 1862. After

John Ericsson

an accident-plagued voyage along the coast, she achieved an historic victory over the CSS *Merrimac* (March 9, 1862). Ericsson received the Thanks of Congress. He went on to design other ironclads for the Union and for foreign countries. He later developed the torpedo technology introduced during the Civil War, as well as heavy guns, superheated steam and the hot air (or gas) engine.

Etheridge, Anna Blair
(b.1844) **Union army nurse**

"Gentle Annie" enlisted with the Union's 2nd Michigan and tended Michigan regiments throughout the war, often working under fire and once being wounded. Union General Philip Kearny died before fulfilling his intention to appoint her a sergeant major, but she earned the Kearny Cross for bravery. She worked for the government after the war.

Evans, Clement Anselm
(1833-1911) **Confederate general**

This George-born judge and legislator fought on the Peninsula, at Fredericksburg, Gettysburg, the Wilderness, Petersburg and Appomattox. He was promoted to brigadier general in 1864 and commanded J. B. Gordon's old brigade both in Jubal Early's Washington raid and during Philip Sheridan's Valley Campaign. Moved by the violence he witnessed at Fredericksburg, Evans became a Methodist preacher after the war. He was active in veterans' organizations and wrote about the war.

Evans, Nathan George
(1824-1868) **Confederate general**

Born in South Carolina and a graduate of West Point, Evans was an Indian fighter before he resigned in 1861 and joined the South Carolina army after the bombardment of Fort Sumter. "Shanks" Evans's career as a cavalry officer began well: he played an important role in the victory at First Bull Run, and he led the Confederate force at Balls Bluff, for which he won the formal thanks of the Confederate congress and a gold medal. In command of the so-called "tramp brigade," he fought at Second Bull Run, Antietam and Vicksburg. But in 1863, after being tried for drunkenness and disobedience, he was relieved of his command, despite being acquitted. In 1864 he returned to the field, only to sustain serious injuries after falling from his horse. He was a school principal in Alabama after the war.

Evarts, William Maxwell
(1818-1901) **Union public official**

Born in Boston, he became a prominent lawyer in New York City and joined the new Republican Party. In 1860 he was secretary of the Union Defense Committee, a moderate group that argued against a definitive split between North and South. In 1863 and again in 1864 he was dispatched by the Union government to England to use his influence and talents to persuade the British to stop building and equipping shops for he Confederate navy. After the war Evarts served as one of the government prosecutors of Jefferson Davis and as one of President Andrew Johnson's defense lawyers during his impeachment trial; his legal and oratorical abilities are credited with keeping Johnson from being convicted of the impeachment charges. Johnson showed his appreciation by appointing him U.S. attorney general (1867-68). In later years Evarts was one of the most prominent lawyers in America, and he served President Hayes as secretary of state (1877-81).

ABOVE: Richard Stoddert Ewell.

BELOW: The remains of Ewell's corps surrenders, April 1865.

Everett, Edward
(1794-1865)
Clergyman, statesman, orator

A classics professor at Harvard and eventually the university's president, Everett also held many high government offices, including U.S. Congressman (1824-1834), governor of Massachusetts (1835-1839), minister to Great Britain (1841-1845) and U.S. Senator (1853-1854). He was noted for brilliant oratory. His many wartime speeches rallied Northern support for the government and were judged by some to be his primary achievement; perhaps the most famous was his two-hour speech preceding Lincoln's brief Gettysburg Address.

Ewell, Richard Stoddert
(1817-1872) Confederate general

Born in Georgetown, D.C., this West Point-trained career officer participated in Indian fighting and the Mexican War. Despite his Unionist sympathies, he became a Confederate brigadier general in June 1861. Ewell was a "fighting" commander. He led the second brigade at First Bull Run; as a major general he won victories at Winchester and Cross Keys and participated in the Peninsular Campaign and at Cedar Mountain and Second Bull Run. Despite the loss of a leg (August 1862), he led the Second Corps as a lieutenant general at Gettysburg, the Wilderness and Spotsylvania. Commanding the Department of Henrico, he was captured by Philip Sheridan at Sayler's Creek in April 1865. He was a Nashville farmer after the war.

Thomas Ewing, Jr.

Ewing, Thomas Jr.
(1829-1896) Union general

A Kansas lawyer and antislavery activist who helped to keep Kansas a free sate, he attended the 1861 Peace Convention in Washington. He resigned from the state supreme court to join the Union army in 1862, fought in Arkansas and commanded the Border District (where he issued the famous Order No. 11, which depopulated western Missouri in order to eradicate the guerrillas) and at St. Louis. He was a prominent Ohio (and, after 1881, New York) lawyer and politician after the war.

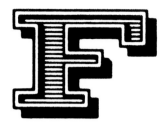

Democratic, then as a Republican. Enlisting as a Union private in 1861, he was soon promoted to captain. He led a regiment in the Iron Brigade at Second Bull Run and was wounded and captured at Gettysburg. Promoted to brigadier general in 1863, he resigned soon after, becoming governor of Wisconsin from 1886 to 1872, then serving as consul in England and Paris and then as ambassador to Spain (1880-1882).

Farnsworth, Elon John
(1837-1863) Union general

This Michigan native left the Utah Expedition against the Mormons to join the Union's 8th Illinois Cavalry in September 1861. He fought in every regimental operation (some 41 engagements) until his death, meanwhile serving as acting chief quartermaster of IV Corps and later as General Alfred Pleasanton's aide-de-camp. Farnsworth was killed while courageously leading a doomed cavalry charge, ordered by General H. J. Kilpatrick on the third day at Gettysburg, four days after his promotion to brigadier general.

Farragut, David Glasgow
(1801-1870) Union admiral

Born in Tennessee, orphaned young, educated in Washington, D.C., and Pennsylvania, he entered the U.S. Navy in 1810, when he was nine, and went to sea the following year in the frigate USS *Essex*. In 1812 the captain of the *Essex*, Farragut's guardian, David Porter, gave the 12-year-old midshipman his first command, a prize of war taken in the Pacific Ocean. Farragut sailed the vessel safely and without incident across the Pacific to the Chilean port of Valparaiso.

After the War of 1812 he served in the Mediterranean for five years. There had not been time for much formal education,

BELOW: David Glasgow Farragut.

OPPOSITE: Farragut on *Hartford*'s quarterdeck (top) and (below) a view of Mobile Bay's Fort Morgan.

Fairchild, Lucius
(1831-1896) Union general

Born in Ohio, Fairchild joined the California Gold Rush in 1849, then returned to Wisconsin to hold public office, first as a

Lucius Fairchild

so he resumed his studies during a nine-month period ashore with the American consul in Tunis. In fact, Farragut always tended to pick up knowledge wherever it was available: in the 1820s, while living in New Haven, he attended lectures at Yale, and he audited lectures at the Smithsonian Institution during a tour of duty in Washington.

Farragut served in the West Indies and in the South Atlantic and commanded the sloop *Saratoga* on blockade duty off Vera Cruz during the Mexican War. He spent many years on shore duty, much of it in Norfolk, Virginia, where he met his first

Edward Ferrero

wife, who died in 1840, and his second, whom he married three years later. In 1854 the navy sent him west to establish a ship-yard at Mare Island, California, and he received the coveted promotion to captain the following year.

Unemployed at the outbreak of the Civil War, he went into a brief period in limbo in New York: the authorities evidently considered his loyalty suspect – he was Tennessee born, with Virginia connections by marriage. He finally received an active appointment on January 9, 1862, when he was given command of the Gulf Blockading Squadron.

Farragut launched the initial Union effort to open the Mississippi on April 18,

1862. "As to being prepared for defeat, I certainly am not," he had written his wife. "I hope for success; shall do all in my power to secure it, and trust to God for the rest." Six days later, on the night of April 23-24, he sailed his flotilla past the guns of Confederate forts Jackson and St. Philip, fought a sharp battle with Confederate warships and captured New Orleans. The victory earned him a promotion to rear admiral and confirmed him as the pre-eminent Union naval commander. It came as he approached his 50th anniversary of naval service.

In 1862 and 1863 Farragut commanded the naval forces in the combined operations against Vicksburg, which finally fell to Ulysses S. Grant's besieging army on July 4, 1863. He sailed to New York City in his flagship, the steam sloop *Hartford*, to a hero's welcome in August. The Navy secretary, Gideon Welles, said of Farragut that he would "more willingly take great risks to obtain great results than any officer in either army or navy." After several months of rest, he returned to the Gulf of Mexico early in 1864 to plan a daring assault on the Confederate defenses in Mobile Bay.

His fleet moved against the Alabama harbor forts early on August 5, 1864. Despite mines – then known as torpedoes – in the channel and an accurate fire from the forts, he pressed on. One of his monitors, *Tecumseh*, struck a torpedo and sank. "Torpedoes ahead," someone called from the sloop-of-war *Brooklyn*, next ahead of Farragut's flagship. "Damn the torpedoes," he replied. Soon the fleet was safely into Mobile Bay. There followed a fierce battle with the defending Confederate fleet, but eventually all the Rebel ships and forts surrendered. The South had lost the use of its greatest remaining port.

Farragut returned to New York City at year's end. Failing health prevented him from taking command of the naval forces assembling to attack Wilmington, North Carolina, the last Confederate port to remain open. After a convalescent leave, he served briefly on the James River in Virginia and was one of the first Northern officers to enter Richmond after the fall of the Confederate capital on April 3, 1865.

Promoted to full admiral in July 1866, he was the first to hold that rank in the U.S. Navy's history. Farragut commanded the European Squadron in 1867 before going into semi-retirement. He never fully recovered from a severe heart attack in 1869. He died on August 14 of the following year in the commandant's house at the navy yard in Portsmouth, New Hampshire.

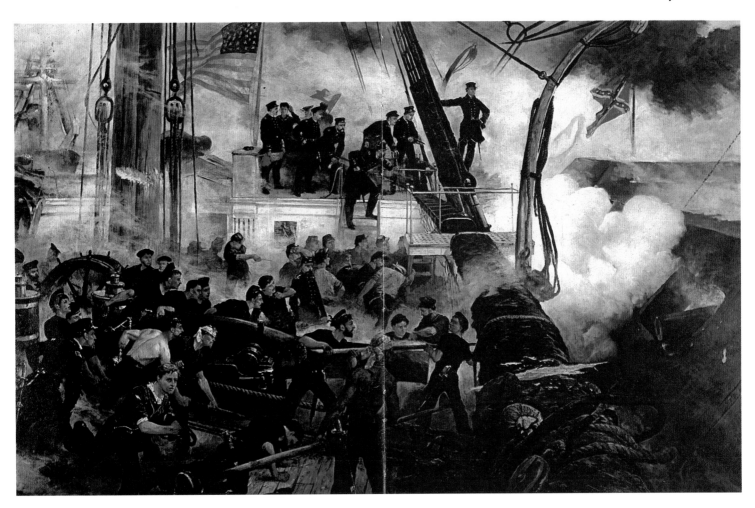

Ferrero, Edward
(1831-1899) Union general

This Spanish immigrant, a New York dancing instructor and militiaman, fought under Ambrose Burnside in North Carolina, led Potomac Army troops from Second Bull Run through Fredericksburg and joined Ulysses S. Grant's army at Vicksburg and Knoxville. He won notoriety at the Petersburg crater by abandoning his black division after ordering them to charge.

Fessenden, James Deering
(1833-1882) Union general

A Bowdoin College graduate and Maine lawyer, he recruited sharpshooters and trained Union volunteers in Virginia in 1861. He was David Hunter's aide-de-camp in the Carolinas in March 1862. He fought at Charleston in spring 1863 and later in the year at Lookout Mountain and Missionary Ridge. His distinguished contribution to the Atlanta Campaign was rewarded with a promotion in administrative posts. While on Hunter's staff Fessenden organized the first black Union regiment, which the authorities, however, disbanded. As a Portland, Maine, lawyer he was later register of bankruptcy (1868-1878).

Finley, Jesse Johnson
(1812-1904) Confederate general

This Tennessee-born lawyer served in the Seminole War, was an Arkansas legislator, a mayor of Memphis, a Whig politician and a judge before he enlisted in the Confederate army in 1862. Appointed a brigadier general in 1863, he fought in Kirby Smith's

Clinton Bowen Fisk

Farragut on *Hartford* during the duel with Fort Morgan in Mobile Bay

Kentucky Campaign, at Chickamauga and in the Atlanta Campaign. He was wounded at Resaca and Jonesboro. He served in the U.S. Congress and Senate after the war.

Fisk, Clinton Bowen
(1828-1890) Union general

A New York-born banker, Fisk was wiped out by the Panic of 1857. A friend of both Ulysses S. Grant and Abraham Lincoln, he joined the Union forces in Missouri and was eventually breveted a major general for war service. After the war Fisk was appointed to the Freedman's Bureau and went on to open an African-American school in Nashville, chartered as Fisk University in 1867. From 1881 to 1890 he was president of the Board of Indian Commissioners. A Methodist and temperance leader, in 1888 he was a presidential candidate for the Prohibition Party.

Floyd, John Buchanan
(1806-1863) Confederate general

Born in Blacksburg, Virginia, and educated at the College of South Carolina, he practiced law and politics and won election to

John Buchanan Floyd

Andrew Hull Foote

Fogg, Isabella
Sanitary Commission worker

She joined a Maine regiment as a nurse when her son enlisted in 1861. Fogg served the Potomac Army in field hospitals, the hospital ship *Elm City* and behind the lines in the Peninsular and Antietam Campaigns and at Fredericksburg, Chancellorsville, Gettysburg and the Wilderness. In January 1865 she was permanently disabled by a fall sustained on a hospital ship.

Foote, Andrew Hull
(1806-1863) Union admiral

The son of a Connecticut Senator, he became a midshipman in 1822 and, as a deeply religious man, worked during his naval career for temperance and other reforms (he was instrumental in abolishing the navy's spirit ration in 1862). He wrote and lectured against the slave trade in the 1850s. From August 1861 to May 1862 he commanded the Union's upper Mississippi naval operations, building the river flotilla and fighting at forts Henry and Donelson. Invalided and promoted to rear admiral, he then directed the bureau of equipment and

the Virginia governorship in 1850. Floyd served as President James Buchanan's secretary of war from 1857 until the end of 1860, when he resigned to try his fortunes with the new Confederacy. Commissioned a brigadier general in 1861, he was in command at Fort Donnelson, Kentucky, when Union forces under Ulysses S. Grant attacked in February 1862. Floyd turned the fort over to his next in command and fled before the Federals captured the place. Jefferson Davis relieved him of his command.

Foote's Mississippi fleet bombarding Island No. 10. This Confederate stronghold fell on April 7, 1862.

recruiting. Foote died of illness in June 1863 en route to assume command of Samuel Du Pont's squadron off Charleston, South Carolina.

Forbes, Edwin
(1839-1895) War artist

He was a New York artist sent by *Frank Leslie's Illustrated Newspaper* to illustrate the Potomac Army's operations. Forbes stayed in the field from 1861 to 1864, sending back a series of sketches of camps and battlefields. Later etched as *Life Studies of the Great Army* (1876), these Civil War sketches remained the highlight of his long career as an illustrator and artist.

Force, Manning Ferguson
(1824-1899) Union general

Born in Washington, D.C., he became a lawyer. He was appointed a Union major in 1861 and fought at Fort Donelson, Shiloh and in the Vicksburg Campaign. Promoted to brigadier general in August 1863, he served in W. T. Sherman's 1864 Meridan and Atlanta campaigns. He was shot in the face just outside Atlanta, but he continued to serve in the March to the Sea. He was eventually (1892) awarded the Medal of Honor for his actions at Atlanta. After the war he was a lawyer, judge and writer.

Forney, William Henry
(1823-1894) Confederate general

This North Carolina-born lawyer had served in the U.S. Army in the Mexican War but in 1861 accepted a commission as a captain for the Confederates. During his career he was wounded at Dranesville, Williamsburg, Salem Church and Gettysburg. He was captured while in the hospital after Williamsburg, and then again at Gettysburg. Though permanently crippled after Gettysburg, he was appointed a brigadier general after his release and fought at Petersburg, Hatcher's Run, High Bridge, Farmville and Appomattox. He was a legislator after the war.

Forrest, Nathan Bedford
(1821-1877) Confederate General

His father, a blacksmith who settled on the Tennessee frontier in 1806, died when he was 16, leaving him to be the sole support for a large family. Forrest had scant education but a surplus of native wit; starting as a farm laborer and building on a small livestock trading business, he bought cotton plantations in Arkansas and Mississippi and gradually amassed a fortune.

In 1849 Forrest moved to Memphis, and for a time was an alderman there. He had had no military training, so when war broke out he enlisted as a private in a Confederate cavalry regiment that he raised and equipped at his own expense. By October 1861 he had risen to lieutenant colonel's rank and had taken command of the regiment. During his first major campaign, at Fort Donelson in February 1862, he argued against surrender of the besieged garrison and, when his arguments failed, led his troopers, with several hundred volunteers from other units, through the Union lines to escape the doomed fort.

Seriously wounded at the Battle of Shiloh in April 1862, he recovered and embarked on a career that would make him one of the greatest cavalry raiders of the Civil War. His first foray, in the midsummer of 1862, took him to Murfreesboro, Tennessee, where he surprised the Federal garrison, captured 1,000 prisoners, destroyed or carried off supplies valued at $1 million and wrecked a long stretch of railroad. Operating from west Tennessee in 1862-63, he raided Ulysses S. Grant's supply lines and seriously impeded his drive on Vicksburg. When Federal forces brought Forrest to bay at Parker's Crossroads, Tennessee, on the last day of 1862, he is reputed to have ordered his cavalry, "Charge them both ways!" In the event,

An Edwin Forbes sketch shows Union troops re-forming at Antietam.

Nathan Bedford Forrest

hard-pressed Confederate troopers kept the two Federal wings from meeting long enough to escape.

In the spring of 1863 Forrest broke up a Federal raid styled after one of his own deep penetrations. After a long, exhausting chase he caught Union Colonel Abel Streight's cavalry at Cedar Bluffs, Alabama, and, through a ruse that involved marching his men and guns in a circle, convinced Streight to surrender his 1,500 troopers to one-third as many Confederates.

He fought at Chickamauga in September 1863 and in the aftermath of the battle clashed with the Confederate commander in Tennessee, Braxton Bragg. After investigating the incident, C.S.A. President Jefferson Davis declined to lay blame on either officer, but he promoted Forrest to major general and transferred him to another command, where he soon resumed his independent and highly successful raiding.

In April 1864 Forrest's command carried out the infamous massacre of black troops

who had tried to surrender at Fort Pillow, Tennessee. Though Forrest denied ordering the killings, he earlier had threatened the Federals with no quarter, a tactic he often used to encourage the enemy to give up. In this instance, the Confederates carried out the threat, killing several dozen black soldiers in cold blood.

From June to November 1864 Forrest led a series of raids on W. T. Sherman's lines of communication and fought several defensive battles against large Federal forces dispatched to track down and destroy him. Sherman vowed to stop Forrest "if it costs ten thousand lives and bankrupts the federal treasury," but his executants were scarcely up to the task. Forrest routed a Federal force with nearly twice his numbers at Brice's Cross Roads, Mississippi, on June 10, capturing 2,000 men, 16 guns and 250 wagons. A month later, again heavily outnumbered, he fought a drawn battle against A. J. Smith's Federals at Tupelo, losing nearly 1,100 men before Smith, low on ammunition and rations, retreated to Memphis to refit. When Smith

returned to the chase, Forrest, in an audacious raid, rode into Memphis with 2,000 men on August 21 and just missed taking two Union generals prisoner before he retired. In October and November, in one of his most successful raids, another foray into west Tennessee, he destroyed four gunboats, 14 river transports and 20 barges, and took or burned nearly $7 million-worth of property.

Forrest commanded the Confederate cavalry in J. B. Hood's disastrous Tennessee Campaign of late 1864 and returned to independent operations after the destruction of Hood's army in December. Promotion to lieutenant general came to him in February 1865, though by then his troops were so worn down by fighting and hunger that they had lost much of their effectiveness. In March and April Forrest could not stop Union General James H. Wilson's raid to Selma, Alabama, perhaps his only important failure of the war. On May 4 his troops were surrendered.

"I went into the army worth a million and a half dollars and came out a beggar," Forrest said. He suffered personal losses too. One of his seven brothers was killed commanding a brigade at Okolona, Mississippi, in February 1864; a second died of pneumonia in Confederate service. Forrest returned to his cotton interests after the war and, for a time, served as president of a railroad that eventually went bankrupt. He had a brief postwar involvement with the Ku Klux Klan in Tennessee, holding office as its Grand Wizard from 1867 to 1869.

Tall, lithe, powerful, mild in repose but fiercely – some said maniacally – aggressive in battle, Forrest had an instinctive genius for soldiering. His colloquial formula for battlefield success, "Get thar fust with the most men," is widely quoted, but the notion that he was uniformly coarse of speech and manner is myth. Someone once asked Gen. Joseph E. Johnston to name the war's preeminent soldier. Johnston answered: "Forrest, who, had he had the advantages of a thorough military education and training, would have been the great central figure of the Civil War."

Fowle, Elida Barker Rumsey (1842-1919) Philanthropist

Too young to enlist as an army nurse, she developed a private wartime relief effort, visiting camps and hospitals and raising money by performing concerts with her fiancé, John Fowle. The pair founded the Soldiers' Free Library in Washington, D.C., and became such famous field nurses that they were married before a joint session of Congress in March 1863. After the war she performed charitable works in New York and Boston.

Fox, Gustavus Vasa
(1821-1883)
Union assistant navy secretary

An Annapolis graduate, Fox resigned from the navy in 1856 and became a manufacturer in his native Massachusetts. In April 1861 he headed a volunteer expedition to reinforce Fort Sumter, arriving in time to observe the bombardment and evacuate the Federals after their surrender: Lincoln commended this operation. The post of first assistant secretary of the navy was created for him, and throughout the war Fox proved an indispensable planner of naval operations. He proposed David Farragut for the New Orleans command and supported the adoption of the ironclad *Monitor*. He afterward returned to his Massachusetts business career.

Franklin, William Buel
(1823-1903) Union general

This Pennsylvania-born West Point graduate was a surveyor in the Mexican war and on Stephen Kearney's Rocky Mountain expedition. Appointed a colonel in May 1861 and promoted to brigadier general three days later, he fought at First Bull Run, in

William Buel Franklin

the Peninsular Campaign and at Antietam. He was blamed by Ambrose Burnside and the Committee on the Conduct of the War for his part in the Union's disaster at Fredericksburg. He was wounded at Pleasant Hill in April 1864 and then was captured that July by Jubal Early's men, only to escape a day later. He never served in the field after his capture but remained in the army until 1866. He was vice-president of the Colt's Fire Arms Manufacturing Company until 1888, then held various public offices.

Frémont, John Charles
(1813-1890) Union general

Raised in South Carolina, he joined the army's topographical corps and began his explorations of the western frontier. In his first major independent expedition he employed Kit Carson as a guide along the route of the Oregon Trail (1842). His spectacular 1843-1844 expedition through Oregon, Vancouver, Nevada, New Mexico and Utah made him a national hero. These explorations were important first steps in settling the western territories. His expedition members formed the "California Battalion" during the Mexican War and helped to secure California, where he was briefly governor (1847). He became rich during the Gold Rush and later led expeditions to identify railroad routes. In 1856 he was the Republican and Know-Nothing presidential candidate. From July 1861 he commanded the Union army's Department of

John C. Frémont (left), as the 1864 Radical Democratic candidate

the West, a difficult job made worse by the flamboyance, recklessness and corruption of his administration and by his excessively harsh policies toward slave-holders (which precipitated his removal). Sent abruptly to the Mountain Department in March 1862, Frémont failed to stop T. J. Jackson in his Shenandoah Valley Campaign of 1862 and was relieved of his command in June when he refused to serve under his old adversary, John Pope. The favored candidate of the Radical Republicans to oppose Lincoln in 1864, he withdrew from the race in September. After the war his fortunes and reputation declined steadily: he went bankrupt as the president of the Memphis and El Paso Railroad (1865-1873). He did, however, serve as a territorial governor of Arizona (1878-1883).

French, William Henry
(1815-1881) Union general

A Maryland-born West Point graduate, he fought in the Seminole and Mexican wars. He held Union commands in the Gulf and in Washington's defenses in 1861-1862 and fought on the Peninsula and at Antietam, Fredericksburg, Chancellorsville and Gettysburg. He lost his command of III Corps after misjudgements in the Mine Run Campaign (1863), ending his wartime field service.

William Henry French

Frietschie, Barbara Hauer
(1766-1862) Patriot

She was the widow of a Frederick, Maryland, glovemaker. According to popular legend, as T. J. Jackson's troops marched out of the border town of Frederick en route to Antietam in September 1862, this 95-year-old patriot defiantly waved a Union flag, winning Jackson's respect. Upon hearing this story, John Greenleaf Whittier composed his 1863 poem "Barbara Fritchie," which made her a national heroine. There is, however, scant evidence that the incident ever took place.

Fry, Birkett Davenport
(1822-1891) Confederate general

He practiced law in his native Virginia and California and was an Alabama businessman before the war. A Mexican War veteran, he joined the Confederate army's 13th Alabama infantry in 1861. Fry was repeatedly wounded (at Seven Pines, Antietam, Chancellorsville and Gettysburg): at Gettysburg he was captured while

Barbara Frietschie (Fritchie), as she was popularly imagined

leading a brigade in Pickett's Charge. Exchanged in April 1864 and promoted to brigadier general, he fought at Drewry's Bluff and Cold Harbor. He later commanded the District of Augusta. After the war he was a cotton trader in Alabama and Virginia.

Birkett Davenport Fry

Gamble, Hamilton Rowan
(1798-1864)
Union governor of Missouri

A Virginia-born Missouri legislator and judge, he left retirement in 1861 to become provisional governor in June when secessionist officials fled the state. Gamble

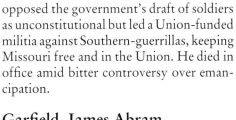

James Abram Garfield

opposed the government's draft of soldiers as unconstitutional but led a Union-funded militia against Southern-guerrillas, keeping Missouri free and in the Union. He died in office amid bitter controversy over emancipation.

Garfield, James Abram
(1831-1881) Union general and 20th president of the United States

Garfield worked his way through an impoverished childhood, was graduated from Williams College and became a teacher and lay preacher. He left the Ohio legislature (1859-1861) for the Union army's 42nd Ohio in 1861 and earned rapid promotions, leading brigades at Middle Creek, Pound Gap and Shiloh. He was William Rosecrans's chief of staff in the Chickamauga Campaign before resigning as a major general in December 1863 to sit in the U.S. Congress (1863-1880). He was a Republican Party loyalist who earned a reputation for his advocacy of sound finance policy. A compromise candidate, he was elected U.S. president in a close election in 1880. He was assassinated by a disappointed office-seeker in July 1861.

Garnett, Richard Brooke
(1819-1863) Confederate general

A Virginian West Point graduate and career officer, he saw fighting in the Seminole and Mexican wars and frontier service before resigning to join the Confederate army in 1861. He led the Stonewall Brigade under T. J. Jackson in the Shenandoah Valley Campaign of 1862 but was relieved of his command for ordering his brigade's withdrawal at Kernstown in March. He commanded George Pickett's brigade in the Maryland Campaign and his own brigade at Fredericksburg. He was killed in Pickett's Charge at Gettysburg.

Kenner Garrard

Garrard, Kenner
(1828-1879) Union officer

This Kentucky-born West Point graduate was captured in April 1861 by Southern sympathizers while in San Antonio, Texas, and then paroled. He was commissioned a colonel in the Union army in 1862 and fought at Fredericksburg, Chancellorsville and Gettysburg, in the Rappahannock and Mine Run campaigns and at Covington and Nashville. He was breveted major general for war service. He resigned in 1866, worked in real estate and studied history after the war.

Gary, Martin Weatherspoon
(1831-1881) Confederate general

This South Carolina-born lawyer was a secessionist leader. As a commissioned captain in what became known as the Confederate army's Hampton Legion, he fought in various battles, including First Bull Run, the battles of the Peninsular Campaign, Second Bull Run, Antietam, Fredericksburg, Chickamauga, Knoxville and Appomattox. Appointed a brigadier general in May 1864, Gary was the last Confederate general in Richmond before its fall. He escorted Jefferson Davis to Cokesbury, South Carolina, where one of the last cabinet meetings was held at the house of Gary's mother. He was a legislator after the war.

Getty, George Washington
(1819-1901) Union general

Born in Washington, D.C., this West Point graduate was a veteran of the Seminole and Mexican wars. He commanded Union artillery batteries in the Peninsular Campaign and at South Mountain and Antietam. As a brigadier general he led a division at Fredericksburg. He constructed entrenched lines at Norfolk and Portsmouth and suffered severe wounds in the Battle of the Wilderness, recovering to participate in the Shenandoah Valley Campaign of Philip Sheridan, the Petersburg siege and the final pursuit of Robert E. Lee. He retired from active service in 1883.

George Washington Getty

John Gibbon

Gibbon, John
(1827-1896) Union general

This Pennsylvania-born West Point graduate served in the Seminole War and on the frontier. He joined the Union army even though three of his brothers chose to fight with the Confederate forces. He began as General Irvin McDowell's chief of artillery and was made a brigadier general in May 1862. He fought at Gainesville, Second Bull Run and Antietam; at South Mountain his command was named the Iron Brigade. He was wounded at both Fredericksburg and Gettysburg. After his recovery after Gettysburg, he fought at the Wilderness, Spotsylvania, Cold Harbor, Petersburg and Appomattox. He was promoted to major general in 1864 and continue in the regular army until 1891. He spent most of his years after the war on the frontier and led the relief column to Little Big Horn in 1876; it arrived in time to bury George Custer and all his men.

Gillmore, Quincy Adams
(1825-1888) Union general

This Ohio-born West Point graduate was an engineer and teacher at West Point before being appointed the Union's acting chief engineer on the Port Royal expedition to South Carolina in 1861. He was injured after falling from his horse in pursuit of Jubal Early in the Shenandoah Valley in 1864. After his recovery he served on various boards and commissions. He became especially well known for the 400 medals – the Gillmore Medal of Honor – he personally issued to the enlisted men who had served under him in Charleston, South Carolina, in a vain effort to recapture Fort Sumter. (The fort surrendered only on April 14, 1865.) After the war, he remained in the regular army, wrote several engineering texts and was president of the Mississippi River Commission.

Gilson, Helen Louise
(1835-1868)
Sanitary Commission worker

A Massachusetts native, she organized a local soldier's aid society before joining the Sanitary Commission in 1862. She began her field work in the Peninsula and accompanied the Potomac Army for two years. She specialized in organizing contraband and freed blacks to provide services to Union troops. Taking over the City Point hospital in Virginia in June 1864, she reorganized a crude operation into a model of efficiency.

Goldsborough, Louis Malesherbes
(1805-1877) **Union naval officer**

He joined the navy as a boy in 1816 and saw action in the first Seminole War and in Mexico. Appointed to command the Union's Atlantic Blockading Squadron in September 1861, Goldsborough led Union naval forces in the successful joint operation with A. E. Burnside along the North Carolina coast in February 1862. He came in for heavy criticism in May 1862 when his James River flotilla failed to capture Rich-

Quincy Adams Gillmore

Helen Louise Gilson

mond. In September, largely as a result of this criticism, he asked to be relieved. Goldsborough held administrative appointments in Washington until the last months of the war, when he commanded the European Squadron. He retired in 1873 after 57 years of service.

Gordon, John Brown
(1832-1904) **Confederate general**

Gordon practiced law in Alabama and was developing coal mines in his native Georgia in 1861. An untrained but gifted officer, he fought with the Confederacy's 6th Ala- bama and then with a Georgia brigade at Seven Pines, Malvern Hill, Antietam, Chancellorsville, Gettysburg and Spotsylvania. Appointed a major general, he led the failed assault on Fort Stedman at Petersburg. His wife, Fanny Haralson Gordon, accompanied him in the field throughout the war. Later, as a popular Democratic U.S. Senator (1873-1880, 1891-1897) and state governor (1886-1890), he promoted Georgia's industrial and commercial development so successfully that he became a revered figure in the state.

Gorgas, Josiah
(1818-1883)
Confederate general, chief of ordnance

This Pennsylvania-born West Point graduate studied military units in Europe before fighting in the Mexican War. He resigned from the U.S. Army in April 1861 and joined the Confederates as chief of ordnance. Appalled at the lack of supplies, by 1863 he had gotten the ordnance bureau running successfully, and by November 1864 he was promoted to brigadier general. After the war he served as chancellor of Sewanee College and president of the University of Alabama. He was the father or William C. Gorgas, who later became the surgeon general.

Granger, Gordon
(1822-1876) Union general

This New York-born West Point graduate served in the Mexican War, and on the frontier as an Indian fighter. He was appointed a major general in the Union army in 1862. Among other battles, he fought at Wilson's Creek, New Madrid and Island No. 10, Tullahoma, Chickamauga, Missionary Ridge, Knoxville and Mobile. He remained in the regular army after the war and died while on duty.

Grant, Ulysses Simpson
(1822-1885) Union general, 18th president of the United States

A tanner's son, born Hiram Ulysses Grant at Point Pleasant, Ohio, he grew up in modest circumstances. His hard-working father eventually attained a degree of prosperity, enabling him to attend school regularly until the age of 17. Hating the tannery, he worked on his father's farm, where he became a master handler of horses. Grant loved animals and disapproved of killing them, even for food. He once explained his distaste for chicken by saying he could not bring himself "to eat anything that goes on two legs."

He arrived at West Point in 1839. Listed incorrectly as Ulysses S. Grant, he dropped Hiram, adopted his mother's maiden name of Simpson and retained the new designation for the rest of his life. His cadet career was uneventful. Commissioned in 1843, he served in Missouri and Louisiana. In 1846-47 he fought in Mexico, earning citations for bravery, and performed ably as quartermaster in Winfield Scott's army during the march on Mexico City.

Grant married Julia Dent in 1848. Assigned to remote Pacific Coast garrisons

where she could not follow, he was miserable, lonely and increasingly bibulous. Higher authority reprimanded him for his heavy drinking, and he resigned from the service in 1854, evidently to avoid being dismissed.

He was a failure in civil life. Unable to make farming pay, he was reduced during one difficult period to selling firewood for a living. In 1860 he went to work as a clerk in his brothers' dry goods store in Galena, Illinois. The advent of the Civil War changed Grant's fortunes at a stroke. In June 1861 he obtained a commission in the Union army as colonel of an Illinois volunteer infantry regiment. By September he had risen to brigadier in command of the Cairo military district. "Be careful," his father wrote. "You're a general now; it's a good job, don't lose it."

In early 1862 Grant set out on the Kentucky-Tennessee River Campaign that would first make him famous. Moving swiftly, with gunboat support, he captured Fort Henry and then Fort Donelson – the latter the most important Union victory of the war to date. At Shiloh, in April, he allowed his army to be surprised and nearly routed, but he recovered on the second day and drove the Confederates from the field. In the aftermath of bloody Shiloh Lincoln rejected calls for his removal. "I can't spare this man," the president said. "He fights."

Quiet and shy, unprepossessing in appearance, Grant proved himself over the next year to be a bold and brilliant strate-

ABOVE: Ulysses Simpson Grant.

OPPOSITE: A haggard Grant after the grisly Battle of Cold Harbor.

gist and a master of the logistical problems of war. In spite of his early trials, he seemed to be without fear of failure. His campaign against Vicksburg, the fortress city controlling the Mississippi River, ended on July 4, 1863, with the surrender of the city. It was probably the war's pivotal Union victory. In November Grant lifted the siege of Chattanooga, Tennessee, decisively defeating the Confederates under Braxton Bragg at Missionary Ridge.

Lincoln appointed Grant commander-in-chief of all the Union armies in March 1864. Making his headquarters in the field with the Army of the Potomac, Grant moved against Robert E. Lee in Virginia while W.T. Sherman, his successor in Tennessee marched into Georgia towards Atlanta. Grant crossed the Rapidan on May 4, and over the next six weeks he and Robert E. Lee clashed in an uninterrupted series of terrible battles – the Wilderness, Spotsylvania, Cold Harbor and Petersburg. "I propose to fight it on this line if it takes all summer," Grant wrote in a famous dispatch from Spotsylvania. His surprise crossing of the James River in June has been called one of the most brilliant operations of the war, for it forced Lee to adopt a static defense behind the lines at Petersburg. But Grant's army had been so

Two Grant victories: Fort Donelson (top) and Lookout Mountain (right). Shown opposite are scenes of his life.

for the presidency and won an overwhelming election victory in November. His two terms were undistinguished and were marked by unprecedented graft and corruption, though scandal never touched Grant himself. He left office with a net worth of only a few thousand dollars. His final years were difficult. He tried business again – and failed again. He pledged his swords and other military memorabilia as credit and lost them. Then a painful throat cancer gradually weakened him. He died on July 23, 1885, not long after he finished his *Personal Memoirs*, one of the great classics of military literature. Grant's friend Mark Twain saw to publication of the manuscript. Royalties from the book left Grant's widow and children financially secure to the end of their lives.

bled that it could not crack the Petersburg defenses. From his crossing of the Rapidan on May 4 to June 19, when Grant suspended the Petersburg offensive and settled down to a siege, the Potomac army had lost 66,000 men – fully half its strength at the start of the campaign.

Grant's last campaign opened on March 29, 1865, with the Union cavalry under Philip Sheridan ranging out beyond the Confederate flank. With strong infantry support, Sheridan turned Lee's right at Five Forks on April 1, forcing the abandonment of Petersburg and the evacuation of Richmond. Lee retreated westward along the Appomattox River, hoping to outrun the Federals and link up with J. E. Johnston's small army in North Carolina. But Sheridan forced the pursuit. "If the thing is pressed I think Lee will surrender," he wrote to Grant after the battle of Sayler's Creek on April 6. Grant passed the message on to Lincoln. "Let the thing be pressed," the president replied.

Grant offered Lee generous terms, including a proviso that Confederate officers and men would be paroled and could go home. Lee signed the surrender document at Appomattox Court House on the afternoon of April 9, and the Army of Northern Virginia passed out of existence.

Over the summer Grant supervised the dismantling of the vast Union war machine. As commander-in-chief of the army, he subsequently oversaw the military aspects of Reconstruction, often finding himself at odds with the martyred Lincoln's successor, Andrew Johnson. In 1868 Grant accepted the Republican nomination

Horace Greeley

Greeley, Horace
(1811-1872) Editor and politician

New Hampshire-born Greeley was a New York printer and newspaper editor after 1831. There he founded the Whig *Tribune* (1841, editor until 1872). The leading Northern newspaper, the New York *Tribune* was a forum for antislavery, anticompromise and emancipation views. Greeley was at first a powerful moral spokesman for the North, but he eroded his popular support by withholding support from Lincoln and opposing conciliatory policies for most of the war and then, towards its end, urging Lincoln to negotiate a peace treaty favorable to the South. As the Democratic presidential candidate in 1872, he was soundly defeated by Ulysses S. Grant. He died, apparently insane, two months later.

Green, Thomas
(1814-1864) Confederate general

Born in Virginia, Green served in the Texas army, as an Indian fighter and in the Mexican War. Commissioned a colonel in the Confederate army in August 1861, he fought in the New Mexico operations, at Galveston, Camp Bisland, LaFourche, Fordoche and Bayou Bourbeau. He was appointed a brigadier general in May 1863 and went to Texas when Union General Nathaniel Banks mounted some half-hearted operations along the Texas coast late in the year. He was killed leading a cavalry attack in Louisiana during the Red River Campaign.

Greene, George Sears
(1801-1899) Union general

Born into an old Rhode Island family, this West Point mathematics teacher and artilleryman had resigned from the army in 1836 to build railroads. On the outbreak of the Civil War he enlisted in the Union army and fought in the Shenandoah Valley Campaign of 1862 and at Cedar Mountain, Antietam, Chancellorsville and Gettysburg. Shot in the face at Wauhatchie, he recovered to participate in W. T. Sherman's North Carolina Campaign. He later engineered major railroad, water, and sewage systems in New York, Washington, D.C., Detroit and other cities.

Greenhow, Rose O'Neal
(*c.*1815-1864) Confederate spy

She was born in Maryland. Married in 1835 to a prominent physician and historian, Robert Greenhow (1800-1854), she was a well-connected Washington political hostess and proslavery activist. She relayed Union General Irvin McDowell's plans for First Bull Run to P. G. T. Beauregard, and her home remained an exchange for Confederate intelligence during her subsequent house arrest. Imprisoned in January 1862, she relayed yet more information to the Confederates from her Washington jail.

George Sears Greene

Tried and exiled to the South, she traveled to England as a Confederate agent but was accidentally drowned while returning home.

Gregg, David McMurtrie
(1833-1916) Union general

A Pennsylvanian, he was a West Point-trained cavalryman and veteran Indian fighter at the outbreak of the Civil War. Commanding various Potomac Army cavalry units, he had a distinguished war career, seeing almost constant action from the Peninsula until his resignation in February 1865. He published an account of the activities of the 2nd Cavalry Division at Gettysburg (1907), where he had been commended for repelling a Confederate attack led by J. E. B. Stuart on the third day of the great battle.

LEFT: The Confederate spy Rose O'Neal Greenhow, shown with her daughter, when she was being held in the Old Capitol Prison in Washington, D.C., in the early months of the grim year (for the North) 1862.

BELOW: David Gregg (seated right).

Benjamin Henry Grierson

Grierson, Benjamin Henry
(1826-1911) Union general

After settling in Illinois as a young man, he taught music for a time before taking up the selling of fresh produce. When the Civil war broke out he volunteered and became the aide-de-camp to Union General Benjamin Prentiss. Although he was reputed to dislike horses, he was commissioned a major in he cavalry in October 1861, and in command of what soon become known as Grierson's brigade he participated in

Charles Griffon

several operations in Tennessee and Mississippi. As a diverson in support of Ulysses Grant's Vicksburg Campaign, Grierson set off from La Grange, Tennessee, on April 17, 1863, riding and raiding through Mississippi until he and his force of 1700 men reached Baton Rouge, Louisiana, on May 2. Having gone some 600 miles, they had destroyed about 50 miles of railroad, captured 1000 mules and horses, taken 500 prisoners and inflicted some 100 Confederate casualties – all at the cost of only 24 Union casualties. Grierson continued to participate in numerous campaigns and battles till the end of the war and ended up a brevet major general. He remained in the regular army, and as a colonel he commanded the 10th Cavalry in campaigns against Indians on the western frontier. He retired from the army in 1890.

Griffin, Charles
(1825-1867) Union general

Ohio-born Griffin was a West Point graduate and veteran artilleryman. His Union artillery company was decimated at First Bull Run. He went on to fight in the Peninsula and at Antietam, Fredericksburg, Chancellorsville and Gettysburg, as well as in the Petersburg and Appomattox campaigns. He finished the war a major general commanding V Corps, and was a surrender commissioner at Appomattox.

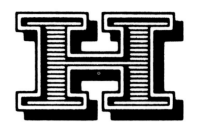

Hagood, Johnson
(1829-1898) Confederate general

A graduate of The Citadel, he was a South Carolina lawyer and planter. Hagood fought for the Confederacy at Fort Sumter and First Bull Run, participated in the defense of Charleston and returned to the field as a brigadier general for the Wilderness and Weldon Railroad battles and the Petersburg Campaign. Returning after the war to his plantation, he contributed much to the modernization of South Carolina's

Johnson Hagood

agriculture and educational system. He served as South Carolina's governor from 1880 to 1882.

Halleck, Henry Wager
(1815-1872) Union general

A farmer's son, he ran away from his Oneida County, New York, home to escape country life and to acquire an education. He earned a bachelor's degree from Union College, then went on to West Point, from which he was graduated, third in his class, in 1839.

Commissioned into the engineer corps, Halleck worked on harbor fortifications in New York and served in California during the Mexican War. A series of lectures he delivered in Boston was published in 1846 as *Elements of Military Art and Science*, and during the long sea passage to California he translated Jomini's *Vie de Napoléon*.

Known as "Old Brains" in the army for these scholarly contributions, he retired in 1854 to practice law in California. He turned down several political opportunities, including a seat on the state supreme court and the office of U.S. Senator, to concentrate on his business affairs; he managed

a quicksilver mine and was president of the Pacific & Atlantic Railroad.

When war broke out Winfield Scott, then commander-in-chief, urged President Lincoln to offer Halleck senior rank. Commissioned a major general in the Union army in August 1861, he took command of the Department of Missouri in St. Louis, where he restored honesty and order after the maladministration of John Frémont.

The success of Halleck's field commanders, Ulysses Grant and John Pope, brought command of the Department of the Mississippi to Halleck. Taking the field after the Battle of Shiloh in April 1862, he moved so cautiously on Corinth, Mississippi, that the outnumbered Confederate army under P. G. T. Beauregard managed to escape without serious harm.

This was Halleck's only field command. In July 1862 he went to Washington as military advisor to Lincoln, with the title of general-in-chief. Almost at once he showed himself ill-equipped for the task. He lacked strategic sense, hampered his field commanders by taking constant counsel of his fears for the safety of Washington and exasperated them with frequent, often offensive, advice.

ABOVE: Henry Wager Halleck.

BELOW: The Battle of Corinth.

Halleck was physically unattractive, with brusque and sometimes grating ways. The qualities that brought him success as lawyer and businessman made him an excellent army administrator, but his lack of charm and leadership ability greatly reduced his effectiveness as a commander and as an operator in Washington power circles. Halleck himself seemed to realize this; he once described his job as "political hell."

In March 1864, after Grant's promotion to lieutenant general, Halleck's job was downgraded to chief of staff. After the Confederate surrender Appomattox he briefly commanded the Military Division of the James, with his headquarters in Richmond. He headed the Military Division of the Pacific from 1865 to 1869, and the Division of the South, his last command, from 1869 to 1872. He died in Louisville, Kentucky, in January 1872.

Halpine, Charles Graham
(1829-1868) Union officer, author

Born in Ireland, he worked for the *New York Times* as their Washington correspondent. Enlisting as a Union private in April 1861, he fought in various battles until his resignation in July 1864, having been breveted to brigadier general for his service at Piedmont, Virginia. In contributing to newspapers about the Civil War, he wrote as "Pvt. Miles O'Reilly." In 1862 he wrote a poem entitled, "Sambo's Right to Be Kilt," referring to the first African-American troops mustered into the Federal forces. He later was active in the Democratic Party in New York City.

Charles Graham Halpine

Hamlin, Hannibal
(1809-1891)
Vice president of the United States

This Maine lawyer was an antislavery Democratic state and national legislator (U.S. Representative 1843-1847, Senator 1848-1861) who turned Republican in 1856 over slavery policy. He served as Abraham Lincoln's first-term vice president (1861-1865) and enjoyed good relations with Lincoln while promoting the Radical Republican emancipation agenda. After the war he represented Maine in the U.S. Senate (1869-1881) and was U.S. minister to Spain (1881-1882).

Hampton, Wade
(1818-1902) Confederate general

Born into the slaveholding aristocracy of upcountry South Carolina, the son and grandson of wealthy planters, Hampton

Hannibal Hamlin (left) and (below) cavalryman Wade Hampton

grew up on the family estate of Millwood, near Columbia, where he learned to ride and hunt in the cavalier tradition. He was graduated from South Carolina College in 1836.

Hampton studied law but decided not to practice, choosing instead to develop his family's Mississippi cotton plantations. He served in the South Carolina legislature from 1852-61. His experiences as a planter caused him to doubt the economic benefits of slavery, and he initially opposed secession. Nevertheless, when war came he raised the Hampton Legion, a mixed command of infantry, cavalry and artillery, and equipped it largely at his own expense.

He commanded the legion at First Bull Run and was wounded there. He recovered in time to lead an infantry brigade during the Peninsular Campaign in the spring of 1862. Wounded again at Seven Pines in May, he returned in late July to take charge of a brigade in J. E. B. Stuart's cavalry corps. Within two months, he had risen to become Stuart's second in command.

Hampton participated in the Antietam Campaign and the raid on Chambersburg, in the Gettysburg Campaign and in the Battle of Gettysburg itself, during which he received his third wound. He was promoted to major general in September 1863.

After Stuart's death in May 1864 he succeeded to the command of Robert E. Lee's cavalry corps. Hampton's troopers blocked Philip Sheridan's Trevilian Raid in June and fought at Sappony Church, Reams's Station and Burgess Mill during the Petersburg Campaign. Circumstances — especially the scarcity of fodder for his horses and the shortage of remounts – kept him largely on the defensive, and his chief responsibility turned out to be the protection of Richmond's lines of communication. In January 1865 he led a part of his command into the Carolinas in search of remounts. Ordered to cover Joseph E. Johnston's retreat, he did not return to the Virginia theater.

Hampton retired to his estates after the war and set about rebuilding his shrunken fortune. He re-entered politics in 1867 and 1868 to oppose Radical Republican Reconstruction policies in South Carolina. Elected governor in 1876 (over the protests of the "carpetbag" incumbent), he helped restore white supremacy to the state. He was re-elected in 1878 and sent to the U.S. Senate shortly thereafter.

Hampton represented a conservative political tradition, the old planter aristocracy. A populist movement developed in South Carolina during the 1880s under the leadership of Benjamin Tillman, whose supporters voted Hampton's conservatives out of office in 1890. Hampton was defeated in a bid for re-election to the Senate the following year.

He died at his home in Columbia in April 1902.

Hancock, Winfield Scott
(1824-1886) Union general

A Pennsylvania native, Hancock was graduated from West Point in 1844, fought in Mexico and was in California when the Civil War began. He returned east in August 1861 to help Union General George McClellan organize and train the Army of the Potomac. Hancock took charge of II Corps in June 1863 and became one of the best of the Potomac army's corps commanders. Seriously wounded at Gettysburg, where he played a major role, he returned to lead II Corps at the Wilderness, Spotsylvania, Cold Harbor and Petersburg. He saw postwar service on the frontier. Tall, dignified, known as "Hancock the Superb," he ran for president as a Democrat in 1880 and lost a close election to James Garfield.

Hardee, William Joseph
(1815-1873) Confederate general

This Georgian was graduated from West Point and fought in the Mexican War. He wrote *Hardee's Tactics* (1855), a definitive infantry manual later used by both sides in the Civil War. After 1956 he was commandant of cadets at West Point. As a Confederate officer he commanded Fort Morgan and, promoted to brigadier general, organized "Hardee's Brigade" in Arkansas. As a major general he led a Kentucky corps at Shiloh and Perryville and, promoted to lieutenant general, commanded the Confederate left wing at Stones River. Commanding the Department of South Carolina, Georgia and Florida, Hardee opposed W. T. Sherman during Sherman's Atlanta Campaign, March to the Sea and Carolinas Campaign. Forced to evacuate Savannah and Charleston, he retreated to North Carolina and surrendered. He was later an Alabama planter and businessman.

Winfield Scott Hancock (seated). With him, from the left: Francis Barlow, David B. Birney, and John Gibbon.

Harris, Eliza
Sanitary Commission volunteer

She distributed food and comforts and helped nurse the wounded from First Bull Run through Gettysburg. Her vivid newspaper accounts of life in the battle zone helped raise large sums for the Sanitary Commission. Mrs. Harris transferred her efforts to Tennessee in the autumn of 1863, returned to Virginia the following year and concluded her war service by nursing the survivors of the Andersonville prison camp.

Nathaniel Harrison Harris

Harris, Nathaniel Harrison
(1834-1900) Confederate general

He was born in Mississippi and was graduated from the University of Louisiana. In 1861 he organized the Warren Rifles in Vicksburg, where he had been practicing law. Joining the Confederate army's 19th Mississippi, he fought in he upper Shenandoah, at Williamsburg, in the Maryland Campaign, at Chancellorsville and Gettysburg and in every major engagement from Spotsylvania through Petersburg, later participating in the defense of Richmond and in the Appomattox Campaign. After the war he was a Vicksburg lawyer, a railroad president and, in later years, a California businessman.

Harrison, Benjamin
(1833-1901) Union officer and 23rd president of the United States

The grandson of President William Henry Harrison, he was an Indianapolis lawyer and Republican politician. He helped to raise the Union army's 70th Indiana and, despite his inexperience, held a series of commands in the Army of the Cumberland and was eventually breveted a brigadier general. He fought in Kentucky and Tennessee before joining W. T. Sherman for the Atlanta Campaign, March to the Sea and Carolinas Campaign. His unsuccessful Indiana gubernatorial race in 1876 brought him to national attention. After serving in the U.S. Senate (1881-1887), he was elected president of the U.S. (1888), failed in a re-election bid, and returned to his Indiana law practice.

Hatch, John Porter
(1822-1901) Union general

This New York-born West Point graduate, having served on the frontier and in the Mexican War, joined the U.S. cavalry at the outset of the war and was promoted to brigadier general by September 1861. He fought at Groveton and Second Bull Run and was so seriously wounded at South Mountain that he thereafter served only as a depot commander and on courts martial. He was given the Medal of Honor in 1893 for his service at South Mountain. He remained in the regular army until his retirement in 1866.

Haupt, Herman
(1817-1905) Union officer

Born in Pennsylvania, he was graduated from West Point in 1835 but soon resigned from the army to go into railroad engineering. He was famed for supervising the construction of the Hoosac Tunnel in western Massachusetts (1856) and for developing an improved pneumatic drill. Commissioned a colonel in the Union army in April 1862, he was placed in charge of the construction and operation of railroads for the Union forces. But he resigned in September 1863, objecting to what he regarded as bureaucratic interference, and went back to railroad building. He wrote several influential books on engineering and bridges.

Hawes, James Morrison
(c.1823-1889) Confederate general

This Kentucky-born West Point graduate served in the Mexican war, taught at West Point, spent two years at the French cavalry school and served on the frontier before resigning in May 1861 to join the Confederate forces as a captain. Promoted to brigadier general in 1862, he led cavalry brigades under A. S. Johnston and then in John Breckinridge's division. He fought at Shiloh, Vicksburg and Galveston Island. He was a hardware merchant after the war.

Hawley, Josph Roswell
(1826-1905) Union general

He was born into an old Connecticut family and there established a law practice. He helped to organize the state's Republican Party and in 1857 became the editor of

Herman Haupt (right) inspecting the construction of a Union railroad

the Republican Hartford *Evening Press* (later the *Courant*). He enlisted in the Union army in April 1861 and fought at First Bull Run, along the Confederacy's east coast and in Virginia, interrupting field service to recruit Northern volunteers. He led a peacekeeping force in New York during the 1864 election, and by the war's end he was Alfred Terry's chief of staff. Later he was Connecticut's governor (1866) and served as a U.S. Representative (1872-1875), (1879-1881) and Senator (1881-1905).

Hay, John Milton
(1838-1905) Author and statesman

He was born in Salem, Indiana, and was graduated from Brown University. Hay's Springfield, Illinois, law office was next to Abraham Lincoln's, and in 1861 he was

John Milton Hay (left), shown with President Abraham Lincoln

appointed Lincoln's private secretary, a job he performed with great ability and discretion throughout Lincoln's presidential years. Appointed an assistant adjutant general detailed to the White House (1864), he was formally the president's military aide during the last year of the war. He then held diplomatic posts in Paris, Madrid and Vienna (1865-1870; much later, he was ambassador to England, 1897). He served as assistant secretary of state (1879-1881), and, named secretary of state in 1898, he sponsored the Open Door Policy toward China (1899-1900) and negotiated the peace after the Spanish-American War and the treaties that made possible the construction of the Panama Canal. In 1903 he settled the Alaskan boundary dispute with Canada. Alongside his diplomatic achievements he earned a reputation as one of the country's leading writers, publishing poems (*Pike Country Ballads*, 1871, and *Poems*, 1890), fiction (*The Bread-Winners*, 1884) and travel sketches (*Castilian Days*, 1871). With

John Nicolay, Hay also wrote the monumental 10-volume study, *Abraham Lincoln: A History* (1890).

Hayes, Rutherford Birchard
(1822-1893) Union general and 19th president of the United States

A Harvard Law School graduate, this Ohio lawyer and politician was commissioned a major in the Union army in 1861 and had an honorable, if modest, wartime career fighting in western Virginia and the Shenandoah Valley Campaigns of 1862 and 1864. He achieved national prominence as Ohio's governor (1868-1872, 1875-1877). As the price for winning the disputed presidential election of 1876, Republican Hayes kept his promise to the Democrats by withdrawing the last Union troops from the South on April 20, 1877, thus ending Reconstruction. He also campaigned to reform the treatment of both the inmates of prisons and the mentally ill.

Rutherford Birchard Hayes

Hazen, William Babcock
(1830-1887) Union general

This Vermont-born West Point graduate, an Indian fighter and teacher at West Point, was commissioned a colonel in the Union army in 1861. He fought at Shiloh, Perryville, Stones River, Chickamauga, Chattanooga, Missionary Ridge, Resaca, Pickett's Mills, Peach Tree Creek and Atlanta. He was promoted to major general in December 1864 and remained in the regular army after the war. He fought Indians on the frontier and went to France to observe the German forces during the Franco-Prussian War. In 1880 he became chief signal officer and head of the Weather Bureau.

Josiah Henson

slowed by his academic deficiencies in philosophy and chemistry, and he needed an extra year at the military academy, eventually being graduated in 1848, 15th in his class of 38.

Commissioned into the artillery, Hill fought in Mexico during the autumn of 1847. He later served in garrisons in Florida and Texas and took part in two Seminole campaigns (1849-50 and 1853-55) in Florida. From 1855 to 1860 he worked in the Washington, D.C., office of the U.S. Coast Survey. In 1859 he married a sister of John Hunt Morgan, soon to become famous as a Confederate cavalry commander.

Ambrose Powell Hill (left) and (below) James Butler Hickok

Henson, Josiah
(1789-1883)
Black leader and clergyman

Henson was born into slavery in Maryland. After escaping to Canada in 1830 he learned to read and write, worked for the Underground Railroad, preached and founded a community and industrial school at Dawn, Ontario (1842). He became an internationally renowned emancipation advocate. Having published his autobiography in 1849 and told his story to Harriet Beecher Stowe, Henson was widely regarded as the inspiration for the character Uncle Tom in *Uncle Tom's Cabin* (1852).

Hickok, James Butler
(1837-1876) Union scout and spy

"Wild Bill" Hickok moved from his native Illinois to Kansas in 1855 and became a stagecoach driver and free-state sympathizer. He served the Federals as a Missouri-based scout and spy in a war career characterized by dramatic adventures, arrests and escapes; in 1865 he publicly killed Dave Tutt, a fellow scout who had defected to the Confederates. He later became an American legend as a fast-drawing Kansas marshal. He was killed by Jack McCall in Deadwood, Dakota Territory.

Hill, Ambrose Powell
(1825-1865) Confederate general

The son of a soldier, born in Culpeper, Virginia, Hill received a standard local academy education before entering West Point in July 1842. His progress was

He resigned his U.S. commission during the secession crisis. Appointed colonel in the Confederate service in the spring of 1861, he commanded the 13th Virginia at the First Battle of Bull Run, where the regiment remained in reserve. He served in western Virginia later in 1861. In February 1862 he was promoted to brigadier general and given command of an infantry brigade.

Hill first achieved prominence as an infantry commander during the Peninsular Campaign of 1862. He fought at Williamsburg and, promoted to major general shortly thereafter, led his subsequently-legendary Light Division, so-called for its speed on the march, in the battles of the Seven Days. His division opened the Battle of Mechanicsville with an impetuous, probably ill-advised attack in the evening of June 26, 1862, and lost heavily. The Light Division fought later in the week at Gaines's Mill and Frayser's Farm.

After he quarrelled with James Longstreet, Hill's division was transferred to Thomas J. Jackson's command in July 1862. He fought with Jackson at Cedar Mountain on August 9 and anchored the left of Jackson's line at the Second Battle of Bull Run three weeks later, repulsing successive Federal attacks on August 29-30.

Hill took part in the capture of Harpers Ferry in September 1862, staying behind to supervise the details of the surrender while Jackson and the rest of the corps rejoined Robert E. Lee at Sharpsburg. On September 17, the day of the Battle of the Antietam, Hill rushed the Light Division from Harpers Ferry to Sharpsburg, reaching the battlefield just in time to stop a potential Federal breakthrough on the right of Lee's line.

He fought at Fredericksburg in December 1862 and participated in Jackson's decisive flank march at Chancellorsville in May 1863. He succeeded briefly to the corps command when Jackson was wounded the evening of May 2. Wounded himself shortly thereafter, he turned the corps over to J. E. B. Stuart for the concluding phases of Lee's great victory.

Promoted to lieutenant general in May 1863, he was given command of the newly-created Third Corps. He led the corps across the Potomac in the Gettysburg Campaign, made the initial contact with Federal forces around Gettysburg and

A.P. Hill fought with distinction in the Battle of the Wilderness.

attacked on July 1, 1863, touching off the great three-day battle. He directed the first day's fighting largely on his own – the only occasion during which he exercised independent command. His corps took part, with Longstreet's, in the indecisive echelon attacks of July 2, and 10 of his infantry brigades supported George Pickett's division during the debacle on Cemetery Ridge on the third day of the battle.

Hill fell ill after the Battle of the Wilderness in May 1864 and missed the Spotsylvania fighting entirely. He returned to command the Third Corps at Cold Harbor in June. He retained this command during the long Petersburg Campaign, taking part in most of the many actions on the Confederate right from 1864 to April 1865.

Hill had once said he did not wish to survive the wreck of the Confederacy. He returned from a brief sick leave on the morning of April 2, 1865, as Ulysses S. Grant was launching his final successful assault on Petersburg, and was shot dead as he rode to the front to rally his troops.

both of the University of Arkansas (1877-1884) and of the forerunner of Georgia Military Academy (1885-1889). In these roles he did much to promote Southern revitalization through industrial and agricultural training.

Hoge, Jane (Mrs. A. H. Hoge)
(1811-1890)
Sanitary Commission worker

Born in Pennsylvania, she had given birth to 13 children and was a wealthy and socially conscious housewife when the Civil War broke out. She helped organize the Chicago branch of the Sanitary Fair in Chicago in October 1863. In addition to lecturing widely to raise money and supplies, she went to camps in the front lines and was tireless in trying to improve the sanitary conditions of the Union troops. After the war she devoted herself to religious and educational causes.

Holabird, Samuel Beckley
(1826-1907) Union officer

Born in Connecticut, Holabird was a West Point-trained career officer who had served in Texas and on scouting duty before the Civil War. He served the Union during the war as a quartermaster to Robert Paterson, Nathaniel Banks, Joseph Mansfield and A. S. Williams, and, after December 1862, he was chief quartermaster of the Department of the Gulf. He continued on active service, retiring as quartermaster general (1883-1890). He wrote a number of military works.

Hollins, George Nichols
(1799-1878) Confederate commodore

A Maryland native, Hollins became a midshipman in 1814 and resigned from the U.S. Navy as a captain in 1861 after distinguished service that included the War of

Daniel Harvey Hill (above) and (right) Jane Hoge

Hill, Daniel Harvey
(1821-1889) Confederate general

He was born in York district, South Carolina. After graduation from West Point he saw seven years of border, garrison and Mexican War service. For 10 years a college mathematics teacher, Hill was superintendent of the North Carolina Military Institute (1859-1861) when the Civil War erupted. After organizing North Carolina's first instruction camp, he led the Confederate army's 1st North Carolina at Big Bethel. Promoted to brigadier general (July 1861) and major general (March 1862), he led a division in the Peninsular Campaign (fighting at Seven Pines, in the Seven Days' Battles and at South Mountain) and at Antietam. At South Mountain he was accused (unfairly, he contended) of allowing Robert E. Lee's famous "lost dispatch" (detailing his Maryland Campaign) to fall into the hands of Union General George McClellan. He defended Richmond during the Gettysburg Campaign. As a lieutenant general (July 1863) he led the Second Corps in the Tennessee Army. He figured prominently in the Chickamauga and Chattanooga campaigns. After signing a petition recommending that Braxton Bragg be removed on the grounds of incompetence, he was himself relieved and sent to a minor command in North Carolina. He surrendered there with J. E. Johnston. Hill was a North Carolina newspaper and magazine publisher after the war and was president

George Nichols Hollins

1812 and the bombardment of Nicaragua in 1854. He commanded the James River defenses for the Confederacy and, as a commodore in command of the New Orleans naval station, broke the Union Mississippi blockade (October 1861). He

Joseph Holt (seated left). R.S. Foster is standing to his left.

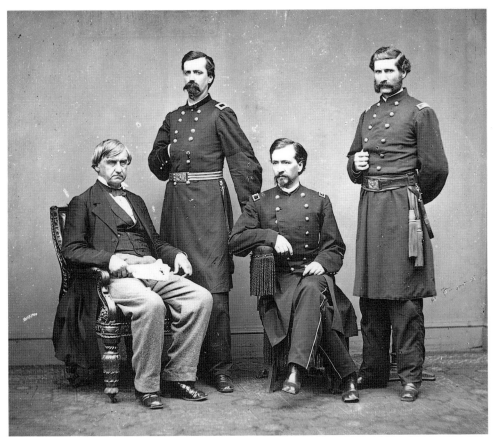

saw heavy fighting while leading the upper Mississippi naval forces until New Orleans fell (April 1862), then sat on naval boards. He worked in the Baltimore city court after the end of the war.

Holt, Joseph
(1807-1894)
Union judge advocate general

This Kentucky-born lawyer and Democratic orator served President James Buchanan as commissioner of patents, postmaster general and secretary of war. After Abraham Lincoln's inauguration he tried to sway Kentucky to stay with the Union and then became the Union army's first judge advocate general in 1862. Granted powers in both civil and military situations, he dealt harshly with many defendants, in particular with those charged with the conspiracy to assassinate President Lincoln. His brand of justice gradually lost favor, and he retired from the military in 1875.

Homer, Winslow
(1836-1910)
Painter, war correspondent

Born in Boston, he trained as a lithographer and was working for a New York publisher when *Harper's Weekly* sent him to Washington to sketch the inauguration of Lincoln in March 1861. He stayed on to sketch the activities – both in camp and in battle – of the Union troops during the early months of the Peninsular Campaign in Virginia. Reproduced as lithographs in *Harper's*, they brought the war to the North with an unaccustomed immediacy and gave Homer a national reputation. Homer returned to New York and soon worked up a number of his sketches into full-fledged paintings, including such famous works as "The Briarwood Pipe" and "Prisoners from the Front" (1866). Homer would go on to gain a reputation as one of America's greatest artists.

John Bell Hood

Hood, John Bell
(1831-1879) **Confederate general**

Born in Owingsville, Kentucky, Hood was graduated near the bottom of his West Point class in 1853. He served on the California and Texas frontiers, and in Texas he became a favorite of his commander, Robert E. Lee. He joined the Confederate cavalry in April 1861. A "fighting general," he commanded John Magruder's cavalry at Yorktown and, as a brigadier general (March 1862), he led the "Texas Brigade" at Gaines's Mill, Second Bull Run and Antietam. Promoted to major general (October 1862), he led a division under James Longstreet at Fredericksburg and Gettysburg (where he led the assault on Round Top on the second day and lost the use of his left arm). He commanded Longstreet's corps at Chickamauga, where Hood lost his right leg and earned a promotion to lieutenant general. He assumed command of the Tennessee Army and, riding strapped to his hose, directed the

disastrous Atlanta and Franklin and Nashville campaigns. Relieved at his own request, he fought under P. G. T. Beauregard in Tennessee. He surrendered in Mississippi in May 1865. "The Gallant Hood," though no match for master tacticians like W. T. Sherman, was an unparalleled brigade and division commander: "Hood's Brigade" set a standard to which other troops aspired. After the war he was a New Orleans merchant. Financially ruined by the yellow fever epidemic of 1878, he himself succumbed to the disease the following year.

Hooker, Joseph
(1814-1879) Union general

Born in Hadley, Massachusetts, the grandson of an officer in George Washington's army, Hooker attended the local school and eventually decided he too would follow the drum. He was graduated from West Point in 1837 near the middle of a class that included the future Civil War generals Braxton bragg, Jubal Early and John Sedgwick.

Hooker served in Florida, on the Canadian border and as adjutant at West Point. He held staff positions during the Mexican War and won brevets for gallantry at Monterrey and Chapultepec. Resigning from the army in 1853, he took up farming in Sonoma, California.

Hooker volunteered to return to the Union service on the outbreak of war but was snubbed at first, possibly because he had feuded with senior officers in California. Obtaining a brigadier's commission finally, he served in the Washington defenses from May through October 1861. He commanded a division at Williamsburg on the Peninsula in May 1862, where he won the sobriquet "Fighting Joe," and performed capably during the Seven Days' Battles and at Second Bull Run.

Promoted to command of I Corps, he won a success at South Mountain on September 14, 1862, and had the lead role in the opening phase of the Battle of Antietam three days later. Hooker's corps appeared to be poised for important gains when he was wounded and carried from the field.

Tall, handsome, incautious, boastful, Hooker could not hold back his biting criticisms of Ambrose Burnside, George McClellan's successor as commander of

OPPOSITE TOP: Joseph Hooker was badly beaten at Chancellorsville.

OPPOSITE BOTTOM: Hooker (second from right, front row) and staff.

ABOVE: Joseph Hooker.

OVERLEAF: The Battle of Missionary Ridge.

the Army of the Potomac. He also spoke openly of the need for autocratic leadership in both the army and the government. After Burnside's debacle at Fredericksburg in December 1862, President Abraham Lincoln named Hooker to the command of the Army of the Potomac in spite of these views. "Only those general who gain success can set up dictators," Lincoln wrote him. "What I now ask of you is military success, and I will risk the dictatorship."

Hooker earned praise for reorganizing the army, improving conditions in the winter camps and building the troops' morale. In early spring he began to plan offensive operations against the Army of Northern Virginia. He set his 130,000-strong army in motion at the end of April 1863. "My plans are perfect," he said. "May God have mercy on General Lee, for I will have none." In a brilliant preliminary, he threw large forces across the Rappahannock and Rapidan rivers and moved up to Chancellorsville in Robert E. Lee's rear.

Then everything went wrong. Lee divided his far smaller army in thirds and defeated Hooker in detail in a masterly war of movement.

Rumor held that Hooker had been drunk at critical moments during the battle of the Chancellorsville. He denied it, saying simply that, "For once, I lost confidence in Joe Hooker." He recovered his nerve in time to maneuver skilfully in step with Lee during the Gettysburg Campaign, successfully screening Washington and Baltimore from attack. But Hooker resigned the Potomac command when the authorities in Washington refused his request for operational control of the garrison at Harpers Ferry. George Meade succeeded him on the eve of Gettysburg.

Staying on in the army just as Burnside had done, Hooker led XI and XII corps

from Virginia to Tennessee to reinforce Ulysses S. Grant in late 1863 and commanded XX Corps during the Chattanooga Campaign. In what became known as the Battle of the Clouds, he captured Lookout Mountain on November 24, 1863, and participated in the decisive victory at Missionary Ridge the following day.

In the spring of 1864 Hooker commanded XX Corps in the opening phases of the Atlanta Campaign: the battles of Mill Creek Gap, Resaca, Cassville, New Hope Church and Pine Mountain. He asked to be relieved of duty in July 1864 when Oliver O. Howard, who had served under him at Chancellorsville, was promoted over his head to the command of one of W. T. Sherman's armies.

Hooker remained in the service, though he did not return to the field, through the war's end. He retired from the regular army in 1868 after suffering a paralytic stroke.

Hough, Daniel
(d.1861) Union soldier

On April 14, 1861, Hough, a private in Battery E, 1st U.S. Artillery, was accidentally killed in an explosion during the Federal evacuation of Fort Sumter, making him the first fatality of the Civil War. He was buried in the grounds of the fort.

Howard, Joseph Jr.
(1833-1908) War correspondent

A businessman-turned-journalist, he earned one of the earliest bylines on the *New York Times* (1860). He sent vivid wartime dispatches from the front, but he is chiefly remembered for a journalistic hoax: in May 1864, as a disgruntled Brooklyn city editor, he helped to forge a presidential proclamation announcing the failure of Ulysses S. Grant's advance on Richmond and calling for 500,000 new Frederal recruits. Two newspapers printed the story: Howard was briefly imprisoned but went on to a successful career as a prolific New York journalist and popular lecturer.

Howard, Oliver Otis
(1830-1909) Union general

A Maine native, he was graduated from and taught mathematics at West Point (1857-1861). He fought for the Union at First Bull Run and in the Peninsular Campaign (losing an arm and earning a Congressional Medal of Honor at Fair Oaks), as well as at Antietam, Fredericksburg and Chancellorsville, where, commanding XI Corps,

Oliver Otis Howard

his troopes were routed in T. J. Jackson's famous flank attack. He subsequently fought at Gettysburg (earning the Thanks of Congress), Lookout Mountain and Missionary Ride, then led IV Corps on W. T. Sherman's Atlanta Campaign, March to the Sea and Carolinas Campaign. He was eventually appointed commander of the Army and Department of the Tennessee. He presided over the Freedmen's Bureau

(1865-1874), was superintendent of West Point (1880-1882) and commanded the Division of the East (1886-1894), retiring as a major general. From 1869 to 1874 he was founding president of Howard University (named for him).

Howe, Julia Ward
(1819-1910) Author, social reformer

Boston-born, she married Samuel, Gridley Howe and with him edited the abolitionist journal *The Commonwealth*. While visiting the Union army camps around Washington, D.C., she was moved to write a poem, and it was published in the *Atlantic Monthly* in the spring of 1862. The editor gave it the name "The Battle Hymn of the Republic." She seems to have written these words for a familiar melody, composed early in the nineteenth century by William Steffe and recently borrowed by Union soldiers for the rousing song "John Brown's body lies a moldering in the grave." In any case, that is the music that has been associated with the words ever since. A prolific writer of both prose and verse, she was the first woman ever to be elected to the prestigious American Academy of Arts and Letters.

Julia Ward Howe

Howe, Samuel Gridley
(1801-1876) **Physician, social activist**

After taking his medical degree from Harvard (1824), he went off to Greece to aid in the revolution against the Turks (1824-1829). On returning in Boston he devoted himself to the education of the blind, prison reform, aiding mental patients and public education. Inevitably, he took a stand against slavery and with his wife, Julia Ward Howe, co-edited the abolitionist newspaper, *The Commonwealth*. He was an early supporter of John Brown, but when Brown's Harpers Ferry raid occurred, Howe tried to disassociate himself from Brown – even fleeing briefly to Canada. During the Civil War he gave his medical talents to the Sanitary Commission, and he thereafter worked for getting the vote and better education for African-Americans.

Andrew Atkinson Humphreys

Huff, John A.
(*c*.1816-1864) **Union soldier**

He won a prize as the best shot in the 1st U.S. Sharpshooters before enlisting in the Union army. He was a private in the 5th Michigan Cavalry when he fatally wounded Jeb Stuart at Yellow Tavern on May 11, 1864. Huff himself died of wounds received at Haw's Shop, Virginia, 17 days later.

Humphreys, Andrew Atkinson
(1810-1883) **Union general**

Son and grandson of naval architects, this Pennylvania-born West Point graduate served as an engineer in the army; he wrote an important *Report upon the Physics and Hydraulics of the Mississippi River* (1861). Assigned to Union General George McClellan's staff in December 1861, he later became General George Meade's chief of staff. He participated in virtually all the major battles in the Eastern theater from the Peninsular Campaign through Antietam, Chancellorsville and Gettysburg to Cold Harbor, the Petersburg siege and the Appomattox Campaign. He was made a brigadier general, became chief of engineers in 1866 and retired in 1879.

Hunt, Henry Jackson
(1819-1889) **Union general**

In the 1850s Hunt, a West Point graduate and career officer, helped to create the light artillery tactics adopted in 1860 and used throughout the war. He trained and commanded Army of the Potomac artillery units, was chief of artillery at Fredericksburg (moving the infantry across the river in boats) and Gettysburg (where his guns stopped Pickett's Charge) and directed the siege at Petersburg for the last year of the war. He held territorial commands before retiring in 1883.

Hunter, David
(1802-1886) **Union general**

Born in Washington, D.C., this West Point graduate and Mexican War veteran was badly wounded at First Bull Run. As a Union major general he held various territorial commands and sat on courts martial and boards. As commander of the Southern Department, Hunter authorized the formation of the first black regiment (the 1st South Carolina). Lincoln annulled his unauthorized proclamation of May 1862 freeing all the slaves in that department. He presided over the trial of Lincoln's assassins. He lived in Washington, D.C., after his retirement in 1866.

Hunter, Robert Mercer Taliaferro
1809-1887)
Confederate secretary of state

This Virginian was graduated from his state university and began a long career in public service. He was a state legislator, a U.S. Representative (1839-1843, 1845-1847), a Senator (1847-1861) and was an ally of John C. Calhoun in promoting states' rights and slavery. He was a wartime Confederate secretary of state (July 1861-March 1862) and senator (1862-1865) and was a commissioner at the Hampton Roads Peace Conference. He was briefly imprisoned after the war, then returned to Virginia, where he helped to organise a conservative party in the state that served to blunt the worst effects of radical Reconstruction. He was state treasurer (1874-1880).

raid into West Virginia that became known as "Jones's and Imboden's Raid." He helped to cover the Confederates' retreat from Pennsylvania after Gettysburg and fought at Piedmont and New Market. After coming down with typhoid fever in autumn 1864, he helped to administer a Confederate prison at Aiken, South Carolina. He was a lawyer, developer and writer after the war.

Iverson, Alfred
1829-1911) Confederate general

This Georgian fought in the Mexican War and resigned to become a lawyer and railroad contractor. He re-enlisted in the cavalry in 1855 and served in Indian fighting and on the Utah Expedition (1858-1860). Joining the Confederate army, he fought in the Seven Days' Battles (wounded) and at South Mountain. He led brigades at Antietam, and, promoted to brigadier general, at Fredericksburg, Chancellorsville and Gettysburg, then organized troops in Georgia. During the Atlanta Campaign he captured George Stoneman at Hillsboro in July 1864. He surrendered after Appomattox and after the war was a businessman and farmer.

Imboden, John Daniel
(1823-1895) Confederate general

A Virginia-born lawyer and legislator, he participated in the arrest of John Brown at Harpers Ferry. After joining the Confederate army he fought at First Bull Run and, in April-May 1863, was joint commander with General William E. Jones of a daring

John Daniel Imboden

Jackson, John K.
(1828-1866) Confederate general

Born in Georgia, Jackson was a lawyer. Commissioned a colonel in a Georgian infantry regiment in May 1861, he fought for the Confederacy at Santa Rosa Island, was promoted to brigadier general in January 1862 and fought at Pensacola, Shiloh, Stones River, Chickamauga and in the Atlanta Campaign. He fought to the end in Florida and in the Carolinas. He returned to his law practice after the war.

John K. Jackson

Jackson, Thomas Jonathan "Stonewall"

(1824-1863) Confederate general

Thomas Jackson's parents died in poverty during his early childhood, and the orphan grew up with few amenities in the Clarksburg, Virginia, household of the uncle who raised him. Jackson's early schooling ill-prepared him for the rigors of West Point. He arrived there in 1842 awkward and behindhand. By dint of hard work he rose to 17th of 59 cadets in a 1846 graduating class that included George McClellan and A. P. Hill.

Jackson attracted the notice of his superiors in the Mexican War, serving with distinction at Vera Cruz, Cerro Gordo and Chapultepec. He found postwar life in garrison tedious, however, and resigned from the army early in 1852 to teach mathematics at the Virginia Military Institute in Lexington. His students graded him a poor teacher – they called him "Tom Fool Jackson" – but he seems to have found consolation in an obsessive Presbyterian piety and in a fulfilling domestic life. His first wife, Eleanor Junkin, died in 1854. He re-married three years later. Jackson and Mary Anna Morrison, like Eleanor the daughter of a Presbyterian minister, lived happily together, adequate compensation, perhaps, for his professional disappointments.

He took no part in secession quarrels, though by happenstance he commanded the cadet detachment at the hanging of abolition insurrectionist John Brown on December 2, 1859. He described war as "the sum of all evils," a view that did not discourage him from obtaining a Confederate commission shortly after the Fort Sumter attack. Soon promoted to brigadier, Jackson led Virginia troops at the First Battle of Bill Run/Manassas on July 21, 1861, so distinguishing himself in repulsing a Federal assault that he acquired the sobriquet "Stonewall."

His soldiers called him "Old Jack." Tall, thin and long-bearded, he looked commonplace except for his pale blue eyes, which – or so nearly everyone who knew him said – blazed up brilliantly in battle. His eccentricities were legendary. He did not smoke, drink or play cards and permitted himself only the sparest of meals. He sometimes refused to march or fight on the Sabbath and often rode about with one arm held above his head. He wore ragged uniforms with few symbols of rank and scorned all military pomp and display. He was a harsh disciplinarian and put tremendous demands on all who served under

him. "I never saw one of Jackson's couriers without expecting an order to assault the North pole," one of his subordinates said. He may have thought war evil but he was a consummate practitioner of its arts.

In November 1861, promoted to major general, Jackson took command of Confederate forces in the Shenandoah Valley. His masterly Valley Campaign of 1862 was the first conclusive evidence of his military genius. He and Robert E. Lee then President's Davis's chief military adviser, had developed a plan to attack the Federal forces in the Valley under Nathaniel Banks as a strategic diversion to prevent reinforcements being sent to Union General George McClellan on the Virginia peninsula. Jackson at first suffered a tactical reverse at Kernstown on March 23 and, in the face of superior forces, retreated slowly up the Valley. But he repulsed a Federal attack on McDowell on May 8, then turned north

Thomas Jonathan Jackson, greatest of Robert E. Lee's lieutenants

again and struck Banks at Front Royal on May 23, driving him back to Winchester. Following up closely, Jackson renewed the attack on the 25th, this time pushing the disorganized Federals all the way back across the Potomac. Alarmed, intent on destroying Jackson, the Federal high command suspended the southward march of a full army corps bound for McClellan and ordered all forces in the Valley to concentrate against Stonewall's little army. "Always mystify, mislead and surprise the enemy," Jackson said. Following his own maxim, he parried each enemy thrust and brought the campaign to a brilliant close with victories at Cross Keys and Port Republic on June 8 and 9.

Jackson's reputation suffered some damage during Lee's battles of the Seven

Jackson at the First Battle of Bull Run. It was here that he acquired his famous nickname, "Stonewall".

OPPOSITE TOP: Jackson is mortally wounded at Chancellorsville in a case of what would today be called "friendly fire".

OPPOSITE BOTTOM: Jackson's death on May 10, 1863. He was 39.

troops, mistaking Jackson's party for Yankees in the twilight, opened fire and brought Old Jack down, forcing him out of the battle.

Though he lost an arm to the surgeon's saw that night, his chances for recovery appeared excellent. But he contracted pneumonia, and on May 10, 1863, he died in a delirium of fever, calling out orders – "Pass the infantry to the front!" – as his life ebbed away. Lee never won another such victory as Chancellorsville, not least because he never found a second Stonewall Jackson. "I know not how to replace him," Lee wrote in a tribute that could also serve as Jackson's epitaph.

James Brothers Desperadoes

Frank (1843-1915) and Jesse (1847-1882) James were born and raised on a farm near Centralia, Missouri, without benefit of much education. Their mother and step-father were Confederate sympathizers; this, along with the fact that Federal militia twice raided the James farm, helped turn the brothers into Confederate guerillas.

They received their criminal apprentice-ship under the bushwhacker chief W. C. Quantrill, famous for the August 1863 sacking of Lawrence, Kansas, in which 150 men and boys were killed and $500,000 worth of property destroyed.

Quantrill did not survive the war, and Jesse James was wounded toward war's end and needed nearly a year of quiet life to recover. He, Frank and Coleman Younger embarked upon their career as brigands in 1866, specializing in bank robberies and, after 1873, train robberies. In April 1882, one of the gang members shot and killed Jesse. Frank James surrendered a few months later. Acquitted in two criminal trials, he lived on blamelessly until February 1915.

Johnson, Andrew
(1808-1875) Lincoln's vice president and 17th president of the United States

Born in Raleigh, North Carolina, he be-came a tailor's apprentice in 1822 and settled in Tennessee. At the age of 18 he married Eliza McCardle, who taught him to read. As a champion of local working men, he was elected mayor or Greeneville, Tennessee (1830-1833); he went on to serve

Days in late June and early July, when Jackson's chronic tardiness, partly the re-sult of physical and nervous exhaustion after the stresses of the Valley, cost the Confederates an opportunity to inflict a serious·defeat on McClellan. But Jackson returned to form at the Second Battle of Bull Run/Manassas in August. Marching 51 miles in two days, his "foot cavalry" destroyed the Union depot at Manassas Junction, laid low for two days, then held off superior forces until Confederate General James Longstreet could bring up

his corps to deliver the blow that sent the Federals retreating back to the Washington lines. In September, commanding Lee's advance guard, Jackson captured the for-tress of Harpers Ferry and reached Antietam/Sharpsburg in time to help Lee check McClellan and escape a serious, per-haps decisive defeat. In December his corps fought the Federals to a humiliating stand-still on Lee's right at Fredericksburg.

Jackson's famous flank march of May 2, 1863, a daylong trek through the Wilder-ness swamps and thickets, made Lee's bril-liant victory at Chancellorsville possible, for Jackson's late-afternoon assault routed the Union right wing. Jackson pressed the pursuit into the evening, but then Rebel

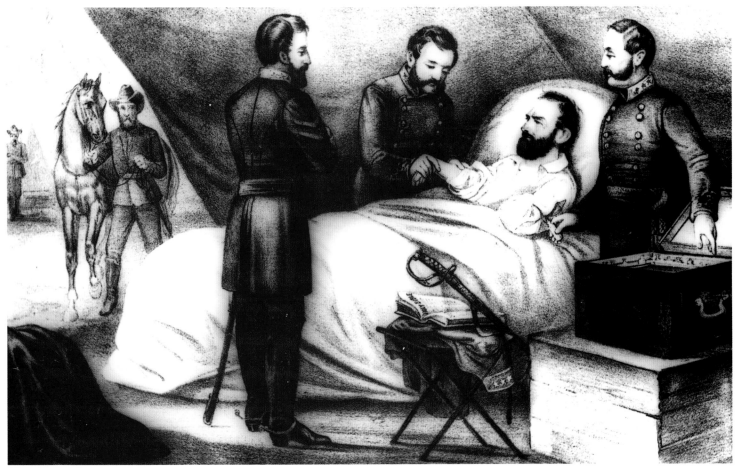

as U.S. Representative (1843-1853), governor of Tennessee (1853-1857), and U.S. Senator (1857-1862). An antislavery Democrat, he was the only Southern Senator to retain his seat after secession, and Lincoln rewarded him with the military governorship of Tennessee (1862-1865). He forged a loyal government there and was consequently nominated as vice president on the National Union-Republican Party ticket in 1864. Succeeding to the presidency after Lincoln's assassination, he issued a proclamation of amnesty, presided over the ratification of the 13th Amendment and succeeded in organizing loyal governments in the former Confederate states. His intention to continue Lincoln's moderate Southern reconstruction policies, however, was foiled by hostile Radical Republicans, who overrode a presidential veto to pass the Reconstruction Act of 1867 and generally impaired his effectiveness. After dismissing Secretary of war Edwin M. Stanton (a Radical Republican) in violation of the Tenure of Office Act, Johnson was impeached on charges of "high crimes and misdemeanors" and acquitted by only a single vote in May 1968. He failed thereafter to moderate the harshness of Congressional Radical Reconstruction policies. He was passed over in the 1868 presidential election and lost U.S. Senate and Congressional bids in 1869 and 1872. Finally elected to the Senate by Tennessee, he served from March to July 1875 before dying of a paralytic stroke.

Andrew Johnson

Bushrod Rust Johnson

Johnson, Bushrod Rust
(1817-1880) Confederate general

Born in Ohio and a graduate of West Point, Johnson served on the frontier and in the Seminole and Mexican wars. He resigned in 1847 to teach, becoming the superintendent of a military college in Tennessee. Commissioned colonel in the Confederate army when the war broke out, he was promoted to brigadier general in January 1862. He escaped through the lines at Fort Donelson, was wounded at Shiloh and fought at Perryville, Stones River, Chickamauga and Knoxville, Drewry's Bluff and the Wilderness and was promoted to major general in May 1864. At Petersburg during the great mine explosion (July 1864), he commanded troops that captured 130 Union soldiers in the crater. He was chancellor of the University of Nashville after the war.

Johnson, Richard W.
(1827-1897) Union general

He was graduated from West Point in 1849 and fought in several Indian campaigns on the frontier. Johnson commanded a Union brigade and then a division at Corinth, Stones River, Chickamauga and Missionary Ridge in 1862 and 1863. Severely wounded at Resaca during W. T. Sherman's Atlanta Campaign, he returned to command XIV Corps and, later, the cavalry corps in the Army of the Cumber-

OVERLEAF: Albert Sidney Johnston was mortally wounded in the first day's fighting at Shiloh in 1862.

Texas seceded. He refused the Union's offer to serve as Winfield Scott's second in command, instead assuming command of the Confederate Western Department as a full general. A powerful personality, Johnston was regarded in 1861 by Jefferson Davis, among others, as "the greatest soldier . . . then living," an assessment not shared by later historians. He captured Bowling Green and began mustering and training an army, but after losses at Logan Cross Roads and forts Henry and Donelson, he withdrew to Nashville, and after D. C. Buell occupied Nashville, retreated to Corinth. He died of a leg wound sustained while leading the Confederates' east flank on the first day of fighting at Shiloh on April 6, 1862, a loss which Jefferson Davis called "irreparable."

Johnston, Joseph Eggleston
(1807-1891) Confederate general

Born in Prince Edward County, Virginia, son of a Revolutionary War veteran, he grew up in Abingdon and received his early schooling at an academy his father had helped to found. He was graduated 13th of 46 in the class of 1829 at West Point and entered the army as a second lieutenant of artillery.

Johnston served on the Black Hawk expedition and in garrison posts before resigning in 1837 to pursue a career as a civil engineer. On an expedition to Florida early in 1838 he took charge of the rear guard when a Seminole war party attacked. He conducted the retreat with such coolness and skill that he won a brevet and a new commission, as a first lieutenant in the elite corps of topographical engineers.

He fought in Mexico at Cerro Gordo and led the storming column at Chapultepec. Five times wounded, he won three brevets for his Mexican service. He later served as chief of topographical engineers in Texas and was lieutenant colonel of the 1st U.S. Cavalry in Kansas during the border disturbances of the late 1850s. He accompanied Albert Sidney Johnston's Utah expedition in 1858. By 1861 he was a brigadier general and chief quartermaster of the army.

Johnston resigned his U.S. commission in April 1861 and entered Confederate service as a major general the following month. Commanding at Harpers Ferry, he withdrew his small army from the enemy's front in time to make a decisive contribu-

Richard W. Johnson (above) and (right) Albert Sidney Johnston

land. Johnson retired in 1875 and later taught military science in Missouri and Minnesota.

Johnston, Albert Sidney
(1803-1862) Confederate general

Born in Washington, Kentucky, and graduated from West Point in 1826, Johnston fought in the Black Hawk War. He resigned from the U.S. Army in 1834 and became commander of the Texas army in 1837 (his appointment occasioning a duel with a disappointed rival officer) and was secretary of war for the Republic of Texas (1838-1840). A Texas farmer in between his military stints, he rejoined the U.S. Army after fighting in the Mexican War, later leading the Utah expedition against the Mormons (1858-1860) and commanding the Pacific Department. He resigned again when

ABOVE: The Battle of Fair Oaks.

OPPOSITE BOTTOM: William E. Jones.

tion to the Confederate victory at Bull Run on July 21, 1861, approving P. G. T. Beauregard's troop dispositions and overseeing the general direction of the battle.

Promoted to full general shortly after Bull Run, Johnston took command of the main Confederate army covering Richmond. Confederate President Jefferson Davis ranked him only fourth in seniority among general officers, however, precip-

itating a feud between the general and the president that would last the full course of the war.

When George McClellan shifted the Union Army of the Potomac to the Virginia peninsula in the spring of 1862, Johnston moved southeast to confront him. As in Florida, he proved himself a master of the fighting retreat, falling back to within a few miles of Richmond before launching a counterattack on May 31, 1862. The Battle of Seven Pines (Fair Oaks) checked McClellan's advance but achieved no decisive result. It did, however, cost Johnston

his command, for he was seriously wounded during the fighting. His successor was Robert E. Lee.

Davis assigned him in late 1862 to overall command in the west, with supervisory responsibility for the armies of Braxton Bragg in Tennessee and John Pemberton in Mississippi. Johnston exercised little operational control, however. Federal forces inflicted a series of defeats that culminated in the loss of the Mississippi River fortress of Vicksburg in July 1863 and the Confederate retreat from Tennessee after the Missionary Ridge debacle in November.

He took command of Bragg's beaten Army of Tennessee in December 1863 with orders to reorganize it and go over to the offensive. Instead, pleading lack of resources, he fought mainly defensively when W. T. Sherman opened the spring campaign in Georgia in May 1864. Sherman steadily forced Johnston back toward Atlanta, and Davis relieved Johnston of command on July 17 on the grounds he had not brought Sherman to battle. Johnston's successor, John Bell Hood, had no hesitancy about attacking, and within six months, in a series of ill-judged offensives,

Hood had completely wrecked the army he had inherited.

Johnston returned to field command in February 1865 at the head of a small army opposing Sherman's advance through the Carolinas. Against Davis's wishes, he capitulated to Sherman in North Carolina on April 26, 17 days after Lee had surrendered the Army of Northern Virginia at Appomattox Court House, Virginia.

After the war Johnston served one term in the U.S. Congress and settled in Washington, D.C. His memoir, *Narrative of Military Operations*, appeared in 1874. Johnston's reputation rested on the fact that he never lost a battle, yet this skilled but cautious and pessimistic soldier never won a major victory either. He died of pneumonia in 1891, not long after he had stood bareheaded in the rain at the funeral of his old adversary, W. T. Sherman.

Jones, William Edmonson ("Grumble")
(1824-1864) Confederate general

This Virginia-born West Point graduate had served on the frontier before resigning from the army in 1857. Commissioned major in the Confederate army in May

Joseph Eggleston Johnston

1861, he fought at Cedar Mountain, Groveton and Second Bull Run. Promoted to brigadier general in 1862, he fought with J. E. B. Stuart at Gettysburg. He had a notable success in what became known as "Jones's and Imboden's West Virginia Raid" in April 1863. He was killed on June 5, 1864, at Piedmont, Virginia.

Kearney, Philip
(1814-1862) Union general

Kearney was graduated from Columbia College, but, after inheriting a fortune in 1836, he opposed the wishes of his socially prominent New York family to fulfill a romantic dream of being a cavalry officer. He studied cavalry tactics in France and fought in Algiers: after 1844 he was aide-de-camp to commanders-in-chief Alexander Macomb and Winfield Scott. He lost an arm in the Mexican War. A dashing leader whose dragoons rode matched dapple-gray horses and whose troops wore distinctive scarlet, diamond-shaped "Kearney patches," he had an outstanding Civil War record, fighting for the Union at Williamsburg, Seven Pines and Second Bull Run. He was killed while reconnoitering at Chantilly in September 1862. Winfield Scott called him "a perfect soldier."

Philip Kearney sketched in action

Kemper, James Lawson
(1823-1895) Confederate general

Born in Virginia, Kemper was a lawyer who volunteered to serve in the Mexican War. He was the speaker of the House of Delegates in Virginia before he joined the Confederate army in May 1861. He fought at Fist Bull Run, Williamsburg, Seven

Erasmus Darwin Keyes

Pines, Frayer's Farm, Second Bull Run, South Mountain, Antietam, Fredericksburg and Gettysburg, where he was seriously wounded and captured. Exchanged three months later, he never returned to the field due to the severity of his injuries. Promoted to major general in September 1864, he ran the Conscript Bureau and was governor of Virginia, (1874-1878) after the war.

Keyes, Erasmus Darwin
(1810-1895) Union general

Keys, a Massachusetts-born West Point graduate and career officer, was a veteran of frontier and Indian fighting who also taught field artillery and cavalry at West Point. He was Winfield Scott's military secretary in 1860-1861. He commanded a Union brigade at First Bull Run and led IV Corps throughout the Peninsular Campaign. During the Battle of Gettysburg he conducted a feint toward Richmond. He resigned in May 1864. Later, his business interests in California included banking, mining and viniculture.

Kilpatrick, Hugh Judson
(1836-1881) Union general

The son of a New Jersey farmer, he was graduated from West Point in May 1861. Severely wounded at Big Bethel in June, Kilpatrick won appointment as lieutenant colonel of a New York cavalry regiment and embarked on a career as one of the most flamboyant Union cavalry commanders of the war. Known as Kill Cavalry, he led the infamous Kilpatrick-Dahlgren Raid on Richmond in 1864 and went west shortly thereafter at W. T. Sherman's request. "I know Kilpatrick is a hell of a damned fool," Sherman said, "but I want just that sort of man to command my cavalry." Kilpatrick led Sherman's mobile forces during the Atlanta Campaign, the March to the Sea and the Carolinas Campaign.

Kimball, Nathan
(1823-1898) Union general

Indiana-born, he had served as a young man in the Mexican War and subsequently became a doctor. Appointed a colonel in the Union army in 1861, he served at Cheat Mountain and Greenbrier. He became a division commander when General James Shields was wounded in the 1862 Shenandoah Valley Campaign, then went on to defeat Stonewall Jackson at Kernstown the following day. He fought at Antietam and Vicksburg and in the Atlanta and Franklin and Nashville campaigns. He was breveted a major general in 1865.

King, Rufus
(1814-1876) Union general

A West Point alumnus, he was an Albany newspaper editor and New York's adjutant general (1839-1843) before editing the influential *Milwaukee Sentinel* (c. 1845-1861). In 1861 he organized Wisconsin's famous "Iron Brigade." As a Union brigadier general King participated in Washington's defenses and led a division at Second Bull Run, where his retreat from Gainesville on August 28 was unfairly blamed for the Federal loss. He retired in ill-health in October 1863. He was U.S. minister to the Vatican when he arrested Lincoln assassination conspirator John Suratt in 1865.

ABOVE: Rufus King.

BELOW: H.J. Kilpatrick (right center).

Lamar, Lucius Quintus Cincinnatus
(1825-1893) Confederate statesman

Georgia-born Lamar moved to Mississippi in 1849. A lawyer and antisecessionist U.S. Representative (1857-1860), he drafted his state's secession ordinance. Lamar led the 19th Mississippi until his health failed in 1862; later he represented the Confederacy in Europe (1862-1863) and served as a judge advocate in the Army of Northern Virginia (1864-1865). A leading Mississippi Democrat and national representative of the "New South," he was a U.S. Representative (1873-1877) and Senator (1877-1885), secretary of the interior (1885-1888) and Supreme Court justice (1888-1893).

Lane, James Henry
(1833-1907) Confederate general

This Virginian, a Virginia Military Institute alumnus and mathematics and tactics teacher, fought in every important engagement of the war with the Army of Northern Virginia, from scouting before Big Bethel in 1861 to the surrender at Appomattox in 1865. Three times wounded, he was a brigadier general at 29; his troops called him "The Little General." He ended his long career in education with a 25-year tenure teaching civil engineering at Alabama Polytechnic Institute.

Lane, Walter Paye
(1817-1892) Confederate general

Born in Ireland, Lane came to Ohio in 1821. He went off to aid Sam Houston in Texas and fought at San Jacinto in 1836. He led an exciting life – as a pirate of sorts in the Gulf of Mexico, an Indian fighter, a soldier in the Mexican War and a goldminer in the

U.S. and South America. Commissioned in the Texas Cavalry, he fought for the Confederacy at Wilson's Creek and Pea Ridge. He was wounded at Mansfield during the Red River Campaign (1864). Ultimately promoted to brigadier general, he became a merchant after the war. He wrote a well-received memoir, *Adventures and Recollections*.

Lawton, Alexander Robert
(1818-1896) Confederate general

A South Carolinian educated at West Point and Harvard Law School, he became a Georgia lawyer, railroad president and leading secessionist legislator. His seizure of Fort Pulaski in 1861 inaugurated hostilities in Georgia. As a Confederate brigadier

Walter Paye Lane (right) and (below) James Henry Lane

general he commanded the Georgia coast and fought in the Shenandoah Valley Campaign of Jackson, in the Seven Days' Battles and at Second Bull Run and Antietam, Wounded and reassigned, he was an effective quartermaster general until the war's end. Returning to his Savannah law practice, he was an influential Democratic politician and was minister to Austria (1887-1889).

Lee, Fitzhugh
(1835-1905) Confederate general

The Virginia-born son of a naval officer and a nephew of Robert E. Lee, he was graduated from West Point in 1856 and served on the frontier. He led a Confederate cavalry brigade under J. E. B. Stuart during the Antietam, Gettysburg and Chancellorsville campaigns and commanded Robert E. Lee's cavalry during the war's last campaign, the retreat to Appomattox. Lee returned to the U.S. army in 1898 to command an infantry corps in Cuba during the Spanish-American War.

Lee, George Washington Custis
(1832-1913) Confederate general

Robert E. Lee's eldest son, he was graduated first in the West Point class of 1854 and saw service with the army's elite engineer corps. He resigned in May 1861 and obtained a Confederate army commission in July. Lee served for most of the war as Jefferson Davis's aide-de-camp. He taught engineering at the Virginia Military Institute after the war and succeeded his father as president of Washington (now Washington and Lee) College in 1871.

George Washington Custis Lee

Lee, Mary Commission worker

A native Briton, she began her war work in April 1861 offering food and drink to U.S. troops passing through Philadelphia. Her Union Refreshment Saloon soon grew to include dormitories, a medical center and other amenities and is said to have served more than 4 million soldiers. Lee volunteered as a Sanitary Commission nurse during the spring of 1862 and served almost continuously in Union field hospitals from the Peninsular Campaign to the Confederate surrender.

Lee, Robert Edward
(1807-1870) Confederate general

The fifth child and third son of Revolutionary War hero Light Horse Harry Lee, he grew up in modest circumstances in Alexandria, Virginia, where his father settled after nearly ruining himself with reckless financial speculations. When the improvident elder Lee died in 1818, care of his invalid widow fell to Robert. Despite such early responsibilities, he excelled in his studies, showing a particular aptitude for mathematics. West Point offered a free education and the prospect of a stable career as a soldier/engineer. After four distinguished years at the military academy, Lee was graduated second in his class in 1829.

He advanced slowly through the grades during 17 years of varied but routine garrison service. He saw combat and was wounded during the Mexican War of 1846-47. He served as superintendent of West Point from 1852 to 1855, a period when, among others, J. E. B. Stuart and the artist James McNeill Whistler were cadets

Robert Edward Lee in 1865.

At the Battle of Chancellorsville Robert E. Lee confers with Thomas J. (Stonewall) Jackson.

Confederacy – developments that might lead to a negotiated end to the war. The gamble failed. In early July 1863, after three days of savage fighting at Gettysburg, Pennsylvania, he led a defeated and badly damaged army back across the Potomac into Virginia.

By the spring of 1864 President Lincoln had at last found Lee's equal in Ulysses S. Grant. With diminishing resources, Lee fought Grant to a stalemate in a series of impressive but costly defensive struggles, from the Wilderness through Spotsylvania to Cold Harbor (where the Confederates claimed one of the most one-sided victories of the war). Then, in mid-June, Grant, in a brilliant tactical maneuver, gained a nearly decisive advantage when he surprised Lee by launching the Union army across the James River and attacking the vital communications center of Petersburg. Grant failed to capture the place, but he pinned Lee in Petersburg's fortifications, depriving him of all freedom of movement. Lee himself recognized the siege as the beginning of the end for his army.

The drain on the Confederacy continued through the winter of 1864-65, and by the time Grant launched his 1865 spring offensive, Lee commanded a doomed army. Grant forced Lee out of Petersburg in the opening phase of the battle. Then, in a swift and powerful drive, he caught and trapped the Army of Northern Virginia near Appo-

there. He commanded the detachment that captured John Brown and his raiders at Harpers Ferry, Virginia, in 1859. By the outbreak of Civil War his superiors and colleagues judged him the most promising officer in the U.S. Army.

Lee opposed secession in 1861, and his moderate political views encouraged President Lincoln to offer him field command of the Union army, but he resigned his commission when Virginia left the Union. His first field campaign, in western Virginia in the late summer of 1861, ended in failure. He afterward served as a military advisor to President Jefferson Davis. On July 1, 1862, at the age of 55, Lee succeeded General Joseph E. Johnston in command of the main Confederate field army in the East. He renamed it the Army of Northern Virginia and, with Union troops in sight of Richmond, launched the offensive known as the Seven Days' Battles. In a week of the bloodiest fighting of the war to date, Lee forced the Federals to retreat down the Vir-

ginia peninsula and, ultimately, to return to Washington.

He followed up with a victory at the Second Battle of Bull Run/Manassas (August 1862), the invasion of Maryland that ended in the drawn Battle of Antietam/Sharpsburg (September 1862) and the great defensive victory of Fredericksburg (December 1862). In May 1863, at Chancellorsville, he responded to a Federal offensive by boldly dividing his army to defeat a far larger enemy force in the battle of maneuver that became known as his masterpiece.

By then Lee's reputation had reached its zenith. But he had failed to destroy the Army of the Potomac at Chancellorsville, and the Federal blockade had begun to suffocate the Southern economy. As time passed, he recognized, the enemy would only grow stronger while the Confederacy expended its non-renewable resources of men and material. Lee thus resolved to try his greatest gamble, a second invasion of the North. A decisive victory on Union soil, he reasoned, would strengthen the Northern peace movement and encourage the European powers to recognize the

Robert E. Lee at the age of 38. He was at that time serving as a captain in the U.S. Army's corps of engineers.

mattox Court House, Virginia. "There is nothing left for me to do but go and see General Grant," Lee told his staff, "and I would rather die a thousand deaths." He surrendered in the front parlor of the Wilmer McLean house at Appomattox Court House on April 9, 1865.

Lee applied for parole in July, partly to set an example for recalcitrant Confederates. He was indicted for treason but not bought to trial, and the Union authorities never troubled him. He remained in Richmond until the autumn of 1865, when he accepted the presidency of Washington

College (now Washington and Lee) in Lexington, Virginia.

Handsome and massively featured, patient and unfailingly courteous, legendary for his kindness to animals, Lee became many Americans' ideal of the gentleman Christian soldier. He was deeply religious, though formal affiliation had come late (he was not confirmed in the Episcopal Church until 1854). As a soldier, Lee's greatest gift was an ability to divine his adversary's intentions. Decisive, willing to run tremendous risks, a master at inspiring troops, he ranks among the greatest of battlefield commanders, though he has been faulted for a strategic short-sightedness that placed too much emphasis on defence of his native Virginia.

Lee died of a heart ailment in Lexington on October 12, 1870. He was the object even then, of his countrymens' veneration, and so he remains.

Lee, William Henry Fitzhugh (1837-1891) Confederate general

Robert E. Lee's second son, he was graduated from Harvard, then entered the regular U.S. Army. Joining the Confederate service in May 1861, he led W. W. Loring's cavalry during the West Virginia Campaign and fought in J. E. B. Stuart's cavalry corps at Antietam and Chancellorsville. Taken captive after the Brandy Station cavalry action in June 1863, he remained in Union custody until the following March. He commanded the Confederate cavalry during the retreat to Appomattox.

The text of Robert E. Lee's farewell address to the men of his famous command, the Army of Northern Virginia

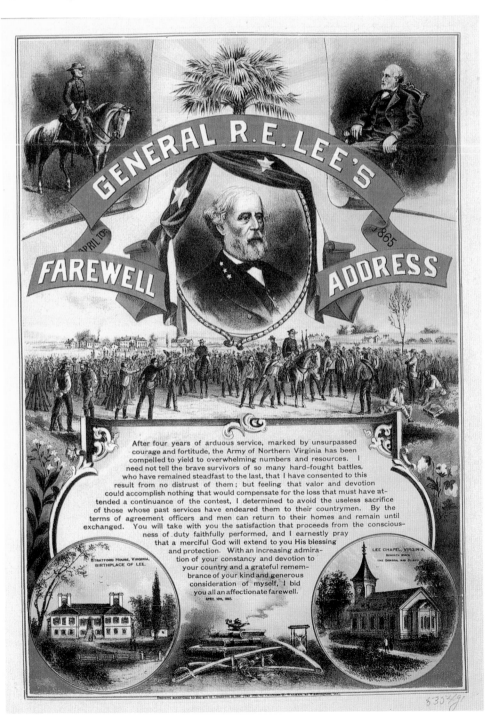

William Henry Fitzhugh Lee

Leggett, Mortimer Dormer (1821-1896) Union general

This Ohio lawyer and school superintendent volunteered as his friend, Union General George McClellan's, unpaid aide-de-camp in 1861 and went on to raise the 78th Ohio, fighting at Fort Donelson, Shiloh, Corinth and Vicksburg, later participating in the Atlanta Campaign and the March to the Sea. The hill he captured and

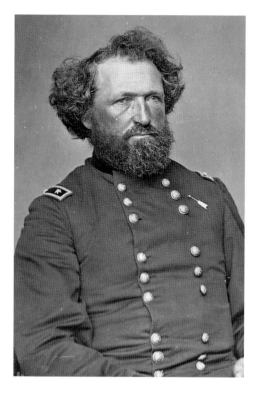

Mortimer Dormer Leggett

held at Atlanta was renamed Leggett's Hill. He reorganized the Patent Office as commissioner of patents (1871-1874), opened a Cleveland law practice and founded Brush Electric Company (1884).

Lincoln, Abraham
(1809-1865)
16th president of the United States

Born in a log cabin near Hodgenville, Kentucky, raised on a frontier farm in Indiana, he attended a "blab" school for a year and furthered his education with close readings of a handful of borrowed books, including The Bible, *Pilgrim's Progress* and Aesop's *Fables*. Lincoln moved to Illinois with his family in 1830 and began to read law in New Salem the following year. He clerked in a store there, managed a mill, split rails and sought other odd jobs to support himself during his long apprenticeship. He served in the militia during the brief Black Hawk War, won election to the state Legislature as a Whig in 1834 and finally received his license to practice as an attorney in september 1836.

Lincoln settled in Springfield, the state capital, established a modestly successful law practice and married the unstable, often-unhappy Mary Todd in 1842. The first of the couple's four children was born the following year. Lincoln left the legislature in 1841 but returned to politics six years later to wage a successful campaign for a seat in the U.S. Congress. After an undistinguished two years in Washington, he decided not to seek re-election and returned to Springfield disillusioned with politics.

Hard-working, fair, honest and well-liked, he rose to top of the legal profession in Illinois. The slavery question finally prompted his return to public life. In the autumn of 1854 he spoke in opposition to the Kansas-Nebraska Act, fellow Illinoisan Stephen A. Douglas's effort to accommodate the pro-slavery forces, but failed to win the Senate nomination. He joined the new Republican Party in 1856 and challenged Douglas for a Senate seat in 1858. Though he lost that election as well, his brilliant performance in a series of debates with Douglas gave him national stature.

He was a striking figure, six feet, four inches tall, thin and bony, with rough unlovely features: coarse hair, deeply sunken eyes, hollow, wrinkled cheeks and a large nose. "On the whole, he is such a mixture of all sorts as only America brings forth," one observer said. "He is as much like a highly intellectual and benevolent satyr as anything I can think of." Lincoln's dress scarcely improve his appearance. He favored tall stovepipe hats and dark, ill-fitting ready-made suits. But he had developed tremendous powers of language, and his political skills were unmatched. The Republicans nominated him as their 1860 presidential candidate on the third ballot at the raucous "Wigwam" convention hall in Chicago. He did not campaign, nor did he try to reassure Southerners who viewed him as a militant abolitionist. "If slavery is not wrong, then nothing is wrong," he had said, and he left it at that. With the Democratic Party hopelessly split over slavery, Lincoln won election as a

BELOW: Abraham Lincoln.

OPPOSITE: The text of Lincoln's great Proclamation of Emancipation.

PROCLAMATION OF EMANCIPATION

BY THE PRESIDENT OF THE UNITED STATES OF AMERICA.

Whereas, On the Twenty-Second day of September, in the year of our Lord One Thousand Eight Hundred and Sixty-Two, a Proclamation was issued by the President of the United States, containing, among other things, the following, to wit:

"That on the First day of January, in the year of our Lord One Thousand Eight Hundred and Sixty-Three, all persons held as Slaves within any State, or designated part of a State, the people whereof shall then be in rebellion against the United States, shall be then, thenceforth, and **FOREVER FREE,** and the *Executive Government of the United States,* including the Military and Naval Authorities thereof, *will recognise and maintain the freedom of such persons,* and will do no act or. acts to repress such persons, or any of them, in any efforts they may make for their actual freedom.

"That the Executive will, on the First day of January aforesaid, by proclamation, designate the States and parts of States, if any, in which the people thereof respectively shall then be in rebellion against the United States, and the fact that any State, or the people thereof, shall on that day be in good faith represented in the Congress of the United States by members chosen thereto at elections wherein a majority of the qualified voters of such State shall have participated, shall, in the absence of strong countervailing testimony, be deemed conclusive evidence that such State and the people thereof are not then in rebellion against the United States."

Now, Therefore, I, ABRAHAM LINCOLN, PRESIDENT OF THE UNITED STATES, by virtue of the power in me vested as **Commander-in-Chief of the Army and Navy of the United States** in time of actual armed rebellion against the authority and government of the United States, and as a fit and necessary war measure for suppressing said rebellion, do, on this First day of January, in the year of our Lord One Thousand Eight Hundred and Sixty-Three, and in accordance with my purpose so to do, publicly proclaim for the full period of one hundred days from the day of the first above-mentioned order, and designate, as the States and parts of States wherein the people thereof respectively are this day in rebellion against the United States, the following, to wit: — **Arkansas, Texas, Louisiana,** (except the Parishes of St. Bernard, Plaquemines, Jefferson, St. John, St. Charles, St. James, Ascension, Assumption, Terre Bonne, La Fourche, St. Mary, St. Martin, and Orleans, including the City of Orleans,) **Mississippi, Alabama, Florida, Georgia, South Carolina, North Carolina, and Virginia,** (except the forty-eight counties designated as West Virginia, and also the counties of Berkeley, Accomac, Northampton, Elizabeth City, York, Princess Ann, and Norfolk, including the cities of Norfolk and Portsmouth,) and which excepted parts are for the present left precisely as if this Proclamation were not issued.

And by virtue of the power and for the purpose aforesaid, I do order and declare that **ALL PERSONS HELD AS SLAVES** within said designated States and parts of States ARE, AND HENCEFORWARD **SHALL BE FREE!** and that the Executive Government of the United States, including the Military and Naval Authorities thereof, will recognize and maintain the freedom of said persons.

And I hereby enjoin upon the people so declared to be free to abstain from all violence, UNLESS IN NECESSARY SELF-DEFENCE; and I recommend to them that in all cases, when allowed, they LABOR FAITHFULLY FOR REASONABLE WAGES.

And I further declare and make known that such persons of suitable condition will be received into the armed service of the United States, to garrison forts, positions, stations, and other places, and to man vessels of all sorts in said service.

And upon this act, sincerely believed to be AN ACT OF JUSTICE, warranted by the Constitution, upon military necessity, I invoke the considerate judgment of mankind and the gracious favor of ALMIGHTY GOD!

In Testimony Whereof, I have hereunto set my name, and caused the seal of the United States to be affixed.

Done at the CITY OF WASHINGTON, this First day of January, in the Year of our Lord One Thousand Eight Hundred and Sixty-Three, and of the Independence of the United States the Eighty Seventh.

[L. S.]

By the President,

William H. Seward

Secretary of State.

A. Lincoln.

J. MAYER & Co. LITH 4 STATE ST. BOSTON.

ENTERED ACCORDING TO ACT OF CONGRESS, IN THE YEAR 1865, BY B.B. RUSSELL & Co. IN THE CLERKS

OFFICE OF THE DISTRICT COURT OF THE UNITED STATES FOR THE DISTRICT COURT OF MASSACHUSETTS

PUBLISHED BY B.B. RUSSELL & Co. 55. CORNHILL BOSTON.

minority president on November 6, 1860.

South Carolina became the first Southern state to secede, in December; in early 1861 six other Deep South states followed. Given the oath as 16th president on March 4, 1861, Lincoln denounced secession in his inaugural address and appealed to ''the mysic chords of memory'' he hoped would bind the nation together and prevent war. Tensions continued to mount. Finally, on April 12, 1861, the Confederates opened fire on federal Fort Sumter in Charleston harbor, touching off four years of civil war.

Lincoln issued an immediate call for 75,000 militia and prepared to force the rebellious states to return to the Union. The first Richmond Campaign went awry at Bull Run in July, a portent of years of military disappointments and frustration to come. Lincoln assumed overall direction of the war effort, gradually extending his powers to near-dictatorial scope. He suspended *habeas corpus*, permitting the jailing of thousands of people on mere suspicion of disloyalty, and there were instances of newspaper suppression. For the first time, the government conscripted men into the armed forces.

At first, to build political support, Lincoln had maintained that the war was entirely about secession. His Emancipation Proclamation of Jan. 1, 1863, transformed the conflict into a crusade against slavery, giving high moral purpose to the Union effort. But it was a crusade that was still floundering militarily, for the Union at first seemed incapable of producing generals as able as their Southern counterparts. And Lincoln was beset by political challenges as well – even from members of his own cabinet, several of whom schemed to replace him in the White House. But Lincoln outmaneuvered all opponents, even the unruly and meddlesome Congress, and kept the Union war effort on a steady course.

He searched nearly three years for a general who could defeat Robert E. Lee, though for a time it looked as though his final choice, Ulysses S. Grant, might cost him the presidency. By the late summer of 1864 Grant's Virginia Campaign, with its unprecedented cost in blood and treasure, appeared to be a failure. The Democrats nominated one of Grant's unsuccessful predecessors, General George McClellan, still immensely popular with the Army of the Potomac, to oppose Lincoln. Then, in early September, Grant's lieutenant, W. T. Sherman, marched into Atlanta in one of the decisive victories of the war. Lincoln won re-election in November, gaining an overwhelming majority of the soldier vote.

He envisaged a generous peace. "With malice toward none, with charity for all . . . let is strive on to bind up the nation's wounds," Lincoln said at his second inaugural in March 1865. In early April, Grant trapped the Army of Northern Virginia near Appomattox Court House and forced Lee's surrender on April 9. Five days later an embittered Southerner, John Wilkes Booth, shot and mortally wounded Lincoln at Ford's Theatre in Washington.

He foretold his own end. In a dream the night before the assassination, Lincoln found himself aboard some "singular, indescribable vessel . . . floating, floating away on some indistinct expanse, toward an unknown shore." He died at 7:22 a.m. on April 15, 1865, in a seedy back room of a boarding house across the street from the theater. "Now he is for the ages," said his war secretary, Edwin Stanton.

Lincoln, Mary Todd
(1818-1882) Wife of Abraham Lincoln

Born into a genteel Kentucky family, she settled in Illinois in 1839 and married Abraham Lincoln in 1842. Her close Southern family ties, political interference, attempts to maintain social life in the capital during the war and unpredictable temperament attracted criticism during Abraham Lincoln's presidency, but his affection for her was apparently unwavering. She tended soldiers in Washington during the war. Her last years, which included much foreign travel, were clouded by mental instability.

Livermore, Mary Ashton Rice
(1820-1905)
Sanitary Commission organizer

This Boston-born teacher married a Universalist minister in 1845 and became active in antislavery and temperance causes. A Chicago writer and editor in 1861, she helped to organize the Sanitary Commission's northwestern branch. She was instrumental in assigning female nurses to the front and in fundraising, and as a national director of the Commission she inspected battlefields and lectured widely. She wrote a popular war memoir (1887). From 1870 to

Mary Todd Lincoln

Mary Ashton Rice Livermore

1895 she became known as "the Queen of the Platform" for her unstinting work as a professional lecturer working for temperance and women's suffrage.

Logan, John Alexander
(1826-1886) Union general

The son of an Illinois farmer, he was erratically educated and interrupted his study of law to fight in the Mexican War. Entering politics as an Illinois district prosecutor and Democratic state legislator in the 1850s, he was a staunch Unionist who opposed the proslavery Lecompton constitution in Kansas. He left his U.S. Congressional seat (1859-1862) to fight for the Union with a Michigan regiment at First Bull Run. He then raised and led the 31st Illinois, compiling a distinguished war record. He was twice wounded, the first time at the capture of Fort Donelson. Promoted to brigadier general and major general in 1862, he fought in the Army of the Tennessee, leading XV Corps in the Vicksburg and Atlanta campaigns, the March to the Sea, and the Carolinas Campaign. An excellent fighter and field commander, despite his lack of formal military training, he twice briefly commanded the Tennessee Army, but his continuing political activity during the war and his impatience with detailed planning deterred his superiors from granting him a permanent major command. Joining the Republican Party after the war, he represented Illinois for two decades as a U.S. Representative (1867-1871) and Senator (1871-1877, 1879-1886). A vocal advocate for veterans, he helped to found the Grand Army of the Republic and the Society of the Army of the Tennessee and established Decoration (Memorial) Day as a national holiday (1868). He wrote *The Great Conspiracy* (1886) and *The Volunteer Soldier of America* (1887).

Logan, Thomas Muldrup
(1840-1914) Confederate general

The valedictorian of the South Carolina College class of 1860, he volunteered to serve the Confederacy at Fort Sumter in 1861, then joined the Hampton Legion as a first lieutenant. He fought at First Bull Run, Gaines's Mill, Second Bull Run and Antietam. Wounded twice and repeatedly promoted for gallantry, he was appointed the army's youngest brigadier general in February 1865 and led a brigade in the last charge of the war at Bentonville (March 1865). A Richmond lawyer after the war, he became a millionaire by organizing the Southern Railway.

Lunsford Lindsay Lomax

Lomax, Lunsford Lindsay
(1835-1913) Confederate general

This Rhode Island-born West Point graduate served as an Indian fighter on the frontier. His father was an army officer from Virginia, so Lunsford accepted a commission as a Confederate captain and then was appointed assistant adjutant general to General Joseph E. Johnston. Promoted to colonel, he fought at Gettysburg, the Wilderness and Petersburg. He was captured at Woodstock and escaped. After the Carolinas Campaign he surrendered with Johnston. He became president of a college in Virginia after the war. He also helped to compile *Official Records* and served as commissioner to Gettysburg National Park.

John Alexander Logan (fifth from the right) with his staff

Longstreet, James
(1821-1904) Confederate general

A farmer's son, South Carolina-born and raised in Georgia and Alabama, Longstreet was graduated from West Point in 1838 near the bottom of a large class that included such future distinguished soldiers as H. W. Halleck, W. T. Sherman and U. S. Grant.

Commissioned an infantry second lieutenant, he saw service in Missouri, Louisiana and Florida. He fought in Mexico with Zachary Taylor and accompanied Winfield Scott on the march to Mexico City. During the 1850s he served in garrison and on the frontier before changing into the paymaster corps; he told friends he had abandoned all dreams of military glory. Then the secession crisis flared. Longstreet resigned his paymaster commission and, in June 1861, obtained a brigadier's appointment in the Confederate army.

Longstreet commanded a brigade at the First Battle of Bull Run and stepped up to command a division under J. E. Johnston on the Virginia peninsula. He fought a tough rearguard action at Williamsburg on May 5, 1862, but reached his assigned position late and thus bore a share of the blame for Johnston's inability to convert opportunity into decisive victory at Seven Pines on May 31.

He came into his own as an infantry commander under Johnston's successor, Robert E. Lee, who called him his "Old War Horse." Lee's most reliable commander during the Seven Days' Battles, Longstreet in consequence had charge of more than half of Lee's infantry during the summer of 1862. Moving up on Stonewall Jackson's right near Manassas on August 29, he launched the powerful counterattack on the 30th that completed the rout John Pope's Union army at the Second Battle of Bull Run.

Promoted to lieutenant general and given charge of the newly-organized First Corps after Antietam, Longstreet's command bore the brunt of the fighting at Fredericksburg in December 1862. He failed to achieve success during a semi-independent assignment in southeastern Virginia during the winter of 1863, and the absence of his two divisions at Chancellorsville in May might have cost Lee a decisive follow-up success there.

Longstreet had strong convictions and a deep stubborn streak, and after Jackson's death he became ever more assertive in his views. He strongly opposed Lee's invasion of Pennsylvania in June 1863, arguing that the Army of Northern Virginia would be better employed in trying to deal with the military crisis developing in the west, at Vicksburg and in Tennessee. He tried to argue Lee out of attacking at Gettysburg on July 2 and bitterly opposed resuming the offensive with Pickett's division on the 3rd. The disastrous outcome of Pickett's Charge appeared to prove him correct.

The Confederate high command ordered Longstreet's corps to Tennessee in early September; his infantry reached the battlefield in time to make a decisive contribution to Braxton Bragg's victory at Chickamauga. He later sharply criticized Bragg for failing to follow up his gains. Again given independent command in November, Longstreet laid siege to Knoxville in eastern Tennessee but found it necessary to retreat after Ulysses S. Grant's decisive victory at Missionary Ridge.

Longstreet returned to Virginia for the spring campaign of 1864. Seriously wounded leading a successful counterattack at the Battle of the Wilderness in May, he missed the Spotsylvania and Cold Harbor fighting, as well as the first several months of the long siege at Petersburg. He returned to duty in the autumn of 1864, took part in the defense of Richmond over the winter and surrendered with Lee at Appomattox on April 9, 1865.

His postwar career fairly burned with controversy. He became an avowed Republican, and Southerners turned violently against him, unfairly blaming him for the Gettysburg defeat and, by implication, for the fall of the Confederacy. He held a series of federal patronage jobs from 1869 until the end of his life, including surveyor of customs in New Orleans, minister to Turkey, U.S. marshal for Georgia and U.S. railroad commissioner. His memoir, *From Manassas to Appomattox* (1896) made him still more enemies among adherents of the Lost Cause, for it dared to criticize the two holiest of Southern icons, Robert E. Lee and Stonewall Jackson.

Loring, William Wing
(1818-1886) Confederate general

He fought against the Seminole Indians while still a youth, became a lawyer and then served with distinction in the Mexican War. He stayed on in the regular army and participated in various actions. He resigned from the Union army in 1861 and accepted a commission as brigadier general in the Confederate army. In what is known as "the Loring-Jackson incident," in January 1862, Loring tried to avoid an order from Stonewall Jackson by appealing over his

James Longstreet

head to the Confederate secretary of war, but Jackson prevailed, and Loring was transferred to the west, where he was engaged in many major campaigns and battles. In 1869 he went to Egypt to serve in its army, and he returned in 1879, highly decorated for his services in battle and created a "pasha."

Lovejoy, Elijah Parish
(1802-1837) Abolitionist

A native of Maine, he studied for the ministry and then became editor of a Presbyterian weekly, the *St. Louis Observer* (1833-36), turning it into an outspoken opponent of slavery. Since St. Louis was hostile to his views, he moved to Alton, Illinois, in 1836 and started the *Alton Observer*. The locals there proved no more sympathetic to his abolitionist message, and he was killed by a mob in 1837.

Lovell, Mansfield
(1822-1884) Confederate general

An 1842 West Point graduate, he served on the frontier and in the Mexican War before resigning in 1849 to become an iron manufacturer. He later was deputy streets commissioner for the city of New York. Given charge of the Confederacy's New Orleans defenses after the outbreak of the war, he failed to stop the fleet from seizing the city in April 1862. Political pressures led to Lovell's removal after the fall of New Orleans; a court of inquiry cleared him, but the Confederacy offered him no further military employment.

Two of James Longstreet's many famous actions: below, The Second Battle of Bull Run (August 29–September 2, 1862) and, overleaf, the murderous Battle of Cold Harbor (May 31–June 3, 1864)

William Wing Loring

Lowe, Thaddeus Sobieski Coulincourt
(1832-1913)
Aeronaut, meteorologist and inventor

Born in New Hampshire, he made his first hot-air balloon ascent in 1858 and began preparing for a transatlantic flight. While investigating air currents on a flight from Cincinnati, he was arrested over the Carolinas on suspicion of spying for the Union in April 1861 (he claimed to have been the war's first prisoner). During the war years he pioneered the Union army aeronautics corps, a balloon fleet used for battlefield observation and communications. He later pioneered the manufacture of artificial ice, improved techniques for manufacturing gas and coke and built an inclined railway in California.

TOP: Thaddeus S. C. Lowe.

ABOVE: Thaddeus Lowe at the Battle of Fair Oaks in 1862 (right, with hand on one of his observation balloons).

Lyon, Nathaniel
(1818-1861) Union general

Born in Connecticut, this West Point-trained career soldier served in the Seminole and Mexican wars and on the frontier. He became a Republican polemicist while stationed in "Bleeding Kansas." Commanding the federal arsenal and troops in St. Louis, he saved the arsenal and captured the pro-secessionist militia gathering at Camp Jackson in May 1861, thereby probably saving Missouri for the Union. Appointed a brigadier general, he was killed at Wilson's Creek in August 1861.

MacArthur, Arthur
(1845-1912) Union officer

Raised in Milwaukee, he joined the Union's 24th Wisconsin Volunteers in August 1862 and fought at Perryville, Stones River, Missionary Ridge, (where he won a Medal of Honor) and in the Atlanta Campaign. Often breveted, he led his regiment in nine battles before he turned 20, making him one of the youngest regimental commanders of the war. He later served in the Spanish American War and was military governor of the Philippines (1900-1901). He retired as a lieutenant general in 1909. General Douglas MacArthur was his famous son.

Mackall, William Whann
(c. 1816-1891) Confederate general

Born in Washington, D.C., this West Point graduate fought in the Seminole and Mexican wars (wounded in both) and on the frontier. He resigned from the U.S. Army in 1861 and joined the Confederate army; he was promoted to brigadier general in 1862. He served at New Madrid and Island No. 10 and then became General Braxton Bragg's chief of staff, a post he left late in 1863 after the Battle of Chickamauga. He served as General Joseph E. Johnston's chief of staff during the unsuccessful campaign to save Atlanta from W. T. Sherman's attack in 1864. He surrendered at Macon, Georgia, in April 1865. He farmed in Virginia after the war.

Mackenzie, Ranald Slidell
(1840-1889) Union general

First in his class at West Point (1862), this New Yorker had a distinguished war record as an engineer officer. He fought for

Ranald Slidell Mackenzie

Magruder, John Bankhead
(1810-1871) Confederate general

He was born in Winchester, Virginia, and educated with a view to a West Point appointment. He was graduated from the academy in 1830, and over the next 15 years he saw service in a succession of garrisons and in the Seminole War.

Magruder commanded a light artillery unit during the Mexican War and was three times recognized for "gallant and meritorious conduct." Though he had a reputation for being restless and short-tempered, Thomas Jackson, for one, sought service with him, knowing that he would be likely to take his guns to wherever the action was hottest.

He earned the sobriquet "Prince John" while stationed in Newport, Rhode Island, where his lavish entertainments were much admired and discussed. He had a "brilliant ability to bring appearances up the necessity of the occasion," someone remarked of him.

Magruder resigned from the U.S. Army in March 1861 and accepted a colonelcy in the Confederate service. His victory at Big Bethel on June 10, which he reported as the first significant land engagement of the war, made him one of the South's first military celebrities. As a result, he was promoted to brigadier in June and to major general in October.

Commanding a force of about 12,000 infantry, Magruder drew on his Newport experiences in the spring of 1862 to bluff the Federals advancing up the Virginia

John Newland Maffitt

the Union in the Army of the Potomac from Kelly's Ford through Petersburg, helped to defend Washington against Jubal Early's 1864 raid and led a brigade in the Shenandoah Valley Campaign of Sheridan and an Army of the James cavalry division during the Appomattox Campaign, suffering three wounds in all. Ulysses S. Grant called him "the most promising young officer in the army." After the war he become one of the army's pre-eminent Indian fighters. He retired from service in 1884

Maffitt, John Newland
(1819-1886)
Confederate naval commander

Born at sea to emigrating Irish parents, Maffitt joined the U.S. Navy in 1832 and served at sea and on the coast survey before resigning to join the Confederate navy. Commanding the Confederate vessels *Savannah*, *Florida*, *Albemarle* and other ships, he was engaged in both combat and blockade-running. He became a commander in April 1863 after running the Federal blockade of Mobile against nearly insuperable odds, and he later captured dozens of Union ships. He retired to North Carolina in 1871.

John Bankhead Magruder

Dennis Hart Mahan

Mahan, Dennis Hart
(1802-1871) Military educator

A New York native raised in Virginia, he was graduated first in his class from West Point in 1824, where he was to teach civil and military engineering for more than 40 years. Among his numerous textbooks, the seminal *Field Fortification* (1836) and *Advance-Guard, Out-Post . . .* (1847, several times revised) were standard military texts for officers in the Mexican War and on both sides throughout the Civil War. His son, Alfred Thayer Mahan (1840-1914), a junior Union naval officer during the war, later became one of the world's greatest naval historians.

Mahone, William
(1826-1895) Confederate general

Graduated from Virginia Military Academy, he was a Virginia railroad president when his state seceded. He was appointed state quartermaster general and helped to capture the Norfolk Navy Yard. As a Confederate brigadier general, "Little Billy" then commanded the Norfolk District until 1862. During his later field service he was promoted to major general for heroism at the Petersburg crater and led "Mahone's Brigade," famous for its *esprit de corps*, through Appomattox. He was later a railroad president, a U.S. Senator (1881-1887) and a Republican power-broker.

peninsula. His improvisations deceived George McClellan, the Union commander, and contributed materially to the success of Confederate operations. Among other ruses, "Prince John" ordered an infantry unit to march in a wide circle for several hours, convincing Federal observers, who saw a continuous line of troops passing their field of vision, that reinforcements were arriving in Magruder's front all the time.

His reputation suffered fatally during the subsequent Seven Days' Battles around Richmond. His bumbling and inefficiency helped deny Robert E. Lee a potentially decisive victory south of the Chicka-hominy. Magruder and Lee quarrelled, and

Lee, deciding he could not work with Magruder, caused him to be transferred to command the District of Texas in October.

Magruder worked to strengthen the Texas coastal defenses and could boast of at least one success. On January 1, 1863, with two cotton-clad gunboats, he took Galveston, captured the cutter *Harriet Lane* and drove off the Federal blockading squadron. His active operations ended in the spring of 1864, when he sent most of his troops to reinforce Richard Taylor in Louisiana.

He refused to ask for parole at war's end and went into exile in Mexico, where he obtained a major general's commission under Emperor Maxmilian. Forced to return to the U.S. after Maxmilian's fall, he settled in Houston, where he died in February 1871.

Stephen Russell Mallory

Mallory, Stephen Russell
(1813-1873)
Secretary of the Confederate navy

Raised in Key West, Florida, and early familiar with shipping and the sea, Mallory was a Key West attorney, county judge and customs collector. He fought in the Seminole War. As a U.S. Senator (1851-1861) he promoted naval reform and opposed secession and the war. When war broke out, however, he resigned to serve as secretary of the Confederate navy (1861-1865), a difficult job, since the Confederates had neither ships nor naval yards. With great resourcefulness he mobilized inventors and construction crews, organized English and French naval construction and advanced naval technology by using ironclads, torpedoes and submarines. Arrested in May 1865, he practiced law in Pensacola after his release.

Marmaduke, John Sappington
(1833-1887) Confederate general

The son of a Missouri governor, he was graduated from West Point in 1857 and participated in the Utah Expedition (1858-1860). He resigned to join the state militia and then the Confederate army. An extremely affective cavalry commander, Marmaduke fought in Arkansas and Missouri. His greatest achievements were his successes under A. S. Johnston at Shiloh (for which he was promoted to brigadier general) and, as a major general in charge of the cavalry, in Sterling Price's 1864 Missouri Raid. He was captured in a rearguard action after Marais des Cygnes in October 1864. After his release in 1865 he became a St. Louis businessman and journal editor. He was governor of Missouri (1884-1887).

Marshall, Humphrey
(1812-1872) Confederate general

This Kentuckian, a West Point graduate and Mexican War cavalry veteran, was a lawyer, Whig U.S. Representative (1849-1852, 1855-1859) and minister to China (1852-1854). Failing to maintain peace in the border states, he became a Confederate brigadier general in 1861. He fought along Big Sandy River, successfully attacked J. D. Cox at Princeton, West Virginia, and participated in Braxton Bragg's invasion of Kentucky before resigning to sit in the Confederate congress (1864-1865). He was later a distinguished Louisville lawyer.

Mason, James Murray
(1798-1871) Confederate statesman

Trained at William and Mary Law School, this Virginia lawyer and member of Congress (U.S. Representative 1837-1839, Senator 1847-1861) was a states' rights Democrat and prominent secessionist; he drafted the Fugitive Slave Act (1850). As a Confederate diplomatic commissioner en route in a British ship to great Britain with John Slidell in 1861, he was captured at sea by the Federals in what became known as the *Trent* Affair, an incident that dangerously strained Anglo-U.S. relations. Despite years of diplomacy, he failed in the end to secure British recognition of the Confederacy.

Humphrey Marshall. His command in 1862, the so-called Army of Eastern Kentucky, a small militia force, was routed by Union troops under future president of the United States James A. Garfield.

Maury, Dabney Herndon
(1822-1900) Confederate general

A West Point graduate, Virginian Maury was a Mexican War and Texas frontier veteran and the author of a standard cavalry manual (1859). In 1861 he joined the Confederate cavalry; he fought at Pea Ridge and, promoted to brigadier general, at Iuka, Corinth and Hatchie Bridge. His command of the District of the Gulf after July 1863 (as a major general) was notable for the loss of Mobile – the use of its harbor to Admiral David Farragut in August 1864 and he city itself to General E. R. S. Canby in April 1865. In Richmond he later organized and chaired the Southern historical Society (1868-1886); he was U.S. minister to Colombia (1885-1889). Famed hydrographer Matthew Fontaine Maury (1806-1873) was his uncle.

Matthew Fontaine Maury

Maury, Matthew Fontaine
(1806-73) Hydrographer and Confederate naval commander

Born near Fredericksburg, Virginia, he was raised on a Tennessee frontier farm. Having joined the U.S. Navy in 1825, he established his reputation with *A New Theoretical and Practical Treatise on Navigation* (1836). After a crippling accident in 1839 ended his seagoing career, he devoted himself to naval administration and research. As superintendent of the navy's depot of charts and instruments (1842-1855, 1858-1861), he oversaw the U.S. naval observatory. He worked on the canal system, the Gulf Stream (which he was the first to describe), deep-sea sounding, the transatlantic cable and other important projects. He compiled his classic work, *Wind and Current Charts of the North Atlantic*, in 1847 and instituted a uniform international system of recording oceano-

Dabney Herndon Maury

graphical data that allowed the extension of these charts to other waters. (The sophisticated pilot charts published by today's Defense Mapping Agency still credit Maury's inspiration and follow his methodology.) This major contribution to international commerce earned him worldwide acclaim. His *Physical Geography of the Sea* (1855, published in numerous languages and many times revised) established oceanography as a major science. Maury resigned from the U.S. Navy in April 1861 and represented the Confederacy as a special agent in England (1862-1865). There he purchased foreign warships and invented a system of laying electric mines, but he returned to America too late for the Confederate navy to make use of his new technology. After a brief exile in Mexico and Europe, he joined the meteorology faculty at Virginia Military Institute (1868) and undertook a survey of Virginia.

Maximilian, Archduke
(1832-1867) Emperor of Mexico

Brother of the Austrian Emperor Franz Joseph, he was asked by Napoleon III of France to accept the "crown" of Mexico, which French troops had captured in 1862 while taking advantage of the unrest attending the Civil War in the United States. Maximilian, assured that he would be welcomed, went off to Mexico to become its Emperor in 1864, and Napoleon III provided French troops to protect him. During the Civil War, Union diplomatic pressure failed to dislodge him, but after the war the Union employed the threat of

military intervention until the French forces withdrew in 1866. Maximilian attempted to continue his reign in Mexico, and he was soon deposed, captured by troops of Benito Juarez and executed.

McCausland, John
(1836-1927) Confederate general

Born in Missouri, he was graduated first in his class from Virginia Military Institute and joined its mathematics faculty. He recruited Confederate troops in the Kanawha Valley, fought at Fort Donelson and defended the Virginia and Tennessee Railroad. As a brigadier general he led a cavalry brigade in the Shenandoah Valley and at Monocacy in 1864 and took part in the burning of Chambersburg, Pennsylvania, in retaliation for David Hunter's destruction in the Shenandoah Valley. He refused to surrender with Lee at Appomattox. He later farmed in West Virginia.

McClean, Wilmer
Virginia farmer

McClean would probably have remained an anonymous farmer in the Virginia countryside some 25 miles southwest of Washington, if, in July 1861, the battle known as First Bull Run had not destroyed his farmhouse. Wishing only to get away from the violence of the war, he moved to a new home at what he believed to be an obscure locale, Appomattox Court House, Virginia. It was in the parlor of McClean's house that, on April 9, 1865, Ulysses S. Grant chose to meet Robert E. Lee and accept the Confederate surrender.

McClellan, George Brinton
(1826-1885) Union general

The son of a distinguished Philadelphia surgeon, he attended preparatory schools and the University of Pennsylvania before entering West Point in 1842. McClellan was graduated second in his class in 1846, joined an engineer detachment and accompanied it to Mexico, where he served with notable competence throughout the war.

McClellan enjoyed a varied career during the next several years. He taught military engineering at West Point, took part in an expedition to the upper reaches of the Red River, worked on river and harbor engineering projects in Texas and surveyed a railroad route in the Pacific Northwest. In 1855-56 the army sent him abroad to study European military organizations. He returned to write a much-admired report on the siege of Sebastopol.

McClellan resigned from the service in 1857 to become chief engineer of the Illinois Central Railroad; three years later

Wilmer McClean's house in Appomattox Court House, Virginia, in 1865

he succeeded to the presidency of the Cincinnati-based Ohio & Mississippi line. He accepted a commission in the Union army as a major general of Ohio volunteers in april 1861, and took command of the Department of the Ohio in May.

His victory at Rich Mountain in early July cleared western Virginia of Confederate troops and made him one of the Union's first heroes, and President Abraham Lincoln soon turned to him to repair the damage caused by the Union defeat at First Bull Run. McClellan reached Washington on July 26, 1861, and set to work immediately to reorganize and train the army and strengthen the Washington defenses.

A brilliant organizer and administrator, McClellan transformed the beaten army almost overnight. But he seemed dilatory when the question of fighting arose. By autumn the president and key Congressmen were growing impatient with his lack of aggressiveness. "If General McClellan does not want to use the army," Lincoln said, "I would like to borrow it." Finally, early in the new year, the president ordered a general advance on Manassas. But McClellan argued for a move on Richmond from the Virginia peninsula, and Lincoln reluctantly approved. In March 1862 McClellan transported the Army of the

LEFT: George Brinton McClellan.

BELOW: McClellan and Lincoln confer in the field after Antietam.

Potomac by water to Fortress Monroe and advanced toward Yorktown. He proceeded up the peninsula at such a deliberate pace that his critics began calling him the "Virginia Creeper." Nevertheless, he had pushed the army to within sight of the spires of Richmond when J. E. Johnston counterattacked at Fair Oaks (Seven Pines) on May 31. Then, in the Seven Days' Battles of early June, Robert E. Lee checked McClellan's advance and forced him to withdraw to his base at Harrison's Landing on the James River, essentially ending the Peninsular Campaign.

Lincoln replaced McClellan with John Pope, then restored him to command after Pope's defeat at the Second Battle of Bull Run in August 1862. McClellan fought a drawn battle at Antietam Creek in Maryland on September 17 but failed to pursue the Confederates when they returned to Virginia. He finally marched in late October, but by then it was too late. Lincoln removed him for the last time on November 7, 1862. He never held another field command.

The troops loved McClellan, whom they dubbed "Little Mac," and many of the Army of the Potomac's senior offices remained devoted to him. His reputation is that of a brilliant failure, though his champions argue that the administration never gave him a fair chance. Lee, for one, thought him the ablest Union commander he faced. Yet the fact remains that McClellan never scored a significant battlefield success. He always wanted more men, more equipment, more time to plan. "He is an admirable engineer," Lincoln said of him, "but he seems to have a special talent for the stationary engine."

McClellan accepted the Democratic nomination for the presidency in 1864. The party platform called for an immediate cessation of the fighting, but McClellan, who supported vigorous prosecution of the war, simply ignored the platform. Even so, he carried only three states in November, and the soldier vote went overwhelmingly to Lincoln. His political ambitions were gratified to a small extent in 1878, when he was elected governor of New Jersey: he served until 1881. McClellan died at Orange, New Jersey, in 1885.

McClernand, John Alexander
(1812-1900) Union general

He was a lawyer, newspaper editor and Democratic politician in his native Illinois who, as a U.S. Representative (1843-1851, (1959-1861) helped to draft the Compromise of 1850. He proposed Congres-

sional war appropriations after First Bull Run, then left Congress to become a Union brigadier general. McClernand proved to be a politically ambitious, sometimes insubordinate and only occasionally effective officer. He commanded troops at forts Henry and Donelson and at Shiloh, and in January 1863 led 30,000 men in the unauthorized and controversial Arkansas Post expedition. Ulysses S. Grant subsequently disbanded McClernand's force and reassigned him to XIII Corps, which he led in the Vicksburg and Red River Campaigns. He resigned in ill health in November 1864 and resumed his legal and political career.

John Alexander McClernand

McCook Family of Ohio
("The Fighting McCooks")

The brothers Daniel (1798-1863) and John (1806-1865) McCook and their 13 sons ("the tribe of Dan" and "the tribe of John") all served the Union with distinction. The elder McCooks served respectively as an army paymaster and surgeon; of their sons, six became generals and three died in the war. The best known of their sons were General Alexander M. McCook (1831-1903, son of Dan), a career soldier who fought at First Bull Run, Shiloh,

Daniel McCook (above) and (above right) Alexander McCook.

RIGHT: Robert McCook

Perryville, Stones River and Chickamauga and General Edward M. McCook (1833-1909, son of John), a brilliant cavalry commander who cut Confederate communications and supply lines and prevented J. B. Hood's reinforcement during the Atlanta Campaign. Edward McCook was later governor of Colorado (1869-1875).

McCullagh, Joseph Burbridge
(1842-1896) **War correspondent**

Born in Ireland, McCullagh was working for the Cincinnati *Gazette* while reporting the Civil War. He volunteered to serve as Commodore Andrew Foote's secretary on the armored gunboat *St. Louis* when General Ulysses S. Grant mounted a combined attack on Fort Donelson in 1862. He later worked for various newspapers in the Midwest before starting the St. Louis *Morning Globe* (which later merged with the *Democrat*).

McDowell, Irvin
(1818-1885) **Union general**

Born in Ohio, McDowell received his early education in France, then returned home to enter West Point. He was graduated in the middle of his class in 1838 and joined the artillery. He taught tactics at the academy, then served on the staff of General John Wool during the Mexican War.

McDowell held various staff assignments up to the outbreak of the Civil War. An early favorite of the Lincoln administration, particularly of treasury secretary Salmon P. Chase, he won promotion to brigadier general in May 1861, helped to organize troops assembling in Washington and took command of the forces south of the Potomac.

Although senior officers considered the army unfit for field operations, political pressures made an attack on the Confederates at Manassas Junction imperative. "You are green, it is true," President Lincoln told McDowell, "but they are green also; you are all green alike." Thus prodded, McDowell marched from Washington on July 16, 1861, to open the brief, disastrous Bull Run Campaign.

McDowell himself had never before held a field command, and he seems to have forgotten his own arguments about the inexperience of his troops when he planned the Bull Run offensive, since he called for a complicated turning operation that required a night march. The flanking column arrived in place hours behind schedule, and in any case, alert Confederates had discovered its presence. After a confused fight lasting several hours, McDowell's army was routed at Bull Run on July 21, the first major battle of the war.

"Both armies were defeated," said William T. Sherman, who commanded a brigade at Bull Run. "Whichever had stood fast, the other would have run."

Yet it was the Federals who ran, and McDowell took the blame: George McClellan superseded him a few days after the battle. McDowell became a division commander; he later led I Corps of the Army of the Potomac. His corps remained behind, covering Washington, when McClellan moved the army to Fortress Monroe in the spring of 1862 to open the Peninsular Campaign.

After the failure of the campaign and McClellan's removal. McDowell's command became III Corps of John Pope's Army of Virginia. His performance at the Second Battle of Bull Run drew heavy criticism, and he was relieved of his command. He called for an inquiry; the investigation exonerated him, but he never again held a command in the field.

McDowell served in California and in the departments of the East and South after the war. He returned to California in 1876 and retired there six years later. As a parks commissioner in San francisco, he is credited with laying out the roads in the Presidio overlooking the Golden Gate. He died in San francisco in May 1885 and was buried in the Presidio.

McKay, Charlotte Elizabeth
Union army nurse

Recently-widowed, McKay left her native Massachusetts to enlist as an army nurse in March 1862. Working in hospitals in Washington and in the field, she nursed men wounded in the Potomac Army campaigns from Winchester through Spotsylvania. She served in City Point hospital during the sieges of Petersburg and Richmond and earned the Kearny cross. After the war she worked with freed blacks in Virginia.

McLaws, Lafayette
(1821-1897) Confederate general

This Georgia-born West Point graduate served on the frontier, in the Mexican war, on the Utah expedition and as an Indian fighter. He resigned from the U.S. Army in 1861 and joined the Confederate army and was promoted to major general in 1862. He fought at Yorktown, helped to capture Harpers Ferry and also served at Antietam, Fredericksburg, Chancellorsville, Peach Orchard and Gettysburg. McLaws was charged by Confederate General James Longstreet of lack of cooperation at Knoxville in 1864, but, cleared of the charges, he went on to fight in the Carolinas Campaign in 1865. He worked for the Internal Revenue and Post Office departments in Savannah, Georgia, after the war.

Meade, George Gordon
(1815-1872) Union general

Meade was born in Cadiz, Spain, where his father served as the United States naval agent, but he was educated in the United States. Entering West Point in 1831, he was graduated four years later, 19th in his class

George Gordon Meade

ABOVE: The Battle of Gettysburg.

BELOW: George Meade's headquarters on Cemetery Ridge at Gettysburg.

of 56. He joined an artillery regiment, served for a year in Florida, where he was laid low with fever for much of the time, and resigned from the army in October 1836.

Meade found work immediately as assistant engineer of the Alabama, Florida & Georgia Railroad and later served as a civil engineer in a survey of the mouths of the Mississippi River. Re-entering the army in 1842, he had several engineering assignments and, during the Mexican War, saw action at Palo Alto, Monterey and Vera Cruz.

He held a succession of army engineering posts during the 1850s. On the outbreak of the Civil War he accepted a brigadier's commission in the Union army and took command of a brigade of Pennsylvania infantry. He fought in the battles of the Seven Days of June and July 1862 and was shot in the hip at Glendale, a wound that would trouble him for the remainder of his life.

Meade commanded a division at Antietam and Fredericksburg and led V Corps at Chancellorsville. On June 28, 1863, a messenger from President Lincoln informed him he had been chosen to replace Joseph Hooker as commander of the Army of the Potomac. When, three days later, advance elements of the armies met at Gettysburg, Meade decided to accept battle there. He has been praised for his masterly handling of the Union troops at Gettysburg, especially on July 2 and 3, but he has also been criticized for failing to counterattack and pursue the vulnerable Army of Northern Virginia in the aftermath of the battle.

He proved to be a solid if unspectacular commander. Tall, gaunt, hatchet-faced and irascible, his unruly temper became legendary in the army. "I don't know any thin old gentlemen with a hooked nose and cold blue eye who, when he is wrathy, exercises less of Christian charity than my well-beloved Chief," Theodore Lyman, one of his staff officers, wrote. In self-critical moods Meade recognized this failing, once describing himself as "an old snapping turtle."

Meade continued in independent command through the inconclusive Rapidan and Mine Run campaigns of late 1863, but he lost much of his authority when Ulysses S. Grant, appointed commander-in-chief, decided to make his headquarters with the army in the field. Meade retained nominal command through the surrender at Appomattox, though Grant apparently considered replacing him, in part because of his frequent quarrels with senior subordinates.

T.F. Meagher leads the Irish Brigade at the Battle of Fair Oaks (1862).

During the pursuit to Appomattox, Grant turned to Philip Sheridan as his chief tactical executive, leaving Meade with only a minor role in the campaign that closed out the war.

Meade commanded military departments in the East and South in the late 1860s. He died in Philadelphia in November 1872 while still on active duty, an indirect result of the wound he had received during the Seven Days' Battles a decade earlier.

Meagher, Thomas Francis
(1823-1867) Union general

A nationalist expelled from Ireland in 1849 for founding the Irish Confederation (1847), Meagher established himself after 1852 as a New York lawyer and newspaper editor, becoming the leader of the city's Irish community. He commanded a company of Union Zouaves, troops distinctive for their exotic costumes, at First Bull Run, and led the Irish Brigade through the Peninsula, Second Bull Run, Antietam, Fredericksburg and Chancellorsville. He later held territorial commands. He was the temporary governor of Montana when he died in a boat accident.

Meigs, John Rodgers
(1842-1864) Union officer

The son of General Montgomery Meigs and a graduate of West Point, he was a Union engineer on Philip Sheridan's staff. He was killed by one of Confederate General Williams Wickham's scouts, and, partly in retaliation, Sheridan ordered all houses within five-miles of Dayton, Virginia, to be burned.

Memminger, Christopher Gustavus
(1803-1888)
Confederate secretary of the treasury

This German immigrant was orphaned in South Carolina and fostered by a state governor. He became a Charleston lawyer and state legislator. A conservative Democrat, he opposed secession until late 1860, then attended the state and Montgomery secession conventions and helped to draft the provisional Confederate constitution.

Thomas Francis Meagher

Christopher Gustavus Memminger

As Confederate secretary of the treasury (1861-1864), he faced difficult choices in financing the war: inflation ballooned, making his treasury notes worthless; the Federal blockade halted cotton exports; all his bond and taxation schemes failed. The C.S.A. congress passed its own funding act in February 1864, and Memminger, held responsible for the collapse of the Confederacy's credit, resigned in June. He was afterward a lawyer and chemical manufacturer.

Merritt, Wesley
(1834-1910) Union general

A New Yorker, this young West Point graduate was aide-de-camp to Union generals Philip St. George Cooke and George Stoneman. Leading Shenandoah Army cavalry units, he saw nearly continuous action for the last two years of the war and ended his brilliant war career as a major general. He later served in Indian fighting and as superintendent of West Point (1882-1887) and held important territorial commands. He commanded the first Philippine expedition (1898) and accepted Manila's surrender with Admiral George Dewey before retiring from the army in 1900.

Miles, Nelson Appleton
(1839-1925) Union general

A Boston store clerk with dreams of military glory, he obtained a commission in the 22nd Massachusetts and advanced rapidly in the Union army, rising to colonel of the 61st New York after Antietam in September 1962. Miles fought at Chancellorsville, the Wilderness, Spotsylvania and Petersburg. At the war's end he commanded the prison guard that watched over Jefferson Davis at Fortress Monroe, Virginia. He later became a famous Indian fighter, saw extensive service on the frontier and led the force that captured Geronimo in 1886. Miles ended a long career as army commander-in-chief from 1895 to 1903.

Morgan, George Washington
(1820-1893) Union general

Morgan was born in Pennsylvania and attended West Point, but left it to study law. He served in the Mexican War and then entered the diplomatic service, serving as U.S. ambassador to Portugal (1858-1861). Upon the outbreak of the Civil War he was made a brigadier general in the Union army, served under Don Carlos Buell in Tennessee, led a division in the Yazoo expedition and led XIII Corps in the capture of Arkansas Post. In June 1863 he resigned due both to ill health and his objections to the Union's use of African-American troops. After the war he served Ohio in the U.S. House of Representatives.

Nelson Appleton Miles

George Washington Morgan

John Hunt Morgan

Morgan, John Hunt
(1825-1864) Confederate general

Morgan was born in Alabama, the son of a merchant who moved his family to a farm near Lexington, Kentucky, in 1830. He was educated in local common schools, volunteered for service in the Mexican War in 1846 and saw action at Buena Vista.

Morgan went into business for himself on his return from Mexico, but the war had left him with a taste for soldiering, and in 1857 he organized a militia unit, the Lexington Rifles. When the Civil War broke out he enlisted in the Confederate army, became a scout and shortly was elected captain of a cavalry squadron.

Promoted to colonel, he commanded Kentucky cavalry at Shiloh in April 1862 and began his career as a raider shortly thereafter, taking 400 prisoners in a raid into Mississippi and Tennessee before the Federals checked him at Lebanon, Tennessee, in early May. By June he had been given command of a brigade. He set out on July 4 on the first of his famous raids into Union-held territory.

Starting from outside Knoxville, Tennessee, with 800 troopers, Morgan advanced into Kentucky, wrecking the railroad, burning stores and harassing the movement of Don Carlos Buell's Federal army toward Chattanooga. He had a sharp fight with militia near Cynthiana on July 17, then began a slow withdrawal. His raiders covered 1,000 miles in 24 days, capturing 1,200 prisoners with a loss of fewer than 100 of their own men.

Morgan carried out two other substantial raids that summer and fall. On his last raid of the year, during the Stones River Campaign in late december 1862, he captured more than 1,800 prisoners and destroyed some $2 million-worth of property at a cost to himself of only two men killed and 24 wounded. This exploit, known as Morgan's Third Raid, won him promotion

John Hunt Morgan on his Second Raid in October 1862. On the 18th he defeated Union cavalrymen, entered Lexington, Kentucky, and seized 125 prisoners.

MORGAN'S GREAT RAID

to brigadier and command of a cavalry division.

In June 1863 he took his 1,800-strong division into Kentucky, crossed the Ohio River on July 2 and led a large force of pursuers on a wild chase, covering as many as 60 miles a day, through southern Ohio and Indiana. Federal troops finally captured him at New Lisbon, Ohio, on July 26. Though this raid has been called a reckless adventure, seemingly without purpose, it did draw substantial Federal troops out of East Tennessee, temporarily easing Union pressures on Confederate forces there.

Morgan escaped from the Ohio Penitentiary in late November, made his way home and resumed his raiding. Taking command of the Department of Southwest Virginia in April 1864, he reorganized his forces and in June launched yet another foray into Kentucky. His losses were heavy this time, and his troopers' plundering brought censure from higher authority. Nevertheless, he immediately began to plot another attack. But as luck would have it, there were to be no more raids. Morgan's whereabouts was known to the enemy. Federal troops infiltrating his lines surprised and killed him in Greenville, Tennessee, on September 4, 1864.

Thomas Jefferson Morgan

Morgan, Thomas Jefferson
(1839-1902) **Union officer**

Born in Indiana, he was commissioned a lieutenant in the Union's Indiana infantry at the outbreak of he Civil War; he would ultimately be breveted brigadier general for his war service. He was particularly known for his actions in enlisting and defending the rights of African-American troops. He became a Baptist minister after the war, worked to provide education for ex-slaves and was U.S. commissioner of Indian Affairs from 1889 to 1893. He was also secretary of the American Baptist Home Mission Society for 10 years.

Mosby, John Singleton
(1833-1916) **Confederate raider**

While attending the university of his native state, Virginia, he was arrested and imprisoned for shooting a fellow student, but he was released when it was determined that the victim had provoked him. In jail he had begun to read law (with the help of his defense lawyer), and he eventually became a lawyer. When the Civil War broke out, he volunteered as a private in the Confederate army and fought at First Bull Run. He was commissioned a lieutenant in February 1862 and began to serve as a scout for Jeb Stuart's cavalry force, helping to guide it during Stuart's ride around George McClellan's forces in July 1862. In January 1863 Mosby was allowed to organize his own small cavalry force, known formally

John Singleton Mosby (center, with a plume in his hat) and some members of his "Partisan Rangers" troop

as the Partisan Rangers or Mosby's Irregulars. He would eventually have as many as 1,000 men in his unit, although he seldom took more than 300 on a single raid. He retained a loose association with Stuart's cavalry, doing advance scouting for him and sending him stolen supplies: Mosby's force usually managed to steal more than enough supplies for themselves from the enemy. Their main function was to impede and disrupt Federal operations, and their first major success came when they raided the Union camp at Fairfax Court House and captured Union General Edwin Stoughton and some 30 other prisoners, plus 58 horses. Eventually Mosby's men attained such control over eastern Virginia that the area was known as "Mosby's Confederacy." Mosby himself was so elusive that he became known as "The Grey Ghost." He simply disbanded his unit at the end of the war and went back to practicing law. He eventually became a friend and political supporter of Ulysses Grant, who had once ordered him hanged. Mosby served as U.S. consul in Hong Kong (1875-

85) and later (1904-1910) as an attorney with the Department of Justice. He wrote *Mosby's War Reminiscences* (1887).

Mudd, Samuel
(1833-1883) Physician

Mudd was the doctor who set John Wilkes Booth's broken leg after the assassination of Abraham Lincoln. As a consequence, Mudd was brought to trial as a conspirator. Convicted and sentenced to life imprisonment in the Dry Tortugas off the Florida Keys, he cared for the garrison and prisoners during a severe yellow fever outbreak there. He returned to Maryland after being pardoned in 1869.

Mumford, William B.
(1820-1862) Confederate patriot

Mumford was a New Orleans gambler who removed a U.S. flag that was hanging over the U.S. Mint after Admiral David Farragut's capture of New Orleans in April 1862. The U.S. commandant in New

James Albert Myer strikes the colors of the U.S. Signal Corps at the end of the Civil War in 1865. Meyer would go on to found the U.S. Weather Bureau.

Orleans, General Benjamin Butler, arrested Mumford and, finding him defiant, saw to it that he was convicted of treason and had him hanged in June.

Myer, Albert James
(1829-1880) Union officer

Trained at Buffalo Medical College, this New York-born army surgeon helped to develop the "wigwag" semaphore signal system in the 1850s: he wrote *A Manual of Signals* (1864). The Union army's first signal officer, he served on the staffs of Benjamin Butler, Irvin McDowell and George McClellan and organized and directed the Signal Corps before being reassigned to the Mississippi in late 1863. Still in active service, he founded, and was the first head of the U.S. Weather Bureau (1870-1880). Fort Myer, Virginia is named after him.

Nast, Thomas
(1840-1902) Cartoonist and illustrator

Born in Bavaria, he was brought to the U.S. as a child. He studied at the National Academy of Design in New York City, and by the time he was 15 he was engaged as a news illustrator for *Frank Leslie's Illustrated Magazine*. In 1859 he began contributing satirical drawings to *Harper's Weekly*, and he joined its staff in 1862. During the Civil War his drawings were so strong and persuasive for the Union cause that President Lincoln called him "our best recruiting sergeant." Recognized now as one of the true inventors of the modern editorial cartoon, he invented the donkey and elephant as emblems of the Democratic and Republican parties, the tiger as the symbol of Tammany Hall and an image of Santa Claus that is the direct inspiration for the one conventionally accepted today. He was credited with having been instrumental in bringing down the corrupt Tweed Ring in New York City. He was U.S. consul general to Ecuador when he died.

Nelson, William
(1824-1862) Union general

Born in Kentucky, Nelson served in the navy during the Mexican war. A brother of a friend of President Lincoln, he was asked in 1861 to report to Lincoln on the situation in Kentucky. He returned there, armed the Kentucky Home Guard and later fought with the Union army at Shiloh, Corinth and Richmond, where he was wounded. While organizing the defenses of Louisville, he was mortally shot by Union General Jefferson C. Davis during a quarrel over Nelson's criticism of Davis.

RIGHT: William Nelson

Oliver, Paul Ambrose
(1830-1912) Union officer

Born on his father's ship in the English Channel, Oliver grew up in Germany, where he studied military science. He was a cotton exporter before the war. Commissioned a lieutenant in the Union army in October 1861, he received the Medal of Honor for his actions at Resaca, Georgia. The inventor of formulas and machinery for making explosives, he owned an explosives factory in Pennsylvania that was ultimately bought by E. I. Du Pont.

Paul Ambrose Oliver

Edward Asbury O'Neal (above) and (right) Emerson Opdycke

O'Neal, Edward Asbury
(1818-1890) Confederate general

This Alabama-born lawyer supported secession and became a Confederate major in 1861. He served in the Peninsular Campaign and was wounded at Seven Pines, Boonsboro and Chancellorsville. He fought at Gettysburg and in the Atlanta Campaign. He spent the end of the war arresting deserters in Alabama. As governor of that state after the war (1882-1886), he played an important role in providing stability during Reconstruction.

Opdycke, Emerson
(1830-1884) Union general

Born in Ohio, he entered the U.S. Army in 1861 and fought at Shiloh, Chattanooga, Chickamauga and Rocky Face Ridge. He was wounded at Resaca, Georgia, and was

credited with saving Union forces at Franklin in 1864 when he led his brigade to cover a gap in the Union line. Later in his life he wrote books about the Civil War and ran a wholesale drygoods business in New York City.

Ord, Edward Otho Cresap
(1818-1883) Union general

This Maryland native was a West Point graduate and 20-year veteran of the Seminole War and Indian fighting when he joined the Harpers Ferry expedition against John Brown (1859). In 1861 he commanded the Union defenses of Washington; he later fought at Dranesville, Iuka and Hatchie. Ord was a corps commander

OPPOSITE: Edward O.C. Ord and family.

BELOW: Peter Osterhaus.

at Vicksburg, Jackson and Fort Harrison, as well as in the Petersburg siege and the Appomattox Campaign. At the war's end he was commander of the Army of the James. Several times wounded, he was repeatedly breveted for bravery. He retired as a brigadier general in 1880.

Osterhaus, Peter
(1823-1917) Union general

Born in Prussia, he emigrated to the U.S. in 1848 and worked as a merchant and bookkeeper in Missouri. He fought for the Union at Wilson's Creek in August 1861 and commanded a brigade at Pea Ridge in March of the following year. Osterhaus led a division during the Vicksburg and Chattanooga campaigns and a corps in the Army of the Tennessee in 1864 and 1865. After the war, he held consular appointments in France and Germany.

Page, Charles Anderson
(1838-1873) War correspondent

A young Treasury official released for war reporting, Page became famous for fast, accurate and vivid dispatches to the New York *Tribune*, which awarded him the unusual distinction of a byline. He covered the Peninsula, Second Bull Run, the Wilderness, Spotsylvania and the Petersburg siege, and was one of the first reporters into Richmond in April 1865. During the temporary ban on reporters in the field he served as a hospital worker with John Pope's army.

Paine, Charles Jackson
(1833-1916) Union general

A Harvard-trained Boston lawyer, Paine recruited a company for the Union army in September 1861. He served on Benjamin

Charles Jackson Paine.

Butler's staff, commanded troops at Port Hudson and, after his promotion to brigadier general in July 1864, led divisions at New Market and Fort Fisher. He became wealthy developing railroads after the war. An internationally renowned yachtsman, he won the America's Cup in 1885, 1886 and 1887.

Halbert Eleazer Paine

Paine, Halbert Eleazer
(1826-1905) Union general

This Ohio-born lawyer and partner of Carl Shurz joined the Union army in 1861 and was commissioned a colonel. While taking his troops to the front he was offered the use of cattle cars; unwilling to allow his men to ride with cattle, he and his regiment stopped a passenger train and boarded it. He was promoted to brigadier general in 1863 and lost a leg at Port Hudson. Always an idealist, he was a Radical Republican in the House of Representatives after the war. Later, as U.S. commissioner of patents, he introduced such changes as the use of typewriters by the office clerks.

Palmer, John McAuley
(1817-1900) Union general

Palmer was a Kentucky and Illinois lawyer and Democratic legislator who was an early convert to the Republican Party and a delegate to the 1861 Peace Convention. Joining the Union Army's 14th Illinois, he was promoted to brigadier general in December 1861. He commanded troops in the Mississippi, Ohio and Cumberland

John McAuley Palmer

armies, fighting at New Madrid, Point Pleasant and Island No. 10 and distinguishing himself at Stones River and Chickamauga. He was governor of Illinois (1869-1873) and, after rejoining the Democrats, U.S. Senator (1891-1897). He ran for president as a National Democrat in 1896.

Parker, Ely Samuel
(1828-1895) Union officer

He was raised on a New York Seneca reservation and, after his education at local academies, represented Indian claims in Washington, D.C. He became a Seneca sachem, (his Indian name was Do-ne-ho-ga-wa) in 1852. Parker trained as a lawyer and then, refused admission to the bar, as an engineer. As superintendent of public works in Galena, Illinois (1857-1862), he befriended Ulysses S. Grant. Commissioned a captain of engineers in the Union

army in May 1863, he was J. E. Smith's division engineer, in September joining Ulysses S. Grant as staff officer and military secretary. Parker transcribed the official copies of Robert E. Lee's surrender. He was commissioner of Indian Affairs (1869-1871) and later a New York businessman.

Parsons, Lewis Baldwin
(1818-1907) Union general

A New York-born lawyer, Parsons went into railroading and, while still a civilian, served as an aide to Union General Francis P. Blair during the capture of Camp Jackson, Missouri. He was commissioned a captain afterward (October 1861) and ran river and rail transportation for the Federal Department of Mississippi. Later running

ABOVE: Lewis Baldwin Parsons.

BELOW: Ely Samuel Parker (far right).

river and rail transportation for the entire country, he was promoted to brigadier general in May 1865. He oversaw the transportation of discharged soldiers after the war and went into banking, railroading and Democratic politics.

Parsons, Mosby Munroe
(1819-1865) Confederate general

This Virginia-born lawyer and legislator who had served in the Mexican War, organized the Missouri State Guard at the outbreak of the Civil War. He was made a Confederate brigadier general in 1862 after fighting at Wilson's Creek and Pea Ridge. He fought in the 1864 Red River Campaign and in Arkansas. Escaping to Mexico after General Sterling Price's unsuccessful raid in Missouri (Price had invaded the state in September 1864 but had been defeated by Union troops by late October), he joined the Republicans in Mexico and was killed during the Mexican rebellion at Camargo on August 17, 1865.

Patrick, Marsena Rudolph
(1811-1888) Union general

A New Yorker, this West Point graduate resigned from the army in 1850 after service in the Seminole and Mexican wars. He left the presidency of New York State Agricultural College to re-enlist in the Union army as a brigadier general in May 1861. After serving on George McClellan's staff and in Washington's defenses, he fought at Second Bull Run, Chantilly, South Mountain and Antietam. He served capably as provost marshal general of the Union army after October 1862. After the war he promoted scientific farming and in his last years supervised an Ohio soldiers' home.

Payne, William Henry Fitzhugh
(1830-1904) Confederate general

This Virginian was graduated from Virginia Military Institute and became a lawyer. Joining the Confederate army as a captain

William Henry Fitzburgh Payne

in the Black Horse cavalry, he commanded cavalry at Williamsburg and Chancellorsville, in Jeb Stuart's 1863 Pennsylvania raid, in Jubal Early's 1864 Raid on Washington and at Richmond. He was repeatedly wounded and was captured three times: twice exchanged, he spent the last months of the war in detention on Johnson's Island. He was Washington-based counsel for the Southern Railroad after the 1880s.

John Pegram

Pegram, John
(1832-1865) Confederate general

The Virginian Pegram was graduated from West Point and served on the frontier and in Indian fighting. As a Confederate officer he fought a varied war. After surrendering to George McClellan at Rich Mountain in 1861, he was chief engineer under P. G. T. Beauregard and Braxton Bragg. He later fought under Kirby Smith, Richard Ewell and Jubal Early, participating at Chickamauga and leading divisions at the Wilderness, Cold Harbor, Winchester, Fisher's Hill and Cedar Creek and in the Petersburg siege. He was killed at Hatcher's Run in February 1865, three weeks after his wedding.

Pelham, John
(1838-1863) Confederate officer

Born in Alabama, Pelham left West Point in 1861 to return to the South and join the Confederate army. He fought at First and Second Bull Run, Williamsburg, Gaines's Mill, Antietam and Fredericksburg. He is famous for Robert E. Lee's description of him at Fredericksburg as "gallant" and courageous. Apparently quite handsome and a ladies man, it was said that three young ladies went into mourning after he was killed in March at Kelly's Ford. "The Gallant Pelham" was posthumously promoted to lieutenant colonel.

Pemberton, John Clifford
(1814-1881) Confederate general

Born into an old Pennsylvania Quaker family in Philadelphia, he was graduated from West Point, fought in the Seminole War and was breveted for bravery in numerous engagements in the Mexican War. He was serving on the northwest frontier at the outbreak of the Civil War. Married to a Virginian, Pemberton refused

John Clifford Pemberton (right) meets with Ulysses Grant outside Vicksburg.

a U.S. colonel's commission and joined the Confederate army in April 1861 as a lieutenant colonel. He organized Virginia's cavalry and artillery and was soon promoted to commands beyond his abilities. As a major general (February 1862) in command of the Department of South Carolina, Georgia and Florida, he built Fort Wagner and Battery "B" at Charleston. Promoted to lieutenant general (October 1862), he took command of the Department of Mississippi, Tennessee and East Louisiana, an assignment that was to cost the South dearly. Besieged at Vicksburg in a brilliant campaign conducted by Ulysses S. Grant, outnumbered, outgunned and under attack from land and water, Pemberton was, confusingly, instructed by Jefferson Davis to hold Vicksburg and by J. E. Johnston to surrender it. In a humiliating defeat for the Confederacy, he accepted Grant's terms of "unconditional surrender" on July 4, 1863; many Southerners, distrustful of his Northern origins, unfairly suspected him of treachery. He was exchanged and resigned his command in May 1864, serving out the war as a colonel and ordnance inspector. He retired to his Virginia farm, and spent his last years in Philadelphia.

Pender, William Dorsey
(1834-1863) Confederate general

This North Carolina-born West Point graduate (1854) served on the frontier until the Civil war began, resigning from the U.S. Army to accept a commission as a cap-

William Dorsey Pender

tain in the Confederate army. He fought in a whole series of battles – Seven Pines, the Seven Days' Battles, Second Bull Run, Antietam, Fredericksburg and Chancellorsville; he suffered three wounds at this last-named battle. A major general by the age of 29, he was mortally wounded on the second day of fighting at Gettysburg, dying on July 19. Pender was highly regarded in the Confederate army and some even compared him to Stonewall Jackson.

Pendleton, William Nelson
(1809-1883) Confederate general

This Virginia-born West Point graduate was a teacher and an Episcopal minister before the war. He was appointed Confederate General Joseph E. Johnston's chief of artillery in July 1861, was promoted to brigadier general in 1862 and then served as Robert E. Lee's chief of artillery (although the value of his contribution in this post has been questioned). He con-

tinued to serve as a minister during the war and was often mistaken for Lee because of their similar appearance. His daughter married Brigadier General Edwin G. Lee.

Perry, Edward Aylesworth
(1831-1889) Confederate general

Born in Massachusetts, Perry was a lawyer before accepting a commission in the Confederate army; he was promoted to colonel in May 1862. He was wounded at Frayer's Farm and was appointed a brigadier general after his recovery in August 1862. He led a brigade at Fredericksburg and Chancellorsville but missed Gettysburg due to illness. He was wounded again at the Wilderness in 1864 and spent the remainder of the war with reserve forces in Alabama. He was a lawyer and Democratic governor of Florida after the war.

Edward Aylesworth Perry was wounded in 1862 and again in 1864.

Pettigrew, James Johnston
(1828-1863) Confederate general

Born in North Carolina, Pettigrew was graduated with the highest marks ever from the University of North Carolina. He went on to become a lawyer and serve in his state's legislature. Although opposed to continuing the slave trade, he sided with the Confederacy from the moment the Federal forces took over Fort Sumter. He led a brigade in the Peninsular Campaign and was wounded and captured at Seven Pines. He was exchanged, and at Gettysburg he led one of the three divisions that made up "Pickett's Charge" on the third day of the battle. He was killed by Union cavalry during the Confederate retreat from Gettysburg.

Pettus, Edmund Winston
(1821-1907) Confederate general

This Alabama-born lawyer and judge had fought in the Mexican War. He was sent from Alabama to persuade his brother, the governor of Mississippi, to bring his state into the Confederacy. He fought for the Confederacy in Kentucky and at Vicksburg and was captured at Port Gibson; he

soon escaped but was recaptured. He was promoted to brigadier general in 1863 and went on to fight at Lookout Mountain and Missionary Ridge and in the Atlanta and Nashville campaigns. He surrendered with J. E. Johnston in he Carolinas. He was a Democratic U.S. Senator after the war.

Phillips, Wendell
(1811-1884) Abolitionist

Boston born, he attended Harvard Law School but soon abandoned a legal career, being drawn to the abolitionist movement by the inspiration of William Lloyd Garrison and Elijah Lovejoy. His impassioned speech at Boston's Funeuil Hall in 1837, protesting the murder of Elijah Lovejoy, launched him on a career as a lecturer against slavery. He took extremely radical positions – attacking the U.S. Constitution, refusing to seek public office and even advocating that the North secede from the flawed union that accommodated slavery. During the war he attacked Lincoln for compromising on slavery. After the war he succeeded Garrison as president of the American Anti-Slavery Society and continued to work for progressive social reforms of all kinds.

Pickett, George Edward
(1825-1875) Confederate general

Born in Richmond, Virginia, he absorbed the rudiments of an education there and in the Illinois law office of an uncle before obtaining a West Point appointment in 1842. He was graduated four years later at the very bottom of his class of 59 cadets.

Assigned to an infantry regiment, Pickett served in Mexico in 1846 and 1847, saw considerable fighting there and took part in the capture of Mexico City. He did duty in a Texas garrison from 1849 to 1856. Transferred to the Pacific northwest a latter year, he commanded an infantry detachment at San Juan Island in Puget Sound during the war scare with Britain in 1859.

He resigned his U.S. commission in 1861 and offered his services to the Confederacy. Commissioned a colonel, he was promoted to brigadier in February 1862. His

BELOW: Pickett's charge.

OPPOSITE: Pickett's charge, the climax.

OVERLEAF: Pickett's final defeat: the Battle of Five Forks, April 1865.

George Edward Pickett

Francis Harrison Pierpont

"Game Cock Brigade" won a good fighting reputation at Williamsburg, Seven Pines and Gaines's Mill during the Peninsular Campaign; Pickett was wounded at Gaines's Mill. Promoted to major general after his recovery, he took command of a division of Virginia troops in October 1862.

Pickett fought at Fredericksburg and accompanied James Longstreet and most of the First Corps on the Suffolk expedition in the winter of 1862-63. Longstreet's corps missed the Battle of Chancellorsville, but rejoined the Army of Northern Virginia in time to cross the Potomac with Lee in his second invasion of the North.

Dapper, somewhat flashily dressed, his long hair worn in ringlets, Pickett thirsted for glory on the battlefield. His chance came at Gettysburg on July 3, 1863. He led one of the divisions that hot afternoon in what became known, inaccurately, as Pickett's Charge, an ill-judged frontal attack ordered by Robert E. Lee that cost the Confederates heavily. Pickett's division alone lost three-quarters of its strength in the disastrous charge. In the aftermath, Lee sent Pickett's shattered division to recuperate in the comparative quiet of the Department of Virginia and North Carolina, but Pickett never wholly forgave Lee for having ordered the charge.

Pickett returned to Longstreet's corps for the Battle of Cold Harbor in June 1864. He served in the Petersburg lines during the siege of June 1864 to March 1865 and was in command on the extreme right of Lee's line when P. H. Sheridan's combined cavalry and infantry attacked at Five Forks on April 1, 1865. Pickett missed the earlier stages of this battle, as he and several of his officers were enjoying a shad bake at a secluded picnic spot several miles away. The rout of the Confederates there turned Lee's right and forced him to evacuate Petersburg and Richmond. Lee is alleged to have decided to remove Pickett from the army after Five Forks, but the surrender of Appomattox on April 9 made the issue moot.

Pickett declined a postwar offer of a generalship in the Egyptian army, went into the insurance business and died in Norfolk, Virginia, in July 1875.

Pierpont, Francis Harrison
(1814-1899) Governor of Virginia

Raised in what would, in 1863, become West Virginia, this lawyer and businessman settled in Virginia in 1842. A Whig activist and Unionist, he supported Lincoln in 1860, and after Virginia's secession he organized the pro-Union forces that declared western Virginia's intention to seek independent statehood within the Union. He was wartime governor of the Federally-controlled Virginia counties (the "restored" Virginia), after the war serving as pre-Reconstruction governor of Virginia (1865-1868) before returning to a West Virginia law practice and public service.

Pike, Albert
(1809-1891) Confederate general

Born in Boston, Pike was educated in Massachusetts and taught school there before venturing west and settling Arkansas in the early 1830s. Pike bought a Little Rock newspaper in 1835 and by the outbreak of war in 1861 had become a wealthy and influential publisher and a writer and poet of national reputation. He entered Confederate service in August 1861 and commanded Indian troops at Pea Ridge in March 1862. After a brief military career marked by friction with his superiors, he resigned in July 1862. Pike had a distinguished postwar career as a lawyer and journalist. His voluminous writings on the rituals of Scottish Rite Masonry were widely read.

Pillow, Gideon Johnson
(1806-1878) Confederate general

This University of Nashville graduate became a well-known criminal lawyer in partnership with James K. Polk, later a close political ally. As president, Polk commissioned the inexperienced Pillow as a brigadier general during the Mexican War. While never holding elective office, Pillow exerted considerable Democratic influence in Tennessee, where he promoted compromise as the Civil War approached. He was the Confederate second-in-command at Fort Donelson, where he and his superior, John B. Floyd, relinquished their commands and fled, leaving Simon B. Buckner to surrender to Ulysses Grant. Pillow was reprimanded for "grave errors of judgment" and received no further significant commands.

Albert Pike in Masonic garb

Allan Pinkerton (seated background, smoking pipe) when he was McClellan's chief of intelligence in 1862

Pinkerton, Allan
(1819-1884)
Detective and Union secret service chief

After emigrating to Illinois (1842), this Scot was a deputy sheriff and Underground Railroad foreman. He opened America's first private detective agency in Chicago (1850). He foiled a plot to assassinate President-elect Lincoln in February 1861. Subsequently recruited to set up the Union army's secret service, he worked under George McClellan in the field and in Washington, where he directed counter-espionage activities under the alias "Major E. J. Allen." The poor quality of the intelligence he supplied contributed to McClellan's lackluster performance in his unsuccessful Peninsular Campaign. After McClellan lost his command, Pinkerton investigated damage claims against the government (1862-1865). He later expanded his agency, won a controversial reputation as a "labor union buster," and wrote 18 popular volumes of detective stories.

Pleasonton, Alfred
(1824-1897) Union general

A native of Washington, D.C., and a graduate of West Point, Pleasonton was a career cavalryman who was breveted for gallantry in the Mexican War and served in Indian fighting and on the frontier. He performed

Alfred Pleasonton (right), with George Custer, in April 1863. He would lead the Union cavalry at Gettysburg in July.

brilliantly for the Union in the Peninsular Campaign, fought at South Mountain, Antietam and Fredericksburg, and earned promotion to major general after helping to stop T. J. Jackson's advance against Joseph Hooker at Chancellorsville. He distinguished himself at Brandy Station and commanded the Union cavalry at the Battle of Gettysburg. He later routed Sterling Price in Missouri at the battles of Westport and Marais des Cygnes (October 1864). He resigned from the army in 1868 and in his last years lived on his army pension in Washington, D.C.

Polignac, Prince Camille Armand Jules Marie de
(1832-1913) Confederate general

This French Crimean War veteran resigned from the French army in 1859 to pursue botanical studies. He was the only alien to hold high rank in the Confederate army, eventually becoming a major general in June 1864. Polignac was P. G. T. Beauregard's chief of staff and fought at Corinth and in the 1864 Red River Campaign. His Texas brigade called him "Polecat." After unsuccessfully seeking French aid for the Confederacy, he retired to his French estate in 1865 and became a noted mathematician and civil engineer.

Polk, Leonidas
(1806-1864) Confederate general

His father had fought in the Revolution and helped found the University of North Carolina, where Polk studied for two years before entering West Point. During his fourth year at the academy he came under the influence of a new chaplain, was converted and led what an early biographer called a praying squad. Polk resigned his army commission six months after he was graduated in order to enter the Virginia Theological Seminary.

Ordained a priest in the Episcopal Church in May 1831, he served as assistant rector of a Richmond parish before failing health forced him to resign. After a sojourn in Europe, he returned to the U.S. to accept an appointment as missionary bishop of the southwest, which at that time meant an area which included Alabama, Mississippi, Louisiana and Arkansas.

Polk became bishop of Louisiana in 1841 and settled on a large sugar plantation. Through an inheritance of his wife's he owned 400 slaves; the bishop is said to have established a Sunday School for them. The plantation enterprise proved a financial failure, however, and Polk returned full time to his pastoral duties.

He helped establish the University of the South, which he hoped would educate a Southern ruling class, laying the cornerstone for the first building at Suwanee, Tennessee, in October 1860. When war broke out the following year Jefferson Davis, who had been a cadet with Polk at West Point, offered him a major general's commission in the Confederate army. Believing the South was fighting for a holy cause, he accepted.

Polk's first military assignment involved the defense of the Mississippi River. His troops occupied Columbus, Kentucky, in September 1861, violating that state's self-declared neutrality and tilting it toward the

Leonidas Polk

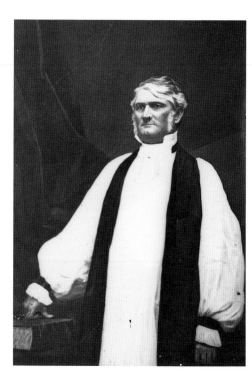

Union. He later became a corps commander under Albert Sidney Johnston (like Davis, a close friend) and fought with Johnston at Shiloh in April 1862.

He was Braxton Bragg's second in command at Perryville on October 8, 1862, and won promotion to lieutenant general later in the month. His performance at Stones River at the year's end and at Chickamauge in September 1863 left a great deal to be desired. His failure to attack at daybreak at Chickamauga prompted Bragg to remove him from command and recommend his court martial. Davis interceded and reinstated him.

Polk's reputation as a corps commander did not stand high with anyone (except, perhaps, Davis), though he probably did as well as could be expected, given his lack of military experience. He was killed near Marietta, Georgia, during the Atlanta Campaign, blown out of his saddle by the sharpshooting crew of a Parrott rifled cannon.

One of his kinsman, James Knox Polk, was the 11th president of the United States (1845-1849).

Pope, John
(1822-1892) union general

Born in Louisville, Kentucky, he was graduated from West Point in 1842 and performed survey work for the army's topographical engineers, first in Florida and later in the Northeast. He served with Zachary Taylor during the Mexican War, winning recognition for his contributions at Monterey and Buena Vista.

Pope served in New Mexico and elsewhere in the Southwest during the 1850s, surveying a potential route for a Pacific railroad. On the outbreak of the Civil War he became the Union army's mustering officer in Chicago. Appointed a brigadier at the end of July, he reported to John Frémont's command in St. Louis and took charge of a division of the Army of Southwest Missouri.

Assigned to command the Army of the Mississippi in the late winter of 1862, Pope scored his first important military successes at New Madrid, Missouri, and Island No. 10 in March (his forcing of the surrender of the island garrison opened the Mississippi River almost to Memphis). His army formed Henry Halleck's left wing on the slow, deliberate advance to Corinth, Mississippi, from April to June.

Lincoln chose him in the summer of 1862 to succeed George McClellan as the senior commander in the Virginia theater. He made himself instantly unpopular with all

ranks. In his famous address on taking command he alienated the troops by calling their courage into question. "Let us understand each other," he wrote. "I come to you from the west, where we have always seen the backs of our enemies; from an army whose business it has been to seek the adversary, and to beat him when he was found; whose policy has been attack and not defense." On the other side, Robert E. Lee conceived an unusually strong dislike for him.

Lee and his chief lieutenants, T. J. Jackson and James Longstreet, thoroughly outwitted and outfought Pope in the Second Battle of Bull Run, August 29-30, 1862. His badly beaten army retreated into the Washington defenses after the Battle of Chantilly on September 1, and Lincoln removed Pope from command the next day.

John Pope, whose defeat at the Second Battle of Bull Run ruined his career

Pope blamed his misfortunes on his subordinates, particularly Fitz-John Porter, a McClellan loyalist who was subsequently removed from command of V Corps and dismissed from the army for alleged failures during the Second Bull Run Campaign. (After a long fight, Porter won reinstatement in 1887). Pope never again had a field command.

Staying on in the regular army after Appomattox, he held a series of military district and department commands in the 1860s and 1870s. He retired from the service as commander of the Department of California in 1886. He died of "nervous prostration" in Sandusky, Ohio, in September 1892.

Porter, David Dixon
(1813-1891) Union admiral

He received a basic education in his native Chester, Pennsylvania, and joined the Mexican navy as a midshipman at age 13. Taken prisoner after an action with a Spanish frigate off the Cuban coast, he spent time in a Havana jail before being repatriated and entering the U.S. Navy in 1829. Midshipman Porter served in the Mediterranean aboard the sailing frigates *Constellation* and *United States* and worked on the U.S. coastal survey for six years. In 1841 he was promoted to lieutenant. Six years later, after a short, dull tour as a recruiting officer in New Orleans, he saw his first action in the Mexican War, taking part in an unsuccessful assault on Vera Cruz. He then commanded the landing party that stormed and captured a coastal fort at Tabasco. The Navy rewarded him with his first command, the steam vessel *Spitfire*.

He returned to coast survey duties after the war. From 1849 to 1855, on leave from the navy, he held several merchant commands. Returning to the navy, he made a cruise to the Black sea, where he had a glimpse of the Crimean War. He was second in command of the Portsmouth Navy Yard in New Hampshire from 1857 to 1860. Frustrated by lack of opportunity, he was preparing to leave the navy for good when, with the Civil War on the horizon, he received command of the steamer USS *Powhatan* with orders to sail to the relief of Fort Pickens, Florida.

Porter participated in the blockade of Pensacola, Mobile and the Southwest Pass of the Mississippi River in 1861. Promoted to commander, he helped plan the New Orleans expedition in early 1862 and recommended David G. Farragut, his foster brother, to lead it. Farragut in turn chose him to command the mortar flotilla assembled to bombard the river forts guarding the city. After Farragut ran the water batteries at forts St. Philip and Jackson, defeated the defending Confederate naval squadron and sailed into New Orleans, Porter demanded the surrender of the garrisons. They capitulated on April 27, 1862

He succeeded to the command of the Mississippi Squadron in October 1862, even though his name was far down on the seniority list. He had a powerful ally in G. V. Fox, the assistant navy secretary, and Gideon Welles, the secretary, thought him brave, energetic and full of dash. His gunboats helped W. T. Sherman capture Arkansas Post in January 1863, and Porter himself received the surrender of the garrison. The river fleet also supported U. S. Grant's operations against Vicksburg; Porter was present when the river fortress capitulated on July 4, 1863. Both Grant and Sherman worked well with Porter and strongly commended his efforts. So did his Navy Department superiors; they promoted his two rungs to rear admiral that summer, skipping he ranks of captain and commodore.

In the spring of 1864 he commanded the naval forces in N. P. Banks's unsuccessful Red River Campaign. Later that year he came east to take command of the 120-vessel North Atlantic Blockading Squadron. His chief offensive assignment was to cooperate with the army in the capture of Fort Fisher, which protected the Confederacy's last important open port, Wilmington, North Carolina. The first attempt, in December, fizzled; Porter blamed the army for the failure. In January a more powerful force, 60 warships and 8,000 troops, succeeded in taking the fort and closing down Wilmington.

David Dixon Porter (opposite) and (below) Porter's squadron running past the guns of Vicksburg in April 1863

David Porter's ships at Baton Rouge in August 1862 (above) and (right) General Fitz-John Porter

Appointed superintendent of the Naval Academy in August 1865, Porter launched a four-year period of reform. He extended his influence navywide in 1869, when President Grant appointed him advisor to the navy secretary. Not all his reform schemes were sensible: among other things, he required steamships to be equipped with auxilary sails long after steam's reliability had been proven. He succeeded Farragut as full admiral in August 1870 and from 1877 until his death headed the Navy Board of Inspection,

Porter embarked on a literary career in his later years, producing his *Memoir of Commodore David Porter* in 1875 and the lively *Incidents and Anecdotes of the Civil War* a decade later. He also wrote several novels.

Porter, Fitz-John
(1822-1901) Union general

He was born in Portsmouth, New Hampshire, the son of a naval captain and the nephew of Admiral David Porter. As a recent West Point graduate, he was wounded and breveted in the Mexican War. He later taught artillery and cavalry at West Point (1849-1855) and was chief of staff to A. S. Johnston on the Utah Expedition. In 1860-1861 Porter inspected Charleston's defenses and restored rail lines north of Washington, D.C., among other duties. As a Union brigadier general, he commanded the siege of Yorktown and fought against Stonewall Jackson in the Shenandoah Campaign of 1862. Promoted to major general, he led V Corps on the Peninsula (distinguishing himself at Malvern Hill) and at Second Bull Run and Antietam. John Pope blamed the Federal defeat at Second Bull Run squarely on Porter's failure to attack Jackson's right flank, and Porter was relieved of his command in November 1862 and cashiered in January 1863, convicted of disobeying battle orders. He spent the next 23 years trying to clear his record. In 1879 an army board ruled in his favor; he received a presidential remission of his lifetime disqualification in 1882 and finally won reappointment as a colonel in the regular army in 1886. Historians still disagree on whether Porter was a competent field commander or on whether the order to attack was feasible, given prevailing battlefield conditions. Porter lived in New Jersey after 1865, holding various jobs there and in New York, where he served variously as commissioner of public works and of the police and fire services.

Powell, Lewis
(d. 1865) Conspirator

Under the alias Lewis Paine he helped John Wilkes Booth plot the assassination of Abraham Lincoln. Powell's assignment was to kill Secretary of State William Seward; he gravely wounded Seward on the night of April 14, 1865. A military court found him guilty of conspiracy and he was hanged on July 7, 1865.

Preston, John Smith
(1809-1881) Confederate general

Born in Virginia, Preston was a planter, art collector, legislator and advocate of states' rights. Having settled in South Carolina, he was sent to Virginia to urge the state to secede in 1861. As a Confederate officer, he aided P. G. T. beauregard at Fort Sumter and First Bull Run. He commanded a prison camp at Columbia, South Carolina, in 1862 and was appointed head of the Bureau of Conscription in July 1863. He continued in that post until 1865. He went to England after the fall of the Confederacy, finally returning in 1868.

Preston, William
(1816-1887) Confederate general

Born in Kentucky, Preston practiced law and served in the Mexican War. A Whig in the U.S. Congress, he then joined the Democrats and became President James Buchanan's ambassador to Spain. He returned to Kentucky to urge the state to secede and was appointed brigadier general in the Confederate army in 1862. He fought at Corinth, Stones River, Vicksburg and Chickamauga. Because of the Federal blockade, he was forced to land in Mexico when he attempted to assume a post as a Confederate minister in Europe. After the war he traveled and then served in the Kentucky legislature.

Price, Sterling
(1809-1867) Confederate general

Born and raised in Virginia, Price attended Hampden-Sydney College there, studied law and moved with his parents to Fayette, Missouri, in 1831. He took up the successful practice of law and politics, serving several terms in the Missouri legislature, and commanded Missouri militia troops during the Mexican War.

Price won election as governor of Missouri in 1852 and led the state capably for four years. Though a conditional Union supporter in 1860, he went with the Confederacy when war broke out in April 1861. Forces under his command defeated a Union army at Wilson's Creek in August,

Sterling Price

establishing him as one of the early Confederate military heroes.

Appointed a major general in the Confederate army in March 1862, Price, nicknamed "Pap," fought at Iuka, Corinth, Helena and during the Red River Campaign of 1864, in which he inflicted a severe defeat on a Union army under Fredrick Steele.

He followed up this victory with an unsuccessful raid into Missouri in September and October 1864. He retreated into Texas in late 1864 and, after the Confederate surrender, went into exile in Mexico. He returned to Missouri after the collapse of Maximilian's empire in 1866 and died in September of the following year.

Pryor, Roger Atkinson
(1828-1919) Confederate general

Pryor was a newspaper publisher and influential Virginia secessionist who resigned from his first term in Congress in March 1861 to join the Confederate army. As a brigadier general, he led brigades at Williamsburg and Seven Pines, succeeding to a division command at Antietam. Impatient with the policies of the Confederate war department, he resigned his commission in August 1863 to fight as a private in Fitzhugh Lee's cavalry. Pryor was captured near Petersburg in November 1864 and was exchanged several months later. A New York lawyer and judge after the war, he eventually served on the New York supreme court (1894-1899).

Roger Atkinson Pryor

Quantrill, William Clarke
(1837-65) Confederate irregular

Quantrill was born in Canal Dover, Ohio. Within the space of a few years he was an Ohio and Illinois schoolteacher, a Kansas homesteader and a Utah gambler (alias

William Clarke Quantrill

"Charley Hart"). In 1859 he drifted back to Kansas and thence into petty thievery and border skirmishing. In December 1860 he betrayed five abolitionists, who were put to death for plotting to free the slaves of a Missouri farmer. He parlayed his involvement in murders, robberies and raids into a Confederate captaincy after taking Independence, Missouri, in August 1862, and continued operating as a guerrilla chief, despite being outlawed by the federal authorities. While his troops continued raiding and sacking pro-Union communities in Kansas and Missouri, Quantrill's own operations included the August 1863 pillaging of the free-state stronghold of Lawrence, Kansas, where he burned a substantial part of the town and murdered at least 150 people. A few months later he murdered 17 noncombatants after defeating Union cavalry at Baxter Springs, Kansas. His troops fractured by internal disagreement, he took 33 men into Kentucky early in 1865 on a fresh series of raids, robberies and killings and was killed there by Union troops at Taylorsville in May 1865. It is likely that he was the officer of whom the South was least proud.

Rains, Gabriel James
(1803-1881) Confederate general

This West Point graduate from North Carolina was a career soldier. A veteran of the Seminole and Mexican wars and a frontier fighting, he became a brigadier general in the Confederate army in September 1861. He directed the first-ever use of land mines and booby traps in the Peninsular Campaign. Superintending the torpedo bureau after June 1864, he sparked controversy by laying land mines in the South. He lived in Georgia and South Carolina after the war. His brother, George Washington Rains (1817-1898), was a leading Confederate munitions specialist.

Ramseur, Stephen Dodson
(1837-1864) Confederate general

This North Carolina-born West Point graduate resigned in 1861 and was commissioned a lieutenant in the Confederate army. He fought at the Seven Days' Battles and was gravely wounded at Malvern Hill. He was wounded again at Chancellorsville but went on to fight at Gettysburg and the Wilderness. He was wounded a third time at Spotsylvania. Promoted to major general in June 1864, he also fought at Cold Harbor and Winchester before he was mortally wounded at Cedar Creek.

Ransom, Robert Jr.
(1828-1892) Confederate general

Born in North Carolina, Ransom was a West Point-trained cavalryman who interrupted his frontier service to teach cavalry at the military academy. He organized the Confederate army's western cavalry and led troops at the Seven Days' Battles, Harpers Ferry, Antietam, Fredericksburg,

Reagan, John Henninger
(1818-1905) Confederate politician

He emigrated to Texas in 1839, received a license to practice law in 1848 and established himself as a leading lawyer/politician. Reagan served in the U.S. Congress from 1857 to 1861 and entered the Confederate congress after Texas seceded. Jefferson Davis appointed him postmaster general in 1861. He retained this post until late in the war, when he became treasury secretary and joined Jefferson Davis in his attempted flight south. The Federals held him prisoner for several months after his capture with Davis in Georgia. Returning to Texas after his release, Reagan practiced law and won re-election to the U.S. Congress, where he sat first as a Representative and later as a Senator.

LEFT: John Henninger Reagan.

BELOW: Thomas E.G. Ransom.

Robert Ransom, Jr.

the Bermuda Railroad defense and Jubel Early's Washington Raid. Ill-health ended his field service. He was later a farmer and civil engineer. His brother, Matt Whitaker Ransom (1826-1904), was also a Confederate general.

Ransom, Thomas Edward Greenfield
(1834-1864) Union general

Trained as a civil engineer, he left an Illinois business career to accept a captain's commission in the Union's 11th Illinois in April 1861. Wounded at Charleston, Fort Donelson and Shiloh, he also fought at Corinth and, after rapid promotions to brigadier general, in the Vicksburg, Red River and Atlanta campaigns. Wounded for the fourth time at Sabine Cross Roads, he finally died in the field of an illness in October 1864. Ulysses S. Grant called him "the best man I have ever had to send on expeditions."

Rawlins, John Aaron
(1831-1869) Union general

A Democratic Illinois politician, he joined the army in August 1861 and became Ulysses S. Grant's "most nearly indispensable" advisor. Trusted for his intelligence, honesty and sound judgment, Rawlins was promoted in tandem with Grant, eventually becoming chief of staff of the U.S. Army in March 1865.

Marcus Albert Reno

out, he joined a Union infantry division and was made a brigadier general in August 1861. After helping to strengthen the defenses of Washington, D.C., he fought at such battles as Mechanicsville and Gaines's Mill. Captured in July 1862 at Glendale (White Oak Swamp) during the Seven Days' Battles, he was exchanged in time to lead a division at Second Bull Run. He fought at Fredericksburg and Chancellorsville as commander of the Army of the Potomac's I Corps. He was very highly regarded, and his partisans held that he, rather than George Meade, should have been chosen in June 1863 to replace Joseph Hooker as commander of the Army of the Potomac. He was killed by a sharpshooter on the first day of fighting at Gettysburg while directing the Union defense to the west of the town.

Alexander Reynolds (left) and (below) John Fulton Reynolds

Reno, Marcus Albert
(1835-1889) Union officer

An Illinois native, he was graduated from West Point in 1857 and served in a Union cavalry regiment for most of the war. He commanded a Pennsylvania volunteer cavalry regiment from January to July 1865. He headed the Freedmen's Bureau in New Orleans in 1865 and 1866. A court of inquiry inconclusively investigated Reno's conduct during George A. Custer's ill-fated campaign against the Sioux in 1876. He was dismissed for unrelated reasons in 1880.

Reynolds, Alexander
(1817-1876) Confederate general

He was graduated from West Point in 1838, saw action in the Seminole War and was dismissed for discrepancies in his accounts in 1855. Reinstated, he was dismissed again after he went absent to join the Confederacy. Reynolds commanded a brigade at Vicksburg and Chattanooga and during the Atlanta Campaign. He joined the Egyptian army in 1869, rising to chief of staff in 1875.

Reynolds, John Fulton
(1820-1863) Union general

Born in Pennsylvania, this West Point graduate fought with distinction in the Mexican War, on the frontier, and in the Utah Expedition. Commandant of cadets at West Point when the Civil War broke

Reynolds, Joseph Jones
(1822-1899) Union general

Born in Kentucky, he was graduated from West Point, then taught there and served on the frontier before resigning from the army in 1857. An Indiana businessman when the war broke out, he was commissioned a Union brigadier general in May 1861 and secured West Virginia for the Union at Cheat Mountain. He led divisions at Hoover's Gap and Chickamauga, was chief of staff of the Cumberland Army at Chattanooga and, among other commands, led VII and XIX Corps and the Department of Arkansas. He remained in the regular army until 1877, then retiring to Washington, D.C.

Rhett, Robert Barnwell
(1800-1876) Confederate politician

This South Carolina planter, lawyer and legislator organized the radical separatist Bluffton movement (later suppressed) in 1844. A U.S Representative (1837-1849) and Senator (1850-1852), he was, after the 1850 Nashville Convention, an influential secessionist. He tirelessly agitated for secession in South Carolina, drafting the state's secession ordnance and calling for the Montgomery Convention; he chaired the committee that drafted the permanent Confederate constitution, over the years fairly earning the nickname, "Father of Secession." His extremist views cost him a Confederate political appointment, and he spent the war years promoting an anti-Jefferson Davis agenda in the *Charleston Mercury*. After the war he engaged in newspaper ventures with his son.

Rhodes, Elisha Hunt
(1842-1917) Union soldier

A sea captain's son, he quit his job as a clerk for a harness maker to enlist in the Union's 2nd Rhode Island Volunteers in 1861. He is remembered for the detailed and eloquent diary he kept of his war service, during which he fought at Bull Run, on the Virginia Peninsula and at Antietam, Fredericksburg, Gettysburg, Petersburg and Appomattox.

Richardson, Albert Deane
(1833-1869) War correspondent

He reported the Kansas troubles in 1857, accompanied an expedition to Pike's Peak, traveled incognito in the South during the secession crisis and covered the fighting in Virginia and the West. Captured with two

Robert Barnwell Rhett (above) and (left) Elisha Hunt Rhodes

other Northern newspapermen near Vicksburg in May 1863, he spent 18 months in a Confederate prison before breaking out and walking 400 miles to his freedom. A jealous husband sought him out in the newsroom of *The New York Tribune*, where he shot and mortally wounded him.

Ripley, Roswell Sabine
(1823-1887) Confederate general

This Ohio-born West Point graduate, after serving in the Mexican and Seminole wars, resigned from the U.S. Army in 1853 to enter business in South Carolina, where he joined the state militia. Entering the Confederate army in May 1861, he soon fell into disagreements with his superiors, generals John Pemberton and P. G. T. Beauregard. He led a brigade that fought at Antietam, where he was wounded. He was then

John Cleveland Robinson

assigned back to Charleston, South Carolina, where he finished out the war after briefly serving in the Army of the West. He went to England after the war and was for a time a manufacturer there. He later lived in Charleston and New York City.

Robertson, Jerome Bonaparte
(1815-1891) Confederate general

He was born in Kentucky and studied medicine at Transylvania University but settled in Texas after participating in the revolution there in 1836. In time he became a prominent doctor, legislator and Indian fighter. In the Confederate service, he led Texan troops in the Seven Days' Battles, Second Bull Run, Boonsboro Gap, Fredericksburg, Gettysburg and Chickamauga. In all, he fought in some 40 battles and was thrice wounded. Never a very successful field commander, he was eventually relegated to leading the Texas reserves. He continued practicing medicine until 1868, then promoted railroads in west Texas.

Robinson, John Cleveland
(1817-1897) union general

A New Yorker, he studied at West Point, fought in the Seminole and Mexican wars and joined the Utah Expedition of 1857-1858. As its commander in April 1861, he saved the Union's Fort McHenry from attack. He led Potomac Army troops continuously and gallantly in the Peninsular Campaign, at Fredericksburg, Chancel-

lorsville, Gettysburg and in the Wilderness. After losing a leg at Spotsylvania, he left field service. He was later active in veterans' organizations. He was awarded a Medal of Honor (1894), and his valiant stand at Gettysburg is commemorated by a statue on that battlefield.

Rosecrans, William Starke
(1819-1898) Union general

Born in Delaware County, Ohio, he was graduated from West Point (1842) and fortified Hampton Roads, Virginia, before returning to the military academy to teach natural and experimental philosophy and engineering. He resigned from the army in 1854 to pursue Cincinnati and Virginia business interests, including coal mining, oil refining and river navigation. He joined Union General George McClellan as a volunteer aide-de-camp in April 1861 and was commissioned in the 23rd Ohio Infantry in June. As a brigadier general he won an early victory at Rich Mountain: commencing the new Department of West Virginia, he expelled the Confederates from his territory, helping to bring West

Virginia to statehood. Succeeding John Pope in June 1862, "Old Rosy" took command of the Mississippi Army, occupied Iuka in September and attacked Corinth in October. Promoted to major general, he led the reorganized Cumberland Army through Stones River (for which he received the Thanks of Congress) and the Tullahoma Campaign. Rosecrans was a gifted strategist, but an error in one of his orders to the front at Chickamauga (September 1863) cost the Federals this crucial battle and Rosecrans his command. He saw no further significant action, commanding the Missouri Department until 1864 and awaiting orders for the duration of the war. After serving as U.S. minister to Mexico (1868, 1869), he pursued Mexican and Californian mining interests, represented California in Congress (1881-1885) and served as register of the U.S. treasury (1885-1893) before retiring to his California ranch.

William Starke Rosecrans (opposite and overleaf) at the Battle of Stones River, December 31, 1862–January 3, 1863.

BELOW: Jerome Bonaparte Robertson.

Rosser, Thomas Lafayette
(1836-1910) Confederate general

He resigned from West Point late in his final year to enter Confederate service. An artillerist at First Bull Run, he saw action with the cavalry during the Peninsular Campaign and led the Fifth Virginia Cavalry in the Second Bull Run, Chancellorsville and Gettysburg campaigns. As a brigade commander, Rosser met his West Point friend George Armstrong Custer in battle in the Shenandoah Valley and during the retreat to Appomattox. The three raids he led into West Virginia in 1864 and 1865 are remembered as "Rosser's Raids." He had a successful postwar career as a railway engineer and commanded a brigade of volunteers during the Spanish-American War of 1898.

Rousseau, Lovell Harrison
(1818-1869) Union general

This self-educated Indiana lawyer and Whig legislator returned to his native Kentucky after fighting in the Mexican War and became a leading Louisville lawyer and legislator. A strong Unionist, he is credited with keeping Kentucky in the Union. He enlisted in the Union army September 1861 and figured prominently in the fighting at Shiloh, Perryville and Chickamauga. From November 1863 to July 1865 Rousseau commanded the District of Nashville. Commissioned a brigadier general in the regular army in 1867, he was sent to receive Alaska from the Russians. He died on active duty.

Ruffin, Edmund
(1794-1865)
Secessionist, agriculturalist, publisher

This Virginian agriculturalist conducted early experiments with crop rotation, fertilizer and drainage. An influential reformer through his lectures and writing, he wrote a seminal *Essay on Calcareous Manures* (1832), founded the *Farmer's Register* (1833-1843) and, as state agricultural surveyor, published a landmark agricultural survey of South Carolina (1843). A committed secessionist, he wrote in defence of slavery and secession in the 1850s. He joined Charleston's Palmetto Guard before the attack on Fort Sumter (where some sources erroneously state he fired the first shot). He left field service soon after First Bull Run, however, and shuttled between his plantations and Charleston until June 1865, Distraught after the surrender, he committed suicide.

Ruggles, Daniel
(1810-1897) Confederate general

A career army officer, Massachusetts-born Ruggles was graduated from West Point in 1833, served on the frontier and in Texas and fought in the Mexican War. He joined the Confederate army as a brigadier general in 1861 and served along the Potomac and at New Orleans. He led a division at Shiloh and at Baton Rouge and, as a major general, commanded the Department of the Mississippi. In 1865 he was commissary general of prisoners. He lived on his Texas and Virginia estates after the war.

Russell, David Allen
(1820-1864) Union general

A West Point-trained career officer and frontier and Mexican War veteran, this New Yorker led the Union's 7th Massa-

Edmund Ruffin

David Allen Russell

chusetts in the Peninsular Campaign and at South Mountain and Antietam. As a brigadier general, he subsequently commanded troops at Fredericksburg, Gettysburg, Rappahannock Bridge (wounded), the Wilderness and Petersburg. After joining Philip Sheridan in the Shenandoah Valley Campaign, he was killed at the Battle of Winchester in September 1864.

Russell, Sir William Howard
(1820-1907) War correspondent

An Irish-born war correspondent famous for his Crimean War dispatches, he covered the Civil War for the pro-Confederate London *Times* in 1861-1862. His effectiveness was compromised by his unpopularity both in the South (because of his antislavery convictions) and in the North (for his unvarnished account of the Federal rout at First Bull Run). Regarded as the first modern special correspondent, he traveled widely covering wars and other world events. He was knighted in 1895.

Salm-Salm, Agnes Elisabeth Winona Leclerq Joy, Princess
(1840-1912) Union nurse.

Born in Vermont or Quebec, she went to Washington at the outbreak of the war and soon married Prussian Prince Felix Salm-Salm. She accompanied him in the field, promoting his career and earning for herself a captaincy for her hospital relief work. She later became famous for her futile but courageous intercession for Mexican Emperor Maximilian's life and for her relief work in Prussian army camps and field hospitals.

Salm-Salm, Felix Constantin Alexander Johann Nepomuk, Prince
(1828-1870) Union officer

A Prussian cavalryman, he fought in the Prussian-Danish War of 1848-49. He sailed to American in 1861 to fight for the North, serving first as aide-de-camp to Louis Blenker, commander of a German division. He later fought with the 8th and 68th New York. He became Emperor Maximilian's aide-de-camp in Mexico immediately after the war. He was killed fighting with the Prussian guards in the Franco-Prussian War of 1870.

Salomon Brothers
Union officers/state governor

These three brothers were Prussian refugees from the 1848 revolution. Carl Eberhard (1822-1881) and Frederick Sigel Salomon (1826-1897) became Union officers. A Wisconsin surveyor and railroad engineer, Frederick joined a Wisconsin infantry regiment and was promoted to brigadier general in June 1862. After the

Frederick Sigel Salomon

war he was surveyer general of Utah Territory. The third brother, Edward Selig Salomon (1836-1913), a prominent Wisconsin lawyer and Republican, was the wartime governor of Wisconsin (1862-1864, lieutenant governor 1861-1862) and a conspicuously successful military recruiter. He greatly improved the state university. After 1869 he practiced law in New York, where he was founding president of the legal aid society (1875-1889); he retired to Germany (1894).

Sanders, John Calhoun
(1840-1864) Confederate general

Born in Alabama, Sanders left college to join the Confederate army. He fought at Seven Pines, Gaines's Mill, Frayers's Farm, Antietam, Fredericksburg, Chancellorsville, Gettysburg, the Wilderness and Spotsylvania. (He was wounded at Frayser's Farm, Antietam and Gettysburg.) Promoted to brigadier general in May 1864, he was killed in August 1864 at Weldon Railroad.

Scammon, Eliakim Parker
(1816-1894) Union general

This West Point-trained Maine native fought in the Seminole and Mexican wars. He left the presidency of Cincinnati College to join the Union's 23rd Ohio in 1861. He fought in West Virginia and Maryland and was promoted to brigadier general in October 1862 for gallantry at South Mountain. His later commands in Missouri and the Carolinas were interrupted by his capture in 1864 and imprisonment at Libby Prison. He spent most of his later years as a college mathematics instructor.

Schenck, Robert Cumming
(1809-1890) Union general, politician

Born in Ohio, Schenck was a lawyer, U.S Congressman, ambassador to Brazil and railroad president before being named a Union brigadier general in 1861. He fought at Vienna and in T. J. Jackson's 1862 Valley Campaign. Wounded at Second Bull Run, he was promoted to major general. He resigned from the army in 1863 after he was elected to the U.S. House of Representatives, where he served until 1870, when he was named U.S. ambassador to England. He sat on the commission that made the treaty of Washington, the Geneva arbitration and the settlement of the *Alabama* claims. He wa forced to resign as ambassador when he was accused of involvement in a fraudulent mine in the American West, but he was never found guilty.

Robert Cumming Schenck (right) and (below) Robert Kingston Scott

Schofield, John McAlister
(1831-1906) Union general

A Baptist clergyman's son, he was graduated from West Point in 1853, taught there and was on a leave of absence teaching physics at Washington University in St Louis at he onset of war. He fought in the Union army at Wilson's Creek in August 1861 and subsequently commanded the Army of the Frontier in Missouri in 1862-63. Schofield led XXIII Corps in the Atlanta Campaign of 1864 and on W. T. Sherman's march through the Carolinas in early 1865. He served as secretary of war in 1868-69, was superintendent at West Point from 1876-81 and rose to commanding general of the army in 1888. Schofield retired in 1895 after 46 years in uniform.

Schurz, Carl
(1829-1906) Union general, social reformer, journalist

Having engaged in revolutionary actions as a young radical in his native Germany, he fled and emigrated to the United States in 1852. He took up farming in Wisconsin (one of the so-called "Latin farmers." highly educated European who took up farming in America), soon spoke out against slavery and became active in the new Republican Party. In 1861 he was sent as Abraham Lincoln's ambassador to Spain, but Schurz returned within months and soon was openly advocating the freeing of all slaves. He was appointed a brigadier general in the Union army in June 1862 and commanded a division at Second Bull Run. He subsequently commanded German-speaking units at Chancellorsville and Gettysburg but was criticized harshly for the unmilitary behavior of these units. He ultimately commanded XI Corps in the Army of the Cumberland. During the presidential campaign of 1864 he campaigned extensively for Lincoln (with whom he corresponded directly even while on active duty). After the war he gained a major reputation as a journalist and political philosopher, with time out to serve as U.S. Senator from Missouri (1869-1875) and secretary of the interior (1877-1881). He is most closely associated with calling for reform of the civil service.

Scott, Dred
(c. 1795-1858) Former slave

Born into slavery, he was purchased in 1832 by John Emerson, an army surgeon, who then took Scott to his military posts in Illinois and Minnesota. (Scott married a

Dred Scott

free black in Minnesota and they had a child born there.) After Emerson brought Scott and his family back to St. Louis, he died (1843) and Scott tried to gain his freedom on the grounds that he was legally a freedman because of his residence in non-slave states. The case was eventually brought up to the Supreme Court, and in 1857 Scott lost his appeal, 7-2, with Chief Justice Roger Taney giving his opinion that no Negro was a citizen under the U.S. Constitution and that slaveholders had the right to take their "property" wherever they went. Within a few weeks, however, Scott and his family were freed, but he lived only another 16 months, working as a doorman at a hotel in St. Louis.

Scott, Robert Kingston
(1826-1900) Union general

Born in Pennsylvania, he had served in the Mexican War. He was commissioned a lieutenant colonel in the Union army in 1861 and fought at Vicksburg, Thompson's Hill, Raymond, Jackson, Champion's Hill and in the Atlanta Campaign. He was promoted to major general in December 1865 and headed the South Carolina Freedman's Bureau until 1868. He was later a Republican governor of South Carolina.

Scott, Winfield
(1786-1866) Union general

Born on his family's estate near Petersburg, Virginia, the year after the Founding Fathers drew up the Constitution, he studied at home under tutors, attended William and Mary College and read law with a Petersburg attorney before entering the army in 1808. A brigade under his command bore the brunt of the fighting in the U.S. victory at Lundy's Lane in 1814.

Scott stayed on in the peacetime army and, among other things, campaigned for temperance; on an 1832 expedition, he decreed then any soldier found intoxicated must dig a grave his own size and study it with the knowledge that he soon would be laid down in it if he persisted in hard drinking. "Old Fuss and Feathers," as Scott was known, also had considerable success as a pacifier. He smoothed over the Nullification crisis in South Carolina in 1832 and settled a vexing boundary dispute between Maine and New Brunswick in 1838. He was mentioned as a possible Whig candidate for the presidency in 1840 and 1844.

Appointed general-in-chief of the army in 1841, Scott took command of U.S. forces in the field during the Mexican War. His army captured Vera Cruz in March 1847, and he then set out with 8,000 men for Mexico City in April. The Mexican capital fell after a series of battles on September 14, 1847. In 1852 Scott became the first officer since George Washington to hold the rank of lieutenant general. In the same year, he ran unsuccessfully for president on the Whig ticket.

Experienced in public as well as military affairs, Scott realized that winning a civil war for the Union would be an enormous undertaking, costly in lives and treasure. Too old, fat and ill to mount a horse, he could not take a field command; instead, he put forward his Anaconda Plan, which called for a complete blockade of the South and control of the Mississippi River, as the essential Union strategy for winning the

Winfield Scott

war. Derided at first, much of the plan eventually became Union policy. President Lincoln ordered the blockade of Southern ports in the early stages of hostilities, and, over time, the strategy contributed enormously to the Union victory.

Scott did not support the appointment of George McClellan to command the Army of the Potomac. McClellan resented this, and the two were unable ever to establish a good working partnership. Scott requested retirement on October 31, 1861, and Lincoln approved it the following day, ending Scott's public career of almost 50 years.

He lived to write a two-volume book of memoirs and to meet the all-conquering Ulysses S. Grant, who had been one of his junior officers in Mexico. In 1865 Scott presented Grant with a gift that bore the inscription, "from the oldest to the greatest general." He died at West Point two weeks before his 80th birthday.

Sedgwick, John
(1813-1864) Union general

This career officer was born in Connecticut and was educated at West Point. A veteran of the Seminole and Mexican wars and frontier service, he was affectionately called "Uncle John" by his men. Competent and hard-fighting, he early won recognition fighting for the Union in the Peninsular Campaign (wounded). He was twice wounded at Antietam but recovered in time to distinguish himself again at Fredericksburg. As a major general (July 1862) commanding VI Corps, he tried unsuccessfully to relieve Joseph Hooker at Chancellorsville. He commanded the Union left wing on the third day at Gettysburg and performed brilliantly in the Mine Run operations. Sedgwick was killed by a Rebel sharpshooter at Spotsylvania.

Semmes, Raphael
(1809-1877) Confederate naval officer

Maryland-born, orphaned at an early age and raised in Georgetown, D.C., by an uncle, he won an appointment as a naval midshipman in 1826. He served in the Mediterranean, read law, earned admission to the bar during leaves of absence and finally received a lieutenant's commission in 1837.

Semmes fought in Mexico in 1846 and 1847, both on blockade duty and ashore with the naval artillery; he marched with Winfield Scott's army to Mexico City. He published *Service Afloat and Ashore during the Mexican War* in 1851.

During the 1850s Semmes commanded

Raphael Semmes standing beside *Alabama's* massive 110-pounder

the storeship *Electra* and the schooner *Flirt*, but spent more than half his time ashore, during which he resumed the practice of law. He resigned from the U.S. Navy in February 1861 and went on a purchasing mission for the Confederacy, actually buying armaments from manufacturers in New England and New York. He took command of the commerce raider CSS *Sumter* in April.

Semmes took 18 prizes during a six-month cruise in *Sumter* before abandoning the ship in Gilbraltar and making his way to England to take command of what became the screw sloop CSS *Alabama*. He set sail in *Alabama* in September 1862 on a commerce destroying cruise that would last nearly two years.

Raiding the whaling grounds in mid-Atlantic, he took and burned 10 whaling vessels, then moved on to the Gulf of Mexico, where he sank the paddlewheeler USS *Hatteras* after a running night action of a quarter-hour. Heading down the coast of Brazil, he preyed on the crossroads of shipping lanes to and from the Pacific, Europe and America.

Semmes called at Capetown, South Africa, in August 1863, then sailed into the Indian Ocean, raided there and in the Arabian Sea, and completed the long run to Cherbourg, France, in June 1864. Altogether, the *Alabama* took, burned, sank or destroyed 69 ships on its 23-month cruise.

He tried to arrange for an overhaul of the ship in the Cherbourg dockyards, but while he awaited permission to enter the harbor the Union screw sloop USS *Keararge* appeared. The two well-matched ships met in battle within sight of land on June 19, 1864. After an exchange of several broadsides the *Alabama* began to take on water. She sank stern first some two and-a-half hours after the action began.

Semmes did not surrender with his ship, escaping to England. He managed to return to the Confederacy before war's end and, promoted to rear admiral, commanded the James River squadron. He burned his ships with the evacuation of Richmond, armed his sailors as infantry and surrendered with Joseph E. Johnston at Greensboro, North Carolina.

Though paroled, Semmes was arrested in late 1865 and held for a time on what amounted to a charge of piracy. He later taught literature, edited a Memphis newspaper and praticed law in Mobile, Alabama. His *Memoirs of Service Afloat during the War between the States* appeared in 1869.

Seward, William Henry
(1801-1872) Union statesman

Son of an Orange County, New York, doctor, he entered Union College at age 15, was graduated four years later, read law and was admitted to the bar in 1822. He began his political career in Auburn, New York, with a successful run for the state senate in 1830, serving four years; he won

William Henry Seward

election to the governorship as a Whig in 1838 and 1840.

Seward's antislavery beliefs drew him into the Republican party in 1856 . In a famous 1858 speech he said that the slavery issue would bring about an "irrepressible conflict," though in fact many of his positions on the subject were relatively moderate. He unsuccessfully sought the Republican nomination in 1860.

Seward joined the Lincoln administration as secretary of state and, during the course of the war, proved to be an able diplomat. He smoothed over the *Trent* controversy with England in 1861, and his efforts helped keep Britain and France from overtly supporting the rebellion, though Britain did build warships and provide other aid to the Confederacy.

Gravely wounded in the Lincoln assassination plot in April 1865, Seward recovered and resumed his cabinet duties. His forward-looking purchase of Alaska from Russia for $6 million in 1867 was called at the time "Seward's Folly." His health failing, he returned to Auburn in 1871 and died there in October of the following year.

Truman Seymour

Seymour, Truman
(1824-1891) Union general

Vermont-born Seymour was a professional artilleryman trained at West Point and seasoned in the Seminole and Mexican wars. He was a captain of artillery at Fort Sumter and fought steadily throughout the war with the Union's Army of the Potomac and in the Department of the South. He was seriously wounded at Battery Wagner and was captured in the Battle of the Wilderness. Exchanged, he fought in the Shenandoah Valley in 1864 and at the siege of Petersburg and led a division at Sayler's Creek. In 1876 he retired to Italy.

Robert Gould Shaw

Shaw, Robert Gould
(1837-1863) Union army officer

This Boston reformer and abolitionist's son attended Harvard and was a New York merchant when the Civil War erupted. Enlisting in the Union army's 7th Massachusetts, he fought steadily in the Eastern theater. He organized and led the Union's first black regiment, the 54th Massachusetts Colored Infantry, which left Boston on May 28, 1863, and saw its first skirmish at James Island, South Carolina, on July 16. Shaw and half of his men were killed amid the heavy Federal losses at Battery Wagner on July 18. As a mark of contempt for this white officer's championing of blacks, Confederates threw his body into a common burial pit with the bodies of his black troops.

Shelby, Joseph Orville
(1830-1897) Confederate general

A wealthy Kentuckian, he joined the Confederate cavalry in 1861 and fought at Wilson's Creek, Lexington and Pea Ridge. He commanded a cavalry brigade on numerous raids in 1863 and 1864. Rather than surrender, "Jo" Shelby led his troopers across the Rio Grande to join Emperor Maxmilian's forces in Mexico. He later settled in Missouri.

Sheridan, Philip Henry
(1831-1888) Union general

The son of immigrants from County Cavan, Ireland, born in Albany, New York, Sheridan grew up in Ohio, where his father had gone in search of work on the canals and roads. Educated in the village school of Somerset, Ohio, he worked as a store clerk there before obtaining a West Point cadetship in 1848. Pugnacious and short-tempered, Sheridan soon found himself in trouble for threatening an older cadet with a bayonet. Suspended for a year, he returned, obeyed the rules (more or less) and was graduated with the class of 1853, 34th of 49.

Sheridan served in Texas and fought Indians in the Pacific Northwest, but his antebellum military career lacked distinction. When the Civil War began he was a quartermaster and commissary for Union General Samuel Curtis's Army of the Southwest. A poor bookkeeper and heedless of procedure, Sheridan was relieved and narrowly escaped court martial. He joined Henry Halleck's staff in Missouri and carried out a series of quartermaster odd jobs, including a roving assignment to buy remounts for Halleck's command.

In May 1862 Sheridan obtained a commission as colonel of the 2nd Michigan Cavalry, rising to the command of a brigade within two months. He defeated a Confederate cavalry force at Booneville, Mississippi, in July during Halleck's Cornith Campaign. At Perryville, Kentucky, in October he capably commanded an infantry division. Sheridan's stubborn defense at Stones River, Tennessee, in December helped save William Rosecrans's army from defeat. Shortly thereafter Sheridan won promotion to major general.

He saw action at Chickamauga in September 1863 and in November, under Ulysses S. Grant, led the infantry charge that carried Missionary Ridge and broke up Braxton Bragg's Confederate army at Chattanooga. When Grant went east as commander-in-chief in March 1864 he took Sheridan with him as commander-designate of the 10,000-strong Cavalry Corps of the Army of the Potomac. He quarreled with Grant's second-in-command, George Meade, over the use of the cavalry during the Wilderness and Spotsylvania campaigns, but his first independent operation in Virginia, the Richmond Raid of May 9-24, proved to be a great success. On May 11 Sheridan's troopers clashed with pursuing Confederates at Yellow tavern near Richmond. J. E. B.

Philip Henry Sheridan (above, on left) and (right) Sheridan's Ride.

PREVIOUS PAGES: The Battle of Winchester.

Stuart, Robert E. Lee's brilliant cavalry commander, was mortally wounded in the action. Sheridan went on to complete a circuit of Lee's army, destroying supplies, tearing up railroad track and defeating the Confederate cavalry in four separate engagements.

In August 1864 Grant sent him to the Shenandoah Valley with orders to destroy Jubal Early's small Confederate army, confiscate livestock, burn crops and render the region unfit as a supply center or base for further Rebel operations. (In July, Early had crossed the Potomac and approached Washington, alarming the politicians and distracting Grant.) When he finished with Early, Sheridan was to turn the Shenandoah into "a barren waste," Grant said, "so that crows flying over it for the balance of this season will have to carry their provender with them."

Sheridan pushed into the Valley and defeated Early at Winchester on September 19 and at Fisher's Hill three days later. His troops began stripping the countryside on October 6. Thinking he had disposed of Early, he made arrangements to return the VI Corps infantry to Grant. But Early regrouped and surprised the Federals at

Cedar Creek on October 19, while Sheridan was absent. The Confederates were on the verge of victory when Sheridan arrived after his famous ride from Winchester and collected troops for a counterstroke that reversed the result. He then continued his work of destruction. In one report to Grant, he claimed to have burned 2,000 barns and 700 mills. In another report, one of his divisional commanders tabulated a precise 3,772 horses, 545 mules, 10,918 beef cattle and 435,802 bushels of wheat among the spoils of the operation.

Sheridan returned to Grant to take the leading part in the Appomattox Campaign of April 1865. His turning of Lee's flank at the Battle of Five Forks on April 1 forced the Confederate commander to begin a disorderly withdrawal to the west. Commanding a mobile force of cavalry and infantry, Sheridan pursued vigorously and blocked Lee's retreat beyond Appomattox Court House. Lee surrendered the Army of Northern Virginia there on April 9.

Hardly five feet tall, squat, with dark, close-cropped hair and a "sun-browned face and sailor air," Sheridan had a natural authority on the battlefield. His troops called him "Little Phil" and rarely failed to respond to his aggressive example. He could be brutal to subordinates whom he judged had failed him. At Five Forks he removed G. K. Warren from command of V Corps for lack of aggressiveness and cast aspersions on his personal bravery; the incident wrecked Warren's career and left him embittered to the end of his life.

In May 1865 Sheridan took command of a force of 50,000 veterans on the Rio Grande in a show of force meant to encourage the French to withdraw troops sent to Mexico to protect the regime of Emperor Maxmilian. He later served as postwar military governor of Texas and Louisiana, where he so rigorously enforced Reconstruction policies that President Andrew Johnson ordered his recall. In the 1870s Sheridan organized a series of punitive campaigns against the Plains Indians, forcing the tribes on to government reservation land. In 1884 he succeeded W. T. Sherman as commander-in-chief of the army. He completed his *Personal Memoirs* (1888) only a few days before his death.

Sherman, John
(1832-1900) Northern legislator

The younger brother of William Tecumseh Sherman, he became a lawyer and a member of the Whig Party, moving over to the new Republican Party only when it became clear that the Whigs had no political future.

He was, in fact, always more moderate than most Republicans. He served Ohio in the House of Representatives (1855-61) and then in the Senate (1861-77), trying vainly to take moderate positions on slavery and, later, on the treatment of the former Confederate states, but constantly being forced by his Republican constituency to vote for radical legislation. After serving as secretary of the treasury (1877-81), he returned to the Senate (1881-97) and put his name on a famous antitrust law (The Sherman Anti-Trust Act of 1890, the first regulatory legislation of its kind). He was secretary of state (1897-98), resigning to protest the decision to go to war against Spain.

Sherman, William Tecumseh
(1820-91) Union general

The son of an Ohio Supreme Court justice, Sherman was born at Lancaster, Ohio, orphaned at the age of nine and raised by a well-to-do connection of his father's, Thomas Ewing. He received his early education at a local academy – schooling sufficient to prepare him for West Point, from which he was graduated, sixth in his class, in 1840, an artillery second lieutenant.

"Cump" Sherman, as he was called, served in Florida and California and saw

William Tecumseh Sherman

limited action in the Mexican War. Bored with garrison life and frustrated by the glacial pace of advancement in the old army, he resigned in 1853 to become a banker in San Francisco. Like his friend Grant, he found the civilian world daunting. When the bank failed, Sherman turned to the practice of law. He lost his only case.

Appointed superintendent of the Louisiana Military Academy (forerunner of Louisiana State University) in 1859, he saw the secession movement close up, agonized over the potential breakup of the Union and viewed the prospect of war with undisguised horror. When it came, Sherman turned down the offer of a Confederate commission and accepted, in May 1861,

The Battle of Kennesaw Mountain (below and opposite top) and Sherman's March to the Sea (opposite bottom)

the colonecy of the 13th U.S. Infantry. In July he commanded a brigade at the First Battle of Bull Run.

Sent west to Kentucky as second-in-command to Robert Anderson in August, he experienced what amounted to a nervous breakdown growing out of his quarrels with his superiors and members of the press over his estimates of the resources of troops and material that would be required to meet the Confederate threat. The politicians responded to his request for 200,000 men to defend Kentucky with ridicule and soon caused him to be removed to a quiet post in Missouri. His forecasts proved, in the event, only too accurate.

After a short stop at Cairo, Illinois, where he forwarded troops and supplies for Ulysses S. Grant's river campaigns of early 1862, Sherman obtained command of a division in Grant's Army of the Ten-

nessee. There began one of the great partnerships of the war. Sherman's division, surprised early on the first day of Shiloh, recovered under his leadership and helped prevent a complete rout. Grant thereafter assigned him leading roles in what became two of the greatest campaigns of the war: Vicksburg in the spring and summer of 1863, and the breakout from besieged Chattanooga in October-November 1863.

When President Lincoln made Grant commander-in-chief of the Union land forces in March 1864, Sherman succeeded him as senior commander in the West. Around this time one of his officers characterized Sherman, with his red hair and beard, thin, sinewy frame and deeply lined face, as "the concentrated essence of Yankeedom." Brilliant, restless, expressive, "he perspired thought at every pore," another observer commented, "with a mood that shifted like a barometer in a tropic sea."

Sherman moved against Joseph E. Johnston in Georgia in May 1864 in a campaign of maneuver that ended with the capture of Atlanta four months later. There he began to articulate views on war that he long had been formulating. "War is cruelty and you cannot refine it," he told Atlantans. Sherman took it as an article of faith that the war could be ended only when its realities were brought home to the civilian population that supported the fighting fronts. He put the theory to the test in Atlanta, authorizing the destruction of all property of potential military value. The result was the near-destruction of the South's second city.

On November 15, 1864, he set out on his famous March to the Sea. "I can make Georgia howl," he told Grant, and his 60,000-man army, traveling light in two wings, cut a 60-mile-wide swath of destruction across interior Georgia. Here Sherman brought the war home to Georgians in the most uncompromising terms, proving as well that the Confederacy could no longer protect its citizens. Casualties, military and civilian, were, however, astonishingly light.

He reached Savannah before Christmas and, after resting his army for six weeks, struck out in February 1865 for the Carolinas and an eventual junction with Grant in Virginia. It was another brilliant success, more impressive – because more difficult – even than the George march. On April 26, 17 days after Lee's surrender at Appomattox, Sherman offered generous terms to large Confederate forces under Johnston in North Carolina. Johnston's acceptance effectively ended the war in the East.

Sherman and his generals: (l. to r.) Howard, Logan, Hazen, Sherman, Davis, Slocum and Mower

In the aftermath of Lincoln's assassination, Sherman's generosity to Johnston inspired much outrage, and leading government officials repudiated his terms. Johnston surrendered anyway, but Sherman never forgave War Secretary Edwin Stanton or the others. The controversy confirmed his contempt for politics and politicians.

He succeeded Grant as commander-in-chief of the army in 1869. His tenure of office saw the completion of the transcontinental railroad and the defeat and resettlement of many of the Plains Indian tribes. He published his excellent *Memoirs* in 1875. Retiring in 1883, he lived thereafter in St. Louis and New York City.

Sherman rebuffed all efforts to draw him into political life. "If nominated I will not accept. If elected I will not serve," he told Republicans who wanted to draft him for a presidential run in 1884. He remained active in veterans' affairs and enjoyed addressing encampments of the Grand Army of the Republic and other soldier organizations. At one such meeting he uttered his famous dictum: "War is all hell."

Some military historians rate Sherman the greatest Federal commander of the war. Certainly his campaigns of 1864-65 were masterworks of conception and execution. In 11 months they carried him from Chattanooga through Georgia and the Carolinas to the verges of Lee's domain and made his name an anathema in the South. Sherman died of pneumonia in his 71st year. His old adversary Joseph Johnston helped carry the casket at his funeral.

Shields, James
(1806-1879) Union general

Irish-born, Shields came to the U.S. about 1820 and became a lawyer in Illinois. He served in the Black Hawk War and the Mexican War and became a Democratic politician. He challenged Abraham Lincoln to a duel because of newspaper criticism, but they were able to resolve their differences and became friends. Shields was made governor of the Oregon Territory and then became a U.S. Senator, first from Illinois, then from Minnesota. Commis-

James Shields

sioned a Union brigadier general in 1861, he served in the Shenandoah Valley Campaign of 1862 and on the Rappahannock. He resigned from the army in March 1863 to become a railroad commissioner in California. Later he would briefly serve as a U.S. Senator from Missouri – thereby becoming the only person in all of U.S. history to serve three different states in the U.S. Senate.

brigadier general in the Confederate army in June 1861, he became commander of the Army of New Mexico and conducted operations in New Mexico and Arizona in 1861-1862 with no great success. He later led commands in Louisiana, south of the Red River. Courtmartialed on charges of refusing orders, he was acquitted – he apparently convinced the court that he was too sick to press an attack. At the end of the war he went to Egypt and served as an artillery general there (1865-1874). He is perhaps known best for his invention, the Sibley tent, which was a lightweight tent capable of holding 12 soldiers and their equipment.

ABOVE: Sickles with S.P. Heintzelman.

RIGHT: Henry Hopkins Sibley.

Sibley, Henry Hastings
(1811-1891) Union general

Born in Michigan, he was a fur trader in Minnesota and served as the latter state's first governor. Commissioned a Union brigadier in September 1862, he fought the Sioux in the Indian rebellion on 1862. Taking 2,000 prisoners, Sibley tried 400 Sioux by court material and executed 38 of them on December 26, 1862. He had post-war success as a banker and merchant.

Sibley, Henry Hopkins
(1816-1886) Confederate general

Born in Louisiana, Sibley was a West Point graduate who fought in the Seminole and Mexican wars and on the frontier. Named a

ABOVE: Daniel Edgar Sickles

Sickles, Daniel Edgar
(1825-1914) Union general

A New York City lawyer, legislator, and U.S. Representative (1857-1861), Sickles seemed to court notoriety. On trial for murder in 1859, he successfully used the first-ever temporary insanity defence. As a Union brigadier general he led New York's Excelsior Brigade in the Peninsular Campaign and at Antietam and Fredericksburg; he led III Corps at Chancellorsville. Without authorization he advanced his unit ahead of the Union line at Gettysburg, possibly helping to stop the Confederate advance but at the cost of half his men. In this action Sickles lost his leg, ending his field career. He won the Congressional Medal of Honor for his role Gettysburg. He was later instrumental in creating a national park at that battlefield. He was dismissed as chairman of the New York state monuments commission (1886-1912) for financial irregularities.

Franz Sigel

Sigel, Franz
(1824-1902) Union general

Forced to flee his native Germany after the 1848 revolution, he settled in New York City and then in St. Louis, where he was director of schools. He obtained a briga-dier's commission in the Union army in May 1861 and fought at Wilson's Creek and Pea Ridge. Sigel held a series of senior com-mands in the Shenandoah Valley in 1864 and suffered a serious defeat at New Mar-ket in May. Though a mediocre general, Sigel materially assisted the Union cause by recruiting thousands of German-Americans. He returned to New York City after the war and became active in journal-ism and politics.

Slidell, John
(1793-1871) Confederate diplomat

A New York native and Columbia Uni-versity graduate, he failed in business in New York and established a New Orleans law practice. As a Democratic Congress-man (1843-1845) and Senator (1853-1861), he became an influential political power-broker. In 1861, in the so-called *Trent* affair, he was captured at sea by Union naval forces while he and James Mason were on a mission to seek Anglo-French recognition for the Confederacy, a goal he never achieved, despite his skilful diplo-matic performance. He did, however, arrange for the French construction of ships and financing for the Confederacy. Union general Ranald Slidell MacKenzie (1840-1889) was his nephew.

Slocum, Henry Warner
(1827-1894) Union general

After graduation from West Point (1852), he became a Syracuse, New York, lawyer and state legislator. He was promoted to brigadier general in the Union army after First Bull Run, where he was badly wounded, and to major general during the Peninsular Campaign. He fought at South Mountain and Antietam and commanded a corps at Fredericksburg, Chancellorsville and Gettysburg, where he held the Union right wing. Toward the end of the Atlanta Campaign he took over XX Corps from Joseph Hooker; his troops were the first into the city. He led W. T. Sherman's left wing during the March to the Sea and in the Carolinas Campaign. He was a Brooklyn lawyer, Democratic politician and U.S. Congressman (1869-1873, 1883-1885) in later years.

Smalley, George Washburn
(1833-1916) War correspondent

Smalley was a Massachusetts-born lawyer and abolitionist who, between November 1861 and October 1862 served as the *New York Tribune*'s war correspondent. He

John Slidell

brought his report from Antietam to New York himself when he was unable to send it. Soon thereafter, Smalley became ill with "camp fever" and worked in the New York office until 1866, when he covered the Prussian-Austrian War. He opened the *Tribune* offices in Europe and then worked for the London *Times* (1895-1905).

Smalls, Robert
(1839-1915) Union sailor, legislator

Born a slave at Beaufort on the Sea Islands of South Carolina, he moved to Charleston, where he worked on the docks and as a sailmaker before becoming an expert boat pilot along the coasts of Georgia and South Carolina. Forced to pilot a Confederate ship, the *Planter*, transporting cotton, on May 13, 1862, he directed his fellow African-American crewmates to sail the ship out of Charleston harbor, past the Confederate guns, and delivered it to the Union fleet. In October of 1862 he went to New York to try to get Northern support for a colony of freed slaves at Port Royal, South Carolina. In June 1864 he was part of a delegation of free blacks who attended the Republican Party convention. After the war he was elected to the South Carolina legislature and then to the U.S. House of Representatives (1875-79, 1882-87), where he fought against many odds to gain fair treatment for his fellow African-Americans. He closed out his career as federal collector of the port of his native town of Beaufort, South Carolina (1889-1913).

Charles Ferguson Smith

Smith, Andrew Jackson
(1815-1897) Union general

He was graduated from West Point in 1838 and saw action on the frontier and in Mexico. Smith led a Union division during the Vicksburg Campaign and the right wing of XVI Corps during the Red River Campaign of 1864. He commanded large formations at Nashville later in 1864 and in operations around Mobile in 1865. He resigned from the regular army as colonel of the 7th Cavalry in 1869.

Smith, Charles Ferguson
(1807-1862) Union general

This Pennsylvania-born West Point graduate served in the Mexican War, on the Utah Expedition and as an instructor at West Point: Ulysses S. Grant had been a cadet under Smith. Serving under Grant in the Civil War, Smith won promotion to major general in March 1862 for a charge he led at Fort Donelson. He died on April 25, 1862, of a foot infection he received while leaping from a boat at the beginning of the Shiloh Campaign.

Smith, Edmund Kirby
(1824-1893) Confederate general

He was born in Florida, the son of a Connecticut lawyer and War of 1812 veteran, and by the age of 12 he had decided to become a soldier. He was graduated from West Point in 1845, joined the 5th Infantry and saw action during the Mexican War at

Edmond Kirby Smith

Palo Alto, Monterey, Vera Cruz, Cerro Gordo and Chapultepec.

Smith's peacetime career and assignments were typical: he served in garrison and on the frontier. He was a botanist on a Mexican boundary commission. He taught mathematics at West Point for three years. He fought Indians in Texas. A leave of absence in 1858 provided him the opportunity to tour Europe. When Florida seceded early in 1861, he resigned his U.S. commission to join the Confederacy.

Chief-of-staff to Joseph E. Johnston at Harpers Ferry, he helped organize the Shenandoah army in the spring of 1861, then took charge of an infantry brigade in Johnston's command. Seriously wounded at First Bull Run in July 1861, he recovered in time to accept a promotion to major general and command of a division in P. G. T. Beauregard's army.

Sent west in early 1862 to head the Department of East Tennessee, Smith launched an invasion of Kentucky in June. He defeated the Federals at Richmond, Kentucky, in August and cleared Cumberland Gap of enemy forces before joining Braxton Bragg for the battle of Perryville in October. He withdrew, along with Bragg, after the drawn battle there.

In February 1863 Smith took charge of he Transmississippi Department, a vast region including Texas, Louisiana and Arkansas, that became known after the fall of Vicksburg as Kirby Smithdom. His chief contribution was to ship cotton and other products through the blockade and to import machinery and other tools of war with the proceeds. Forces under his command deranged the Federal Red River Campaign of 1864 and later blunted a Union offensive in Arkansas.

Smith surrendered the last Confederate army to Edward Canby at Galveston, Texas, on June 2, 1865. He thought of settling in Mexico, but returned to the U.S., headed the Atlantic and Pacific Telegraph Co. for a time and considered entering the Episcopal ministry. From 1870 to 1875 he was president of the University of Nashville, then taught mathematics at the University of the South.

He and his wife, whom he met while recuperating from his Bull Run wound, raised 11 children.

Smith, Gustavus Woodson
(1822-1896) Confederate general

He was graduated from West Point in 1842, fought in Mexico and worked as a civil engineer, serving as New York City streets commissioner from 1858-61. Commissioned a major general in the Confederate service, he briefly commanded the army after Joseph E. Johnston's wounding at Seven Pines on May 31, 1862, stepping aside next day in favor of Robert E. Lee. Smith later resigned in a seniority dispute in February 1863. He commanded a Georgia militia division during W. T. Sherman's March to the Sea in late 1864. After the war Smith became the first insurance commissioner of Kentucky.

Gustavus Woodson Smith

ABOVE: William (Extra Billy) Smith

Smith, William
(1796-1887) Confederate general

A lawyer, he served in Congress and as governor of Virginia (1846-49). He became known as "Extra Billy" on account of the large government subsidies he received for his mail-coach service from Washington to Milledgeville, Georgia. He commanded a Confederate regiment at First Bull Run, on the Peninsula and at Antietam and a brigade at Gettysburg. Smith carried out his duties as a Confederate congressman between campaigns. He took office a second time as the governor of the state of Virginia in January 1864.

Smith, William Farrar
(1824-1903) Union general

An 1845 West Point graduate, he fought for the Union at the First Battle of Bull Run and led a brigade, then a division, during the Peninsular Campaign. Sent west in 1863, he organized Ulysses S. Grant's defenses at Chattanooga and helped open the "Cracker Line" to supply the besieged city. Smith led XVIII Corps in the initial assault on Petersburg in June 1864, but the attack was dilatory and failed to carry the city. Had Smith succeeded, he might have shortened the war by a year. He was relieved in consequence and did not hold another field command.

Soulé, Pierre
(1802-1870) Confederate general

Born in France, educated in Jesuit schools there, he went into exile at the age of 15 after being accused of conspiring against the Bourbon monarchy. After many adventures he settled in New Orleans, read law and entered politics, serving in the U.S. Senate from 1847 to 1853. He was a clandestine Confederate operative early in the war. Commissioned brigadier in 1863, he served on the staff of P. G. T. Beauregard in Charleston. He resumed his New Orleans law practice after the war.

Sprague, Kate Chase
(1840-1899) Washington hostess

At the age of 15 she began serving as a precocious hostess for her widower-father, Salmon P. Chase, then governor of Ohio. When he became Abraham Lincoln's secretary of the treasury, she went with him to Washington and soon became known for her extravagant parties. In 1863 she married William Sprague, a Senator from Rhode Island. During the war they continued to be social leaders, although their marriage soon began to fall apart. Kate schemed to have her father replace Lincoln as the Republican candidate in 1864 and even had the bad grace to complain when Lincoln named Chase chief justice of the Supreme Court later that year. In 1868 she schemed again to get her father the Democratic presidential nomination. When her father died in 1873 she lost all control, drank heavily, carried on a scandalous friendship with N.Y. Senator Roscoe Conkling (whom William Sprague attacked with a shotgun in 1879) and finally divorced William in 1882. She lived in Europe for a while, returning to her father's estate near Washington later in life, an eccentric and disappointed woman.

Stanton, Edwin McMasters
(1814-1869) Union secretary of war

Ohio-born Stanton was a successful Northern lawyer before serving as U.S. attorney general for the last four months of James Buchanan's presidency. He was Abraham Lincoln's secretary of war after January 1862. An outstanding executive, he efficiently manned, equipped and reorganized the military, rooted out fraud and corruption and instituted harsh security measures such as press censorship and arbitary arrests. He was widely resented, however, for his abrasive personality and interference in field tactics.

Edwin McMasters Stanton (above) and (right) James Blair Steedman

Initially opposed to Lincoln, Stanton became one of his most ardent supporters. His dismissal by President Andrew Johnson in 1868 provided an opportunity for Stanton's Radical Republican Congressional colleagues to impeach the president, whose Reconstruction policies they had long opposed. Stanton died four days after his confirmation as a U.S. Supreme Court justice.

Steedman, James Blair
(1817-1873) Union general

Steedman, a Toledo, Ohio, newspaper editor and Democratic state legislator, joined the Union army's 14th Ohio in 1861. He fought at Perryville, Stones River and in the Tullahoma Campaign and later, with great gallantry, at Chickamauga, where his division provided crucial aid to George

Thomas in his successful effort to prevent a Union rout. As a major general (April 1864), he commanded the post of Chattanooga, and during the Battle of Nashville he led the District of Etowah. He returned to Toledo journalism and public service after the war.

Steele, Frederick
(1819-1868) **Union general**

Born in New York, a West Point graduate and a veteran of fighting on the frontier and in the Mexican War, Steele was a major at the outbreak of the Civil war. He was promoted to major general in the Union army in 1862 and fought throughout Missouri and Arkansas. He served with distinction under Ulysses Grant in the Vicksburg Campaign. He led the Arkansas Campaign of 1864, a basically disastrous expedition, and ended the war by assisting in the final operations around Mobile, Alabama. Remaining in the army, he died when he fell from a horse-drawn vehicle after suffering an apoplectic attack.

Alexander Hamilton Stephens (above) and (left) Frederick Steele

Stephens, Alexander Hamilton
(1812-1883) **Confederate vice president**

This prominent lawyer and Congressman (1843-1859) helped to secure passage of the Kansas-Nebraska Act. He was a voice for moderation while serving as Jefferson Davis's vice president. Instrumental in drafting a moderate Confederate constitution, he worked for prisoner exchanges and opposed Davis's centralization of power and suspension of civil rights. He attended the Hampton Roads Peace Conference and wrote a constitutional study of the war. He again served in Congress (1873-1882) and then as Georgia's governor (1882).

Steuart, George H. ("Maryland Steuart")
(1828-1903) **Confederate general**

This Maryland-born West Point graduate served on the Utah Expedition and as an Indian fighter before resigning from the U.S. Army in 1861. Appointed a lieutenant colonel in the Confederate cavalry, he fought at First Bull Run and in the 1862 Shenandoah Valley Campaign, at Gettysburg, the Wilderness, Spotsylvania and Petersburg. A brigadier general since 1862, he was captured at Spotsylvania but exchanged in time to lead a brigade at Petersburg. He farmed in Maryland after the war.

Stevens, Thaddeus
(1792-1868) **Radical Republican**

This Dartmouth graduate settled in Pennsylvania in 1816. An uncompromising abolitionist lawyer and Congressman (Whig 1849-1853, Republican 1859-1868), Stevens was a formidable debater, famous for the ferocity of his oratory. He opposed the Compromise of 1850 and the Fugitive Slave Law. As wartime chairman of the House Ways and Means Committee, he controlled military appropriations, providing the government critical financial support. A founder and leader of the Radical Republicans, he advocated harsh treatment of the Confederates during and after the war. He was instrumental in securing passage of the Civil Rights, Freedmen's Bureau and radical Reconstruction Acts and in the impeachment of President Johnson.

Thaddeus Stevens (above) and (below) George H. Steuart

Carter Littlepage Stevenson

Stevenson, Carter Littlepage
(1817-1888) **Confederate general**

This Virginian career officer trained at West Point and served in the Seminole and Mexican wars and on the frontier. He joined the Confederate army, becoming a brigadier general in March 1862 and a major general the following October. After fighting with Braxton Bragg in Tennessee and Kentucky, he commanded Confederate troops in the Vicksburg Campaign, at Chickamauga and Missionary Ridge and in the Atlanta, Nashville and Carolinas campaigns. He was later a civil and mining engineer.

Stone, Charles Pomeroy
(1824-1887) **Union general**

This Massachusetts-born West Point graduate served in the Mexican War and then resigned from the army in 1856 to engage in business in Mexico. He was a banker in San Francisco when the Civil War began and accepted a U.S. commission as a colonel. He was promoted to brigadier general in May 1861 and led the capture of Alexandria, Virginia. His brigade and division became known by his name, but after the Union's disaster at Balls Bluff (October 1861), Stone was arrested and held in prison for over six months; although never charged, he was suspected of treason. He

returned to service but remained under suspicion and so resigned in 1864. From 1869 to 1883 he was in Egypt, serving as its army's chief of staff. Later he served as chief engineer for the building of the pedestal of the Statue of Liberty.

Stoneman, George
(1822-1894) Union general

He was graduated from West Point in 1846, fought in Mexico and served on several southwestern expeditions. Stoneman commanded the Union Army of the Potomac's cavalry division during the Peninsular Campaign and the newly established Cavalry Corps at Chancellorsville. Leading W. T. Sherman's cavalry during the Atlanta Campaign, he and 700 of his troopers were captured on what is known as Stoneman's Macon Raid.

Stowe, Harriet Elizabeth Beecher
(1811-1896) Abolitionist author

ABOVE: Charles Pomeroy Stone.

BELOW: George Stoneman (4th from rt.)

Born in Litchfield, Connecticut, she moved with her family to Cincinnati in 1832 and as a schoolteacher there began writing stories and sketches. Her antislavery novel *Uncle Tom's Cabin* (1851-1852) sold over a million copies in 10 years and was the subject of numerous dramatizations. Reviled by Southerners, it became a potent abolitionist weapon in the North and did much to define and solidify pro- and antislavery camps. The novel made Stowe an international celebrity, a position she used to raise large sums for the antislavery movement. Her later works include *Dred* (1856), another antislavery novel. A leading lecturer in later years, she lived after 1863 in Hartford, Connecticut.

Stuart, James Ewell Brown "Jeb"
(1833-1864) Confederate general

"Jeb" Stuart was born at Laurel Hill plantation, Patrick County, Virginia, the seventh of 10 children of a prosperous family. His father, Archibald Stuart, served a term in the U.S. Congress. Educated at home and at Emory and Henry College, young Jeb entered West Point in 1850. He proved to be a popular cadet, generally well-behaved and quietly religious, though prone to fighting (He seems to have been

beaten more often than he prevailed in his many brawls.) He was graduated in 1854, 13th of his class of 46.

Stuart served in Texas and Kansas, where he crossed paths with the radical abolitionist John Brown: during a leave of absence in 1859 he accompanied Robert E. Lee to Harpers Ferry as a volunteer aide and helped identify Brown as the leader of the raid on the U.S. armory there. In January 1861, as the secession crisis deepened, he wrote Jefferson Davis to request a commission in the "Army of the South."

He fought at First Manassas/Bull Run on July 21, 1861, as colonel of the 1st Virginia Cavalry, leading his troopers in a timely charge that contributed to the Confederate victory. Promoted to brigadier general in September, he brought his enlarged command to a peak of efficiency over the autumn and winter. His brigade effectively screened the army during the withdrawal up the Virginia peninsula in May 1862. On June 11, in an operation that began with a request from Robert E. Lee to report on Federal positions, Stuart set out on his first ride around the Army of the Potomac. He returned four days later with 165 prisoners and 260 captured horses and mules – a morale-building victory for the Confeder-

LEFT: Harriet Beecher Stowe.

BELOW: An 1862 Cavalry skirmish during "Stuart's First Ride Around McClellan."

ABOVE: James Ewell Brown Stuart.

RIGHT: Jeb Stuart's battlefield gravestone.

of effort into playing the part. He always rode a magnificent charger. He wore a fine gray cloak, trimmed in red, and a cavalier's cocked hat with a gilt star and a long peacock's plume. He enjoyed music and dancing and cutting a figure at parties and balls, though he discouraged drinking and his jollifications were nearly always temperate. He led a stolidly conventional private life, quite at odds with his romantic appearance.

Though his critics accused him of glory-hunting, Stuart's reputation rested on solid ground. He was Lee's best source of information on his adversarys' movements – the "eyes of the army," Lee called him. In December 1862 he carried out several strikes against Union General Ambrose Burnside's lines of communication, including the elaborate Dumfries Raid at year's end. In a six-day excursion, Stuart's troopers skirmished, stole horses and seized or burned supplies, and returned to the Confederate lines with some 200 prisoners. He skilfully held the Rappahannock outposts during the winter of 1862-63 and kept Lee fully informed of Union General Joseph Hooker's operations in the initial phases of the Chancellorsville Campaign in late April 1863. He handled the II Corps efficiently after Stonewall Jackson's fatal wounding on the night of May 2. But Lee did not retain Stuart in corps command, evidently because he found him irreplaceable as his chief of cavalry.

Stuart's troopers recovered from a surprise dawn strike from the much-improved ates and an embarrassment for George McClellan's Union army.

Stuart was promoted to major general in July and given command of all the cavalry in the Army of Northern Virginia. During the preliminary phases of the Second Manassas/Bull Run Campaign he raided Federal commander John Pope's headquarters, making off with important documents and one of Pope's uniforms. His Chambersburg, Pennsylvania, raid of October 9-12, 1862, further embellished his popular reputation for brilliance and dash. In this second ride around the Union army, Stuart's 1,800 troopers covered 126 miles – the final 80 miles without a halt – and returned with another 500 captured horses.

These early exploits confirmed Jeb Stuart one of the great heroes of the Confederacy. A striking figure, with his flowing beard and powerful build, he put a lot

Federal cavalry at Brandy station on June 9, 1863, to fight a drawn battle in the largest cavalry action of the war. Though the Federals lost nearly 1,000 men – twice Stuart's toll – they did learn that Lee had begun the northward march that would take him to Gettysburg. After Brandy Station, Stuart threw an impenetrable screen over Lee's flank, holding off the hard-charging Federals in engagements at Aldie, Middleburg and Upperville in mid-June.

With what he interpreted as Lee's full approval, Stuart set off on June 24 on his Gettysburg Raid, an ill-advised operation that nearly became the ruin of his reputation. Passing Hooker's rear and right flank, he crossed the Potomac and harried Federal communications in Maryland and Pennsylvania. He captured 125 new wagons, took 400 prisoners and fought skirmishes at Fairfax, Westminster, Hanover and Carlisle. But he had strayed a long way from Lee, and meantime Hooker's (soon to be George Meade's) army had gotten between him and the Army of Northern Virginia. He thus left Lee in ignorance of the enemy's whereabouts for several critical days that culminated in the fateful Battle of Gettysburg. It is said that this was the only time Lee ever showed displeasure with him.

Stuart's cavalry covered Lee's movements during the Wilderness Campaign in May 1864. On May 9, Stuart led 4,500 troopers in pursuit of the 12,000-strong Federal Cavalry Corps under Philip Sheridan. Setting a furious pace, his command reached Yellow Tavern just ahead of Sheridan early on May 11 and took up a position astride the Richmond road. The Confederates turned Sheridan away from the direct route to the capital after an all-day fight, but at the cost of Stuart. He was shot in the abdomen late in the afternoon and died in Richmond the following day. "He never brought me a false piece of information," Lee said when he learned of Stuart's death.

Sturgis, Samuel Davis
(1822-1889) Union general

This Pennsylvania-born West Point alumnus and career officer served in the Mexican War, on the frontier and in Indian fighting. When his officers resigned to join the Confederate army in April 1861, he saved Fort Smith, Arkansas, for the Union. He commanded the defenses of Washington, D.C., and fought at Second Bull Run, South Mountain, Antietam, Fredericksburg and in Kansas, Tennessee and Mississippi. He attracted criticism for his actions at Wilson's Creek, and his disas-

trous loss to Nathan B. Forrest at Brice's Cross Roads in June 1864 was the subject of an official investigation. After the war he was a cavalry commander and Indian fighter: he retired from the army in 1886.

Sumner, Charles
(1811-1874) U.S. Senator

Born in Massachusetts and educated at Harvard Law School, this Massachusetts lawyer and orator was first elected to the U.S. Senate (1851-1874) on the strength of his antislavery views. As a Radical Republican Senator, Sumner was an uncompromising abolitionist whose fiery oratory made him profoundly influential. Narrowly surviving a retaliatory beating on the Senate floor in 1856 after denouncing a South Carolina member, he maintained his staunch advocacy of emancipation and equal rights for blacks throughout and after the war.

Surratt, John and Mary
Confederate conspirators (?)

John Surratt served the Confederacy as a dispatch rider and spy in the early years of the war. His mother Mary ran a Washington boardinghouse that served as the meet-

Charles Sumner, Massachusetts Senator and staunch abolitionist

ing place where John Wilkes Booth and his conspirators planned the murder of Abraham Lincoln. John Surratt fled to Canada after the assassination. His mother was arrested, accused of conspiracy, convicted by a military court and hanged on July 7, 1865, though she appears to have been innocent of any involvement in the plot. Her son returned to the U.S. in 1867; his trial ended in a hung jury. John Surratt later settled in Maryland and worked as a clerk. He died in 1916.

Swinton, William
(1833-1892) War correspondent

Born in Scotland, he emigrated with his family to Canada in 1843. As a young *New York Times* reporter he was sent to the front as a special war correspondent in 1862. His constant verbal attacks on generals and his underhanded methods of news-gathering – including eavesdropping on a Meade-Grant conference during the 1864 Virginia campaign – finally led the War Department to ban him from the field in July 1864. He later wrote several books about the war, as well as many textbooks.

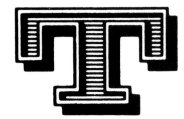

Taliaferro, William Booth
(1822-1898) **Confederate general**

He studied law at Harvard and fought in the Mexican War, returning home to sit in the Virginia legislature. In the Confederate army he served with distinction in 1862 under Stonewall Jackson in the Shenan-

Roger Brooke Taney

doah Valley and led the Stonewall Brigade at Cedar Mountain, Second Bull Run and Fredericksburg. He later commanded at Fort Wagner and James Island, ending the war a major general. He surrendered with J. E. Johnston (April 1865) and resumed his Virginia law and political career.

Taney, Roger Brooke
(1777-1864)
Chief justice of the Supreme Court

Born into a wealthy Maryland family, he became a lawyer and prominent Federalist in his home state. He was U.S. attorney general (1831-1833) and acting secretary of the treasury (1833-1834). He closely advised President Andrew Jackson during the "bank war" in these years. Taney became chief justice of the U.S. Supreme Court in 1836, and during his 28-year tenure ruled on cases that highlighted the growing North-South rift. The most explosive of these was *Dred Scott v. Sandford* (1857), in which the court held blacks to be unentitled to sue in the federal courts and Congress to be powerless to outlaw slavery in the territories. The case is generally regarded as one cause of the Civil War.

Tattnall, Josiah
(1795-1871) **Confederate commodore**

This Georgian began his long naval career in 1812. He fought West Indian pirates and was wounded in the Mexican War. Opposed to secession, he nevertheless accepted a Confederate naval captaincy and directed coastal defenses. As commander of CSS *Virginia* (formerly *Merrimac*) after her fight with USS *Monitor*, he ordered her destruction during the evacuation of Norfolk. He later challenged the Federal blockade and defended the Savannah River until Savannah fell (December 1864). He surrendered with J. E. Johnston. He was later port inspector of Savannah.

Taylor, Richard
(1826-1879) **Confederate general**

Zachary Taylor's son, he was born in Kentucky and educated in Edinburgh and France before graduation from Yale. He became a Louisiana planter, legislator and secessionist. As a Confederate brigadier general he led the Louisiana Brigade in the Shenandoah Valley Campaign of 1862 and in the Peninsular Campaign. As a major general (July 1862) he commanded the District of Western Louisiana, where he stopped Nathaniel Banks's Red River Campaign of 1864 with a victory at Sabine Cross Roads, earning a promotion to lieutenant general. Taylor commanded other Gulf departments before surrendering the last Confederate army east of the Mississippi to Edward Canby in May 1865. His *Destruction and Reconstruction* (1879) is a highly regarded military memoir.

Terry, Alfred Howe
(1827-1890) **Union general**

This Yale-educated lawyer was a New Haven, Connecticut, court clerk before the war. He served the Union at First Bull Run, led the 7th Connecticut in the Port Royal Expedition (November 1861), helped to capture Fort Pulaski (April 1862) and led a division in the attack on Fort Wagner (summer 1863). He later held James Army corps commands. He received the Thanks of Congress for his greatest wartime achievement, the taking of Fort Fisher in January 1865. Later a famous Indian fighter he directed the campaign against the Sioux in 1876 and himself led one of the three U.S. columns, that approaching from the east. Part of his command was George A. Custer's 7th Cavalry, soon to become famous for its part in the Battle of the Little Big Horn.

ABOVE: George Henry Thomas.

BELOW: Chickamauga, the battle that made Thomas's name a household word.

Thomas, George Henry
(1816-1870) Union general

The Virginia-born Thomas studied law briefly before obtaining an appointment to West Point, where he was graduated with W. T. Sherman and R. S. Ewell in the class of 1840. Commissioned into the artillery, he joined his unit in Florida and took part in the campaign against the Seminole Indians there. He later served in several garrisons in the South.

Thomas saw extensive action during the Mexican War, earning brevets for gallantry at Monterey and Buena Vista. He returned to Florida after the war, taught gunnery and cavalry tactics for three years at West Point and did garrison duty in California and Arizona. He later served in Texas with the 2nd Cavalry, whose officers' roll included many soon-to-be-famous names, A. S. Johnston, Robert E. Lee and Fitzhugh Lee among them. Wounded in an Indian skirmish, he was on convalescent leave when the Civil War began.

Though a Virginian, Thomas remained loyal to the Union. He commanded a brigade in the Shenandoah Valley in the early weeks of the war and went to Kentucky in August 1861 to organize new troops. He then took command of the 1st Division, Army of the Ohio, and led it to victory at Mill Springs (also known as Logan's Cross Roads) in January 1862. He commanded the division at Shiloh in April and during the advance on Corinth, Mississippi, later in the spring.

He returned to Kentucky for the campaign against Braxton Bragg. He declined an offer to succeed the army commander, Don Carlos Buell, who had fallen into disfavor; he was Buell's second in command at Perryville in October 1862. In late October, when William Rosecrans replaced Buell, Thomas took command of XIV Corps in what was now styled the Army of the Cumberland. He led the corps competently at Stones River at the year's end and in the 1863 Tullahoma Campaign.

A large, powerfully built man, he had a reputation for deliberateness that earned him the nickname "Slow Trot." His troops, who greatly admired him, also called him "Pap." He won his most famous nickname at Chickamauga Creek on September 20, 1863. There Thomas held out

for several hours against a violent Confederate attack, enabling the broken remnants of William Rosecran's other formations to retreat safely into Chattanooga. Henceforth, he was known as "the Rock of Chickamauga."

Ulysses S. Grant, newly appointed to the supreme command in the West, relieved Rosecrans and put Thomas in his place at the head of the Cumberland army. His first order to Thomas directed him to hold besieged Chattanooga at all hazards against the Confederate siege. "We will hold the town till we starve," Thomas answered. He did so until, with reinforcements, Grant managed to reopen a supply line and prepare for offensive operations. On November 25, 1863, Thomas's command stormed

Missionary Ridge, routing the Confederates under Bragg and forcing them out of Tennessee altogether.

Thomas marched with W. T. Sherman for Atlanta in the spring of 1864; elements of the Cumberland army received the surrender of the city on September 2. When Sherman set out on his March to the Sea, he left Thomas behind to oppose the Army of Tennessee, now under John B. Hood. Hood went off in the opposite direction to that of Sherman. Thomas's field force checked him at Franklin, Tennessee, on November 30, then retreated into the Nashville lines.

Grant ordered an immediate offensive against Hood. Thomas delayed, protesting he was not yet strong enough. Grant decided to relieve him. He stayed the order, then reissued it when Thomas still

failed to act. Grant actually ordered a replacement to Nashville, but before he could arrive, Thomas had fought the Battle of Nashville, one of the most crushing victories of the entire war: in two days of fighting, December 15 and 16, Hood's army was all but destroyed.

Thomas remained in command in Tennessee through the end of the war and into the early postwar period. He took charge of the Military Department of the Pacific in 1869 and died of apoplexy on active service in San Francisco in March 1870.

Thompson, Meriwether Jeff
(1826-1876) **Confederate general**

Virginia-born Thompson was the mayor of St. Joseph, Missouri, at the outbreak of the Civil War. After organizing a Confederate battalion in 1861, he inaugurated a notable war career leading his so-called "Swamp Rats" on border raids against J. C. Frémont's forces in southeastern Missouri. He later fought with Earl Van Dorn in the Transmississippi, and in 1864 he led Shelby's Brigade in Sterling Price's Missouri Raid. An eccentric but brilliant leader and a daring scout, he was a brigadier general by the end of the war. He surrendered in Arkansas in May 1865.

Tompkins, Sally Louisa
(1833-1916) **Confederate nurse**

Daughter of a wealthy Virginia family, even as a young woman she was noted for her care of the sick. As soon as the Civil

Meriwether Jeff Thompson

Sally Louisa Tompkins

War broke out she began a hospital in Richmond; so successful was she that she was made a captain by Jefferson Davis when the Confederate government took over medical services – the only woman ever given a regular commission by the Confederate army. After the war she continued to engage in charitable work and was always treated by Confederate veterans as one of them.

Toombs, Robert Augustus
(1810-1885) Confederate general

He studied law at the University of Virginia and returned to his native Georgia, where he was a planter, lawyer and politician. In the U.S. Congress (1845-1853) and Senate (1853-1861), Toombs consistently supported compromise measures, finally turning secessionist after the failure of the Crittenden Compromise in 1860. After losing the Southern presidency to Jefferson Davis, he was briefly and unhappily secre-

Robert Augustus Toombs

tary of state in the provisional Confederate government before joining the army in July 1861. Opposed to the South's defensive strategy and denied promotion after Malvern Hill and Antietam, he resigned in March 1863. He returned to his legal and political career after the war and opposed Radical Reconstruction in Georgia.

Townsend, George Alfred
(1841-1914) War correspondent

This Delaware native reported the Seven Days' Battles and Cedar Mountain for the *New York Herald*, then promoted the Union cause in articles and lectures in England (1862-1863). He became famous for his fine New York *World* coverage of the last battles of the war and of Lincoln's assassination. After 1867 he lived mostly in Washington, D.C., publishing political and social commentary under the pseudonym "Gath" in nearly 100 newspapers. In 1896 he erected a monument to 157 Civil War correspondents on the South Mountain battlefield.

Isaac Ridgeway Trimble

Trimble, Isaac Ridgeway
(1802-1888) Confederate general

This Kentuckian was graduated from West Point and spent 10 years as an army surveyor before resigning to become a railroad engineer. He disrupted Union supplies in 1861 by destroying railroad bridges north of Baltimore. As a Confederate army engineer, he constructed Potomac River batteries and fought in the Shenandoah Valley Campaign of Jackson, the Seven Days' Battles and at Second Bull Run (wounded). Leading a division in "Pickett's Charge" at Gettysburg, he lost a leg and was captured; he was imprisoned until February 1865. He was later a Baltimore engineer.

Tubman, Harriet
(1820?-1913) Abolitionist

She was born into slavery on a plantation in Dorchester County, Maryland, the granddaughter of Africans brought to America chained in the holds of slave ships. She worked as a house servant, nursing children and doing maid's chores, and as a fieldhand. She evidently was a refractory servant and was often punished: an overseer once struck her in the head with a heavy object, doing her an injury from whose ill effects she suffered intermittently for the rest of her long life.

She married a free black, John Tubman, in about 1844 and in the late 1840s worked in the household of a Methodist parson. She made her escape to free soil in 1849, leaving behind her husband, who declined

Harriet Tubman (far left), shown with some slaves she helped to escape

to accompany her. She soon discovered her true vocation: helping slaves escape to the free states. She made nearly 20 trips into Maryland in the 1850s. No exact accounting is possible, but estimates of the number of slaves she escorted north range from 60 to 300.

Tubman operated much as a secret agent would, setting out on trips south from her home base in St. Catharines, Ontario. She passed easily as an ordinary slavewoman traveling on her master's business. She carried a handgun for her own protection and – it was said – to encourage prospective runaways afflicted with 11th-hour doubts. She announced her coming with oracular messages: "Tell my brothers to be always watching unto prayer," ran one, "and when the good old ship of Zion comes along, to be ready to step on board." Her success caught the attention of Maryland slaveholders. Rewards of as much as $40,000 were offered for her capture.

She was plain-looking, uneducated, deeply religious. "Harriet was a woman of no pretensions, indeed, a more ordinary specimen of humanity could hardly be found among the most unfortunate-looking farm-hands of the South," an abolition colleague wrote of her. "Yet, in point of courage, shrewdness and disinterested

exertions to rescue her fellowmen, she was without her equal." She believed her actions were guided by a providential hand, and she remained always attentive to dreams and omens that might reveal the divine purpose.

Well known in abolition circles, Tubman became a regular speaker at anti-slavery conventions. In 1858 she advised John Brown as he planned his Harpers Ferry raid. (He afterwards referred to her as General Tubman.) At around this time William Seward, the Republican abolitionist leader, sold her the small farm near Auburn, New York, that would be her home for the rest of her life.

Tubman actively served the Union cause in the Civil War. In early 1862 she traveled to Beaufort, South Carolina, recently siezed by Federal forces, to volunteer as a spy and scout. She collected intelligence from slaves behind the Confederate lines and assisted newly freed slaves in Beaufort. Toward the war's end she worked as a nurse at a freedmen's hospital at Fortress Monroe, Virginia. The great abolition leader Frederick Douglass saluted her for her contributions. "Excepting John Brown," he wrote her in 1868, "I know of no one who has willingly encountered more perils and hardships to serve our enslaved people than you have."

Returning to her farm after the war, Tubman established the Harriet Tubman

Home for Indigent Aged Negroes, promoted educational opportunity for freedmen and proselytized for the African Methodist Episcopal Church. A short biography, *Harriet Tubman: The Moses of Her People*, appeared in 1869; the author, Sarah Bradford, donated the royalties to her. But she had barely a subsistence income, and in the late 1860s she began her long campaign for payment for her wartime services. She kept at the government for nearly three decades before Congress finally granted her a small monthly pension.

She died of pneumonia in March 1913.

Tucker, John Randolph
(1812-1883)
Confederate naval commander

The Virginian Tucker began his long naval career in 1826. During the Civil War, as a Confederate commander, he directed the James River defenses, commanding the gunboat *Patrick Henry* at Hampton Roads. He later attacked the Federal blockade and commanded a squadron at Charleston and the fleet off Drewry's Bluff. He destroyed his ships when Charleston was evacuated and created a naval brigade which fought at Sayler's Creek. He was later a rear admiral in the Peruvian navy and in 1873 led an Amazon surveying expedition.

Turchin, John Basil
(1822-1901) Union general

Born Ivan Vasilevitch Turchinoff in Russia, he fought in the Crimean War before emigrating in 1856 to Chicago, where he became a raildroad engineer. Joining the Union's 19th Illisnois in 1861, he served in Missouri, Kentucky and Alabama and fought at Stones River, Chickamauga and Missionary Ridge. Turchin's wife accompanied him as a nurse throughout his campaigns, once even leading his regiment into battle. He resigned in October 1864. He established the Polish farming community of Radom, Illinois (1873).

Turner, Nat
(1800-1831) Slave leader

Born into slavery on a plantation in Southampton County, Virginia, he found a vocation as a gospel preacher. Convincing slaves on his own and neighboring plantations that he was divinely inspired to lead them in revolt, he touched off a short, violent insurrection on August 21, 1831, in

The capture of Nat Turner

which more than 50 whites were murdered. Troops quickly restored order and killed or captured the rebellious slaves. Turner remained at large for several weeks but was taken, tried and condemned; he was hanged on November 11, 1831. Fifteen of his supporters were also put to death. The insurrection had widespread repercussions in the South, leading to a strengthening of the slave codes and the erosion of support for gradual emancipation.

Twiggs, David Emanuel
(1790-1862) Confederate general

The son of a Revolutionary War general, he entered the army in 1812 and saw service during the war with Britain. After a long period out of uniform, he returned in 1825. Twiggs fought in Mexico in 1846 and 1847 and served as a department commander, mainly in the South, during the 1850s. In February 1861, in command in Texas, Twiggs surrendered all Union troops and stores to the Confederates. Though he entered Confederate service, he never took the field for the Confederacy. He died near his birthplace outside Augusta, Georgia, in July 1862.

Upton, Emory
(1839-1881) Union general

This New Yorker was commissioned second lieutenant upon his 1861 West Point graduation. He saw continuous action with the Union's Army of the Potomac from 1861 to 1864, then joined the Army of the Shenandoah in fighting at Opequon and in Alabama and Georgia. Several times wounded and repeatedly cited for gallantry, he became one of the Federals' leading tacticians and most celebrated war heroes. He was West Point commandant of cadets (1870-1875). He committed suicide while commanding the Presidio, San Francisco. His military works include the outstanding *Military Policy of the United States* (posthumously published in 1904).

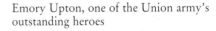

Emory Upton, one of the Union army's outstanding heroes

Vallandigham, Clement Laird
(1820-1871) Democratic politician

He was an Ohio lawyer, journalist and Democratic politician who strenuously opposed the war. As a U.S. Congressman (1858-1863), he was prominent among the "Copperheads," or Peace Democrats, and tried to obstruct war-related legislation. Abraham Lincoln banished him to the

Clement Laird Vallandigham

South after his conviction of treason in 1863 for speaking against the war in defiance of a military prohibition. Vallandigham re-entered the North via Canada and campaigned vigorously against Lincoln's re-election in 1864, while hurting the Democrats' chances by inserting an antiwar plank in their election platform. He opposed Reconstruction policies, but his influence on both political parties and on the public at large was waning and never revived.

Van Dorn, Earl
(1820-1863) Confederate general

An 1842 West Point graduate, he fought in Mexico and in many Indian campaigns. He took command of the Confederate Transmississippi Department early in 1862. Van Dorn's army was beaten at Pea Ridge, Arkansas, in March, and in October William Rosecrans inflicted a serious defeat on his forces at Corinth, Mississippi. A commission absolved Van Dorn of any blame in the Corinth defeat, and he led John Pemberton's cavalry at Holly Springs, Mississippi, in December. Van Dorn was shot and killed in May 1863 by a man who accused him of carrying on an affair with his wife.

Van Lew, Elizabeth L.
(1818-1900) Union spy

A Virginian educated in Philadelphia, she early opposed slavery. Ardently Unionist, Van Lew lived in Richmond throughout the war, and in addition to her relief work at Libby Prison she both gathered vital intelligence for the Union and helped Federal prisoners to escape. Disguising her spying with eccentric behavior, she earned the nickname "Crazy Bet." Her role became known after the war, and she was an outcast in Richmond society until her death.

Velazquez, Loreta Janeta
(1842?-1897)
Confederate officer and spy

Born in Cuba to an aristocratic Spanish family, she was educated in New Orleans. The wife of a U.S. Army officer (married 1856), she accompanied her husband into the Confederate army, raising and leading a volunteer battalion disguised as "Lieutenant Harry Buford." After her husband was killed early in the war, she fought at First Bull Run and Fort Donelson. She was unmasked in 1863 but continued to spy behind Federal lines. She later wrote *The Woman in Battle* (1876).

Villard, Henry
(1835-1900) War correspondent

Born in Bavaria, he emigrated Illinois and studied law before becoming a journalist. In an 1861 scoop he reported W. T. Sherman's views on the Union's lack of preparedness and the probable scope of the war, leading Union authorities to judge Sherman unbalanced and remove him from command of the Kentucky Department. Villard later reported for Horace Greely's *New York Tribune* and became one of the war's leading correspondents. He married a daughter of the famous abolitionist leader William Lloyd Garrison.

Von Steinwehr, Adolph
(1822-1877) Union general

Born into a Prussian military family, he came to America to fight in the Mexican War and later became a farmer in Connecticut. Chosen colonel of the Union's all-German 29th New York at the outbreak of war, Von Steinwehr led a brigade at the Second Battle of Bull Run and a division at Chancellorsville and Gettysburg. He briefly commanded XI Corps in Virginia and Tennessee. He taught military science at Yale after the war.

Mary Edwards Walker

Waddell, James Iredell
(1824-1886) **Confederate naval officer**

This North Carolinian, a career officer, became a midshipman in 1841. He returned from Asia at the outbreak of the Civil War and enlisted in the Confederate navy in March 1862. He helped to turn back a Union flotilla supporting the Peninsular Campaign, then joined the battery at Charleston. As commander of the raider *Shenandoah* after October 1864, he secured a number of prizes in the Pacific, some after the war ended (for he had not heard of the Confederate surrender). He became a civilian skipper after the war.

Wade, Benjamin Franklin
(1800-1878)
Radical Republican Senator

Born in Massachusetts, Wade practiced law in Ohio and became a strong abolitionist in the Republican party. As a U.S. Senator,

Benjamin Franklin Wade

Wade joined Representative Henry W. Davis in drafting a Reconstruction plan in 1864 that opposed Abraham Lincoln's policies, which they felt to be too moderate. After Lincoln vetoed the plan, Wade and Davis wrote a manifesto denouncing him. Not surprisingly, Wade later opposed President Andrew Johnson's moderate Reconstruction policies.

Walker, Leroy Page
(1817-1884) **Confederate general and secretary of war**

A lawyer, outspoken secessionist and Democratic power in Alabama, he was chosen for the sake of regional balance to be the first Confederate secretary of war (February-September 1861). Inexperienced and overwhelmed, he resigned in broken health and was commissioned brigadier general but, denied a field command, resigned in March 1862. He presided over an Alabama military court during the last year of the war, later returning to his Huntsville law practice and political deal-making.

Walker, Mary Edwards
(1831-1919) **Union surgeon**

This New Yorker was certified by Syracuse Medical College in 1855. For the first three years of the Civil War she was an army nurse and sometime spy. In 1864 she was commissioned as the first woman assistant surgeon in the U.S. Army: she dressed like her male colleagues in trousers and a greatcoat (she wore male dress throughout her life). After the war she was a Washington, D.C., physician, inventor and active suffragist.

Wallace, Lewis
(1827-1905) **Union general**

Indiana-born Wallace had a varied career in politics, journalism and the law before the war. He fought for the Union at Romney and Harpers Ferry, and, earning rapid promotions (brigadier general Sepember 1861, major general March 1862), he led divisions

infantry regiment, and later a brigade, early in the war, then became chief engineer of the Army of the Potomac, playing a decisive role at Gettysburg in directing reinforcements to the Federeal left on Little Round Top. Warren commanded V Corps at the Wilderness, Spotsylvania, Cold Harbor and Petersburg. Philip Sheridan relieved him for lack of aggressiveness during the Appomattox Campaign; a court of inquiry cleared him of Sheridan's charges in 1881.

ABOVE: Stand Watie

Lewis Wallace (above) and (right) Gouverneur Kemble Warren

at Fort Donelson and Shiloh and saved Cincinnati from Edmund Kirby Smith. He led VIII Corps at Monocacy, where, although he lost the battle, he was commended by Ulysses Grant for saving Washington, D.C., from capture. His substantial administrative service included the courts martial of Abraham Lincoln's assassins and Andersonville Prison commandant Henry Wirz. A prolific novelist, "Lew" Wallace became famous for his *The Fair God* (1873) and more so for his *Ben Hur* (1880). He was governor of New Mexico (1878-1881) and minister to Turkey (1881-1885).

Warren, Gouverneur Kemble
(1830-1882) Union general

An 1850 West Point graduate, he joined the army engineer corps and later taught mathematics at the academy. He led a Union

Watie, Stand
(1806-1871)
Cherokee leader, Confederate general

His father was a full-blooded Cherokee and his mother half-Indian. He attended mission schools in Georgia, where he grew up to become a fairly prosperous planter, as well as the publisher of a newspaper for the Cherokee. He was one of four Cherokee who signed a treaty in 1835 agreeing to give up their tribal lands in Georgia and to move to Oklahoma; some Cherokee who bitterly opposed this killed the three other signers (including Watie's brother), but he escaped and became the chief of the Cherokee who supported the treaty. When the Civil War broke out, a number of Cherokee formed an alliance with the Confederacy, and Watie was commissioned a captain and assigned command of a Cherokee unit in the Confederate army. As a colonel, he led his unit, the Cherokee Mounted

Rifles, through several battles, including Pea Ridge (Elkhorn Tavern), Arkansas. In 1863 most of the Cherokee repudiated the alliance with the Confederacy, but Watie still upheld it, thus becoming the effective chief of those Cherokee who stayed with the Confederacy. In May 1864 he was promoted to brigadier general, and he was one of the last Confederate generals to surrender (June 1865). After the war he went back to being a planter.

Waud, Alfred R.
(1818-1891) War artist, correspondent

Waud was the principal war artist for *Harper's Weekly* and produced hundreds of sketches from the frontlines, depicting some of the war's most important events. Because of the state of mid-nineteenth century printing technology, few of Waud's contemporaries ever saw his original sketches reproduced, but only hasty and often coarse wood-block prints made from them by *Harper's* engravers. Many of his sketches survive, however, and continue to provide an invaluable record of the Civil War. (His brother William was also a war artist.)

RIGHT: Alfred R. Waud.

BELOW: A Waud sketch of Fair Oaks.

Webb, Alexander Stewart
(1835-1911) Union general

This New York-born West Point graduate, having served in the Seminole War and taught at West Point, was commissioned a lieutenant in the Union artillery in April 1861. He served at First Bull Run, Yorktown, Mechanicsville, Gaines's Mill, Malvern Hill, Antietam, Chancellorsville, Gettysburg, and the Wilderness and Spotsylvania, where he was wounded. Due to his injuries, he was out of service until January 1865 but returned to duty for the end of the siege of Petersburg. He was breveted a major general and remained in the regular army until 1870. He received a Medal of Honor for his role at Gettysburg, and his statue stands at the Bloody Angle, Spotsylvania. He long served as president of City College of New York (1869-1902).

Alexander Stewart Webb (standing right of flagpole, center of tent entrance)

Weisiger, David Adams
(?-1899) Confederate general

Weisiger served in the Mexican War and then, while a merchant, in the Virginia militia. Assigned the rank of colonel, he led the Confederate forces that seized the Norfolk Navy Yard. He fought at Seven Pines, Charles City Cross Roads, the Seven Days' Battles, Second Bull Run, the Wilderness and Petersburg. He was wounded at Second Bull Run and was promoted to brigadier general in November 1864 for his service in Petersburg. He was wounded three times at Appomattox and lost two horses before finally surrendering there.

Welles, Gideon
(1802-1878)
Union secretary of the navy

A Connecticut native, he edited the *Hartford Times* (1826-1836) and brought much public service experience to Washington as

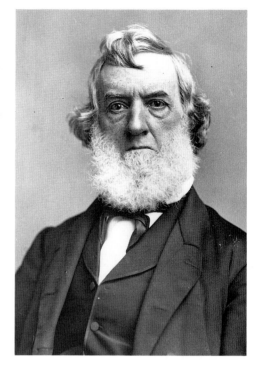

ABOVE: Gideon Welles

secretary of the navy (1861-1869). Welles served ably throughout the war. Despite a serious loss of personnel to the Confederates, Welles quickly established a Federal shipbuilding program and assembled a navy (during the war he increased Union naval strength from 90 to 670 ships and from 9000 to 57,000 men). He defined strategy, promoted new technology, including ironclad ships, and enforced the blockade of the South. The Union's naval successes made him influential in Lincoln's cabinet. His *Diary* (3 vols., 1911) is an important Civil War record. He later founded the *Hartford Evening Press*, one of New England's earliest Republican newspapers.

Wheat, Chatham Roberdeau
(1826-1862) **Confederate officer**

An Episcopal minister's son, he saw action in the Mexican War, practiced law and

Joseph Wheeler

politics in New Orleans, fought in Nicaragua during the Walker filibuster in 1856 and served with Garibaldi's army in Italy. Wheat returned home in time to lead the Louisiana Tigers battalion at First Bull Run, where he was shot through both lungs. "I don't feel like dying yet," he said when told he had been mortally wounded. Wheat recovered, fought with Jackson in the Valley but was killed at Gaines's Mill in June.

Wheeler, Joseph
(1836-1906)
Confederate cavalry officer

This Georgian was graduated close to the bottom of his West Point class. He left frontier fighting when the war broke out. He fought for the Confederacy at Shiloh, Perryville and Stones River, reorganized and commanded the Army of the Mississippi's cavalry and led raids against Federal communications. One such raid on Union

supply lines (October 1-9, 1863) nearly forced the besieged Federals in Chattanooga to evacuate th city. He wrote *Cavalry Tactics* (1863). By spring 1864 he was the senior Confederate cavalry officer. He participated in the Knoxville and Atlanta campaigns and fought W. T. Sherman during his March to the Sea. "Fightin' Joe" was said to have fought in 1000 engagements and skirmishes before his capture in May 1865. He represented Alabama in Congress (1880-1882, 1884-1899).

William Henry Chase Whiting

Whiting, William Henry Chase
(1824-1865) **Confederate general**

He was graduated at the head of his West Point class in 1845 and held engineering appointments in the old army. Joining the Confederate service, he planned the Charleston harbor defenses and led an infantry division during T. J. Jackson's Shenandoah Valley Campaign and on the Virginia peninsula in the spring and summer of 1862. Whiting later commanded the military district of Wilmington on the North Carolina coast. He was mortally wounded at Fort Fisher, North Carolina, in January 1865.

Whitman, Walt
(1819-1892) **Poet**

The second of nine children, born in West Hills, Long Island, New York, he moved with his family to Brooklyn, then a small city of 10,000 people, in 1823 and was educated in the public schools there. When he was about 13 years old he went to work,

Lincoln's funeral, inspiration for Walt Whitman's "When Lilacs in the Dooryard Bloom'd" and "Oh Captain! My Captain"

first as a lawyer's office boy and later as a printer's devil for the *Long Island Patriot*.

Whitman worked for newspapers as a compositor and sometime contributor during the first half of the 1830s and taught school in several Long Island communities in the latter years of the decade. He edited the *Long Islander* in Huntingdon in 1838-39 and began contributing verse to various other newspapers. People who knew him during these years described him variously as morose, lazy, untidy and rude to children. As one obsered, "He was a genius who lived, apparently, in a world of his own."

He moved restlessly from newspaper to newspaper during the 1840s. In 1841 the *Democratic Review*, a leading literary journal, began publishing his short stories: Nathaniel Hawthorne, Edgar Alen Poe and Henry David Thoreau were among the review's contributors. In January 1846 he became editor of the Brooklyn *Eagle*, and he used its editorial page to campaign for various reforms. His advocacy of the antislavery cause cost him his job early in 1848.

With his characteristic knack for finding jobs, Whitman landed a position as a writer on the New Orleans *Crescent* and journeyed south in the winter of 1848. He remained for only three months, however, returning to Brooklyn and a lonely, unstable freelancer's life. All the while he continued to write, and over the next few years he found his poetic voice. His *Leaves of Grass*, published in 1855, established him as

a leading poet. In an anonymous review of his own book, he described himself – as presented through the poems, one of which he later titled "Song of Myself" – as "of pure American breed, large and lusty, a naive, masculine, affectionate, contemplative, sensual, imperious person."

Though a critical success, *Leaves of Grass* was a commercial failure, and Whitman had to continue to support himself with newspaper work while producing more than a hundred new poems from 1856 to 1860. In them, he further developed the main themes of his work, love and death. The outbreak of Civil War gave both these themes a public dimension. The war had a tremendous imact on Whitman. In 1862 he published four articles on hospitals for a New York newspaper, and he wrote the first of the poems that would later appear in the *Drum Taps* collection. Then, late in the year, word came that his brother George had been wounded in Virginia, serving with the Union's 51st New York. Whitman found him in Falmouth, on the Rappahannock opposite Fredericksburg, where he had his first exposure to the immediate aftermath of the fighting.

He settled in Washington, D.C., and began to visit the wounded and sick in the city's military hospitals, distributing sweets, cool drinks and tobacco, reading to the convalescents and writing letters for them. "I can testify that friendship had literally cured a fever," he wrote, "and the medicine of daily effection, a bad wound."

Whitman's poem "A March in the Ranks Hard-Prest" is a poetic response to what he saw in a field hospital after the battle of Chancellorsville in May 1863:

Walt Whitman

Faces, varieties, postures beyond
   description, most in obscurity, some of
   them dead,
Surgeons operating, attendants holding
   lights, the smell of ether, the odor of
   blood,
The crowd, O the crowd of bloody
   forms, the yard outside also fill'd,
Some on the bare ground, some on
   planks or stretchers, some in the death-
   spasm sweating. . . .

Drum Taps appeared in 1865, with Whitman's most famous poem, "When Lilacs in the Dooryard Bloom'd," appended as a supplement. He brought out new editions of *Leaves of grass* in 1867 and 1871. Some of his collected prose, including wartime writings, appeared in *Specimen Days* (1882-83). By the 1870s Whitman had become a famous man of letters, though his critical reputation tended to fluctuate. He passed his last years quietly in Camden, New Jersey, where he died in March 1892.

Wickham, William Carter
(1820-1888) Confederate general

Born in Richmond, this Virginia planter, lawyer, and legislator opposed secession at his state's secession convention. At the outbreak of war he raised a Confederate cavalry company and fought steadily, participating at First Bull Run, on the Peninsula (wounded at Williamsburg) and under J. E. B. Stuart at Second Bull Run, Antietam, Fredericksburg, Chancellorsville and Gettysburg. Promoted to briga-

dier general (September 1863), he fought at the Wilderness, Spotsylvania and Cold Harbor, then joining Jubal Early for the fighting in the Shenandoah Valley. He resigned from the army in November 1864 to sit in the Confederate congress: he attended the Hampton Roads Peace Conference. After the war he was a Richmond lawyer and railroad president.

Wilcox, Cadmus Marcellus
(1824-1890) Confederate general

This North Carolina-born West Point graduate served in the Mexican and Seminole wars and taught at West Point; he was a member of Ulysses S. Grant's wedding party in 1848. He was stationed on the western frontier when he resigned to

William Carter Wickham (left) and (below) Cadmus Marcellus Wilcox

accept a commission in the Confederate army. He fought at First and Second Bull Run, on the Peninsula, at Fredericksburg, Chancellorsville, Bank's Ford, Gettysburg, the Wilderness, Spotsylvania and Petersburg, finally surrendering at Appomattox. He had been promoted to major general in 1863. After the war, he held government jobs in Washington and wrote and translated books on military subjects.

Wild, Edward Augustus
(1825-1891) Union general

Born in Massachusetts, he was a doctor who served as a medical officer in the Turkish army during the Crimean War. He was commissioned a U.S. Army captain in May 1861 and fought at First Bull Run. Wounded at Fair Oaks, he was mustered out in July 1862. He then helped to raise African-American forces in Massachusetts. Recommissioned as a brigadier general in April 1863, he led African-American units for the next year. He was arrested in 1864 when he refused to replace his quartermaster, but the charges were set aside and he continued to serve till the end of the war. He was with the Georgia Freedman's Bureau when mustered out in 1866. He went on to mine silver after the war.

Wilkes, Charles
(1798-1877) Union naval officer

He entered the U.S. Navy as a midshipman in 1818 and built a reputation as a surveyor and hydrographer. Wilkes led a six-ship scientific expedition to Antartica from 1838 to 1842. Commanding USS *San Jacinto*, his arrest of the Confederate envoys James Mason and John Slidell on board a British ship on the high seas on November 8, 1861, caused a serious diplomatic breach with England, though the *Trent* Affair, as it was known, made him a temporary hero. Assigned to command a squadron formed to hunt down Confederate raiders in the West Indies, he was recalled in June 1863 after several countries complained of violations of neutrality.

Wilmot, David
(1814-1868) Northern statesman

He was a lawyer and Democratic politician in his native Pennsylvania. As a U.S. Representative (1845-1851) he introduced the Wilmot Proviso (August 1846), a clause in a Mexican War appropriations bill that outlawed slavery in any territory acquired from Mexico. Passed 87-64 in the House, the measure failed in the Senate and failed again when reintroduced the following year. The acrimonious debate surrounding the bill deepened the growing rift between North and South and led to the foundation of the Free-Soil Party (1848) and later the Republican Party (1845). Wilmot joined both parties in his later career as a Pennsylvania and federal judge and U.S. Senator.

Wilson, James Harrison
(1837-1925) Union general

Graduated from West Point in 1860, this Illinois native was a Union major general by 1865, having served under W. T. Sherman, David Hunter and George McClellan; directed the Cavalry Bureau; and, in 1864-1865, led a cavalry corps. An outstanding commander, he led several spectacular raids: during the Petersburg siege Wilson and August V. Kautz destroyed many miles of vital railroad track, and, in May 1865, in a sensational finale to his brilliantly successful Selma Raid, Wilson's force captured Jefferson Davis. He built railroads and wrote military works in later life, and, following his re-enlistment for the Spanish-American War, he helped to suppress the Boxer Rebellion.

Winder, John Henry
(1800-1865)
Confederate provost marshal general

Born in Maryland, Winder was a West Point graduate and veteran of the frontier and the Seminole and Mexican wars. As a Confederate brigadier general his most significant commands were Libby, Belle Isle and Andersonville Prison: in November 1864 he became commissary general of all

OPPOSITE: James Harrison Wilson (sprawled on steps) and staff.

BELOW: John Henry Winder.

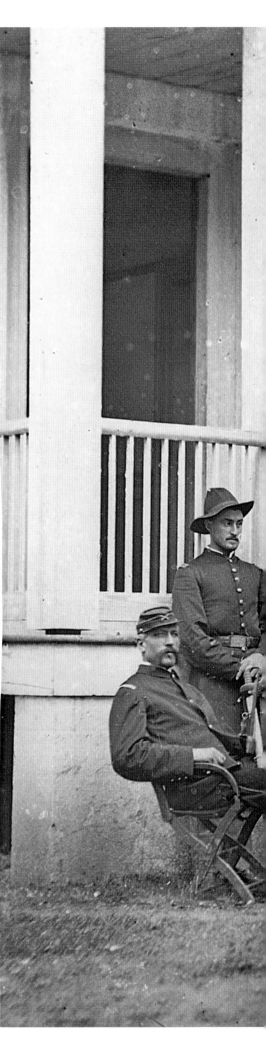

ABOVE: The execution of Henry Wirz, commandant of Andersonville Prison.

RIGHT: Henry Alexander Wise.

prisoners of war in the East. The degree of Winder's responsibility for the appalling conditions in prisons under his purview remains unresolved. His death was attributed to fatigue and strain.

Wirz, Henry
(1822-1865) Confederate officer

Swiss-born Wirz emigrated to the U.S. in 1849 and settled in Louisiana as a physician. During the Civil War he was a Confederate clerk in Libby Prison, fought at Seven Pines (wounded) and conducted a Confederate mission to Europe. He returned early in 1864 to become commandant of Andersonville Prison, Georgia, a prison camp notorious for its utter lack of shelter and sanitation, its overcrowding and its brutal guards: 13,000 Federal prisoners died there. The only person executed for war crimes after the war, he was hanged in November 1865 for conspiring to murder prisoners.

Wise, Henry Alexander
(1806-1876) Confederate general

A lawyer and politician, he served in Congress and was governor of Virginia (1856-1860). He opposed secession initially but volunteered for Confederate service and obtained a brigadier general's commission in May 1861. Wise served in western Virginia and at Roanoke Island, North Carolina, where one of his sons was mortally wounded. He later fought in the Petersburg and Richmond defenses and surrendered with Robert E. Lee's army at Appomattox. Wise returned to the practice of law after the war and died in Richmond in September 1876.

Wood, Thomas John
(1823-1906) Union general

Born in Kentucky, he was graduated from West Point in 1845 and participated in the Mexican War, frontier fighting and the Utah Expedition. He mustered 40,000 Indiana troops for the Union at the beginning of the Civil War. He commanded an Ohio Army division at Shiloh, Corinth and Perryville. He then fought in the Army of

Thomas John Wood (left) and (above) John Ellis Wool

the Cumberland at Stones River, in the Tullahoma Campaign, at Chickamauga, Missionary Ridge and Knoxville, and in the Atlanta Campaign. He commanded IV Corps at Nashville. He retired as a brigadier general in 1875.

Wool, John Ellis
(1784-1869) Union general

Wool raised a New York regiment for the War of 1812. As a brigadier general, he became a Mexican War hero by leading a superbly organized march through Chihuahua and securing victory at Buena Vista. He lived to become the fourth-ranking Union general in the Civil War. He saved Fort Monroe, occupied Norfolk and Portsmouth after the Confederate evacuation and commanded the Department of the East, the Middle Department and VIII Corps, retiring from active duty in August 1863 at the age of 79.

Worden, John Lorimer
(1818-1897) Union naval officer

This New Yorker was a 25-year navy veteran when the Civil War broke out. He earned national celebrity (and the Thanks of Congress) after commanding USS *Monitor* in the historic combat against CSS *Virginia* (ex-*Merrimac*) on March 9, 1862. Worden commanded the ironclad USS *Montauk* in the South Atlantic Blockading Squadron early in 1863 and spent the remainder of the war supervising the con-

struction of ironclad warships in New York. he retired as a rear admiral in 1886. He was also a superintendent of Annapolis (1869-1874).

Wright, Horatio Gouverneur
(1820-1899) Union general

Born in Connecticut, Wright was a West Point graduate. He became an army engineer who worked on harbors and fortifications. As chief engineer assigned to destroy the Union's Norfolk Navy Yard when the Civil War broke out, he was captured by the Confederates but was soon released. He served the Union at Fist Bull Run and on the Port Royal expedition, and fought in South Carolina and Florida, at Rappahannock Bridge and on the Bristoe Campaign. He led VI Corps from the Wilderness through the Petersburg assaults and on to Appomattox, then went to South Carolina to confront General Joseph Johnston's force. He was breveted a major general for his actions at Petersburg. He remained in the army until 1884.

Wright, Marcus Joseph
(1831-1922) Confederate general

A Tennessee court clerk, he joined the Confederacy's 154th Tennessee in 1861. He was wounded at Shiloh, and, promoted to brigadier general, led a brigade at Chickamauga and Chattanooga and participated in the defense of Atlanta. He surrendered as a Mississippi territorial commander. After the war he was a Memphis lawyer. Appointed to collect the C.S.A. archives (1878-1917), he made his major contribution to history by collecting, compiling, and editing the Southern records of the Civil War.

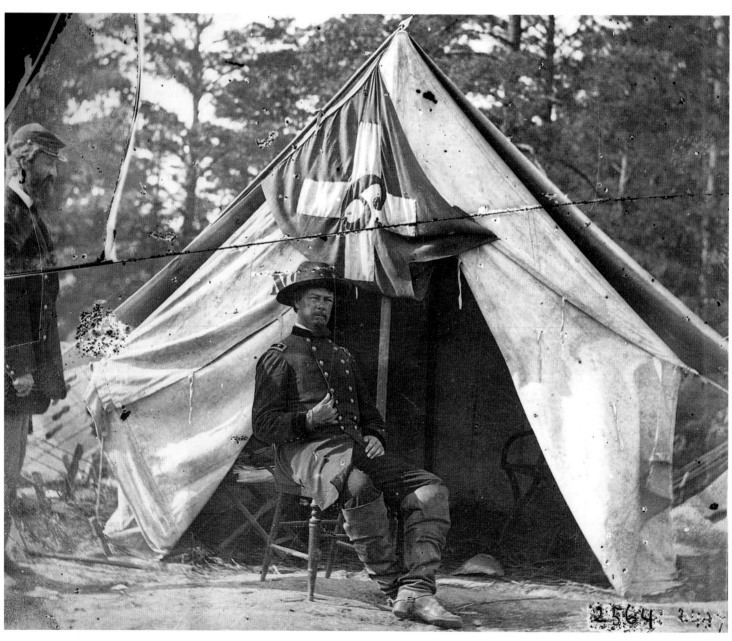

John Lorimer Worden (left) and (below) Horatio Gouverneur Wright

Yancey, William Lowndes
(1814-1863) **Confederate legislator**

After graduation from Williams College, this Georgian returned south, where he was a newspaper editor, lawyer and legislator. He settled on an Alabama plantation. Yancey resigned his Congressional seat (1844-1846) to agitate for states' rights. He countered the Wilmot Proviso with the Alabama (or Yancey) Platform (1848) seeking the codification of slaveholders' rights. The Compromise of 1850 drove him to radical secessionism; he became a leader of the "Fire-Eaters," delivering hundreds of speeches and becoming a pivotal figure in the secessionist movement. He drafted Alabama's secession ordnance. In Europe (1861-1862) he sought diplomatic recognition of the Confederacy. He died in office in the Confederate senate.

Young, Pierce Manning Butler
(1836-1896) **Confederate general**

Born in South Carolina, Young resigned from West Point just before graduation to join the Confederate army. He was wounded at South Mountain and Fredericksburg, fought at Gettysburg, defended Augusta against W. T. Sherman and was promoted to major general in December 1864. After the war he became a planter, served in the U.S. House of Representatives, was a member of the West Point Board of Visitors and held various diplomatic posts.

Zollicoffer, Felix Kirk
(1812-1862) **Confederate general**

This Tennessee-born newspaper editor and Whig politician fought in the Seminole War, held various offices in Tennessee and served in the U.S. House of Representatives (1853-59). Although a staunch supporter of states' rights, he worked to avoid a confrontation between North and South and attended the 1861 peace conference in Washington. He was made a Confederate brigadier general in July 1861 and commanded a brigade in eastern Tennessee. He was killed in his first major battle, at Logan's Cross Roads (Mill Springs), Kentucky, in January 1862.

William Lowndes Yancey

Pierce Manning Butler Young

Felix Kirk Zollicoffer

The publisher would like to thank the Library of Congress and the National Archives for the pictures that appear in the Great Battles section of this book as well as the following photo archives.

The Bettmann Archive, New York, NY: pages 158 (bottom left), 172 (top), 176 (bottom right), 177 (bottom right), 180 (top right), 184 (top right), 185 (top), 187 (top right), 195 (bottom right), 218 (top right), 221 (top left), 225 (top left), 227 (bottom right), 231 (bottom), 237 (bottom), 256 (top left, bottom right), 268, 269 (bottom), 280 (bottom right), 295, 312 (bottom right), 314–15, 328 (bottom right), 329 (top), 337 (bottom center), 344, 345 (bottom), 355 (bottom), 356 (bottom right), 362, 363 (bottom left).

Boston Public Library, MA: page 339 (top center).

Brompton Picture Library: pages 189, 272–73, 342 (bottom right).

Brown University, Providence, RI/Anne S.K. Brown Military Collection: pages 158, (bottom center), 246 (top left), 247, 257, 296 (top left), 303 (bottom), 329 (bottom center), 336 (top center), 359 (top left).

John Hay Library: pages 172 (bottom), 239 (bottom right).

Chicago Historical Society, IL: pages 224 (top right), 236 (top center, bottom), 251 (top right), 356 (top left), 359 (bottom).

Library of Congress: pages 158 (top, bottom right), 160, 161, 162 (bottom left, top right), 163 (bottom right), 164 (top left), 165 (both), 166, 167 (bottom left), 170 (top left), 171 (both), 174 (bottom right), 175, 176 (top), 177 (top left), 178 (top right), 180 (top left), 181 (both), 182 (bottom left), 184 (top, bottom left), 186 (both), 188, 190, (top right), 191 (bottom left), 192 (both), 194 (both), 195 (top), 196 (bottom left), 197 (top left), 198 (bottom right), 199 (both), 200 (both), 202 (top right, bottom), 203 (both), 204, 205 (all three), 206 (both), 207 (top left), 208 (bottom left, right), 209 (both), 212 (top left, right), 215, 216–17, 218 (bottom left), 219 (all three), 221 (bottom right), 222–23, 224 (bottom left), 226 (all three), 227 (top left), 228 (right), 229, 230, 231 (top left, right), 232 (bottom left), 234–35, 236 (top left), 238, 239 (bottom left), 240 (bottom left, right) 241 (both), 242 (both), 243 (bottom left), 246 (bottom right), 248 (bottom right), 249 (both), 250 (top left, bottom right), 251 (bottom), 252 (all three), 253, 254 (both), 255 (bottom right), 256 (top center), 258 (top left), 259 (all three), 260 (bottom), 261, 262–63, 266 (both), 269 (top), 270 (both), 271 (top), 274–79, 281 (top left), 281 (both), 282 (top left), 283, 285 (top right, bottom), 286 (top right), 287 (bottom), 288–89, 291 (both), 292 (top left), 293 (top left), 294 (both), 296 (bottom), 297, 298 (all three), 299, 300–1, 302 (both), 303 (top), 305, 306, 307 (top right, bottom right), 307–11, 312 (top left), 316–17, 318 (both), 319 (bottom left), 320–27, 328 (top center), 330–31, 332–33, 335 (top left), 336 (bottom left), 337 (top left), 339 (left), 340–1, 345 (top), 346 (bottom right), 347 (right, bottom center), 348–354, 358, 361 (both), 364, 366 (top left, right), 367 (both), 368 (bottom), 369–71, 372 (left), 374 (bottom), 375–77.

Louis A. Warren Lincoln Library and Museum, Fort Wayne, IN: pages 183, 284.

The Museum of the Confederacy, Eleanor S. Brockenbrough Library, Richmond, VA: pages 173, 201 (right), 202 (top left), 260 (top).

National Archives: pages 163 (top), 169 (bottom left), 170 (bottom right), 174 (top), 178 (bottom left), 285 (bottom), 291 (bottom right), 296 (top left), 201 (bottom left), 208 (top left), 210, 211 (all three), 212 (bottom center), 214 (both), 220 (bottom right), 224 (bottom left), 228 (bottom left), 232 (bottom right), 233 (both), 244, 248 (top left), 250 (bottom left), 267, 271 (bottom), 272 (bottom right), 290 (both), 293 (bottom right), 304 (bottom), 312 (bottom left), 313 (both), 319 (top right), 334, 338 (bottom right), 342 (top), 343, 346 (top), 347 (top left), 355 (top left), 357, 365 (both), 366 (bottom center), 368 (top right), 373.

National Portrait Gallery, Smithsonian Institution, Washington, D.C.: page 363 (bottom right).

U.S. Army Military History Institute, Carlisle Barracks, PA: pages 164 (center), 167 (both right), 168 (both), 169 (bottom right), 179, 182 (bottom right), 187 (bottom left), 193 (bottom center), 197 (bottom right), 198 (top right), 213, 220 (top right), 240 (top right), 243 (top right), 255 (bottom left), 258 (bottom right), 285 (top left), 292 (top right), 304 (top center), 307 (bottom left), 328 (top left), 335 (top right), 360 (bottom left).

U.S. Military Academy Archives, West Point, NY: page 245.

U.S. Navy, Naval Photographic Center, Washington, D.C.: page 238 (top).

University of Maryland Baltimore County, Photographic Collections: page 374 (top).

The Valentine Museum, Cook Collection, Richmond, VA: pages 162 (center), 207 (top right), 287 (top left), 360 (bottom right).